British Avant-Garde Fiction of the 1960s

British Avant-Garde Fiction
of the 1960s

Edited by Kaye Mitchell and
Nonia Williams

EDINBURGH
University Press

Edinburgh University Press is one of the leading university presses in the UK. We publish academic books and journals in our selected subject areas across the humanities and social sciences, combining cutting-edge scholarship with high editorial and production values to produce academic works of lasting importance. For more information visit our website: edinburghuniversitypress.com

© editorial matter and organisation Kaye Mitchell and Nonia Williams, 2019, 2020
© the chapters their several authors, 2019, 2020

Edinburgh University Press Ltd
The Tun – Holyrood Road
12(2f) Jackson's Entry
Edinburgh EH8 8PJ

First published in hardback by Edinburgh University Press 2019

Typeset in 11/13 Adobe Sabon by
IDSUK (DataConnection) Ltd

A CIP record for this book is available from the British Library

ISBN 978 1 4744 3619 9 (hardback)
ISBN 978 1 4744 3620 5 (paperback)
ISBN 978 1 4744 3621 2 (webready PDF)
ISBN 978 1 4744 3622 9 (epub)

The right of Kaye Mitchell and Nonia Williams to be identified as the editors of this work has been asserted in accordance with the Copyright, Designs and Patents Act 1988, and the Copyright and Related Rights Regulations 2003 (SI No. 2498).

Contents

Acknowledgements   vii

Introduction: 'The avant-garde must not be romanticized. The avant-garde must not be dismissed'   1
    Kaye Mitchell

1. Muriel Spark and the Possibility of Popular Experiment   20
    Marina MacKay

2. B. S. Johnson: The Book as Dynamic Object   36
    Joseph Darlington

3. Giles Gordon: *Beyond the Words* and Beyond the Language of Experimentalism   54
    David Hucklesby

4. Brigid Brophy's Aestheticism: The Camp Anti-Novel   72
    Len Gutkin

5. Alexander Trocchi: Man at Leisure   90
    Christopher Webb

6. Anna Kavan: Pursuing the 'in-between reality' Hidden by the 'ordinary surface of things'   107
    Hannah Van Hove

7. J. G. Ballard: Visuality and the Novels of the Near Future   125
    Natalie Ferris

8. Ann Quin: 'infuriating' Experiments?   143
    Nonia Williams

9. Contradiction, Incongruity and Fragmentation: Political and Avant-Garde Compromise in the Work of Alan Burns 160
   Kieran Devaney

10. Eva Figes: Tracing the Survival of a 'Poetry of the Inarticulate' 176
    Chris Clarke

11. Christine Brooke-Rose: The Development of Experiment 193
    Stephanie Jones

12. Aspirations Inevitably Failing: Hope and Negativity in Rayner Heppenstall's Experimental Fiction of the 1960s 210
    Philip Tew

13. Maureen Duffy: The Politics of Experimental Fiction 231
    Eveline Kilian

14. Not the Last Word on the Sixties Avant-Garde: An Afterword 248
    Glyn White

Notes on Contributors 262
Index 266

Acknowledgements

We would particularly like to thank Jackie Jones of Edinburgh University Press for her faith in the project, as well as for the feedback and practical guidance along the way, from proposal to submission. We also thank Ersev Ersoy for the excellent administrative support and incredibly helpful guidance (and patience) with the finer details of the typescript, as well as Rebecca MacKenzie for help with organising our wonderful cover image. For this artwork we have Ron Sandford to thank, for giving us permission to use his striking composition, which comes from *The Invisible Years* project of 1976 – a collaboration with J. G. Ballard for *Ambit Magazine*. Our Edinburgh University Press peer reviewers helped us to refine and shape the project at an early stage and we would like to acknowledge the helpfulness of their feedback.

In January 2018, we organised a conference to discuss the project-in-progress, and we thank the Modern and Contemporary Writing research group at the University of East Anglia for hosting and funding this event. We were very lucky to have wonderful respondents to lead the conference discussion; so thank you, Julia Jordan, Carole Sweeney and Glyn White for doing that so well, and thank you to everyone who attended and participated in the discussion. And finally, this book would not exist without our contributors, whose wonderful, curious, probing and thoughtful work on the 1960s authors included in this collection has made this project possible: grateful thanks to each and every one of you.

Introduction: 'The avant-garde must not be romanticized. The avant-garde must not be dismissed'[1]

Kaye Mitchell

> For a long time now I have felt that writing which is not ostensibly self-conscious is in a vital way inauthentic for our time. For our time – I think every statement should be dated. Which is another way of saying the same thing. I know of no young man who is not either an ignoramus or a fool who can take the old objective forms for granted. Is there no character in the book large enough to doubt the validity of the book itself?[2]

This statement, delivered apropos of nothing as part of Alexander Trocchi's meandering, fragmented, discursive, moving, sometimes shocking *Cain's Book* (1960), touches on many of the concerns informing the writers whose sixties' output comes under analysis in this collection: a concern with authenticity and truth that expresses itself sometimes, but not always, through overt devices of literary self-consciousness (some of which would later be deemed 'metafictional'); an acute awareness of the (changeable, antagonistic, hopeful, hopeless) times through which they are living; a desire to challenge or even overturn 'the old objective forms'; and through these experiments (formal, thematic, metaphysical, material), to throw into doubt 'the validity of the book itself' – its shape, its purpose, its political remit, its future.

Each chapter that follows devotes itself to the work – mainly the 1960s work – of one author, thereby presenting them as distinct but related. The focus on a single author per chapter allows a fuller introduction to authors, some of whom remain relatively unknown or little studied; across the range of chapters, the continuities and points of contact become visible, via a process of illuminating juxtaposition. The diversity and distinctiveness of the work produced during the decade illustrate the difficulty, but also the value, of grouping these British avant-garde writers of the 1960s together. Writing in 1967, B. S. Johnson averred that 'There are not many of us, and in the English way we do not form a "school"' – that tentative 'we' includes Christine Brooke-Rose, Alan Burns, Maureen Duffy, Rayner Heppenstall and Ann Quin, all of whom feature in this volume.[3] Yet, as Julia Jordan notes, Johnson's piece is wilfully contradictory: he claims this 'we' and yet 'refuses the collectivisation' of a 'school'; titles his piece 'Experimental British Fiction' and yet claims that the authors in question 'object to being called "experimental"', because of 'the pejorative sense the term bears for most English critics'; and asserts that 'there is no point in doing something that has been done before', while also claiming that their 'greatest debt is owed to James Joyce, of course'.[4] Jordan's analysis of Johnson reveals, also, the sense of divided inheritance and conflicted possible futures affecting the sixties avant-gardists:

> In his anxious movement between self-effacement and self-conscious inheritance, Johnson and his 'we' display characteristically late-modernist traits. And yet, as a generation they were also responding to new artistic impetuses from the continent and America, to the dissolution of Empire and the migration of colonial subjects to England. As products of the post-war political settlement, their inheritance was not just modernism but the cultural and political conditions of late modernism itself.[5]

Jordan's comments reveal the complexity of the British avant-garde of the 1960s, which is not a 'school' in any clearly defined, coherent sense; which is diverse in its aesthetic practices and (sometimes) divided in its politics; which both embraces and shuns its own description as 'experimental' or 'avant-garde'; which takes on myriad influences, yet often in a piecemeal fashion, from Europe and the USA; which should not be read in isolation from its historical contexts and from the continuing fallout (social, economic and psychological) of the Second World War and of the decline of the British Empire; which looks back to modernism, while declaring itself weary of literary traditions to date; which often seems to hold in tension the exhilaration of innovation and the torpor of a kind of aesthetic exhaustion.

Johnson also claims that the British avant-garde writers of the 1960s form only a 'small' group and yet one contention of this collection is that the 1960s is a much livelier period of literary experimentation in Britain than might previously have been supposed – and that the experimental writing produced in Britain in that period invites, deserves and rewards our renewed attention to it. In this Introduction, I will consider the contexts of that work's production and reception, its influences and allegiances, its formal and thematic continuities and discontinuities, its continuing legacies, and the ways in which it might speak to various of our twenty-first-century concerns.

'Avant-garde, avante garde, avant guard'

We must at the outset, however, tackle the issue of terminology. If Johnson prickles at the use of 'experimental', writers and critics during the sixties and since have expressed similar ambivalence towards the terms available. The editors of a 1964 special issue of the *Times Literary Supplement* on the 'avant-garde' opine that:

> Avant-garde, avante garde, avant guard: there is a certain doubt about the spelling, even among its most enthusiastic supporters, and it corresponds to a certain vagueness about the institution itself. This avant-garde has long been one of Western culture's great myths: one of those dynamic but ill-defined concepts which drive men to attitudes if not to action. You are for it or you are against it: you distrust it or you die for it, but always instinctively, without pausing to think out just what it is.[6]

Can the term and the 'myth' be separated? What connotations and consequences does that myth carry with it? Can the more negative connotations ('attitudes' rather than 'action') be neutralised? Can that 'vagueness' be dispelled? In the same issue of the *TLS*, Jonathan Miller asserts more acerbically that 'the idea [of the avant-garde] is simply old hat'.[7] Bernard Bergonzi, in his introduction to a collection entitled *Innovations* (1968), is kinder but still insists that:

> [T]he 'avant-garde' label has come to seem a little old-fashioned, as it must inevitably do, having been in continuous use for about sixty years, and although a basic avant-garde tenet is the desirability of 'perpetual revolution' this concept is too paradoxical to convey much meaning to a sceptical mind.[8]

He chooses, instead, the word 'innovation' – 'an innocuous but precisely descriptive term', and one seemingly more acceptable to the 'sceptical mind' of the 1960s.[9] Does an adherence to the concept of the 'avant-garde' require, then, a persistent idealism? If the accounts of the avant-garde in this period evince a forthright suspicion of 'myth', idealism and the more romantic manifestations of avant-gardism, they nonetheless struggle to jettison that terminology, and those aims, altogether.

In the same collection, Frank Kermode sidesteps the issue somewhat by recommending a distinction 'between two phases of modernism, [. . .] palaeo- [sic] and neo-modernism' – that is, the modernism of the late nineteenth and early twentieth centuries, and the (neo-)modernism of the 1960s – and claims that 'they are equally devoted to the theme of crisis, equally apocalyptic; but although they have this and other things in common, they have differences which might, with some research, be defined, and found not to be of a degree that prevents our calling both "modernist"'.[10] On the 1960s version, 'neo-modernism', Kermode writes:

> There seems to be much agreement that the new rejection of order and the past is not quite the same thing as older rejections of one's elders and their assumptions. It is also agreed that this neo-modernist anti-traditionalism and anti-formalism, though anticipated by Apollinaire, begins with Dada.[11]

This 'new' modernism of the 1960s, then, on Kermode's reading, is different in kind from its precursor, but the two share thematic and formal characteristics to some degree (apocalypticism, crisis, anti-traditionalism, anti-formalism). I will return to some of these historical sources – particularly the *TLS* special issues of 1964 and Bergonzi's *Innovations* – in more detail in due course because they provide interesting insights into the attitudes and anxieties of the period as regards the 'avant-garde'.

Misgivings about appropriate terminology persist into the present. The editors of a recent *Routledge Companion to Experimental Literature* (2012) concede that they use 'avant-garde', 'innovation' and 'experiment' 'more or less interchangeably', while acknowledging that 'there are import nuances of difference in connotation, especially between *experimental* and *avant-garde*'; the latter 'begins its career in the military context, but then migrates to the political sphere', and 'aesthetic avant-gardism continues to be allied with political radicalism'.[12] That is one question that this collection poses – without necessarily offering a definitive answer: to what extent does the *aesthetic* radicalism of the sixties avant-gardists indicate a corresponding *political* radicalism? Our use of the descriptor 'avant-garde' should not necessarily imply that correspondence; as in so many other respects, the authors featured here are not united. To give one example: Brigid Brophy (in *In Transit*) and Duffy (in *The Microcosm*) might challenge what we would now term 'gender normativity', but Quin and Anna Kavan's writing, respectively, is harder to pin down in terms of its gender politics, suffused as it is with intimations of sexual violence, feminine masochism and bodily disgust; meanwhile, entrenched forms of chauvinism are to be found in the work of Trocchi and Johnson (which is not to denigrate them – merely to suggest that they are conservative in some respects and not in others).

Is there a preferable term to 'avant-garde'? Francis Booth is uneasy with 'experimental novel' – 'It is certainly not an ideal description; experimentalism implies that the author didn't know what s/he was doing or would happen.'[13] In this he echoes B. S. Johnson's oft-quoted objection that '"experimental" to most reviewers is almost always a synonym for "unsuccessful"'.[14] Booth concedes, however, that 'neither I nor anyone else as far as I know has come up with a better term',[15] although he then proceeds to elaborate a distinction between 'two modes of writing: the "internal" and the "external"', claiming that it is this 'internal mode' that 'has characterised much of the experimental novel writing in Britain in this century, and especially since the beginning of the 1960s'.[16] Sebastian Groes, meanwhile, identifies what he calls the 'Extreme Sixties': 'made up of hardcore experiments in anti-novelistic writing by J. G. Ballard, Christine Brooke-Rose, R. C. Kenedy, Eva Tucker, Ann Quin, Elspeth Davie, Alan Burns and B. S. Johnson, whose work radically seeks new literary aesthetics',[17] though it might be objected that these writers' experiments take very different forms and that they practise their 'extremity' in diverse manners, from collage (Burns) to constraint (Brooke-Rose) to 'psychopathic hymn' (Ballard).[18] Jennifer Hodgson claims that 'the vague, slippery epithet "experimental" generally euphemises aesthetic or commercial failure or, worse, a questionable politics and a narcissistic artistic dandyism, and has tended to preclude rigorous critical engagement with the effects and affects of literary innovation'.[19] She opts, then, to present the sixties writers as continuing a (broadly defined) modernism, and employs Kermode's idea of 'neo-modernism', defined as 'a "rejection of order" that "prefers and professes to do without the tradition and the illusion" of form'.[20] However, as Hodgson acknowledges, 'this neo-modernist contempt for form actually entails formal innovation' and constitutes rather 'a battle [. . .] against the false orders that narrative convention imposes upon human experience'.[21]

There are other terms, of course, that come into play when discussing particular works under consideration in this volume – notably, metafiction and postmodernism. R. M. Berry, then, includes Johnson's *Albert Angelo* (1964) and Brooke-Rose's *Out* (1964) in his list of 'fictions of the sixties and seventies most often prefixed meta, sur, or super', alongside works by Nabokov, Coover, Pynchon and Calvino, among others.[22] Such readings of sixties texts are, of course, retrospective, and fuller theorisations of metafiction would not emerge until the 1970s and 1980s (by Larry McCaffery and Patricia Waugh, for example), even if those theorisations then belatedly lay claim to much earlier literary texts as exemplars of the metafictional and the postmodern. As Glyn White notes in the Afterword to this volume, while the works of these authors might fulfil the requirements and anticipate the later developments of postmodern fiction, they are working without the benefit of a governing framework or terminology in that respect: 'avant-garde writers who felt something very different was called for were searching for what that was without the benefit of theory. Even in the late 1960s, common usage of postmodernism as a literary term was at least a decade away.' From White's perspective, it is fiction of the eighties – by the likes of Rushdie and Carter – that more neatly fits the category of the postmodern.

At first glance, Brian McHale's distinction between modernism and postmodernism would also seem to place the sixties experimentalists within the former category – note his claim that 'Postmodernist fiction experiments with individuals, and also with models – which explains its affinity for science fiction – but beyond that it experiments as well with the very *process of world-modeling*,' while modernist fiction 'experimented with consciousness'.[23] Yet McHale's distinction between modernism and postmodernism on the grounds of 'dominant' (epistemological and ontological, respectively) does not easily map on to the work of the sixties avant-garde.[24] Many of the texts covered here are centrally concerned with consciousness, and seem to be innovating in order to express and explore the structure and operations of consciousness, memory and the inner life better – this is perhaps particularly the case with Kavan's writing, before and during the 1960s, but it is arguably a feature of Heppenstall and Trocchi's work too, and of Quin's use of free indirect discourse to blur the boundaries between inner and outer worlds. And yet McHale does include various 1960s titles in his lists of exemplary postmodern fiction, notably John Fowles's *The French Lieutenant's Woman* (1969) and John Barth's *Giles Goat-Boy* (1966), as well as a later work by Brooke-Rose, *Thru* (1975). Moreover, some of the works discussed in the succeeding essays might be read as governed by ontological questions about the nature of the world(s) depicted and the nature of the book itself – notably Kavan (with her surreal dreamscapes), Ballard (with his hyperreal worlds) and Johnson (due to his experiments with the very form and materiality of the book).

'A distrust of the new and exceptional'?

The *TLS* quotation with which I opened the last section hints at a very British kind of reserve – even suspicion – as far as the avant-garde is concerned. The common story about the mid-century period of British literary history has been that it was characterised by a 'distrust of the new and exceptional' and that 'most of the postwar writers conscientiously rejected experimental techniques in their fiction as well as in their critical writings, and turned instead to older novelists for inspiration': this according to Rubin Rabinovitz.[25] Raymond Williams, writing in 1961, asserted that:

> [T]he 1950s could be fairly characterized [. . .] as a period of return to older forms, and to specifically English forms, especially by comparison with the most widely discussed work of the 1920s and 1930s, which was largely experimental in form and cosmopolitan in spirit.[26]

For Williams, then, the 'return' is not merely to realism; it also implies a narrowing of perspectives in terms of influences from outside the British Isles.[27] Reassessing the 'situation of the novel' in the mid-century, from the later standpoint of 1970, Bergonzi concludes, pessimistically, that the novel, by reason of its very form, was resistant to 'modernisation', that 'nearly everything possible to be achieved [in or with the novel] has already been done',[28] and that

> [D]emands for the total modernisation of the novel are likely to be defeated by the stubbornly traditional qualities of the verbal medium, and by the further limitations that words are likely to assume when they are set down in a printed book. The lesson seems to be that the *avant-garde* novelist will find greater possibilities in other media, notably the cinema.[29]

Thus, even though he thinks the novel will survive in some form, he does not believe 'that the future novel will be characterised by stylistic dynamism, by a constant orientation towards novelty'.[30] (We might, of course, agree that a *constant* 'orientation towards novelty' is neither possible, nor desirable.) More adventurous and speculative critics such as Robert Scholes predicted the passing of the *realist* novel, thanks in part to competition from cinema, boldly asserting that 'the novel may be dying, but we need not fear for the future' because what would take its place would be 'fabulation'.[31] Those of a more conservative mindset, such as David Lodge, made a case for realism and for 'liberalism' – 'the aesthetics of compromise go naturally with the ideology of compromise' – and for 'reality', concluding that 'It is this sense of reality which realism imitates; and it seems likely that the latter will survive as long as the former.'[32]

Yet as Booth – rightly – claims, even in the 1950s 'the hegemony of neo-realism was never complete' and 'the tendency towards non-realism and stylistic innovation never died out in Britain even during the period when it was all but swamped by a flood of anger' (a reference to the 'Angry Young Men' writers).[33] He cites, among other examples, the publication of William Golding's *Lord of the Flies* and Brophy's *Hackenfeller's Ape* in 1954, and John Fowles's *The Collector* in 1958. We could add to this Muriel Spark's *The Comforters* (1957) and Iris Murdoch's *Under the Net* (1954), both of which incorporate self-reflexive (that is, putatively metafictional) elements that are in productive tension with those texts' more 'realist' elements.[34] As I have argued elsewhere, the richness, diversity and inventiveness of women's literary output in the mid-century – works by authors such as Ivy Compton-Burnett, Anna Kavan, Iris Murdoch, Angela Carter, Jean Rhys and Muriel Spark – '[preclude] any easy distinction between, or categorisation as, "realism" or "experimentalism"'.[35] Two sources in particular from the 1960s might give us more nuanced insights into the views on the avant-garde at the time: the two *TLS* special issues of 1964 and Bergonzi's collection, *Innovations* (1968). What these reveal is that the situation is not as simple as the accepted accounts appear to suggest – that realism and experimentalism co-existed (and even overlapped), and that attitudes to avant-gardism held in tension seemingly contradictory views as to its utility and worth, its promise and its limitations.

Thus the editors of the 6 August (1964) issue of the *TLS*, subtitled 'The Changing Guard', assert that:

> The whole scene has been transformed since 1945. Already before the war it was plain that the truly spectacular avant-garde movements had all run their course: surrealism, the last of them to develop, was still feebly kicking, but the age of the -Isms seemed to be over and the great innovators, men born mainly in the 1870s and 1880s, were occupied with exploiting and consolidating their earlier discoveries.[36]

Despite – or perhaps because of – this seeming exhaustion of the avant-garde imperative, the editors identify an increasing assimilation of the avant-garde into the mainstream: through its institutionalisation (such as support from museums and public funding bodies) and popularisation (through television, advertising and pop culture more generally). The tone here wavers between relief (at the renewed tolerance of avant-garde art in the postwar years, following its persecution by the Nazi and Russian regimes) and regret (at the loss of 'the old sense of shock', and at the putative transformation of the practitioners of the avant-garde into 'a band of hired entertainers whose function is to astonish a passive and indulgent audience').[37] This anxiety about popularisation is evident elsewhere in the issue: in Clancy Sigal's comment that 'The fruits of [the] avant-garde are borrowed, bought or purloined almost as soon as they are created. Where walls once stood now are transmission belts' (Sigal himself professes 'friendly indifference' towards avant-garde art and literature);[38] in Ken Baynes's article, entitled 'Far Out or Sell Out?', which asserts that 'the avant-garde today is institutionalized' and 'avant-garde activity has become almost an autonomous *style*', and which asks, pertinently, how a set of practices apparently distinguished by 'esotericism' can exist 'in a context of mass literacy and mass media';[39] and in Miller's statement that the 'popularization of the avant-garde' is one of the things that has effectively killed it.[40]

And yet, despite these obviously critical views dotted throughout the issue, the editors, in their introduction and in the editorial to 'The Changing Guard' issue, seek to counter the idea that the avant-garde might be 'unimportant', instead insisting that 'the silliest-looking avant-garde movement may turn out in twenty or fifty years' time to have been an instinctive anticipation which the historians will pounce on. There is life in the old avant-garde yet, and the critic's job is to spot where it lies.'[41] If the *TLS* is – hubristically – attempting to set itself up as national gatekeeper here, its writers nevertheless concede that 'we cannot do that in two issues', though they do wish to 'slough off the dying myth' and be 'less romantic' about the avant-garde: 'Then we can begin to distinguish between the difficult and the merely unintelligible, the extreme and the merely disgusting, the experimental and the merely affected.'[42] Even in this wording, they reveal the common (mis)perceptions and grievances levelled at the avant-garde, at its supposed obscurity, obscenity and pretentiousness. It seems apt, therefore, that the editors' two governing principles, with which they conclude, seek to position them between two equally disagreeable, and yet utterly opposed, standpoints: 'The avant-garde must not be romanticized. The avant-garde must not be dismissed.'[43] That these are negative principles rather than positive (say, to *celebrate* or *champion* the avant-garde work of the period) might give us pause.

The essays collected together in Bergonzi's *Innovations*, all of which originally appeared 'in British, American and Canadian magazines between 1963 and 1967', evince a similar ambivalence (even, in some cases, hostility) towards avant-gardism and aesthetic experiment.[44] Despite bringing together this wealth of material on 'the contemporary avant-garde', from illustrious contributors such as Kermode, Ihab Hassan, David Lodge, Marshall McLuhan and Edwin Morgan, Bergonzi describes himself as an 'unusually detached' editor, due to being 'in the position [. . .] of being deeply interested in a good many things he does not particularly like', and he confesses that he finds 'the aesthetic theories of neo-modernism more interesting than the works of art they are intended to explain and justify'.[45] Within the wider collection, Leslie Fiedler – in an essay tellingly titled 'The New Mutants' – displays a barely concealed distaste for 'the new irrationalists' who 'seek an anti-language of protest as inevitably as they seek anti-poems and anti-novels';[46] for the young who 'celebrate disconnection';[47] for Burroughs's *Naked Lunch* (which he deplores as 'a nightmare anticipation [. . .] of post-Humanist sexuality');[48] for the elevation of 'the schizophrenic' to the status of a 'new culture hero';[49] and for readers who 'respond sympathetically to the 'flirtation with incoherence and disorder' that they find in the writings of some contemporary authors.[50] Lodge, meanwhile, in his 'Objections to William Burroughs', laments what he sees as the unwarranted and over-hasty elevation of certain experimental writers of the period. For Lodge, the praise of Burroughs and the 'smooth acceptance and accommodation' of his work (examples of which Lodge finds to be 'indecent' and 'tedious') epitomise 'the institutionalisation of the adversary culture of modernism', and, he declares, 'I do not see this process as a symptom of cultural health.'[51]

Even the much more measured intervention by Kermode, reprinted in *Innovations*, is ultimately rather critical of what he terms neo-modernism. On the subject of chance, randomness and the irrational in the modernisms, Kermode comments:

> Aleation in the arts [. . .] pushes into absurdity a theory based on observation, that chance or grace plays a role in composition. In so far as palaeo-modernism pretended to be classical, it played this down; but between it and neo-modernism stands surrealism, and other manifestations of irrationalism. [. . .] Aleatory art is accordingly, for all its novelty, an extension of past art, indeed the hypertrophy of one aspect of that art.[52]

This is no positive enlargement or 'extension', however. On Kermode's reading, 'the theoretical bases of neo-modernism, in so far as they show themselves in relation to form, chance, humour, [. . .] are not "revolutionary". They are marginal developments of older modernism,'[53] and he concludes that:

> [T]here has been only one Modernist Revolution, and [. . .] it happened a long time ago. So far as I can see, there has been little radical change in modernist thinking since then. More muddle, certainly, and almost certainly more jokes, but no revolution, and much less talent.[54]

In short, he believes that the experimental literary output of the mid-century cannot live up to the promise of its modernist forerunner.

'Island View'

A much more positive view on the 1960s avant-garde emanates from the publisher who was responsible for bringing many of its members into print in the UK: John Calder. In an editorial – really a thinly disguised promotional piece – by Calder Publications in the *TLS* special issue of 6 August 1964, the publisher claims of 'The New British School' that 'the younger writers are moving to a new kind of novel, rivalling the achievements that have already been made by younger writers in the theatre', and ending a decades-long period of relative stylistic stagnancy.[55] Of the Calder stable of British authors, they write that 'Ann Quin has discovered a style that, while owing much to the "nouveau roman," is completely English in atmosphere and presentation'; Trocchi they characterise as 'an ex-patriot adherent of the American "beats"' (Trocchi spent time living in both Paris and New York); Burns's *Europe After the Rain* is described as 'a very original, highly important, experimental work', and they suggest that 'Kafka and Robbe-Grillet and some modern painters are major influences.'[56] In addition to publishing Quin, Trocchi and Burns, Calder was responsible for publishing and promoting experimental writing from the USA and continental Europe (particularly France) during this period. What is notable here is the way all three British writers – whatever the 'Englishness' of the out-of-season seaside town setting of Quin's *Berg* (1964) – are described in relation to overseas influences. According to the editorial to the issue as a whole ('Island View'):

> Appreciation of avant-garde movements has never been this country's strong suit. We are notoriously stickier in our reactions than any of the other principal nations of the West; we lack the Frenchman's quick

interest in all the latest artistic fashions, the German's slightly guilty sense of obligation to almost any innovator, the American's prodigality in support of anything new.[57]

Two things are perhaps not surprising, then: firstly, that relatively few British writers are featured in the *TLS* special issue of 6 August 1964, and that the follow-up issue (3 September 1964) focuses entirely on avant-garde writing from continental Europe and from further afield, with articles on Situationism, the Vienna Group, concrete poetry, Lettrism and Dada, and examples of writing from Jean Arp, Augusto de Campos, Eugen Gomringer, Günther Grass and Miroslav Holub.[58] Secondly, the British avant-garde writers of this period looked beyond these shores, taking inspiration, in a deliberately piecemeal and partial fashion, from a disparate range of 'foreign' and/or radical sources, including, but not limited to, Dada, Surrealism, the *nouveau roman*, concrete poetry, the Beats, the Black Mountain poets, Beckett, jazz, and visual and performance art.

The *nouveau roman* is a frequent reference point in critical responses to key works of this period. As Danielle Marx-Scouras explains, 'The term *nouveau roman* gained currency in 1957 thanks to the Academician Emile Henriot, who used the expression in his review of Robbe-Grillet's *La Jalousie [Jealousy]* (1957) and Sarraute's *Tropismes [Tropisms]* (1939/1957) in *Le Monde* (22 May 1957).'[59] The *nouveau roman* is characterised by 'its so-called objective description, devoid of traditional psychology', and by 'the disappearance of the traditional character, the deconstruction of plot, formal experimentation with space and time, the critique of realism and psychology, the re-examination of author/reader relationships, and a new use of description'.[60] For Calder, the *nouveau roman* is 'the most important post-war literary movement [. . . ,] more significant and exciting than anything produced here in the last 30 years',[61] and it becomes a way of describing and accounting for the seemingly un-British experimentalism of novels such as *Berg*, Brooke-Rose's *Out* and Spark's *The Driver's Seat* (1970). In *Out*, the stripped-back object-ness of objects, of which Robbe-Grillet writes in *Towards a New Novel* (1956) – evoked via an emphasis on their spatial or geometric arrangement and relation to each other, is especially evident. The narrator of *Out* becomes, consequently, a point of observation, a position within the geometric arrangement of objects, even an object among other objects, rather than a fully fleshed-out person of depth and psychological verisimilitude. In fact, and although Brooke-Rose had written admiringly of 'anti-novels [. . .] which for various purposes turn the form inside out, hold it up, perhaps, to ridicule, and give it a thorough beating, or at least an airing', she grew to dislike this particular descriptor of her work.[62] Writing to her editor Michael Schmidt in 1984, in the lead-up to Carcanet's publication of *Amalgamemnon* (1984), she asks, 'Can you avoid the "French" & "anti-novel" label. Every reviewer plonks me there,' claiming that this applied only to *Out*: 'I am completely different & keep falling between 2 stools.'[63]

A less direct but nonetheless important influence during this period is concrete poetry. Concrete poetry emerged in Switzerland and Brazil in the 1950s, typified by the work of Eugen Gomringer and the Noigandres group (the de Campos brothers), respectively. The varied examples of 'concrete poetry and prose' that Joe Bray discusses in the *Routledge Companion to Experimental Literature* are unified in 'their desire to experiment with the possibilities afforded by the page, and in particular to explore the potential of that often-overlooked site of meaning [. . .] : white space'.[64] While, as Bray points out, experiments in typography, visual design and page lay-out have a long history, concrete poetry does wield a certain influence in the 1950s and 1960s. In the UK, it is epitomised by the work of the Scottish poets Ian Hamilton Finlay and Edwin Morgan (both of whom feature in the *TLS* special issue of August 1964) but, as Bray also notes, this experimentation with(in) the space of the page is evident also in prose of the 1960s and 1970s; he mentions Brooke-Rose's *Thru* and Johnson's *Albert Angelo* as particular examples. Concrete poetry can be seen as opening further the possibilities of experimentation with white space (which is evident in some of Quin's work, such as *Three*); with typography, page layout and visual design (as we see in some of Brooke-Rose's later work and in Brophy's *In Transit*, for example); and with collage (as practised by Burns). If 'concrete prose', as McHale terms it, '[focuses] attention on the ontological "cut": on the one side of the cut, the world projected by the words; on the other side, the physical reality of ink shapes on paper', then the writers featured in this collection, in their various ways, can be read as extending their innovations to both the 'world[s] projected' and 'the physical reality' of the page.[65]

Quin's work also, notably, bears the influence of the Black Mountain poets in the US, thanks to her relationship and correspondence with Robert Creeley. Benjamin Lee claims in turn that mid-century American poetry movements such as the Beats, the Black Mountain poets and the New York School 'adopted jazz or painting as primary aesthetic models' and that this comprised 'a way of rejecting the prevailing notions of literature and literary tradition, which these poets perceived as static, unimaginative, and excessively polite'.[66] It is worth noting in conclusion here, then, that this influence, in the context of the 1960s avant-garde(s), can be seen as working across the boundaries of different media, art forms and genres, with experimental writers taking inspiration from music, film, visual and conceptual art, and performance (of various kinds).

'Shandyean digression' / 'Fluttering around a canon'

This book sets out to rectify what we are claiming as a kind of critical lacuna in the history of British writing in the twentieth century. That history has tended either to skip the 1950s and 1960s, in its awkward leap from (late) modernism to postmodernism (as my earlier discussion shows, the sixties avant-gardists are not easily assimilated into either category); or to dismiss the experimental writings of the 1960s as a temporary aberration or, worse, a literary embarrassment. As Hodgson opines:

> The literary-historical fate of the British experimental novel of the 1960s – that of B. S. Johnson, Ann Quin, Christine Brooke-Rose, Brigid Brophy and Alan Burns, amongst others – was to become a Shandyean digression in the master narrative of British literary history. [...] Positioned as an adjunct to the post-war re-emergence of realism in the 'situation of the novel' debates of the time, it was perceived as belatedly and exhaustedly modern, out of time and overshadowed by its modernist predecessors. [...] Subsequent critical accounts of the period seem content to rehearse the old realist-experimentalist divide, to pitch the experimental novel against its realist counterpart and find the former lacking – in popular success, in a tenable politics – and dismiss it to the peripheries of literary history.[67]

It can be argued, furthermore, that women experimental writers have enjoyed even less acclaim, have been even more significantly disregarded, than male experimental writers: doubly marginalised on the grounds of their formal innovation and their gender. As Ellen G. Friedman and Miriam Fuchs assert in their highly influential *Breaking the Sequence: Women's Experimental Fiction* (1989):

> Despite their pioneering work, women were cut out or subordinated in the first assessments of early twentieth-century experimentalism, fixing the response to succeeding generations of women. However, this neglect is also partially a legacy of the last decades of feminist criticism, which

has hunted subtexts and muted texts to uncover a feminine discourse while overlooking the texts by women experimentalists who may be writing that discourse in deliberate, open, and varied ways.[68]

Brooke-Rose, in turn, has lamented the tendency for women experimental writers to be marginalised as 'minor' members of a particular movement and/or defined by their relationships with male writers of that movement:

> Perhaps one of the safest ways of dismissing a woman experimental writer is to stick a label on her, if possible that of a male group that is getting or (better still) used to get all the attention. Fluttering around a canon. The implication is clear: a woman writer must either use traditional forms or, if she dare experiment, she must be imitating an already old model. [. . .] [W]omen are rarely considered seriously as part of a movement when it is 'in vogue'; and they are damned with the label when it no longer is, when they can safely be considered as minor elements of it.[69]

Friedman and Fuchs, in their own 'archaeological and compensatory' work, seek to 'recover' and celebrate 'the rich tradition of women's experimental fiction' in the twentieth century.[70] In doing so, they divide their chosen twentieth-century authors into three 'generations' – the early modernists (before 1930), such as Dorothy Richardson and Virginia Woolf; a 'second generation' of 1930–60; and a 'third generation' positioned 'after 1960'. Only the chapters on Marguerite Young (Miriam Fuchs), Ann Quin (Philip Stevick) and literature in translation (Germaine Brée) directly engage with works produced in the 1960s (Brée discusses sixties texts by Nathalie Sarraute and Monique Wittig). And yet, the 1960s was an incredibly generative period for women experimentalists, as this volume's inclusion of chapters on Brooke-Rose, Quin, Brophy, Spark, Duffy, Kavan and Figes attests, perhaps bearing out Jordan's point that, 'already-marginalised experimental writing has overall been more open to women writers and articulations of women's experiences'.[71] These women writers are not merely 'fluttering around a canon', and their work has been at the forefront of recent revivals of interest in mid-century and later avant-gardes.[72]

In compiling this collection of essays, we do not insist on the equal value of all the texts under consideration – undoubtedly some might be dismissed, still, as 'Shandyean digression'. We do, however, suggest that, read collectively, they constitute that most un-British of things: an avant-garde – as fraught, fleeting, divided and divisive as avant-gardes often are, but also, importantly, informed by and radically reworking the complex legacies of an earlier modernism, influenced by some of the most exciting, challenging aesthetic experimentation happening worldwide in the 1960s, and anticipatory of many later formal and thematic preoccupations (metafiction, multimodalism, hypertext, apocalypticism and the post-Beckettian problematics of failure). To the extent that they are united, the chapters that follow seek to reveal the richness and intricacy of this 1960s British avant-garde fiction, opening it up to new readings, new connections forwards and backwards in time, and – we hope – new audiences.

Notes

1. 'The Changing Guard' [Introduction to special issue on the avant-garde], *Times Literary Supplement*, 6 August 1964, pp. 675–6, p. 676.
2. Alexander Trocchi, *Cain's Book* [1960] (London: Calder, 2017), p. 47.
3. B. S. Johnson, 'Experimental British Fiction', unpublished transcript, 20 August 1967, p. 1; quoted in Julia Jordan, 'Late Modernism and the Avant-Garde Renaissance', in *Cambridge Companion to British Fiction Since 1945*, ed. David James (Cambridge: Cambridge University Press, 2015), pp. 145–59, p. 145.
4. Johnson, 'Experimental British Fiction', p. 1; Jordan, p. 145.
5. Jordan, p. 146.
6. 'The Changing Guard', p. 675.
7. Jonathan Miller, 'Jokers in the Pack', *TLS*, 6 August 1964, pp. 703–4, p. 703.
8. Bernard Bergonzi, 'Introduction', in *Innovations: Essays on Art and Ideas*, ed. Bernard Bergonzi (London: Macmillan, 1968), pp. 11–22, p. 11.
9. Ibid. p. 12
10. Frank Kermode, 'Modernisms', in *Innovations*, pp. 66–92, p. 73.
11. Ibid. p. 76.
12. Joe Bray, Alison Gibbons and Brian McHale, 'Introduction', in *Routledge Companion to Experimental Literature*, ed. Joe Bray, Alison Gibbons and Brian McHale (London: Routledge, 2012), pp. 1–17, p. 1.
13. Francis Booth, *Amongst Those Left: The British Experimental Novel 1940–1980* (Lulu Press, Inc., 2012), p. 12.
14. B. S. Johnson, *Aren't You Rather Young to Be Writing Your Memoirs?* (London: Hutchinson, 1973), p. 19. See also Ronald Sukenick's comment that the real meaning of 'experimental novel' is 'no sales of subsidiary rights', and Christine Brooke-Rose's complaint that '"Experiment" is often regarded as "merely" formal, tinkering with technique'. Sukenick, *In Form: Digressions on the Act of Fiction* (Carbondale: Southern Illinois

University Press, 1985), p. 55. Brooke-Rose, 'Illiterations', in *Breaking the Sequence: Women's Experimental Fiction*, ed. Ellen G. Friedman and Miriam Fuchs (Princeton: Princeton University Press), pp. 55–71, p. 64.
15. Ibid.
16. Ibid. pp. 37, 41.
17. Sebastian Groes, *British Fictions of the Sixties* (London: Bloomsbury, 2016), p. 16.
18. This is Ballard's own description of *Crash*, the novel which most obviously develops the material of his earlier *Atrocity Exhibition* – though he had previously described it as a 'cautionary tale'. J. G. Ballard, Preface, *Crash* [1973] (London: Harper Perennial, 2008), n.p.
19. Jennifer Hodgson, '"Such a Thing as Avant-Garde Has Ceased to Exist": The Hidden Legacies of the British Experimental Novel', in *Twenty-First Century Fiction: What Happens Now*, ed. Siân Adiseshiah and Rupert Hildyard (Basingstoke: Palgrave, 2013), pp. 15–33, p. 21.
20. Kermode, *Innovations*, pp. 76, 77.
21. Hodgson, p. 23
22. R. M. Berry, 'Metafiction', in *Routledge Companion*, pp. 128–40, p. 131.
23. Brian McHale, 'Postmodernism and Experiment', in *Routledge Companion*, pp. 141–53, p. 146.
24. For an explanation of this 'dominant' idea, see Brian McHale, *Postmodernist Fiction* (London: Methuen, 1987), pp. 6ff.
25. Rubin Rabinovitz, *The Reaction Against Experiment in the English Novel 1950–1960* (New York: Columbia University Press, 1967), p. 2.
26. Raymond Williams, 'A Changing Social History of English Writing', *Audience*, 8:76 (Winter, 1961). Quoted in Rabinovitz, p. 5.
27. Jed Esty is interesting on this point in *A Shrinking Island: Modernism and National Culture in England* (Princeton: Princeton University Press, 2004).
28. Bernard Bergonzi, *The Situation of the Novel* [1970], 2nd edn (Basingstoke: Macmillan, 1979), p. 19.
29. Ibid. p. 30.
30. Ibid.
31. Quoted in David Lodge, 'The Novelist at the Crossroads', *Critical Inquiry*, 11 (1969), pp. 105–32, p. 107.
32. Lodge, 'The Novelist at the Crossroads', p. 131.
33. Booth, p. 54.
34. For my reading of the proto-experimental elements of *Under the Net* and *The Comforters*, see Kaye Mitchell, 'Post-War Fiction: Realism and Experimentalism', in *The History of British Women's Writing, 1945–1975*, ed. Clare Hanson and Susan Watkins (London: Palgrave, 2017), pp. 19–36.
35. Ibid. p. 20.
36. 'The Changing Guard', p. 675.
37. Ibid. p. 676.

38. Clancy Sigal, 'The Haunted House', *TLS*, 6 August 1964, pp. 681–2, p. 681.
39. Ken Baynes, 'Far Out or Sell Out?', *TLS*, 6 August 1964, p. 694.
40. Miller, p. 703.
41. 'The Changing Guard', p. 676.
42. Ibid.
43. Ibid.
44. Bergonzi, 'Introduction', p. 11.
45. Ibid. pp. 11, 22.
46. Leslie A. Fiedler, 'The New Mutants', in *Innovations*, pp. 23–45, pp. 28, 31.
47. Ibid. p. 34.
48. Ibid. p. 37.
49. Ibid. p. 44.
50. Ibid.
51. David Lodge, 'Objections to William Burroughs', in *Innovations*, pp. 200–12, p. 201. In many accounts of the literary avant-gardes, Burroughs functions as either poster boy or bête noire – so, for John Calder, he is 'the most important writer so far thrown up by the American "beat" movement' and 'the principal American post-Joycean' [untitled editorial by John Calder Publications], *TLS*, 6 August 1964, p. 690.
52. Kermode, pp. 84–5.
53. Ibid. p. 88.
54. Ibid. p. 89.
55. Calder editorial, p. 690.
56. Ibid.
57. 'Island View' [editorial], *TLS*, 6 August 1964, p. 695.
58. As the introduction to 'The Changing Guard, pt 2' makes clear, the focus is more on movements than individuals than in the first issue, and the contents 'have perhaps more of the traditional avant-garde flavour' and 'give a picture of something much more coherent and less parochial than did their British and American opposite numbers'. *TLS*, 3 September 1964, pp. 775–6, p. 775.
59. 'The Nouveau Roman and Tel Quel', in *Routledge Companion*, pp. 89–100, p. 94.
60. Ibid.
61. Calder editorial, p. 690.
62. Christine Brooke-Rose, 'Samuel Beckett and the Anti-Novel', *London Magazine*, 5:12 (1958), pp. 38–46, p. 38.
63. Handwritten letter, CBR to MS, 14/03/84, held in the Carcanet archive.
64. Bray, 'Concrete Poetry and Prose', *Routledge Companion*, pp. 298–309, p. 298.
65. McHale, *Postmodernist Fiction* (London: Methuen, 1987), p. 184. For a more extensive and substantial discussion of experiments with the 'graphic surface' of the book, see Glyn White, *Reading the Graphic Surface* (Manchester: Manchester University Press, 2005).

66. Benjamin Lee, 'Spontaneity and Improvisation in Postwar Experimental Poetry', in *Routledge Companion*, pp. 75–88, p. 77.
67. Hodgson, p. 21.
68. Ellen G. Friedman and Miriam Fuchs, 'Contexts and Continuities: An Introduction to Women's Experimental Fiction in English', in *Breaking the Sequence*, ed. Ellen G. Friedman and Miriam Fuchs (Princeton: Princeton University Press, 1989), pp. 3–51, p. 6.
69. Brooke-Rose, 'Illiterations', p. 35.
70. Friedman and Fuchs, 'Preface', in *Breaking the Sequence*, p. xi.
71. Jordan, p. 153.
72. For example, the posthumous publication of Quin's *Unmapped Country* and various short stories by And Other Stories in 2018; in 2014, at the Cinecity festival in Brighton (Quin's hometown), the exhibition of a film set installation for an imaginary screen version of *Berg*, to celebrate the fiftieth anniversary of its publication, as well as screening a series of sixties films and hosting a public discussion about Quin; a special issue of *Women: A Cultural Review*, 28:4 (2017) on Anna Kavan; a forthcoming special issue of *Contemporary Women's Writing* on Brigid Brophy; renewed interest in Brooke-Rose since her death in 2012, including a symposium on her work at the Royal College of Art in 2013 and the founding of a Brooke-Rose Society; and numerous events and publications for the Muriel Spark centenary in 2018.

Chapter 1

Muriel Spark and the Possibility of Popular Experiment

Marina MacKay

In Muriel Spark's *Loitering with Intent* (1981), narrator Fleur Talbot is walking on Hampstead Heath with world-weary journalist Solly Mendelsohn and ancient Lady Edwina. It is 1949 and Fleur has just lent the manuscript of her first novel to her lover's wife, Dottie.

> I said, 'Dottie's sort of the general reader in my mind'.
> 'Fuck the general reader', Solly said, 'because in fact the general reader doesn't exist'.
> 'That's what I say', Edwina yelled. 'Just fuck the general reader. No such person'.[1]

The episode is amusing because the obscenity is so at odds with Spark's usually elegant wit, and is even more absurdly discordant coming from the elderly Lady Edwina. As with many of Spark's ancillary characters, it is never clear that Edwina is conscious of the meanings of the words that leave her mouth – she soon loudly echoes Solly's advice that Fleur should urge her unreliable publisher 'to wipe his arse' with their meaningless contract.[2] But what of Fleur's 'general reader'? This chapter proposes that the kind of ventriloquism Edwina represents here was fundamental to Spark's creation of a body of popularly experimental fiction.

Popularly experimental may seem a contradiction in terms. '"Experimental" is the dirtiest of words, invariably a synonym for "unsuccessful",' complained B. S. Johnson in 1965.[3] Spark's fiction clearly escaped this stigmatising label, with its connotations of the unsellable and the unreadable. When she became Dame Muriel Spark in 1993, the honour confirmed what the national reception of her fiction had long implied: a widely reviewed and Booker-nominated novelist of upper-middlebrow appeal and literary seriousness whose novels had been adapted for theatre, film and television. Reading her fiction in the USA suggests a slightly edgier Spark. Although she was a *New Yorker* author from the 1960s onwards – they published the best known of her twenty-two novels, *The Prime of Miss Jean Brodie*, in 1961 – much of her back catalogue is published by New Directions, a house associated with experimental writing ever since its founding by the poet and modernist promoter James Laughlin in 1937.[4] Recent critics such as Victoria Stewart and James Bailey see affinities between Spark and avant-garde contemporaries, particularly her friend Christine Brooke-Rose, and Spark openly acknowledged the influence of the *nouveau roman*.[5] Yet in *For a New Novel* (1963), its major practitioner Alain Robbe-Grillet expressed dismay at being cast as 'a "difficult" author' when really he 'was eager to write for the "reading public"'.[6] '"Difficult"' here does the same work as Johnson's '"experimental"': reaching a mainstream readership with formally tricky, anti-realist, metafictional novels was an unusual achievement on Spark's part.

An admiring Leo Robson notes her simultaneous 'popularity' and 'postmodernism', her worldly wit and her testing of the whole concept of fiction: 'the beady, troubled and troublesome offspring of Jane Austen and B S Johnson'.[7] She is a novelist who defies easy classification, we might say, were we to resort to the type of clapped-out formula that – as I suggest in what follows – her novels exploit to unsettling effect. She is certainly unusual in the postwar canon for producing novels at the far fringes of realism that are not merely written about but also read. A 'proto Post-Modernist', John Lanchester calls her: 'The great flaw in Post-Modernism, however, has always been that the writer's freedom to expose the fictionality of fiction tends to be precisely paralleled by the reader's freedom not to care what happens in the book.'[8] Yet it is probably not at the level of plot that Spark holds her readership. In her most instantly popular novels, either her signature use of prolepsis announces 'what happens in the book' (as in *The Prime of Miss Jean Brodie*) or the plot resolution is too abnormal to be remotely satisfying (the enigmatic caller in *Memento Mori* (1959) is 'death' – but what could that even mean?). Instead, what connects the conventional and the experimental in Spark's fiction is her attention to the automatised verbal forms of everyday life, and particularly the cliché. In what follows, I describe, firstly, how her fiction emphasises the repurposing of ordinary language and, secondly, how her rendering of personhood as mere ventriloquism of second-hand discourse suggests the distinctive moral conditions out of which many mid-century experiments emerged.

'My own voice and nobody else's': Spark and the Ready-Made

Thinking about Spark as a mid-century writer, as *Loitering with Intent* encourages, we might read her interest in recitation by looking backwards to late modernism or forward to postmodernism. Discussing the late works of the high modernists, John Whittier-Ferguson finds that, by the late 1930s, 'Make it new' has become 'Make it again'.[9] Thus, in his striking account of Virginia Woolf's final novels, we find that little 'could be mistaken for something Woolf would have written in the 1920s', not, ironically, because she is cultivating new idioms but because she turns to the overused: 'the world's ordinary language, . . . passing platitudes, hackneyed phrases, received ideas, and familiar, if botched, quotations from English literature'.[10] Her late work recovers 'catchphrases, clichés, conversational filler . . . the ordinary and the unredeemed, the repetitive, the banal, the common bits and pieces of the languaged world'.[11] Or, if we read Spark forward, her recourse to the ready-made might anticipate Roland Barthes's 'From Work to Text' (1971), in which 'the citations which go to make up a text are anonymous, untraceable, and yet *already read*: they are quotations without inverted commas'.[12] Considering Spark in this transitional context between a late modernism newly accommodating the verbal texture of everyday life and a postmodernism advancing citationality as a fundamental condition of writing helps to explain why her fiction is both experimental and deeply readable. Her simultaneous verbal and social attentiveness makes for deceptive familiarity – even Spark's titles are usually derived from old tags and clichés – at the same time as the overall effect is to defamiliarise the recognisable social environments that she purports to be describing.

Spark's attention to cliché is closely connected to the interest in voice evidenced from her earliest fiction: the protagonist of her first novel, *The Comforters* (1957), is tormented by a disembodied narrative voice that anticipates or recounts her activities, while one of Spark's earliest collections, a compilation of short stories and radio features ('all were written on the same creative wavelength'), is instructively titled *Voices at Play* (1961).[13] A concern with voice *as such* is a familiar feature of the mid-century avant-garde, reaching its bleak apotheosis in Samuel Beckett's *Not I* (1972), which consists entirely of the otherwise disembodied 'Mouth' emitting her lines at furious speed on a blacked-out stage. Many critics have noticed Spark's auditory aesthetic. Describing the problematics of hearing people speak in a Second World War culture saturated by the dangerous sounds of authority, Lyndsey Stonebridge argues that 'the voice itself becomes an object of scrutiny' in Spark's war-set *The Girls of Slender Means* (1963).[14] Most recently, Amy Woodbury Tease suggests that Spark's media-saturated fiction extends modernism's attention to the wireless and telephone into the age of surveillance: 'Haunted by disembodied voices, terrorized by anonymous callers, and subjected to twenty-four-hour surveillance, Spark's characters are suspicious, untrustworthy, and cunning.'[15] I share their sense of the centrality of voice, and would add that Spark is particularly attentive to unowned voice, automated speech and unconscious ventriloquism. Like mid-century political writers from Hannah Arendt to George Orwell, Spark considers speech a test of good faith: like them, she is concerned not simply with what people say but also with how far they are really in control of what they are saying. For Spark, this sense of ownership marked the difference between the artist and everyone else: 'I am aware of my own voice, always', she explained in a late interview, 'because I speak with my own voice and nobody else's.'[16]

Her semi-autobiographical Fleur encounters early in her career the distinction between writing in one's own voice and merely serving as an unreflective conduit for the words of others. 'I've been writing ever since with great care,' Fleur announces. 'I always hope the readers of my novels are of good quality. I wouldn't like to think of anyone cheap reading my books.'[17] The joke is about literary rather than social class, for Fleur's nemesis is the supremely snobbish Sir Quentin Oliver, of whom she writes sardonically that he is 'far too democratic for the likes of me. He sincerely believed that talent, although not equally distributed by nature, could be later conferred by a title or acquired by inherited rank.'[18] For Fleur, 'readers ... of good quality' are those sophisticated enough to appreciate her overturning of clichés ('democratic', 'good quality', 'cheap').

Sir Quentin's literary insensibility becomes clear when Fleur reads with a connoisseur's delight his thumbnail sketches of the members of his Autobiographical Association:

> Major-General Sir George C Beverley, Bt., CBE, DSO, formerly in that 'crack' regiment of the Blues and now a successful, a very successful businessman in the City and on the Continent. General Sir George is a cousin of that fascinating, that infinitely fascinating hostess, Lady Bernice 'Bucks' Gilbert, widow of the former chargé d'affaires in San Salvador, Sir Arthur Gilbert, KCMG, CBE (1919) whose portrait, executed by that famous, that illustrious, portrait painter Sir Ames Baldwin, KBE, hangs in the magnificent North Dining Room of Landers Place, Bedfordshire . . . .[19]

Spark often excerpts and indents literary text like this, bringing it into the foreground for critical inspection. Fleur calls Sir Quentin's autobiographical sketch 'a kind of poem' in its effort to make his misfit acolytes sound as socially grand as possible.[20] What makes it a very bad poem is its recourse to the same trite formula of amplification, what we might call mandarin anaphora: 'a successful, a very successful businessman', 'that fascinating, that infinitely fascinating hostess', 'that famous, that illustrious, portrait painter'. Indeed, Sir Quentin's verbal taste is so poor that he is captivated by Fleur's redescription of Lady Edwina's urinary incontinence as 'fluxive precipitations': in a slyly obscene analogy that marks the difference between the authentically and the spuriously literary, Fleur describes Sir Quentin repeating the phrase 'as if he were tasting a wine new to his experience, but which he was prepared to go more than half way towards approving'.[21]

However, Sir Quentin is not the novel's only bad writer, for Fleur is having an affair with Leslie, husband of 'the general reader', Dottie. Among Leslie's verbal offences, as Fleur cuttingly informs Dottie, is 'that dreadful recurrent phrase of his, "With regard to . . ."':

> I meant to tell her more about Leslie's prose, its frightful tautology. He never reached the point until it was undetectably lost in a web of multi-syllabic words and images trowelled on like cement.
> She said, 'You didn't say this when you were sleeping with him'.
> 'I didn't sleep with him for his prose style'.[22]

Bad writing is overwriting. Leslie anticipates Hector Bartlett, the devastatingly nicknamed 'pisseur de copie' ('he urinates frightful prose') of *A Far Cry from Kensington* (1988), another retrospective novel drawing on Spark's early career. Hector's prose 'writhed and ached with twists and turns and tergiversations, inept words, fanciful repetitions, far-fetched verbosity'.[23] Worse, he speaks only in clichés, as when he asks the protagonist to advance his plan to adapt the fiction of his (talented) lover, Emma Loy:

> 'It would be preferable to procure an introduction from Martin York', he said. 'It would be let us say a decided feather in Martin's cap. You yourself should have a word in Martin's ear with regard to the possibility of transmuting this fine work of fiction to a saga of the silver screen. Nepotism is still I believe the order of the day'.
> How could Emma Loy stand him?[24]

The absence of the expected commas around 'let us say' and 'I believe' further diminishes the sense of an actual consciousness at work selecting his words. Indeed, Hector speaks not in words but in phrases, to borrow a distinction from Orwell: '*phrases* tacked together like the sections of a prefabricated hen-house' or 'prefabricated phrases bolted together like the pieces of a child's Meccano set'[25] – a feather in one's cap, a saga of the silver screen and the order of the day.

Loitering with Intent and *A Far Cry from Kensington* were published in the 1980s but Spark's comic defamiliarisation of bad style goes back to the mid-century period she revisits there. The demonic Dougal Douglas of *The Ballad of Peckham Rye* (1960) is, appropriately enough, a ghostwriter. As he drafts the memoirs of forgotten actress Maria Cheeseman, his notebook ('Phrases Suitable for Cheese') underscores how bad writing is always ghosted:

> Memory had not played me false.
> He was always an incurable romantic
> I became the proud owner of a bicycle.
> He spoke to me in desiccated tones.
> Autumn again. Autumn. The burning of leaves in the park.
> He spelt disaster to me.
> I revelled in my first tragic part.
> I had no eyes for any other man.
> We were living a lie.
> She proved a mine of information.
> Once more fate intervened.
> Munificence was his middle name.[26]

The mere excerpting of the clichés is obviously funny in an ordinary mocking way – in every sense, the ghostwriter knows his 'Cheese' – but it is also as estranging as poetry, since we suddenly see anew the peculiar surreality of defunct metaphors (would the ludicrous 'Munificence' be a worse middle name than other nominalised virtues such as Patience or Faith?). The possibility of meaningfulness suddenly bubbles up from what overuse has rendered low-content page-filler. Characters mystified by Dougal's list wonder if he is writing in code; for the reader, the compilation recalls found poetry.

'Predominantly a poet': Ventriloquism in Verse

Spark told an interviewer that she liked her language 'to be very correct, very accurate, and I don't like to spread myself too much' – she clarified, 'I mean I don't like long involved sentences.'[27] In her memoir, she recalled that early editorial positions had taught her 'how to copy-edit tactfully. I recall that I took out a great many adjectives.'[28] Her surrogate Fleur likewise observes 'how little one needs, in the art of writing, to convey the lot, and how a lot of words, on the other hand, can convey so little'.[29] Perhaps this identification of good writing with economy helps to explain why, despite the fact that her reputation depends on her fiction rather than her verse, she argued that 'the novel as an art form was essentially a variation of a poem' and considered herself 'predominantly a poet'.[30] She offered an interviewer her definition of 'poetic vision': 'being aware of the value of words, sometimes in their etymology, in two or three senses, in a very quick flash'.[31]

Yet her fiction typically associates poetry with cliché and impersonated feeling, and her poets seem only dimly aware that individual words have any meaning at all, let alone several. Decrepit survivor of the decadent 1890s, Percy Mannering in *Memento Mori* responds to the memento mori of the telephone calls with a sonnet entitled 'Memento Mori', for which Spark writes three endings:

> Out of the deep resounds the hollow cry,
> *Remember—oh, remember you must die!*
>
> But slowly the reverberating sigh
> Sounds in my ear: *Remember you must die!*
>
> And from afar the Voices mingle and cry
> O mortal Man, *remember you must die!*[32]

The phony 'Memento Mori' is not a poem about death but an unselfconscious mimicry of obsolete ways of writing about death. It serves as ludicrous contrast to the novel of the same title in which it appears, with its crisp prose factuality about biological finitude, about the pains and humiliations of ageing.

In a novel published the following year, Spark associates poetic recitation with outright fraud. Séance medium Patrick Seton in *The Bachelors* (1960) seduces credulous victims through poetry as well as spiritualism:

> As a young man he memorizes the early poems of W. B. Yeats and will never forget them. Now, on his first visit to the Western Isles he first encounters an unfortunate occurrence, having sat up reciting to an American lady far into the night and the next morning being accused of having taken money from her purse.[33]

'He recites poetry so beautifully. He's a sort of a real artist,' says Alice, the girlfriend whom he plans to murder. 'I'll agree,' her friend replies: 'he's a first-rate medium.'[34] This is not the non sequitur it appears, for it is always the words of others that pass through Seton: the fact that the novel's plot hinges on his forging of someone else's handwriting seals the implied connections among mediumship, poetry and fraudulent impersonation. Seton is no 'real artist' but his gifts as a ventriloquist might indeed make him 'a sort of a real artist', as Alice puts it. At the same time as Spark mimics the redundant tics of ordinary speech ('a sort of a'), she invites the attentive reader to catch another meaning here, where artistry is no longer defined by the absolutely original but incorporates the ersatz and ready-made.

'He used to recite "Season of mists and mellow fruitfulness"', one victim recalls: 'it was a deepening experience.'[35] In Spark's most-read novel, the charismatic Miss Jean Brodie uses the very same line to introduce her pupils to her fictional lover Hugh Carruthers, a composite of Keats, Burns and the poetic war dead from Flodden to Flanders – and Miss Brodie is nothing if not 'a sort of a real artist'.[36] Miss Brodie is so recognisable as to be a figure of myth in a way that must be unique in postwar British fiction – it is hard to think of a mid-century character with comparable cultural status, except, perhaps, in certain institutional environments, Anthony Powell's ebullient climber Kenneth Widmerpool – and yet her distinctive speech (we see her only from the outside) is essentially a composite of pre-existing catchphrases. In our first glimpse of her classroom, she is, instructively, having the girls recite poetry:

> 'It lifts one up', Miss Brodie usually said, passing her hand outward from her breast towards the class of ten-year-old girls who were listening for the bell which would release them. 'Where there is no vision', Miss Brodie had assured them, 'the people perish. Eunice, come and do a somersault in order that we may have comic relief'.[37]

Only a few paragraphs later, her most famous phrase makes its first appearance:

> 'I am putting old heads on your young shoulders', Miss Brodie had told them at the time, 'and all my pupils are the crème de la crème.'[38]

Miss Brodie speaks substantially in borrowed phrases: 'Where there is no vision, the people perish' is a quotation from the scriptural book of Proverbs (29: 18); 'comic relief', 'old heads on . . . young shoulders' and the 'crème de la crème' are ordinary clichés. This most popular of Spark's novels is, in fact, among her most self-referential and citational; it is a book about the construction of charismatic individuality out of repurposed saws and catchphrases.

Miss Brodie's girls come only slowly (if at all) to see through her literal fabrications. The adult reader, in contrast, apprehends much earlier that Miss Brodie's voice may be absolutely original but mainly in the way a patchwork is original. Spark underscores the point through Jenny's and Sandy's sweetly juvenile scrutiny of barely understood maxims, as they celebrate Sandy's tenth birthday with pineapple cubes and cream:

> 'Little girls, you are going to be the crème de la crème', said Sandy, and Jenny spluttered her cream into her handkerchief.
> 'You know', Sandy said, 'these are supposed to be the happiest days of our lives'.
> 'Yes, they are always saying that', Jenny said. 'They say, make the most of your schooldays because you never know what lies ahead of you'.
> 'Miss Brodie says prime is best', Sandy said.
> 'Yes, but she never got married like our mothers and fathers'.
> 'They don't have primes', said Sandy.
> 'They have sexual intercourse', Jenny said.
> The little girls paused, because this was still a stupendous thought, and one which they had only lately hit upon; the very phrase and its meaning were new. It was quite unbelievable.[39]

Working through the axioms of Miss Brodie and others, they evaluate claims about schooldays, primes and sex as statements of literal fact. (Although they are ready to accept most of these claims, the most factual – or the facts of life, as customarily euphemised – is ironically the only one that they find 'quite unbelievable'.)

Breaking away from Miss Brodie means becoming sceptical about her characteristic language. Churchgoing Eunice pleads off an outing with Miss Brodie 'because of something else she had to attend which she described as "a social"'. '"Social what?" said Miss Brodie, who always made difficulties about words when she scented heresy.'[40] After she betrays Miss Brodie, and 'betrayal' becomes the broken Miss Brodie's new catchword, protégée Sandy starts making her own 'difficulties about words': 'If you did not betray us it is impossible that you could have been betrayed by us,' she tells Miss Brodie: 'The word betrayed does not apply . . . .'[41] Sandy is going too far – to borrow an earlier warning from Miss Brodie – in stretching words beyond their received meanings in order to license her own actions; loyalty may be conditional in practice but it is not inherently so, since one can remain loyal to a person by whom one has been or felt betrayed. Sandy knows how to wrench old words into new meanings, just like her mentor, and, of course, her author.

'A speaking machine ... gone wrong': Violence and Automated Speech

Spark's narrator does precisely this at the start of her next novel, *The Girls of Slender Means*. 'Long ago in 1945 all the nice people were poor,' she announces in an opening line that she soon qualifies: 'All the nice people were poor; at least, that was a general axiom, the best of the rich being poor in spirit.'[42] Within the space of the first paragraph, 'poor' has lost its literal meaning and gained an exculpatory metaphorical one, while the novel's brutal events will eviscerate the snobbish conflation that gives 'nice' its double meaning of genteel and kind. Even by Spark's standards, *The Girls of Slender Means* is remarkably preoccupied by second-hand speech. Among the publishing assistant Jane's jobs is discovering the exploitable vulnerabilities of the firm's authors. She hits on what she believes is a winning formula: 'What is your raison d'être?' she asks aspirant writers, oblivious to the formula's crushing triteness. But Jane comes unstuck when she puts the question to Nick Farringdon, whose subsequent death prompts the flashbacks that comprise the main body of the novel. Nick merely looks at her 'as if she were a speaking machine that had gone wrong'.[43]

Jane credits the question to one of her 'brain-waves': along with 'brain work', this phrase is associated with her, largely by herself, throughout the novel, often several times per page.[44] Spark's joke is that the term 'brain-wave', especially when endlessly reiterated, points directly to mechanistic mindlessness. Jane's 'brain work' is essentially ventriloquism:

> First, and secretly, she wrote poetry of a strictly non-rational order, in which occurred, in about the proportion of cherries in a cherry-cake, certain words that she described as 'of a smouldering nature', such as loins and lovers, the root, the seawrack and the shroud. Secondly, also secretly, she wrote letters of a business intention.[45]

Her 'letters of a business intention' are frauds. Jane impersonates suffering women – released convicts, tuberculosis patients, unmarried mothers – to write fan mail to famous authors in the hope of eliciting lucrative handwritten replies. Her poetry is no less a form of mediumship, for she merely transmits the clichés of 1940s neo-Romantic poetry ('Dear Dylan Thomas', begins one of her bogus letters[46]). Jane's last name is 'Wright': both an ingenuously commonplace name and a warning about Jane's status as a maker or fabricator. This is a good example of how Spark asks the reader to look suspiciously into what at first glance sounds socially unremarkable to the point of banality.

Jane is only one of the novel's 'speaking machines'. Débutante Dorothy speaks in Sloane 'phrase-ripples': '"Filthy lunch." "The most gorgeous wedding." 'He actually raped her, she was amazed.'"[47] Beautiful Selina recites her 'Two Sentences', a form of autosuggestion that begins: 'Poise is perfect balance, an equanimity of body and mind, complete composure whatever the social scene . . . .'[48] Its success is darkly confirmed when Selina re-enters the burning hostel where the novel is set, not to rescue her friends but to steal another girl's gown ('Poise is perfect balance. It was the Schiaparelli dress').[49] Vicar's daughter Joanna is, of all things, an elocution teacher, of whom we are told that it is unusual for her 'to quote anything for its aptitude'.[50] When she finally quotes wholly aptly it is also, no less unsettlingly, by purely unconscious habit; as the hostel burns, she recites 'mechanically' and 'compulsively' the correct liturgy for the date, the 27th of the month.[51] Vassiliki Kolocotroni identifies the creepiness of Joanna's voice: 'uncannily, eerily mechanical, as if disembodied or agentless'.[52] As Stonebridge writes, there is 'finally, perhaps, nothing human . . . about the voices in *The Girls of Slender Means*'.[53] Ian Gregson objects to Spark's fiction on these grounds, for the identification of characters with their speech patterns 'suggest[s] the repetitions of a mechanism rather than the growth of an organism. They invoke, not the branching roads of the humanist self, but the cul-de-sac of caricature.'[54]

'Caricature' seems the wrong word for Spark's characters: the fictional world of caricature is one in which characters recall such familiar types that a few exaggerated pencil strokes can signify their essence. On the contrary, the eerie effect of many of Spark's characters comes from their composite formation, and the reader's sense that there may be no singular underlying essence distinct from their dissemination of the words of others. More consequentially, the 'humanist self' is probably not the most relevant model for mid-century fiction. Robbe-Grillet argued that '[t]he novel of characters belongs entirely to the past, it describes a period: that which marked the apogee of the individual'.[55] This is in keeping with Robbe-Grillet's broader arguments about the need for contemporary novelists (and reviewers) to surrender their unreflective attachments to obsolete forms. But he said more than this when he clarified immediately that it was not 'an advance' that the humanist sense of the person was irrelevant in a world in which people are merely 'administrative numbers'.[56] As he dryly wrote of nineteenth-century realism, '[i]t was something to have a face in a universe where personality represented both the means and the end of all exploration'.[57] For Robbe-Grillet, these changed conditions for personhood were a new factor with which the mid-century novel needed to reckon.

And Spark did. Her pre-eminent instance of a 'speaking machine gone wrong' is not, in the end, endearing, silly Jane but a figure drawn from life in the novel Spark was then finding much harder to write, *The Mandelbaum Gate* (1965). Barbara Vaughan is attending what is ironically described as 'a boring phase' of the trial of Adolf Eichmann in Jerusalem:

> Minute by minute throughout the hours the prisoner discoursed on the massacre without mentioning the word, covering all aspects of every question addressed to him with the meticulous undiscriminating reflex of a computing machine. Barbara turned the switch of her earphones to other simultaneous translations – French, Italian, then back to English. What was he talking about? The effect was the same in any language, and the terrible paradox remained, and the actual discourse was a dead mechanical tick, while its subject, the massacre, was living. She thought, it all feels like a familiar dream, and presently located the sensation as one that the anti-novelists induce.[58]

This is not an attack on the anti-novel but a reflection on the historical conditions from which it emerged. As Arendt famously argued, Eichmann's total moral insensibility could be understood in relation to totalitarian 'language rules' ('itself a code name; it meant whatever in ordinary language would be called a lie'), whereby dispossession, torture and murder could never be named as such: 'Eichmann's great susceptibility to catch words and stock phrases, combined with his incapacity for ordinary speech, made him, of course, an ideal subject for "language rules".'[59] He is a speaking machine of the most dangerous kind imaginable.

The shape of her mid-century career shows that Spark's attendance at the Eichmann trial was not the cause of her attention to automated speech, but it confirmed why that interest was of deeper moral and historical significance than was apparent in her earlier work, where, even in the case of the fascist-sympathising Miss Brodie, the endless recourse to recitation is more funny than sinister. It seems significant that the novels Spark wrote immediately after *The Mandelbaum Gate* were simultaneously among her most violent and those she considered most indebted to the *nouveau roman*, whose mood Eichmann's inhuman ventriloquism had summoned for Barbara Vaughan.[60] Among them was Spark's declared favourite, *The Driver's Seat* (1970).[61] Like many of the others, it begins with a cliché: the driver's seat is a tired metaphor for an autonomy that is shockingly overturned when protagonist Lise is denied even the chance to determine the circumstances of her planned self-destruction, a suicide by murderer, if she can find the right man to kill her. Nowhere in Spark's œuvre does cliché do such devastating work as when this young single woman ('You're young and you have your life in front of you') goes on holiday in the sun ('I'm going to have the time of my life') in pursuit of the right man, the one who 'will recognize me right away for the woman I am', the man who is exactly her 'type'.[62] Flipping all the verbal formulae of the holiday romance, *The Driver's Seat* exposes in the most lacerating way the significance of cliché for thinking about the un-freedom of the would-be autonomous human subject, and about the power and violence of the forces that speak through her.

Finally, when he discusses Spark's early work in relation to the undervalued experimentalism of British fiction in the 1950s, Nick Bentley finds that Spark is 'asking similar questions to Robbe-Grillet in French fiction, Sartre in philosophy, and Beckett in drama'.[63] The real surprise, though, is that such questions as those we identify with the postwar avant-garde and which I have associated here with Spark – questions of autonomy, ontology and the determining force of language – could be asked in so approachable a way. The 'general reader' proved to be a more teachable creature than Fleur's aptly named 'Dottie', for at the same time as Spark calls upon the reader's ordinary social competence, she offers a training in discrimination by showing how the most common verbal currency can be made to yield deeper and more disconcerting new meanings.

Notes

1. Muriel Spark, *Loitering with Intent* (London: Virago, 2012), p. 55.
2. Ibid. p. 56.
3. B. S. Johnson, 'Holes, Syllabics and the Succussations of the Intercostal and Abdominal Muscles', in *Selected Prose and Drama of B. S. Johnson*, ed. Jonathan Coe, Philip Tew and Julia Jordan (London: Picador, 2013), p. 396.

4. See Lisa Harrison, '"The Magazine That Is Considered the Best in the World": Muriel Spark and the *New Yorker*', in *Muriel Spark: Twenty-First-Century Perspectives*, ed. David Herman (Baltimore: Johns Hopkins University Press, 2010), pp. 39–60. See also Martin Stannard, *Muriel Spark: The Biography* (London: Weidenfeld & Nicolson, 2009), pp. 269–82.
5. Victoria Stewart, *The Second World War in Contemporary British Fiction: Secret Histories* (Edinburgh: Edinburgh University Press, 2011), pp. 20–54. James Bailey, 'Salutary Scars: The "Disorienting" Fiction of Muriel Spark', *Contemporary Women's Writing*, 9:1 (March 2015), pp. 34–52. Pressed by an interviewer on the influence of the *nouveau roman*, Spark explained that 'I was thinking the same thoughts that they were thinking, people like Robbe-Grillet. We were influenced by the same, breathing the same informed air. So, I naturally would have a bent towards the *nouveau roman* but in fact I was very influenced by Robbe-Grillet.' Martin McQuillan, '"The Same Informed Air": An Interview with Muriel Spark', in *Theorizing Muriel Spark: Gender, Race, Deconstruction* (Basingstoke: Palgrave, 2002), p. 215, p. 216. See also Robert Hosmer, 'An Interview with Dame Muriel Spark', *Salmagundi*, 146/7 (Spring–Summer 2005), p. 135.
6. Alain Robbe-Grillet, *For a New Novel: Essays on Fiction*, trans. Richard Howard (Evanston: Northwestern University Press, 1996), p. 8.
7. Leo Robson, 'Cold Mistress', *New Statesman*, 10 August 2009, pp. 40, 41–2.
8. John Lanchester, 'Introduction', in Muriel Spark, *The Driver's Seat* (London: Penguin, 2006), pp. vi, vii.
9. John Whittier-Ferguson, *Mortality and Form in Late Modernist Literature* (Cambridge: Cambridge University Press, 2014), p. 6.
10. Ibid. p. 10, p. 9.
11. Ibid. p. 26.
12. Roland Barthes, 'From Work to Text', *Image Music Text*, ed. and trans. Stephen Heath (London: Fontana, 1977), p. 160.
13. Muriel Spark, *Voices at Play: Stories and Ear-Pieces* (London: Macmillan, 1961), p. v.
14. Lyndsey Stonebridge, *The Writing of Anxiety: Imagining Wartime in Mid-Century British Culture* (Basingstoke: Palgrave Macmillan, 2007), p. 118. See also Alan Pero's Lacanian reading of Spark, '"Look for One Thing and You Find Another": The Voice and Deduction in Muriel Spark's *Memento Mori*', *Modern Fiction Studies*, 54:3 (Fall, 2008), pp. 558–73.
15. Amy Woodbury Tease, 'Call and Answer: Muriel Spark and Media Culture', *Modern Fiction Studies*, 62:1 (Spring, 2016), p. 74.
16. Hosmer, 'An Interview', p. 149.
17. Spark, *Loitering*, p. 171.
18. Ibid. p. 13.

19. Ibid. p. 11.
20. Ibid. p. 12.
21. Ibid. p. 20.
22. Ibid. p. 79.
23. Muriel Spark, *A Far Cry from Kensington* (London: Penguin, 1989), p. 109, p. 46.
24. Ibid. p. 49.
25. George Orwell, 'Politics and the English Language', *A Collection of Essays* (Orlando, FL: Harcourt, 1981), p. 159; George Orwell, 'The Prevention of Literature', *The Collected Essays, Journalism and Letters Volume 4*, ed. Sonia Orwell and Ian Angus (Boston: David R Godine, 2000), p. 66.
26. Muriel Spark, *The Ballad of Peckham Rye* (New York: New Directions, 1999), p. 91.
27. Sarah Smith, 'Columbia Talks with Muriel Spark', *Columbia: A Journal of Literature and Art*, 30 (Fall, 1998), p. 205.
28. Muriel Spark, *Curriculum Vitae: A Volume of Autobiography* (London: Penguin, 1993), p. 165.
29. Spark, *Loitering*, p. 60.
30. Ibid. p. 206.
31. Stephen Schiff, 'Muriel Spark Between the Lines', *The New Yorker*, 24 May 1993, p. 41.
32. Muriel Spark, *Memento Mori* (New York: New Directions, 2000), p. 198.
33. Muriel Spark, *The Bachelors* (New York: New Directions, 1999), p. 132.
34. Ibid. pp. 15–16.
35. Ibid. p. 152.
36. Muriel Spark, *The Prime of Miss Jean Brodie* (New York: Perennial, 1999), p. 9.
37. Ibid. p. 4.
38. Ibid. p. 5.
39. Ibid. pp. 14–15.
40. Ibid. p. 65.
41. Ibid. pp. 135–6.
42. Muriel Spark, *The Girls of Slender Means* (New York: New Directions, 1998), p. 7.
43. Ibid. p. 41.
44. On the 'brain-wave', see Spark, *Girls*, p. 41, p. 45, p. 46, p. 47 and *passim*. On 'brain work', p. 34, p. 35, p. 36, p. 37 and *passim*.
45. Ibid. p. 37.
46. Ibid. p. 82.
47. Ibid. p. 44.
48. Ibid. p. 50.
49. Ibid. p. 125.

50. Ibid. p. 12.
51. Ibid. p. 126, p. 129.
52. Vassiliki Kolocotroni, 'Poetic Perception in the Fiction of Muriel Spark', in *The Edinburgh Companion to Muriel Spark*, ed. Michael Gardiner and Willy Maley (Edinburgh: Edinburgh University Press, 2010), p. 18.
53. Stonebridge, *The Writing of Anxiety*, p. 129.
54. Ian Gregson, *Character and Satire in Post-War Fiction* (London: Bloomsbury, 2013), p. 107.
55. Robbe-Grillet, *For a New Novel*, p. 28.
56. Ibid. p. 29.
57. Ibid. p. 29.
58. Muriel Spark, *The Mandelbaum Gate* (New York: Welcome Rain, 2001), p. 187.
59. Hannah Arendt, *Eichmann in Jerusalem: A Report on the Banality of Evil* (London: Penguin, 1994), pp. 85–6.
60. McQuillan, '"The Same Informed Air"', p. 215.
61. Ibid. p. 229.
62. Spark, *The Driver's Seat*, p. 60, p. 6, pp. 60–1. The pseudo-romantic 'type' appears on pp. 27, 31, 32, 38, 58, 64, 77, 84, 86, 89 and 98 – sometimes several times on a single page.
63. Nick Bentley, *Radical Fictions: The English Novel in the 1950s* (Oxford: Peter Lang, 2007), p. 170.

Chapter 2

B. S. Johnson: The Book as Dynamic Object

Joseph Darlington

When it comes to British avant-garde writing in the 1960s, B. S. Johnson's name is often at the forefront. His novels pushed the limits of what was technically possible in the medium of print at that time. This began with experiments with font and page layouts (described as 'graphic devices' by Glyn White);[1] his unbound 'book-in-a-box', *The Unfortunates* (1969); and, finally, cross-media works involving film, text and image. Johnson's insistence on blunt, straightforward prose and unsentimental imagery led fellow 1960s avant-gardist, Christine Brooke-Rose, to describe his writing as 'fashionable drab social realism'.[2] Johnson's standoffish personality and militant approach to promoting himself and his allies in a 'campaign for the good stuff'[3] also served to alienate much of the British literary establishment in his lifetime. Over the years, however, many of these negatives have been reframed as positives. Since the publication of Jonathan Coe's *Like A Fiery Elephant: The B. S. Johnson Story* in 2004, there has been a concerted effort by scholars and fans to reconnect to Johnson's avant-garde vision as a whole, seeing in his apparently disparate and contradictory approaches a recognisable literary position. This chapter argues that Johnson's innovations have the political intention of disrupting traditional reading patterns. In his philosophy, these traditions are synonymous with complacency; the innovative novel is therefore conceived as a force for modernisation and the disruption of a political establishment.

The chapter proceeds in three sections. The first considers Johnson's novels as dynamic objects and borrows from the language of design theory to describe how they encourage active readership. The second utilises materials from the Johnson archive to unpack Johnson's conflicted relationship with his working-class origins and to consider how a political commitment to truth and authenticity emerges from this in opposition to bourgeois elitism. The third and final section brings these two aspects of Johnson's writing together to reread *The Unfortunates* as a text that is avant-garde in both its form and its political implications. Johnson's commitment to communicating truth is embodied in a novel requiring the complicity of the reader to shuffle its pages. He demonstrates how direct communication requires the creation of space by the speaker for audience interpretation and response.

B. S. Johnson and the Book

Figure 2.1 is taken from the opening pages of *Albert Angelo* (1964), Johnson's second novel and the first of the recognised œuvre.[4] In the novel, we follow Albert, the visionary architect of the section below, as he works as a substitute teacher to support his architectural hobby, goes out with friends, and is revealed to be a construct of the author who is 'trying to tell you something of what I feel about being a poet in a world where only poets care anything about real poetry through the objective correlative of an architect who has to earn his living as a teacher'.[5] This 'almighty aposiopesis'[6] is one of a number of devices, physical and otherwise, that draw explicit attention to the novel as

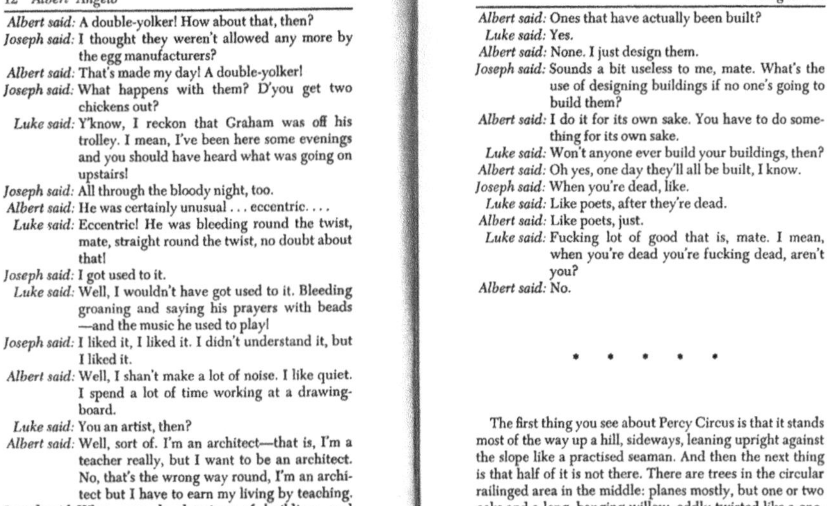

12 *Albert Angelo*

Albert said: A double-yolker! How about that, then?
Joseph said: I thought they weren't allowed any more by the egg manufacturers?
Albert said: That's made my day! A double-yolker!
Joseph said: What happens with them? D'you get two chickens out?
Luke said: Y'know, I reckon that Graham was off his trolley. I mean, I've been here some evenings and you should have heard what was going on upstairs!
Joseph said: All through the bloody night, too.
Albert said: He was certainly unusual . . . eccentric. . . .
Luke said: Eccentric! He was bleeding round the twist, mate, straight round the twist, no doubt about that!
Joseph said: I got used to it.
Luke said: Well, I wouldn't have got used to it. Bleeding groaning and saying his prayers with beads —and the music he used to play!
Joseph said: I liked it, I liked it. I didn't understand it, but I liked it.
Albert said: Well, I shan't make a lot of noise. I like quiet. I spend a lot of time working at a drawing-board.
Luke said: You an artist, then?
Albert said: Well, sort of. I'm an architect—that is, I'm a teacher really, but I want to be an architect. No, that's the wrong way round, I'm an architect but I have to earn my living by teaching.
Joseph said: What, you do drawings of buildings and things?
Albert said: Yes.
Luke said: What buildings have you done, then?

Prologue 13

Albert said: Ones that have actually been built?
Luke said: Yes.
Albert said: None. I just design them.
Joseph said: Sounds a bit useless to me, mate. What's the use of designing buildings if no one's going to build them?
Albert said: I do it for its own sake. You have to do something for its own sake.
Luke said: Won't anyone ever build your buildings, then?
Albert said: Oh yes, one day they'll all be built, I know.
Joseph said: When you're dead, like.
Luke said: Like poets, after they're dead.
Albert said: Like poets, just.
Luke said: Fucking lot of good that is, mate. I mean, when you're dead you're fucking dead, aren't you?
Albert said: No.

* * * * *

The first thing you see about Percy Circus is that it stands most of the way up a hill, sideways, leaning upright against the slope like a practised seaman. And then the next thing is that half of it is not there. There are trees in the circular railinged area in the middle: planes mostly, but one or two oaks and a long, hanging willow, oddly twisted like a one-legged circus tumbler. There is a little grass there, too, and rubbish of various kinds littered around—bicycle wheels, bottomless enamel buckets, tins, rotting cardboard. Some

Figure 2.1 B. S. Johnson, *Albert Angelo* [1964], in *B. S. Johnson Omnibus* (London: Picador, 2004), pp. 12–13.

a constructed object. This conforms to the 'ontological break'[7] that McHale prescribes as a defining feature of postmodernism, suggesting Johnson prefigures the concept. Rather than distance the reader through irony, however, that other defining postmodern characteristic, Johnson's text uses these techniques to open a dialogue with the active reader, to encourage them to challenge their immersion in narrative and actively undertake interpretation of the object before them, and, in doing so, become, at least nominally, a co-writer of the text: a fellow poet in a world that cares about poetry.

The opening scene in question is implicitly domestic: three characters bumbling over the stove. The characters' banter is jovial but competitive. It is not an environment in which cultivated and refined intellectual discussion would be forthcoming. When the subject of Albert's architecture is raised, it is met with a statement that could only be a performance of wilful ignorance: 'what, you do drawings of buildings and things?'[8] Albert eventually has to admit, after a satirical back-and-forth, that he *does* in fact believe in the transcendence of cultural creation beyond the present life of its creator. This faith in the power of art is not only one that Albert subscribes to, but also something he builds his life around: 'I'm an architect but I have to earn my living by teaching.'[9] Albert's visionary aspirations are diminished by the implied values of his setting, and his commitment to art is immediately perceived by the other characters as incongruous.

However, as White has already commented about Johnson's work, what 'promises great intimacy ... simultaneously devalues it, questions the honesty of the process by which it is achieved and challenges the motives that drive us to seek it'.[10] In this instance, we can look to the presentation of this dialogue, its physical appearance on the page, as a defamiliarising subtext inviting a more ambiguous reading of the opening scene. The immediate appearance of the text suggests drama rather than prose. Each character's name appears prior to their statements, and the setting of the scene is framed by context clues in the dialogue rather than third-person description. The scene is staged. The technique of withholding his hero from the first scene and using supporting characters to provide exposition is well established in drama, its usage going back to Shakespeare.[11] In this case, we might take Albert as one of these supporting characters, his architecture (or Johnson's 'poetry') taking the role of hero-to-be-announced. And yet, there is something at odds with this reading as well. Johnson includes 'said' after every character's name. This is clearly a novelistic device, and somewhat of a cliché that Johnson plays with on other occasions too, such as in *Christie Malry's Own Double-Entry* (1973) when he writes '"What I would like to", said Headlam, "Do is to make a discovery,"'[12] drawing attention to the convention of interjecting the speaker's name between clauses by intentionally introducing it mid-clause instead. There is an ambiguity here, with Johnson staging the novel form as much as his characters' interactions, inviting the reader to visualise the dramatic scene while also revealing the mechanics of its description. The text is ultimately irreducible to either the language on the page or the graphic device which presents it; both aspects hang in questioning relation to each other, whole and yet apart, awaiting the active reader to enter into interpretative dialogue with the book and contribute their own quota of speculative meaning to the text.

Our engagement with these opening pages of one of Johnson's novels reveals what is at stake with much of his project. David Hucklesby has described Johnson's 'argument' as one citing 'the specificity of the medium, the technical and formal possibilities offered by print, and the exploratory potential of language as key positions'.[13] Hucklesby describes how the history of books, language and the novel form are never taken for granted in Johnson's work. Each becomes a tool for disrupting expectation. To these, I would add the vital ingredient of the reader, who Johnson invites into his discourse and proceeds to challenge and threaten more than console. His work is a negotiation between the object's signifying potential and the expectations that precede textual consumption. Readers bring expectations to texts ranging from personal desires and preferences, through socially informed codes of taste, right down to the expectation that a novel is a work of fiction bound into book form with prose text aligned in a uniform pattern from top left to bottom right. It is true to an extent that Johnson 'upsets' these expectations but that is not his sole intention. Many of his avant-garde approaches to form, including the infamous 'book-in-a-box', were adaptations of formal experiments already conducted by others. The 'book-in-a-box' was tried by Marc Saporta, for example, while the black page in *Travelling People* is an obvious borrowing from Sterne. Johnson's focus was on learning from these experiments in order to unlock additional expressive potential from the novel form. His graphic devices allow novels to be metaphorical in their physical presentation as well as their written content.

Johnson's concern with physical presentation is tied to the ubiquity of design thinking in Britain during the 1960s. The Design Council (at that time the Council for Industrial Design) played a central role in promoting design philosophies and modernist practice across the now booming consumer goods industries. Council housing fell under the spell of modernism, and the Le Corbusier-inspired Brutalist movement in particular, in its campaign to demolish Victorian 'slum' housing and replace it with modern concrete tower blocks. Johnson found a key influence in Alison and Peter Smithson, Brutalist architects and designers of the (now infamous) Robin Hood Gardens project, going on to produce a BBC documentary, *The Smithsons on Housing* (1970), in order to promote their message. There are closer parallels between Johnson's approach to text and Le Corbusier's conception of houses as 'machines for living' than there are between Johnson's 'machines for reading' and any literary critics' theories that existed at the time of his writing.

Under these terms, we might think of Johnson as a designer of books. His textual production always followed considerable planning efforts; his archive reveals plans for plot, structure and presentation of novels years before the novels' publication and yet, for all this planning, very little in the way of written manuscripts. In an interview with Alan Burns, Johnson hints at this approach and sets it in a technological and class context:

> I learned typing at fourteen. I failed the eleven-plus and went to commercial school where they taught me shorthand, typing and book-keeping. Useful. While I'm typing I can't revise, I can't think. The manuscript gets into such an involved state because I have to do all the creative work before I start typing ... I [get] bored stiff, not by reading it because I wasn't reading it, but by the mechanical act of typing.[14]

Johnson's writing, as well as being funny, is also often extremely intimate, confessional in style and anguished in tone. This does not seem to fit with the 'mechanical act' described above: writing as merely a typing up of thoroughly planned-out material. The prose itself seems too fraught with emotion. We can perhaps square his writing with his account of its conception by considering the reader. The 'honest' is performed for their sake, with a planned structural effect in mind. As we will investigate further below, Johnson had an almost puritanical commitment to writing reflecting a writer's personal truth ('the truth of my truth'[15]), but this raw material only becomes a novel when it is structured, packaged and presented to an audience. This process is a design process. It corresponds to what Donald Norman has described as an 'appropriate conceptual model for [interaction]'[16] or, to return to the literary-theoretical mode, the text is produced in correspondence with the implied reader. If we might introduce a new term to bridge the theoretical gap between design language and textual theory, Johnson's texts are dynamic objects. They exist as potential narrative experiences. The reader receives the text while interacting with its mode of presentation. The 'novel' proper emerges as the accumulation of relevant interpretations. Working towards this end, Johnson designs the book with the reader's interaction in mind. An expected reader response is implicated in the book's design.[17]

To present a concrete example, let us consider pages 176 and 177 of *Christie Malry's Own Double-Entry* (Fig. 2.2). Across these pages Christie, the novel's eponymous protagonist, discovers he has cancer and relates this to his girlfriend, 'the Shrike', and her 'Old Mum'. As one may gather from their names, these characters are not fleshed out in the realist sense but rather exist metafictionally as self-aware narrative functions. As the novel progresses, however, Johnson uses all the techniques of traditional character development (sympathetic details, backstories, believable dialogue and so on), such that – in spite of the author repeatedly 'unveiling' them as fictions – we become emotionally invested in them. The reader's willingness to root for these fictions *as fictions*, as things that they *know* they are imagining, is essential for the dramatic and emotional core of key scenes like this to operate successfully. By constantly reminding us of these characters'

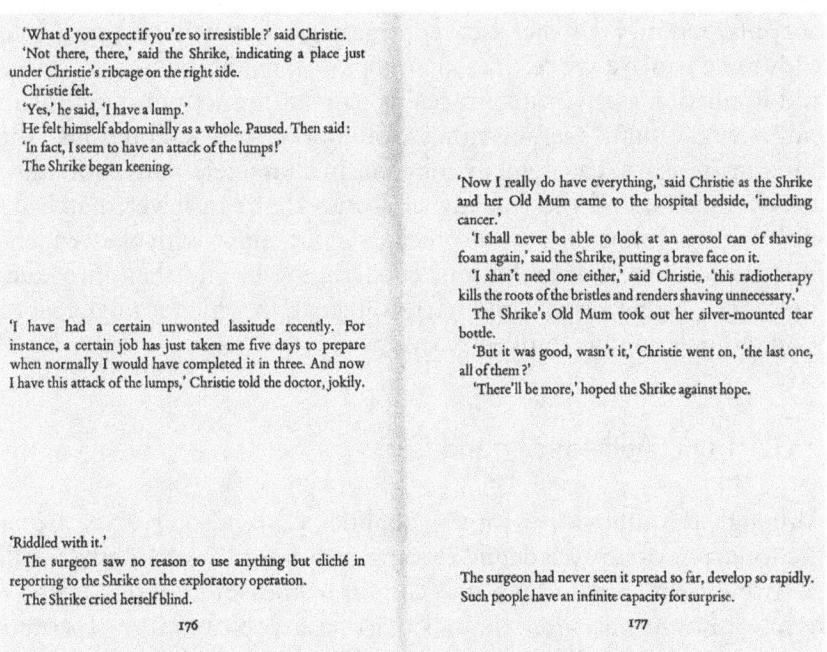

Figure 2.2 B. S. Johnson, *Christie Malry's Own Double-Entry* [1973] (London: Picador, 2001), pp. 176–7.

fictional status, Johnson is making present their lack, showing us the blanks, demonstrating that our emotional engagement with the text may begin with the page but soon expands beyond it through interpretation and imagination. As the author figure complains, 'What writer can compete with the reader's imagination!'[18]

Now return to the page. We see gaps in the text. We see blank space. At the very least these are pauses, causing our eye to take a fraction of a second to move from the close of one sentence to the opening of another. Reading the text, it becomes clear that these breaks in reading also reflect breaks in narrative time. We jump forward chronologically with each break. The language of cinema, with its quick 'cuts' between the most relevant moments (cutting out the irrelevant), is invoked, encouraging us to visualise our reading, to fill out the sparse descriptions with images of hospitals – perhaps those we have known or those from other works. These images, merely implied, also carry a particular tone: a tone of melodrama, fraught emotions, despair and consolation. Compare this to the actual dialogue of the characters – 'Now I really do have everything,' jokes Christie, who began the novel by wanting everything – and the authorial descriptions, which are sparse at best: 'The Shrike cried herself blind.'[19] Through the use of negative space, Johnson has designed our interaction with the text, contrasting what we are being told with the narrative space that surrounds it. The interaction of stated and implied narrative encourages us to read the written humour in pathetic relation to the unwritten around it. It is 'black humour', the humour of death, the comedy inherent in characters that know they are characters, and the tragedy of stories that can never match up with reality. Johnson is by no means 'competing' with the reader's imagination here but guiding it, encouraging it, and then introducing spaces, both physical and narratological, in which it might set to work completing his implied story.

Truth, Authenticity and Class

Although the innovative formal qualities of Johnson's texts are at the forefront of any academic reading of Johnson's work, his overall contribution to British literature cannot be measured purely in these terms. Johnson was, after all, only one of a sizeable number of writers experimenting with form during the 1960s.[20]

A comprehensive-schooled, working-class lad from London, Johnson worked his way into the world of literature after having seemingly already been assigned the role of accounting clerk by his post-fourteen 'vocational' education. He went to night classes and attended a pre-university foundational course at Birkbeck College, before managing to pass the entrance examination to King's College London. The connections that Johnson made by editing the journal *Universities Poetry* as an undergraduate helped to establish him as a known writer but the journey up to this point was a difficult one. This process hardened Johnson. His plain speaking style and distrust of abstract verbiage – his insistence upon concrete and palpable realities – make up an intentional pose adopted against what he described in his notebooks as 'very COMFORTABLE people'.[21] White has described how taking Johnson at his word often leads to critics 'regarding [him] as a confused and beleaguered figure [and] tempts us to revert to psychologism and cast him as a martyr to experimental literary Puritanism'.[22] Indeed, Paul D'Eath praises Johnson for this 'stoic pragmatism'.[23] Yet this stoicism is not a product of Johnson's literary-conceptual mission, it is a precursor to it and a force that drives it. The belligerence in Johnson's work targets a cosmopolitan elite whose carefully cultivated attitudes have acted as a curbing and domesticating force in Johnson's version of literary history.

Johnsons' writings, both public and private, conform to many of Richard Hoggart's observations about the working-class intellectual in *The Uses of Literacy* (1957), most particularly those concerning traditional modes of thought brought into conflict with middle-class sophistications:

> In the root-attitudes themselves there is no marked change. There does seem to be a difference in what might be called the attitude-to-the-attitudes. The old appeals – to the plain man, friendliness, cheerfulness, home, love, and the rest – are still to be found, but now in an increasingly self-conscious form.[24]

Johnson's 'root-attitudes', his commitment to truth and authenticity over abstraction and irony, come under constant self-critical exploration in his works but are never neglected or negated by new ideas. At the root of this is Johnson's mission to tell the 'truth of my truth' and his belief that, in the wrong hands, 'telling stories is telling lies'. The traditional novel, written from a position which takes the novel form for granted, represents in Johnson's eyes a smug complacency. His manifesto-like essay, 'Aren't You Rather Young to be Writing Your Memoirs?', presents a nightmare vision of the novel, created by generations of innovators, now relegated to rehashing old formulas and presenting the world in Victorian forms. By the same measure, Johnson refused to abandon his belief in monogamy and the family in favour of a sexual revolution, which he saw as simply the same old louche middle-class hypocrisy with a new linguistic sheen over it: 'old wine in new bottles'.[25] In both cases, Johnson is writing against the blasé, 'COMFORTABLE' middle class. What first appears as inconsistency is revealed as a working-class modernism.[26]

What characterises Johnson's ideological position in all of its abrasiveness and seeming self-contradiction is his attitude to truth. In spite of his acceptance that truth can be subjectively experienced, he nevertheless was adamantly opposed to any form of relativism when discussing truth as a concept. Coe quotes Johnson's friend Joebear Webb, saying, 'he could get quite angry about it . . . these words, [truth, fiction, subjectivity,] strange little words . . . were like red rags to him'.[27] I have previously described Johnson's truth-imperative as a 'rebel truism',[28] a foundation on which to ground himself against sophisticated linguistic deconstructions. Julia Jordan has described how this 'truism' lends Johnson's œuvre a repetitive quality, a sense of perpetually recurring themes and phrases, until eventually:

> We see repetition itself emerge as a characteristically Johnsonian rhetorical device: for Johnson, certainty is achieved through accumulation, through the testing and extension of his ideas. Johnson's repetitions display him in the act of gaining certainty through these accretions.[29]

Johnson's repetition of the same mantras about truth represents a defence of his working-class identity in a literary milieu where sophistication and its partner, cynicism, represent the cultural norm. He refuses to give ground in debate, preferring to emphasise the irreconcilability of what he perceived as a classed conflict.[30]

Writing what's Present, Writing what's Passed

Bearing Johnson's attitudes and practice in mind, we can return to his particular avant-garde vision with a clearer sense of how he envisioned novel writing as political praxis. The key to his engagement lies in what he describes as 'the technological fact of the book'.[31] The 1960s was a decade of progress and, specifically, of progress framed in the discourse of scientific management. Harold Wilson's 'white heat' speech is a key example here, but one can look at almost any non-fiction book published between 1964 and 1973 and find evidence for the technocratic fascination with statistics and regulation that predominates within the era's political imagination. Johnson, in his own way, adopts these attitudes in relation to literature. In his clearest statement on writing, 'Aren't You Rather Young to be Writing Your Memoirs?', Johnson points to the progress of literature as a fundamentally technological one:

> Joyce saw this at once, and developed the technique of interior monologue within a few years of the appearance of cinema. In some ways the history of the novel in the twentieth century has seen large areas of the old territory of the novelist increasingly taken over by other media ... that is what he should be exploring, rather than anachronistically fighting a battle he is bound to lose.[32]

Joyce, in Johnson's reading, was writing at the historical moment when powerful descriptive storytelling was being accomplished more effectively in cinema. He then used that moment to transform the novel into the dominant medium for depicting the internal psyche. Realism, forever associated in Johnson's writings with the Victorians, was an anachronism from this point onwards. 'The novelist cannot legitimately or successfully embody present-day reality in exhausted forms,'[33] he argues. Instead, the novelist must commit to understanding the possibilities of the novel as they exist technologically, in order to produce work capable of connecting to the society in which they are writing.

Looking into the Johnson archive, his engagement with technology is visible throughout. Burns congratulates him on the 'superb edition of HOUSE MOTHER NORMAL' he was sent, as 'the book is so good to have: paper, binding, colours – beautiful production'.[34] Johnson takes credit for every element of production. 'A film becomes the sum of its technicians,'[35] he writes to himself in 1969 in the midst of bringing his book-in-a-box, *The Unfortunates*, to print. Even in the presentation of his texts one can witness the inclusion of brand new printing practices in order to reach higher levels of graphic mimesis. Compare the section from *Albert Angelo* (1964) quoted below (a section that used the page in an innovative way but was nevertheless produced using traditional hot metal typesetting) with the presentation of Christie's accounts in *Christie Malry's Own Double-Entry* (Fig. 2.3). The inclusion of pages like the above within the text was made possible by xerography, a precursor of photocopying that allowed for faster and cheaper image reproduction, and

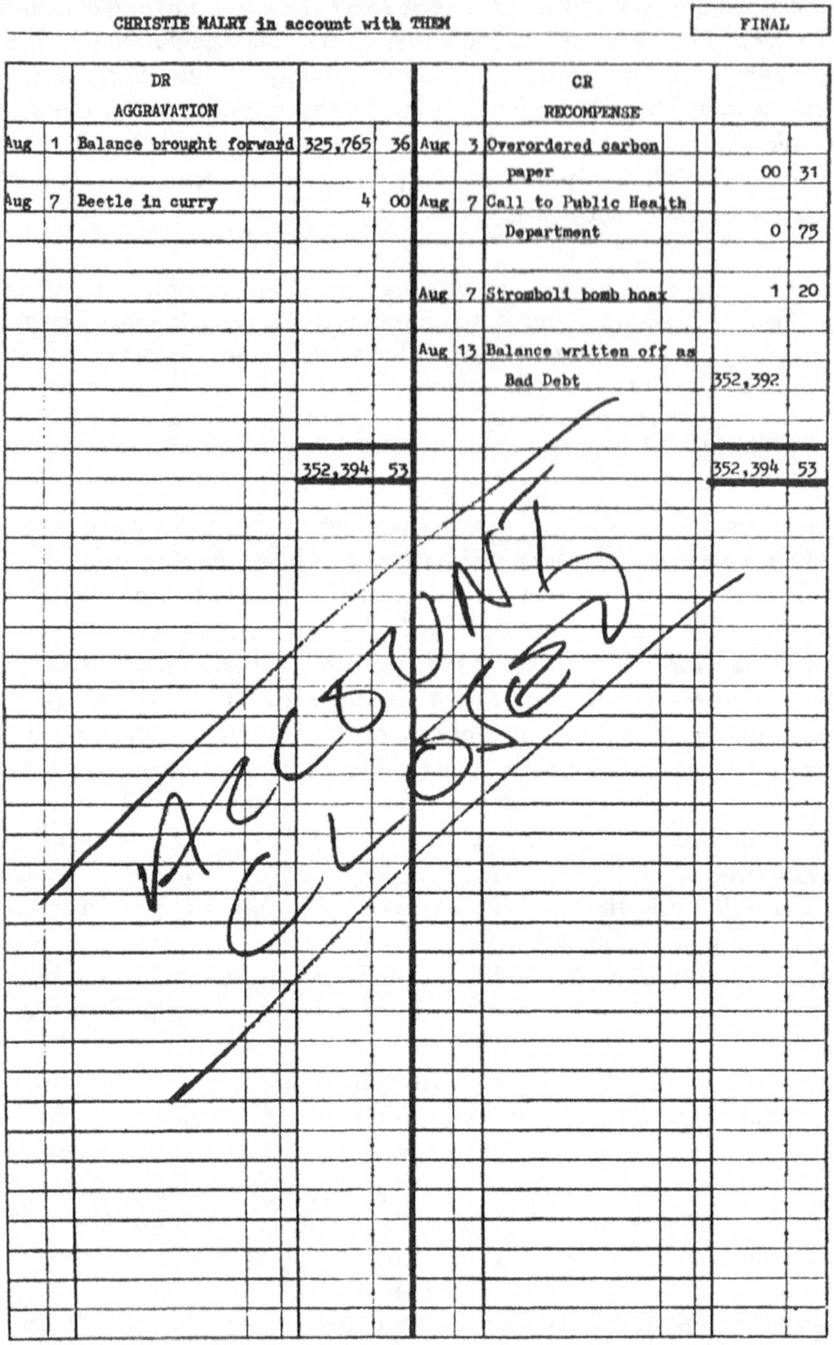

CHRISTIE MALRY in account with THEM						FINAL	
DR AGGRAVATION				CR RECOMPENSE			
Aug 1	Balance brought forward	325,765	36	Aug 3	Overordered carbon paper	00	31
Aug 7	Beetle in curry	4	00	Aug 7	Call to Public Health Department	0	75
				Aug 7	Stromboli bomb hoax	1	20
				Aug 13	Balance written off as Bad Debt	352,392	
		352,394	53			352,394	53

ACCOUNT CLOSED

Figure 2.3 B. S. Johnson, *Christie Malry's Own Double-Entry* [1973] (London: Picador, 2001), p. 187.

by phototypesetting, which simplified text printing such that images could be presented next to text much more easily, rather than given a separate page. This is Johnson making use of contemporary technology for his own artistic purposes and, in spite of the charge often put against him of indulging in novelty for its own sake, he is also being subtle in its inclusion.

Johnson is far from a technophile; his usage of the most up-to-date printing methods available to him is an extension of his truth-mantra into design. One cannot, in Johnson's philosophy, separate the technological fact of the book from the story it tells. Just as any given novel is culturally shaped by the literary history preceding it and surrounding it, so a book is technologically shaped by the particular mode of production that reproduces and disseminates it. Form, by which we refer to the organisation of elements in a work of art, reflects the organisation of society in a number of important ways. To attempt a political intervention without addressing formal boundaries would, for Johnson, be fundamentally to misunderstand the nature of the novel, or, as Zulfikar Ghose, another close ally of Johnson, wrote in a review of his first novel, *Travelling People* (1963):

> About four thousand novels are published in Britain every year and during the course of the year, the novel form suffers some four thousand deaths. It is the task of the serious novelist to revitalise the form, to recreate it for himself and thus to re-establish the literary worth of the form by demonstrating its historical progress.[36]

Serious novelists are those who shoulder the burden of history and do that legacy some justice in the present. They pass the baton forward, to use another Johnsonian image, in a relay race most writers do not even recognise that they are running in.

So what results did all this stringent theorising of the novelist's role actually produce? We can turn to *The Unfortunates*. From a literary critical perspective, it is important to understand Johnson's mission, yet when we approach *The Unfortunates* we find it a rather conventional treatment of grief and loss. The speaker attends a football match while reminiscing about a friend from the same town who died of cancer. The prose is brutally honest, at times heart-breaking, but not, on the surface of things, innovative in itself. The novel is not an exercise in precisely depicting grief in general; as Johnson writes, 'not how he died, not what he died of, even less why he died, are of concern, to me, only the fact that he did die, he is dead, is important: the loss to me, to us'.[37] This is not a novel about losing a friend to cancer, the speaker assures us; it is about *this* specific incidence of loss. There is something in the specificity, or more rightly the communication of that specificity, which is essential to 'us': the reader–writer alliance sharing in the experience of this novel. The novel's form, unbound sections to be read in random order, has been said to represent both the disordered experience of remembering and the unpredictable nature of cancer growth.[38] The reader acts out the jumbling of Johnson's memories and the growth of Tony's cancer in each shuffle. The truth of Tony's death, the specific truth, is altered every time. We are not allowed to generalise, not allowed to say that this is a book on the theme of cancer: it is about this one particular and true death, not death as a general theme or abstract concept.

The football match that brings Johnson back to the town where his friend died may, on first reading, appear in arbitrary relation to the past event: a Proustian invocation of memory based upon a small coincidence. However, considered in relation to specificity and truth, it becomes clear that Johnson is utilising his biographical experiences covering City versus United to shape the narrator's response to Tony's death, his own mortality as a person and his legacy as a writer. The section 'Away from the ground . . .' begins with Johnson's invocation of the 'Heavy Mob'[39]: the professional sports reporters who he has described in a different section as 'household names' whose 'money . . . I'm envious of'.[40] On this occasion, their images are strewn across the ground on discarded newspapers, litter and programmes. The game has ended and the Heavy Mob, and all their works, are reduced to 'rough forecourt litter'.[41] Johnson, by contrast, has held his programme tight with him, telling us 'I keep mine, still, I always used to keep them, still do, for reference, am neurotically attached to any piece of paper which has had anything to do with me.'[42] Johnson collects the detritus that others discard. The famous writers of the day, the Heavy Mob, are ephemeral by contrast. They write the programmes that locate the game within a wider narrative of league tables, historical rivalries and personalities; they then comment upon it as it plays out, phone in their reviews at the end and leave. There is a parallel here with Tony and, more specifically, what Tony represents to Johnson as a literary academic. Johnson distrusts and envies the academics as much as the Heavy Mob because they are better paid than him and yet, in his mind, inferior. They are 'parasites on the living body of literature'.[43] In Johnson's mind, the academics set up the narrative, watch the game play out, cast judgement and leave without ever considering the specifics of the event, of the particular novel, upon the specific terms of its writing.

Bearing the narrator's symbolic attachment to programmes in mind, it is then possible to consider the section 'Time! It's after two! ...' as formally mimicking a programme. The six-page section is slight but densely packed with text. It does not use large gaps and spaces in the way that many other sections do. The section depicts the narrator negotiating the match-day crowds during his approach to the stadium. He buys a football paper to crib facts from, thanking Christ that 'I don't have to write that sort of preliminary speculative meaningless crap. Just my own kind of crap.'[44] The narrator's 'own kind of crap' here acts like a programme for the match; it establishes the match in the wider narrative – in this case remembering Tony, positions the narrator in relation to the game (he is indifferent to it, 'United's team picks itself'[45]) – and, most importantly, sets up the stakes of the game in relation to the personalities in *The Unfortunates*. On the one side there is the narrator, providing details and descriptions as and when they truly arrive, memories of Tony in the real contexts of their appearance, unstructured. On the other there is the Heavy Mob, the writing establishment, who:

> seem to look alike ... armed to the teeth with Colour and Mixed Metaphors, ready to defend their principles to the death as long as they do not conflict with their financial interests, the well-paid pseuds who write their reports from prepared telling phrases, and make the football fit whatever it is they imagine their readers want them to say.[46]

These are the forces of inauthenticity against which Johnson rails in his demand for truth, who would tell any story in any order with any message, the better to appeal to an uncritical mass readership. They are also the forces in power, the ones who make the rules and dictate what the job of writing is, attacking or corrupting those writers 'writing as though it mattered'.[47] Most importantly, these are writers who have conceded that their words are impermanent and their writing ephemeral; they simply add their general comments to the general discourse, adding language to more language. By reducing each football game to a set of clichés and moulding it into a shape that sells, the Heavy Mob betray their lack of concern for the game at hand. By contrast, when the narrator talks to Tony on his deathbed, telling him 'I'll get it all down, mate,'[48] he depends on the specificity of writing, its truth, to allay death in some way, to prolong memory in the face of impermanence and generalisation. Writing staves off death in Johnson's world: hence his 'neurotic, psychotic' attachment to 'any piece of paper which has anything to do with me'.[49] Johnson has to trust that he lives on in the pieces of paper we hold in our hands, though his narrator's neurosis reveals the delusion in this. The dramatic irony is painful.

It is perhaps for this reason that Johnson avoids any long and drawn-out description of either Tony's death or the football game itself. The narrator's article about the game is printed on the inside of the box rather than in one of the unbound sections of text, physically representing its separation from the body of text comprising *The Unfortunates* proper and appearing as an appendix to sate the curious reader. The names of the teams have been removed in the same way as the name of the city in which the novel is set. Tony, too, dies off stage; in the tiny, single-paragraphed section 'June rang on the Saturday . . .', we are told that 'there was no need for us to come down now, on Sunday, for he had died that evening' and that, prior to his death, Tony's mind cleared and 'for the first time [he and his wife June] had talked about death'.[50] We are not told the specifics of any of these moments. The moments around which the rest of the novel revolves, those that would represent the climax of the action in any traditional narrative structure, are denied to us and made intentionally opaque – that is, until we consider what Melanie Seddon has described as Johnson's mission to 'bridge the gap between the novel and the world by creating an assemblage with the world rather than a representation of an external reality'.[51] In the most painful moments of the text, Johnson, the designer of the book, is depending upon the active participation of the reader to understand and recognise the limits of the narrator addressing them. The commitment to authentic detail over fictional cliché and authentic ordering over archetypical structures can take Johnson only so far in presenting the 'truth of his truth'. He depends, ultimately, upon the reader's own subjective experience of truth – their shared awareness of how those specific moments cannot be conveyed in their entirety – in order to direct their reading experience towards that realisation on a formal level. Rather than present the story in generalisations, in deference to the reader's expectations, perhaps with a glorious deathbed scene in which Tony's passing is made meaningful in a universal way, Johnson gives us the specifics of the circumstances, as they truly happened, then invites us in to complete the experience ourselves. It is the opposite of mythmaking, where story can explain the world away. By writing what amounts to a non-fiction novel, Johnson disrupts our association of the novel with fictionality. He instead tries to tell a true story, meeting the limits of writing's capacity for description.

Conclusion

In his writing on the aleatoric novel, Sebastian Jenner describes how Johnson 'seems to respond to the contemporary interpretation of "nothingness" not as signifying a hopeless chaotic void, but as indicating a state of chaogenous possibility'.[52] I would add that these possibilities are integrated and framed in Johnson's work, built in by design, as part of his literary philosophy. As editor of *BSJ: The B. S. Johnson Journal*, I have witnessed the reach of Johnson's influence within contemporary culture at first hand. His 'cult' status is not the sole province of literary scholars but reaches into music, film and comedy, with his works being especially popular with creators of digital media. Johnsonian influence is larger than literary history often gives it credit for and will only grow as we come to take chance elements and interactivity as givens in our cultural experiences. It is essential, however, that in revisiting Johnson's works as formal innovations we do not lose the meaning within them. The depth of Johnson's writing often baffles our initial presumptions based on his more ostentatious avant-garde techniques. These unexpected subtleties contain the deepest of Johnson's insights.

Notes

1. Glyn White, *Reading the Graphic Surface* (Manchester: Manchester University Press, 2005), p. 6.
2. Tom Boncza-Tomaszewski and Christine Brooke-Rose, 'The Texterminator', *The Independent on Sunday*, 27 March 2005, p. 28.
3. Jonathan Coe, *Like a Fiery Elephant: The Story of B. S. Johnson* (London: Picador, 2004), p. 399.
4. Johnson's first published novel, *Travelling People* (1963), was later disowned by the author and his estate has refused to republish it to this day.
5. B. S. Johnson, *Albert Angelo*, in *Omnibus* (London: Picador, 2004), p. 168.
6. Ibid. p. 167.
7. Brian McHale, *Postmodernist Fiction* (London: Routledge, 1994), p. 35.
8. Ibid. p. 12.
9. Ibid.
10. Glyn White, 'The Sadism of the Author or the Masochism of the Reader?', in *B. S. Johnson and Post-War Literature*, ed. Julia Jordan and Martin Ryle (London: Palgrave, 2014), pp. 153–66, p. 161.
11. Anthony Brennan, *Shakespeare's Dramatic Structures* (London: Routledge, 1988), p. 19.

12. B. S. Johnson, *Christie Malry's Own Double-Entry* (London: Picador, 2001), p. 172.
13. David Hucklesby, 'B. S. Johnson, Giles Gordon and a "New Fiction": The Book, The Screen and the E-book', in *B. S. Johnson and Post-War Literature*, pp. 202–16, p. 210.
14. Alan Burns, 'Interview with B. S. Johnson', in *The Imagination on Trial*, ed. Alan Burns and Charles Sugnet (London: Allison and Busby, 1981), p. 90.
15. Johnson, *Albert Angelo*, p. 167.
16. Donald A. Norman, *The Design of Everyday Things* (Cambridge, MA: MIT Press, 2013), p. 31.
17. Although I am drawing here upon the structuralist term 'implied reader' (Iser, Barthes, Foucault), the discussion of readers in this chapter does not prescribe a formal relationship between an implied reader and the text in the same manner as these writers. Structuralist and post-structuralist theory often overstates the case when presenting either an 'implied reader' structurally enclosed by the text (Barthes) or an infinite multiplicity of potential readers, each with a unique set of interpretations and affects (Deleuze and Guattari). Drawing instead on design theory, 'reader' is here analogous with 'user': a term describing a predictable average response. 'User' aims neither to prescribe limits of use nor to account for every possible use.
18. Johnson, *Christie Malry's Own Double-Entry*, p. 51.
19. Ibid. p. 176.
20. Joseph Darlington, *Contextualising the British Experimental Novelists of the Long Sixties* (PhD Thesis: University of Salford, 2014) focuses upon the links between Johnson, Eva Figes, Ann Quin and Alan Burns in particular.
21. Johnson, *Notebook 3*, held in the British Library, 1958, n.p.
22. White, *Reading the Graphic Surface*, p. 67.
23. Paul M. D'Eath, 'B. S. Johnson and the Consolation of Literature', *The Review of Contemporary Fiction*, 5:2 (1985), pp. 77–81, p. 79.
24. Richard Hoggart, *The Uses of Literacy* (London: Penguin, 1957), p. 228.
25. Johnson, *Notebook 3*, n.p.
26. In spite of using many techniques now associated with postmodernism, Johnson's framing of literature as a form developing like a 'relay race' is far more in keeping with modernist conceptions of culture's historical development and political potential (Owen Hatherley, *Militant Modernism* (London: Zero Books, 2009), p. 26).
27. Coe, *Like a Fiery Elephant*, p. 397.
28. Darlington, '"A Sort of Waterfall": Class Anxiety and Authenticity in B. S. Johnson', in *BSJ: The B. S. Johnson Journal*, 2 (2014), pp. 69–110, p. 101.
29. Julia Jordan, 'Foreword', in *Well Done God!*, ed. Jonathan Coe, Julia Jordan and Philip Tew (London: Picador, 2013), p. xvi.

30. See Darlington, '"A Sort of Waterfall"'.
31. B. S. Johnson, *Aren't You Rather Young to be Writing Your Memoirs?* (London: Hutchinson, 1973), p. 12.
32. Ibid.
33. Ibid. p. 16.
34. Alan Burns, letter to B. S. Johnson, 25 May 1971, held in the British Library.
35. Johnson, *Notebook 8*, 1973, held in the British Library, p. 9.
36. Zulfikar Ghose, 'Review of *Travelling People*', 1963, included in letter to B. S. Johnson, held in the British Library.
37. Johnson, 'Last', in *The Unfortunates* (London: Picador, 1999), p. 6.
38. Coe, White, Jenner, Kirby and Mitchell have each proposed distinct interpretations of the novel's presentation. See: Coe, *Like a Fiery Elephant*; White, *Reading the Graphic Surface*; Sebastian Jenner, 'B. S. Johnson and the Aleatoric Novel', in *B. S. Johnson and Post-War Literature*, pp. 71–86; Alan Kirby, *Digimodernism* (London: Continuum, 2009); Kaye Mitchell, 'The Unfortunates: Hypertext, Linearity and the Act of Reading', in *Re-Reading B. S. Johnson*, ed. Philip Tew and Glyn White (London: Palgrave, 2007).
39. Johnson, 'Time!', in *The Unfortunates*, p. 1.
40. Ibid. p. 5.
41. Ibid. p. 1.
42. Ibid.
43. Johnson, 'The Opera Singer', in *The Unfortunates*, p. 2.
44. Johnson, 'Time!', p. 3.
45. Ibid.
46. Ibid. p. 4.
47. Johnson, *Aren't You Rather Young To Be Writing Your Memoirs?*, p. 29.
48. Johnson, 'So He Came', in *The Unfortunates*, p. 5.
49. Johnson, 'Away from the Ground', in *The Unfortunates*, p. 1.
50. Johnson, 'June Rang on the Saturday', in *The Unfortunates*, p. 1.
51. Melanie Seddon, 'Reading the Matrix: B. S. Johnson's See the Old Lady Decently', in *BSJ: The B. S. Johnson Journal*, 2 (2010), pp. 5–40, p. 38.
52. Jenner, 'B. S. Johnson and the Aleatoric Novel', p. 80.

Chapter 3

Giles Gordon: *Beyond the Words* and Beyond the Language of Experimentalism
David Hucklesby

In his 1993 memoir *Aren't We Due a Royalty Statement?*, Giles Gordon offers a brief explanation of his struggle as autobiographer:

> I am not [says Gordon] famous, although I have always wanted to be. To achieve what others perceive as fame has long seemed to me the only justification for the mediocrity of my life. I only slipped into *Who's Who* along with about 28,000 others in 1991 when I was half a century old.[1]

When Gordon satisfied this 'mild obsession',[2] his father's response was that the piece 'was too long; it was much more dignified to keep the vital statistics of one's "career" and the facts of one's life to the minimum'.[3] Key aspects of Gordon's career have been afforded such 'dignity'; any perception of Gordon's fame rests on his career as a literary agent and editor – counting Sue Townsend, Fay Weldon and Peter Ackroyd amongst his clients, along with members of the British royal family (as mischievously punned upon in his memoir's title) – but the 'vital statistics' of his fiction-writing are largely overlooked. They reveal a dual commitment, supporting and contributing to a burgeoning movement of British avant-garde writing in the 1960s. Though not the surest route to the pages of *Who's Who* – some notable avant-gardists like Anthony Burgess would find themselves there, whilst others like B. S. Johnson and Ann Quin would not – it is Gordon's response to the innovative writing of the 1960s, made manifest in his novels and editorial projects in the early 1970s, which will be the focus of this chapter.

Initially, this chapter examines Gordon's critical perspective on the 1960s novel, his appreciation for the work of Johnson, Quin and others culminating in the publication of *Beyond the Words: Eleven Writers in Search of a New Fiction* (1975). In particular, the chapter examines Johnson's and Gordon's condemnation of established realist traditions for failing to respond to modernism, whilst refuting the perceived experimentalism in their own writing. Following Johnson's lead, Gordon attempts to position a generation of 'experimental' writing as a new kind of realism, an aim more akin to their modernist forebears than is commonly recognised. After this, the chapter examines Gordon's fiction, focusing on introductory sections from his 1970 prose collection *Pictures from an Exhibition* and his 1974 novel *Girl with Red Hair*. Though Gordon's major literary and critical publications are produced after the turn of the decade, his authorship is moulded by the 1960s avant-garde, with substantial influence drawn from his *Beyond the Words* contributors.

In Search of a New Fiction

The intent behind *Beyond the Words* is twofold. On one hand, it reacts against Karl Miller's 1968 anthology *Writing in England Today*.[4] On the other, it is a collaborative editorial project for Gordon and Johnson, representing a generation of avant-garde writers in 1960s Britain. Though Johnson's suicide in 1973 delayed the project, Gordon's reasoning for joining forces with Johnson is central to his criticisms of Miller. Gordon's opening comments in *Beyond the Words* clarify the book's origins, recalling that he 'suggested [to Johnson] that he and I might compile an anthology of previously unpublished work by those we considered to be among the most worth while [sic] of contemporary British writers'.[5] Gordon's enthusiasm for this collaboration stems from Johnson's *Aren't you Rather Young to be Writing your Memoirs?* (1973), a prose collection bearing an acerbic introductory essay on readership, the modern novel and Johnson's writing priorities. Though identified by critics and biographer Jonathan Coe as 'Britain's one-man literary avant-garde of the 1960s',[6] Johnson's involvement in *Beyond the Words* is evidence of the potential for collaboration that this generation of writers had. Since the anthology represents a culmination of Gordon's critical perspective on avant-garde writing of the period, clarity is needed about how the perspectives expressed in *Beyond the Words* were formed, and Johnson's influence is central to this process.

Coe describes Johnson's introduction to *Aren't you Rather Young* as 'a belligerent critique of the conservatism of modern British writing'.[7] Johnson's most widely referenced comment upon the novel asserts that 'life does not tell stories. Life is chaotic, fluid, random; it leaves myriads of ends untied, untidily [. . .] telling stories really is telling lies.'⁸ Johnson reveals his modernist influence here, arguing against the artifice of traditional realism and proposing to embrace the chaos of life as it is lived. This is confirmed by Johnson's admiration for James Joyce's recognition of cinema's potential to supplant written fiction, as he declares Joyce 'the Einstein of the novel'.⁹ Johnson posits this argument in the form of an accusation: to pursue the old comforts of realist narrative is to make one a liar, 'perversely anachronistic, [. . .] a literary flatearther'.¹⁰ 'The novelist', he asserts, 'cannot legitimately or successfully embody present-day reality in exhausted forms.'¹¹ His remedy is that 'the novel may not only survive but evolve to greater achievements by concentrating on those things it can still do best: the precise use of language, exploitation of the technological fact of the book, the explication of thought'.¹² Perhaps most surprisingly, Johnson never explicitly identifies his conclusion as an apologia for experimentalism. Indeed, David James describes Johnson as 'abhorring the label "experimental"',¹³ and *Aren't You Rather Young* clarifies this perspective:

> What I have been trying to do in the novel form has been too much refracted through the conservativeness of reviewers [. . .]. 'Experimental' to most reviewers is almost always a synonym for 'unsuccessful'. I object to the word *experimental* being applied to my own work [. . .], where I depart from convention, it is because the convention has failed, is inadequate for conveying what I have to say. The relevant questions are surely whether each device works or not, whether it achieves what it set out to achieve, and how less good were the alternatives.¹⁴

Here, Johnson reveals a commitment to literary innovation, but simultaneously a resistance to the language of experimentalism so commonly applied to it. 'Success', in Johnson's terms, is determined by the functionality of his devices; to depart from convention is seriously and productively to seek viable alternatives to failing conventions, rather than whimsical gimmickry. To experiment, for Johnson, is to pose a question. To publish a novel, with carefully chosen devices, is to propose solutions long after the process of experimentation is complete: 'Certainly I make experiments, but the unsuccessful ones are quietly hidden away and what I choose to publish is in my terms successful: that is, it has been the best way I could find of solving particular writing problems.'¹⁵ Gordon's response to Johnson's essay is recorded in his Introduction to a 2001 edition of Quin's *Berg* (1964), as follows:

> In 1973 the leading British 'experimental' novelist (I put the adjective in quotes because, to me, experimental in the context implies unsuccessful)

B. S. Johnson published a collection of short fictions, [. . .]. It was prefaced with a wonderfully polemical and didactic introduction, arguing for a new seriousness and honesty in fiction.[16]

For Gordon, Johnson's essay is clearly formative in its ambition to celebrate the 'seriousness' and 'honesty' present in avant-garde writing, and to distance it from the 'experimental' label. In doing so, Johnson also supplies ammunition, and a target, in the form of a lingering reliance on nineteenth-century realism and the reading culture it promoted.

Gordon would raise similar objections to Johnson's in *Beyond the Words*, about contemporary literature, reading culture and the language of experimentalism. Gordon focuses on the rise of mass-produced newspapers in the nineteenth century:

We are conditioned to read thousands of words every day. There are probably more of them in a single issue of *the Times* or *the Guardian* or the *Daily Telegraph* than there are in the average new novel; and we're conditioned, because we lead such 'busy' lives, to read these words – whether in newspaper or book – as fast as we're able to assimilate them. In practice, this means a general understanding of the surface meaning, the 'factual' content, rather than being persuaded, beguiled, influenced, stimulated, and altered by the words. But the craft of even our best journalist is one thing, the art of our better novelists quite another. Or should be.[17]

Like Johnson, Gordon alludes to a form of complacency; modern novelists pander to, rather than challenge, the habits of the reading public. Despite a pervasive self-consciousness and sense of irony, Gordon's critique of contemporary mainstream literature is clearly stated. The risk of lingering on the traditions of realist fiction is obsolescence; it would 'make novel writing and reading a more private, more elitist activity than hitherto. It accepts both the limitations and the strengths of the position in which fiction now finds itself: that it is no longer a popular art.'[18] Gordon's arguments are coloured by a changing technological culture surrounding reading. The main argument which emerges from Gordon's observation is that novelists must view the fundamentals of their craft in relation to other media and demonstrate that their goals and means are unique:

Most people, in daily currency, use words in what they think of as a fairly literal way. Consequently they are made uneasy if a writer does not use them similarly. They expect a novelist to know more words than they do, and to employ them with greater expertise than they can. Basically though, they expect a 'story' to begin at the beginning (wherever that may be). If the first four words aren't literally 'Once upon a time', the reader should be able to assume they're taken for granted.[19]

Here, Gordon aligns himself with Johnson's view that established realist modes are hamstrung by the artificiality of the very narrative conventions they espouse. His solution is also similar to Johnson's: a new understanding of realism, informed by modernism and not reliant upon the traditional forms that preceded it. Gordon writes:

I'm asking for a *more* critical approach to fiction – by authors, reviewers and readers, I'd like the reviewer or reader to say to himself: 'Mr X appears to be doing such and such, [. . .] he uses words in his latest artefact in a way that, if not peculiar to him, is not how they are used in this sentence. He's intrigued and fascinated by them, by sentences, paragraphs, pages as sounds, shapes, rhythms as well as senses. His meanings aren't necessarily mine, but that's no reason to dismiss them.'[20]

The sense of 'dismissal' outlined here appears symptomatic of the same conservative mainstream critical landscape observed by Johnson – and again, like Johnson, Gordon holds this responsible for sustaining an objectionable status quo. The language of experimentalism again comes to the fore – Johnson objected to the application of such terminology to writing methods he saw as necessary, and Gordon saw such an application as logically impossible in the first place:

If content and form are inseparable, both essential aspects of a single artefact, a novel which with skill portrays its author's individual contemporary vision cannot be experimental or avant garde. It can only be itself, a work of fiction.[21]

Positioning himself and Johnson as leaders of a charge against traditionalism, yet rejecting the terminology that would identify them as vanguards, Gordon is subject to similar criticism as Johnson: he seems contradictory and inconsistent. Nevertheless, Gordon indicates a pressing issue in the critical identification of the literary moment he is keen to highlight: if the mainstream of literary fiction and criticism in the 1960s had successfully responded to the lessons of modernism, such measures would never need to be identified as avant-garde. Though 'experimental' in relation to an observed conservatism, the goal outlined by Johnson and highlighted by Gordon is not to pose questions or to test waters, but to supply solutions to observed problems. In doing so, both encourage a generation of writers to produce complete and conclusive literary works which take their cue from modernism, reject a rising traditionalism and reshape the novel's relationship with realism. That they continue to be labelled 'experimental' serves to confirm the validity of their arguments; within this period, their views are made to feel anomalous by this labelling, and the serious critical attention due to writers like Johnson or Quin is – according to Gordon, as well as Johnson himself – neglected as a result.

Johnson and Gordon aimed to challenge British reading and writing culture to evolve in the wake of modernism – and to recognise writers acting as potential catalysts for such an evolution. In attempting to enact such a change, assumptions about experimentalism would also need to be challenged, so that the methodologies and strategies promoted by the avant-gardists might take hold in the mainstream. It seems for these reasons that Gordon describes *Beyond the Words* as an 'antidote' to *Writing in England Today*.[22] Johnson perceived a perverse anachronism in continuing to pursue traditional realism in a world already reshaped by modernity, and Gordon employs a similar tone: 'The book was not only idiosyncratic, it was perverse. It omitted any writer whose abilities and inclinations were remotely divorced from the, so called, "realistic".'[23] In *Royalty Statement*, Gordon clarifies his intentions:

> Our anthology was to be different in kind and tone from the usual run of realist fiction approved by the literary editors of the time. [. . .] Bryan and I wanted to provide an antidote, a counterblast to that admittedly influential anthology, something which would get an argument going.[24]

If the 'usual run of realist fiction' celebrated in *Writing in England Today* exemplifies a failure to learn from the innovations of modernism, then *Beyond the Words* is an overt attempt to amend this. Gordon accuses Miller of having 'eulogised fiction [. . .] as a division of journalism, of deadening social realism',[25] an objection closely related to his observation of readerly complacency in relation to news media. Miller, however, states his intention to 'give a picture of the work of the younger writers, in the main, and of the way in which themes and styles have behaved',[26] with an emphasis on truthfulness and realism. Whilst Gordon's anthology also collects writing by young British authors, the two differ substantially in the nature of the praise offered. Gordon celebrates new, innovative forms, drawn from contemporary culture and mimetic of newer media. Miller cites Richard Ellmann and Charles Feidelson Jr's *The Modern Tradition* to promote quite the opposite:

> Committed to everything in human experience that militates against custom, abstract order, and even reason itself, modern literature has elevated individual existence over social man, unconscious feeling over self-conscious perception, passion and will over intellection and systematic morals, dynamic vision over the static image, dense actuality over practical reality.[27]

Both anthologies promote a kind of realism but offer opposing ideas of how a modern realism can be achieved. Miller describes modernism as 'ancient history', exhibiting 'awkwardness' and 'scabrousness', expanding on Ellmann and Feidelson's claims that international influences have corrupted British writing: 'the fever for American literature which succeeded the "French flu" in this country has resulted in a philistine condescension towards native writers'.[28] Ultimately, the future of literature outlined by Miller is 'tired of the international, experimental avant-garde and of mandatory modernity, [. . .] tired of the romantic individualism, the religiosity, the martyred sensitiveness that had been favoured by writers during the war'.[29] One of Miller's key selections is a group of poets who 'attracted a name which conferred the maximum degree of anonymity consistent with the purposes of identification and publicity: they painted themselves battleship-grey and were called "The Movement"'.[30] Miller credits Robert Conquest's *New Lines* anthology with providing the definition of The Movement's goals, and Donald Davie with establishing The Movement as 'a people's literature'. Miller lists Kingsley Amis, D. J. Enright, Philip Larkin and John Wain alongside Conquest and Davie as key figures in The Movement who adopted 'reversions to ordinary speech and moral earnestness', and were 'polite in the eighteenth-century sense – by virtue of a concern for manners and morals'.[31] Writing by all six is featured in Miller's anthology, constituting a body of critical and creative works encapsulating the models of realism esteemed therein.

If Miller's anthology is partially responsible for confining Gordon's favoured writers to the experimental fringe, then Gordon's is explicit in bringing them to the fore. In doing so, Gordon constructs the critical landscape his own fiction would later occupy; his intention is to supply the critical dialogue for the 1960s avant-gardists to gain traction. This itself represents Johnson's and Gordon's collective thesis: for too long, an approach to realism built upon modernism has been dismissed as 'experimental', when it ought to be recognised as a reimagining of tradition – and at that, a more aesthetically and methodologically successful one, and truer to its contemporary era, than the fare offered by Miller's selected writers.

Gordon's perspective is distinctly shaped by his observations of the previous fifteen years, and influenced by Johnson, a key innovative novelist who was publishing consistently throughout that period. Although Gordon would produce collections of poetry and short stories during the mid- to late 1960s, book-length publication of his writing did not begin until the 1970s. Yet, as critic and author, he carries a staunch commitment to those writers of the previous decade he sees as regrettably confined to the fringes, and the desire to ensure that their early forays were not lost. Indeed, his ambition seems to be to remove writers most willing to learn from modernism, like Johnson, Quin or others collected in that anthology, from the fringes. Further to this, Gordon would expose how the literary strategies they developed shaped his understanding of a new kind of 'realistic' fiction, rooted in individualism and dismissive of conventions deemed artificial or superficial. What remains to be seen is the extent to which Gordon's own fiction is imperative in understanding this project – a body of work not *of* the 1960s but overtly emerging *from* it, intelligent to its landscape and actively employing its methodology.

Pictures from an Exhibition (1970)

Gordon would consistently publish short stories throughout the 1960s, as a contributor to the *Penguin Modern Stories* series, and his first book-length collection of prose works would emerge in 1970. Of the works therein – a total of twenty-eight stories and prose compositions – it is the titular sequence of five that opens the collection, and demonstrates Gordon's affinity with writers such as Johnson, Quin and their fellow 1960s avant-gardists. The book's liner notes suggest as much:

> He makes you feel what the pictures at the exhibition can give you, which art critics don't do. [. . .] He doesn't write neat Somerset Maugham short stories with a catch ending, but he has a wit and economy – a style – all of his own.[32]

This statement is significant when compared to the critical views which Gordon would later express. The reference to the Somerset

Maugham stories reads like apology but also defiance: a statement of intent to pursue Gordon's own individual style despite the implied expectation of 'neatness'. Also noteworthy is Gordon's comment on the visual arts and it is here that the reading of his stories is best begun. Johnson asserted that the borrowing and reworking of styles from other media was a technique unique to the written word, key to the evolution of fiction. Gordon in turn argued that the skill of the fiction writer ought to differentiate itself fully from that of the journalist or critic. The stated attempt to capture in prose what artist or critic could not would constitute Gordon's first attempt to enact his critical viewpoint as a writer of fiction, long before the *Beyond the Words* project was begun.

Immediately clear, in 'Pictures from an exhibition 1', is Gordon's adoption of an impressionistic, near-Cubist sketching of scenery reminiscent of Gertrude Stein's *Tender Buttons* (1914); if Johnson was critical of writers who had failed to learn the lessons of modernism, Gordon would not be amongst them. Refusing, as promised, the neatness of traditional short story form, Gordon's title implies plurality rather than an enclosed stand-alone work, both in its use of the word 'pictures' and in its numeration. In this, its visual presentation and its narrative perspective, Gordon's fiction is fragmented from the start, presenting an image that we, as readers, are not party to:

> LIKE A FLAYED OX. A flayed ox.
> A body, though, ping-pong, a human body. A male body, the body of a man, oh yea, a very masculine man, at that, a man prepared to show his body, naked, part naked, part uncovered, his hands at least not buried in gloves, not covered with mitts to keep out the cold, the air. His hands, in fact, out of the picture, beyond the frame (there is no frame), lost in the pigment.[33]

Gordon's opening line initially denies the reader access to the subject. The incomplete simile gives a loose impression of the 'picture', before being cut off entirely in favour of a more direct observation of the subject: the image of a partially naked man, confirmed as a painting by references to frame and pigment. Repetition acts as reinforcement, as the subject is observed and reobserved, adjusted and corrected with affirmations like 'oh yea' and 'in fact'. Gordon's device here is a familiar modernist strategy, embodying in prose that first experience of viewing, moving around a subject, noting impressions and associations, without providing an artificially precise, direct description. On its own, this might be mere reminiscence of modernist works – like

Stein's – which predate Gordon's by over half a century. The same is true of other writers later included in Gordon's *Beyond the Words*. Quin's *Berg*, for instance, is described by Gordon as 'intense, linguistically precise, [...] sophisticated, [...] it deliberately fails to pin down an objective reality'[34] – a statement which celebrates Quin in the very terms that would deem her writing unacceptable to the mainstream of literary realism. Gordon's own writing in 'Pictures' could be described similarly, when compared to a passage from Quin:

> The partition swayed: a boat without sails, anchored to a rock, yet revolving outside its own circumference. I an albatross, never to fly in a direction taken a million times before. Berg looked at the crack in the ceiling. Follow on the dream, the beginning conjured up in a single second, an isolated thought hooked out of the mainstream of chance.[35]

Gordon is keen to draw attention to Quin's use of familiar modernist techniques, describing the manner in which her narrative perspective 'changes constantly, kaleidoscopically'.[36] Comments like this indicate a clear allegiance to writers such as Quin, and echo Johnson's complaints about the experimental terminology used to describe them; there emerges a logic to Gordon's own adoption of concretion and shifting narrative perspectives in his own writing. The lessons of modernism are not yet learned; the ghosts of nineteenth-century narrative realism are not yet exorcised. The tone set by the liner notes to *Pictures from an Exhibition* illuminates the fact that writing in such a mode still required apology, or confrontation, in the wake of anthologies like Miller's.

Gordon's image of a 'flayed ox' recurs throughout this short text, as if that first impression is re-evaluated as each of the painting's visual cues is expanded upon with sensory imagery: 'A three-dimensional flayed ox, the third dimension being the pig-ment, the pigment being the bod-y, a male torso, naked to the waist, devoid of covering other than skin and the sweat you can smell, suck up your nostrils via your eyes.'[37] Gordon's narrator supposes that the body 'stands, no, no, hangs, is suspended, suspends, is in suspension',[38] and that the figure is 'caught in some act, some right, caught in motion [...] in benediction, in surrender, in forgiveness, in defence of the flayed ox'.[39] This grasping for meaning is crucial – if we are to follow Johnson's suggestion – to assessing whether Gordon's device works or not. Johnson, for instance, suggests that 'film is an excellent medium for showing things, but it is very poor at taking an audience inside characters' minds, at telling it what people are thinking'.[40] Gordon appears to highlight written text's ability to 'take an audience inside' in this piece, and, through the various reiterations and recalculations, he also brings to light the ability of prose fiction to employ even its perceived weaknesses and failures to great effect. Where Johnson asserts that 'life is not like that', rejecting the neatness of traditional realist narrative, the fact that Gordon's text refuses to settle on an image and ends with an unpunctuated half-sentence highlights his refusal to be what Johnson might call a liar. Gordon's short prose is frustrating and frustrated, mimicking sensations of unfamiliarity and grasping for meaning. In this, the version of realism Gordon aims for is clarified: a portrayal of internal experience, devoid of the artificial trappings of traditional description. As cited in the section above, in *Beyond the Words* Gordon would describe his desire for readers to be 'intrigued and fascinated by [words], by sentences, paragraphs, pages as sounds, shapes, rhythms as well as senses' – and his body of work published in 1970 reinforces this 'fascination'. In turn, this confirms that Gordon's fiction is written with the direct intention to respond to and reflect upon the previous decade's avant-garde literature.

The other 'Pictures' from Gordon's collection also employ specific modernist devices, revisited in the context of his own growing critical perspective. In particular, the second story exhibits a further suspicion toward traditional realist representation, rejecting narrative description in favour of visual concretion. In '2', Gordon describes a violent relationship, between the reader and an implied 'picture', but also with words themselves:

> You are breathing heavily, wildly, are jumping up and down. Your fingers tear at the words, pick at them, hack at the letters. Nothing will move, not one word. You concentrate on one letter, an 'e'. If you could dislodge that one the others would follow. You gouge at it with your finger nails, your thumbs.[41]

As the text adopts a second-person perspective, the reader is thrust into a relationship with the 'picture' and attributed with violent acts enacted upon an image of a face. Gordon depicts this face loosely in the form of a simple concrete poem:

```
                forehead
    eye                         eye
                nose
        cheek           cheek
                mouth
                chin
```
[42]

The face is crudely made manifest by a simplistic construction of words – and yet, through the narrative perspective, and repetitions of 'she', 'her eyes' and '*I loved your eyes*',[43] Gordon places his reader in an uncomfortably aggressive position, enacting violence upon an impression of a face. The fourth 'Picture' piece employs even briefer fragments, whilst both this and the fifth employ a cold, directorial tone when stating '*end of first fragment*'[44] or 'end of inventory of her outward appearance'.[45] The devices, again, are not unfamiliar, but their purpose warrants investigation – Gordon expressed concerns about a readership content with mere surface meaning, and it is crucial to recognise that *Beyond the Words* is preceded by a body of short prose which forces an engagement with language beyond the superficial and the descriptive. Gordon encourages his reader to examine each word in the passage above as visually representative and enactive of the human face, in addition to its meaning as a linguistic signifier. The effect is exaggerated by Gordon's consistent positioning of his writing in relation to the visual arts, drawing clear attention to the unique capacity of written literature to reflect and remediate. Gordon's approach here highlights his belief in literature as a means to interrogate other media, whilst simultaneously accounting for the act of interrogation itself – a process familiar in writing contributed to *Beyond the Words*, such as Eva Figes's dramatic characters resisting the trappings of narrative fiction in 'On Stage' or Maggie Ross's subversion of the interview format in 'Interview'.

As an author of short prose, Gordon self-consciously toys with form, all the while drawing attention to the functions and faculties of language in contrast to other media, creating vivid impressions of the images which inspire each piece whilst pushing his language towards collapse. The fact that each of Gordon's devices performs this function, mimetic of linguistic and cognitive faculties, suggests that the notion of 'success' – again following Johnson – needs revision in terms of modernism's iteration of realism. The stability of surface reading is denied in Gordon's writing – a failure in Miller's terms but perhaps a success in Johnson's. Gordon closely mirrors the shifting, mercurial narratives exhibited by Quin, the quiet experiential chaos of Robert Nye, the sharp fragmentation of Alan Burns – or, most significantly of all, the broad, defiant drive to revitalise the sense of realistic writing championed by Johnson. The attempt to render other media through literary form is echoed in Elspeth Davie's contribution to *Beyond the Words*, a short prose piece titled 'Concerto' which transliterates music into written words by toying with urgency, pauses and slow reveals: 'the crash has coincided to a split second with the quietest bars of the concerto – that point where not only the soloist but all other players have lowered their instruments – all, that is to say, except the flute'.[46] The association between these writers is perhaps best described as a form of literary mimesis, albeit one self-consciously detached from nineteenth-century realism by its modernist influence, and anticipatory of postmodernism. The awareness this implies of the specific 1960s literary context within which these works were produced – and the critical perspectives Gordon would come to formulate as a result of the experience – reveal a coherent and consistent endeavour in both his critical and creative outputs to abandon tradition and pursue a new fiction.

Girl with Red Hair (1974)

Girl with Red Hair is Gordon's third novel, though by comparison to *The Umbrella Man* (1971) and *About a Marriage* (1972), it is by far his most formally unusual novel written prior to the publication of *Beyond the Words*. Whilst *The Umbrella Man* would employ a multitude of narrative voices and perspectives, *About a Marriage* is largely autobiographical. *Girl with Red Hair* constitutes a comprehensive challenge to the novel form as a whole, fragmentary from the start, non-sequential in narrative chronology and internally contradictory throughout.

Two devices, recurrent in Gordon's own writing and familiar from that of his 'eleven writers', are immediately clear from the opening chapter and set a consistent tone for the novel as a whole. Firstly, as with Gordon's 'Pictures', the reader is given a vivid sensory description of a subject which is obscured. The novel opens in the aftermath of an explosion, devoid of context:

> FIRST the rubble was cleared away. Dust blew about, inside buildings and outside. It lay on pianos, sofas, beds, chairs, tables. It latched onto food. It became ingrained in static, sleeping bodies for hundreds of feet around. And the noise of the cranes, mechanical shoves, drills, bulldozers, trucks, pickaxes, spades. Hammers.[47]

Gordon's narrative employs fragmented sentence structures, lists of furniture and construction tools, repeated anaphoric uses of 'it', and the brief, disconnected staccato of 'hammers' which seems more onomatopoeic joke than direct narrative. The sense of unease created by a text which refuses to abide by the familiar comforts of description, tonal consistency or narrative precision is further reflected in Gordon's second device – the use, again, of the second-person narrative perspective:

> Outside, in the street, you looked up, knowing one of the windows was hers. Was she there, awake or asleep? Did she sense your presence? Would she look out, rub her nose against the glass so that, around her nose, it would steam up? Oh that she would, oh that she would.
> Wanting to see her anew. To renew. How she was before you were married, before you lived together, before you met. To renew. No, a start; not a new start. A birth, not a rebirth.[48]

Brian McHale briefly discusses the employment of second-person narration in *Constructing Postmodernism* (1992), outlining the challenging position in which it places a reader, interpreting this 'you' on one hand as 'the protagonist's self-address', and on the other as 'an extra-diagetic narrator',[49] directly addressing the reader. If Gordon can again be identified as owing much to the modernists, it is perhaps as a counterpoint to Virginia Woolf's missing protagonist in *Jacob's Room* (1922). Similarly overshadowed by an unseen violence (Woolf's in the future, with the looming threat of the First World War, and Gordon's in an obscured but traumatic past), Woolf's protagonist's absence consistently implies his untimely death, whilst Gordon's is rendered uncomfortably present and participatory. Also notable here are the same revision and correction exhibited by the narrators of Gordon's 'Pictures' as, rather than following an omniscient narrator in command of objective facts, we join an impression at the moment of its formation, and witness its growth in detail and specificity as it is observed. Whether this act of observation is attributed to us as readers or placed very directly into our attention by positioning us fully within the consciousness of the protagonist, the effect is confrontational. Gordon demands that his reader read 'more critically', in a manner the journalist, the critic or indeed the traditional realist might not, engaging with the intrigue and fascination of words.

Girl with Red Hair develops into a murder mystery, albeit one fractured throughout in its presentation of short, non-sequential scenes which demand participation in reconstructing a coherent narrative. Quin's *Berg* again provides apt comparison here, as a novel revolving around – but never quite settling upon – a potential murder, never quite committed by the protagonist whose internal monologue the reader follows. *Girl with Red Hair* explores similar ambiguities, describing the scene of a shooting without settling on objective details:

> No one. He could see no one. He turned round, began to run. He didn't even know in which direction. Away from the body, from the centre of the superbly manicured lawn. Began to run. He did not look round to see if the man was pursuing him, the body. He did not look round to see if the man was grimacing, clutching himself, doubled up with pain, coughing bloody, dying. If he was crawling, about, like a worm chopped in two by a spade, if he was pouring blood into the green. If he had run in an opposite direction, not wanting to encounter again the man who had tried to kill him.[50]

Gordon describes the scene in terms of what is not seen, rather than what is – as witness to these events, the reader is provided only with doubts and suppositions. The notion of witnessing and, by extension, the reliability of description available to realist narrative, are called into question as Gordon captures the intense wondering and searching for meaning, rather than the facts of the event. David Plante similarly explores this ambiguity of seeing in 'Preface' – a short work of prose written for *Beyond the Words* in which the narrator repeatedly confesses his failures to observe:

> I tried to see this: her sadness, round, circumscribing him, square, the circles and squares revolving on one another, and, finally, separating from them, rising up around their heads in great and greater arcs and angles, expanding out into the air, over the land, until they might have thought their sadness was the sadness of the county they inhabited.
> I don't know why they were unhappy. Perhaps they didn't.[51]

The imprecision created by these texts is deliberate, revealing the artifice and impossibility of fully occupying another's mind, whilst simultaneously portraying extreme acts and circumstances. In doing this, Gordon and his selected writers challenge their reader to become the very readership which is lacking from their contemporary mainstream, coaxing them 'beyond the words' into a reading of form and style entirely separated from nineteenth-century realism, and favouring a form of experiential realism more familiar to the modernists.

Conclusion: The Language of Experimentalism

One of the crucial links between Johnson and Gordon is their insistence that the devices and strategies they employ in the writing of fiction are not innately experimental. Though certainly the product of experimentation, their literary strategies are instead complete, fully realised aspects of contemporary writing in a mimetic form of realism derived from the modernists. The terminology of experimentalism allows such writing to remain confined to the avant-garde, and allows editors like Miller to construct widely influential anthologies and critical studies which entirely omit writers falling outside the realms of traditional realist fiction. Fundamentally, both Johnson and Gordon draw critical and creative influence from modernism to arrive at a similar conclusion; each asserts that his wilfully unconventional approaches to fiction are not 'experimental' in nature, but also that a modernist definition of 'realism' is necessary in order to classify them as such. The frustration which permeates their critical writing rests upon the notion that such a classification does not exist in mainstream circles – or exists within modernism but has been overlooked as regards works of the 1950s and 1960s. When they reject the 'experimental' label, this seems due more to the complacent habit of conflating the term with experimentalism than to the notion of critical and methodological innovation, for which both Johnson and Gordon clearly strive.

The outcome of examining Gordon's writing in this way, and the extent to which it confirms and supports other avant-garde writing of the 1960s, reveal a clear need to assess this writing from the perspective of its rejection of the experimental label. If 'experimental' is indeed indicative of 'failure', as both Gordon and Johnson assert, then it can be read as a failure as it relates to the contemporaneous understanding of realism, as exhibited by Miller's anthology. A reading placed in terms of Gordon's critical relationships to realism and modernism is able to view his writing within a wider context of literary innovation and identify him alongside Johnson, Quin and others of this 1960s British avant-garde, as vital figures in the constitution of an emergent literary movement during this period. Though this movement would ultimately collapse in the wake of Johnson's and Quin's deaths, and Burns's departure for America, Gordon continued this pursuit: a 1970s writer shaped by the 1960s, determined to enact its new fiction and sustain its critical legacy.

Notes

1. Giles Gordon, *Aren't We Due a Royalty Statement?* (London: Chatto & Windus, 1993), p. 2.
2. 'Obituary: Giles Gordon', *The Telegraph*, 15 November 2003, available at <http://www.telegraph.co.uk/news/obituaries/1446732/Giles-Gordon.html> (accessed 25 October 2017).

3. Gordon, *Aren't We Due a Royalty Statement?*, p. 2.
4. Specifically, Gordon saw a lack of innovation in Miller's selection of Kingsley Amis, D. J. Enright, Philip Larkin, John Wain, Robert Conquest and Donald Davie, and rejected what he considered to be the book's conservative, anti-modern and anti-international biases.
5. Gordon, 'Introduction', in Gordon (ed.), *Beyond the Words: Eleven Writers in Search of a New Fiction* (London: Hutchinson, 1975), pp. 9–15, p. 9.
6. Jonathan Coe, *Like a Fiery Elephant: The Story of B. S. Johnson* (London: Picador, 2004), p. 3.
7. Ibid. p. 13.
8. B. S. Johnson, *Aren't You Rather Young to be Writing Your Memoirs?* (London: Hutchinson, 1973), p. 14.
9. Ibid. p. 12.
10. Ibid.
11. Ibid. p. 16.
12. Ibid. p. 12.
13. David James, 'B. S. Johnson Within the Ambit of Modernism', *Critical Engagements: A Journal of Criticism and Theory*, 4.1/4.2 (2011), pp. 37–53, p. 39.
14. Johnson, *Aren't you Rather Young to be Writing your Memoirs?*, p. 19.
15. Ibid.
16. Gordon, 'Introduction', in Ann Quin, *Berg* (Chicago: Dalkey Archive Press, 2001), pp. vii–xiv, p. xiii.
17. Gordon, *Beyond the Words*, p. 9.
18. Ibid. p. 14.
19. Ibid. p. 12.
20. Ibid. p. 14.
21. Ibid. p. 15.
22. Ibid.
23. Ibid.
24. Gordon, *Aren't we Due a Royalty Statement?*, p. 154.
25. Ibid. p. xiii.
26. Karl Miller, 'Introduction', in Karl Miller (ed.), *Writing in England Today: The Last Fifteen Years* (Harmondsworth: Penguin, 1968), p. 13.
27. Ibid.
28. Ibid. pp. 24–6.
29. Ibid. p. 13.
30. Ibid.
31. Ibid. p. 15.
32. Gordon, *Pictures from an Exhibition*, Front Liner Notes (London: Allison and Busby, 1970).
33. Gordon, 'Pictures from an exhibition 1', *Pictures from an Exhibition*, pp. 9–10, p. 9.
34. Gordon, 'Introduction', p. xi.

35. Quin, *Berg*, p. 22.
36. Gordon, 'Introduction', p. xi.
37. Gordon, 'Pictures from an exhibition 1', p. 9.
38. Ibid.
39. Ibid. pp. 9–10.
40. Johnson, *Aren't you Rather Young to be Writing your Memoirs?*, p. 12.
41. Gordon, 'Pictures from an exhibition 2', *Pictures from an Exhibition*, pp. 12–13, p. 12.
42. Ibid. p. 11.
43. Ibid. pp. 11–12.
44. Gordon, 'Pictures from an exhibition 4', *Pictures from an Exhibition*, pp. 16–17, p. 16.
45. Gordon, 'Pictures from an exhibition 5', *Pictures from an Exhibition*, pp. 18–21, p. 19.
46. Elspeth Davie, 'Concerto', in *Beyond the Words*, pp. 89–95, p. 92.
47. Gordon, *Girl with Red Hair* (London: Hutchinson, 1974), p. 7.
48. Ibid. p. 9.
49. Brian McHale, *Constructing Postmodernism* (London: Routledge, 1993), p. 95.
50. Gordon, *Girl with Red Hair*, pp. 46–7.
51. David Plante, 'Preface', in *Beyond the Words*, pp. 234–5.

Chapter 4

Brigid Brophy's Aestheticism: The Camp Anti-Novel

Len Gutkin

Brigid Brophy, famous in her day but now more or less forgotten, was an eccentric mid-century genius whose novels, social theory, music writing and literary criticism constitute one of the most intense and singular literary corpuses in postwar Britain.[1] Born in 1929, Brophy began publishing in the fifties but the sixties was by far her most fruitful decade – between 1962 and 1969 she published four novels, a play, studies of Mozart and Aubrey Beardsley, a collection of occasional criticism and the unclassifiable *Black Ship to Hell* (1963), an idiosyncratic 500-page Freudian account of 'man as a destructive and, more particularly, a self-destructive animal'.[2] Her productivity continued at a respectable but more moderate pace into the 1970s, during which she produced a massive biography of Ronald Firbank, her literary hero, as well as a biography of Beardsley. This decade also saw the publication of Brophy's final novel, *Palace Without Chairs* (1978), a touching, absurdist romance set in 'Evarchia', an Eastern European monarchy riven by Cold War intrigue. In 1981, Brophy was diagnosed with multiple sclerosis; she died in 1995, writing very little in the final years of her life.

Brophy's posthumous neglect is more than a mere vagary of literary history; it is, it seems to me, written into her texts, courted deliberately (or at least anticipated) as an effect of her peculiar aesthetic commitments. Her remarks on 'minorness' in *Prancing Novelist: A Defence of Fiction ... in Praise of Ronald Firbank* (1973) are a key to her own work. Opposed to what she calls the 'social-mirror' model of artistic evaluation – in which the larger the slice of sociohistorical reality a novel seems to capture, the better it is – Brophy's defence of Firbank involves a rejection of the major/minor binary altogether: 'The moment you drop the social-mirror theory as untenable, you see major and minor fictions according to a quite different scale, and you stop seeing the history of fiction as a scale at all.'[3]

Brophy's form of minorness was, explicitly and self-consciously, a species of high camp, and her novels of the 1960s can clarify, with the benefit of retrospect, the important place of camp aesthetics in the broader formal experimentalism of the British (and American) novel of the period.[4]

Brophy's *Firbank* and the Aestheticist Baroque

Firbank, Brophy says, is an artist of 'modernity' but, 'like most of the great modernities in art, [Firbank's] consisted partly and importantly, though not mainly, of revivalism'.[5] We might say the same for Brophy, whose 1963 novel *The Finishing Touch* is a frank Firbank pastiche, a work of overt revivalism. More generally, Brophy's work revives two period styles, about which she writes often in her criticism: the decadent aestheticism of the *fin de siècle* and eighteenth-century baroque. With a high degree of theoretical self-consciousness, Brophy brought these periods and styles to bear on the radical experimentalism of the sixties and seventies. Brophy's modernity, to borrow her formula on Firbank, consisted partly and importantly in a playful renegotiation of a literary and aesthetic past appropriated and adapted under the sign of 'camp'. Along with Muriel Spark, Brophy was the great camp experimentalist of postwar British fiction.[6]

Brophy, in fact, is 'The Great Camp King' of the British avant-garde; or is it 'the Great Camp Queen-Pin herself'?[7] As these character-figments from her 1969 gender-bending fantasia *In Transit* suggest, 'camp' is, for Brophy, inextricably tied to gender performance and sex mutability. These are arguably the great themes of all of Brophy's work. Brophy's 'camp' (a word she uses frequently in both her fiction and her criticism) has a specific aesthetic history; indeed, as one of the most learned of camp's practitioners, Brophy herself should probably be considered a principal historian and theorist of the term. Brophy's camp derives from a synthesis of the baroque and the classical (understood as eighteenth-century period styles) on the one hand and of nineteenth-century aestheticism on the other. These period styles, though, are not revived without modification – instead, they are decked out in the modish garb of the experimental 1960s.

This synthesis took some time to achieve. Brophy's artistic self-understanding at the beginning of the sixties claims a debt to the classical *at the expense of* aestheticism. She writes that George Bernard Shaw, one of her heroes, 'rescue[d] . . . English prose from Art for Art's Sake and Style for Style's . . . restoring prose to its eighteenth-century rigour and giving style a new lease of life by re-attaching it to meaning'.[8] A stark opposition is here proposed: between a weak, thoughtless *fin de siècle* and a stylish but 'vigorous' eighteenth century. As she puts it a little later in the same volume, 'artists might do without [science], but only at the risk of locking themselves into the infertile cul-de-sac of art-for-art's sake'.[9]

Even at this early stage, however, Brophy is not quite as opposed to the *fin de siècle* as these proclamations might suggest. She sees aestheticism[10] as a 'reaction' whose greatest figures are Baudelaire, Beardsley and Firbank:

> The rush to hell was an exaggeration of the eighteenth-century habit of going to the dogs. It swept on, still without forfeiting its dandyism, carrying Rimbaud down to pass une saison en enfer in 1873, illuminating another underworld in the brothel scenes of Toulouse-Lautrec, creating genuinely Baudelairean images in the stylish and perverse images of Aubrey Beardsley. By that time, however, the decadents were unintentionally giving back to the Hell tradition a little of Mrs. Radcliffe's absurdity [. . .]. All the decadents' hints about nameless vice boiled down to one predilection which, as its propagandists knew quite well, is not a vice and which is explicitly, if monotonously, nameable. Oscar Wilde and the Yellow Book authors [. . .] preserved little from their Baudelaire–Rimbaud lineage except an obsessive connexion [*sic*] between homosexuality and Roman-Catholicism. Yet even within these limits, and well into the twentieth century, the Baudelairean line produced in Ronald Firbank one last, left-over, washed-out but authentic fleur du mal [. . .].[11]

In this compressed account of what are, after all, her chosen literary antecedents, Brophy admits the importance of '*ce dandysme sobre*' to her own interests, an importance each of her sixties novels bears out in its own way.[12]

Her denigration of Wilde, though, still suggests a bit of protesting-too-much. By the other side of the decade, her criticism of Wilde will have softened, as will her somewhat dismissive attitude towards what Eve Sedgwick called 'the homosexual topic'.[13] In *Prancing Novelist*, Brophy observes that because 'Firbank was . . . a militant (defensive in the positive sense) homosexual', he was 'free to make rational aesthetic decisions at a time when the arts were still suffering the trauma of the Wilde trials and when [therefore] heterosexuals and apologetic homosexuals treated the whole subject of aesthetics as taboo'.[14] Far from being 'monotonously' obsessed over by Yellow Book fad-followers, homosexuality has become, in Brophy's critical vision, integral to any understanding of 'the whole subject of aesthetics'. And Wilde himself is no longer 'merely silly' but one of the 'pioneers of the future', a status achieved 'partly by virtue of reviving the methods of the 18th century'.[15] By making Wilde into an eighteenth-century revivalist, Brophy reconciles her twinned attachments to aestheticist *l'art pour l'art* on the one hand and the eighteenth century (baroque and classical both) on the other.

Brophy's comments on fiction in *Prancing Novelist* should be taken as a kind of justification or explanation for her own novels of the 1960s. In the twentieth century, Brophy says, 'selfconsciousness crept upon both novelists and readers. Naturalism died, as any artistic convention must when that happens, because both sides found themselves unable any longer to believe it.'[16] In Brophy's campy experimental fictions, not only is naturalism dead, but so too are both gender and ethnic/national essence. Brophy's experiments are heavily preoccupied with the waning belief in the validity of what were once quite naturalised codes of being. Such scepticism is, of course, very much a feature of the various sixties countercultures, but by yoking countercultural anti-traditionalism to the aestheticism of the *fin de siècle*, Brophy achieves a literary and argumentative texture uniquely her own.

Brophy's most valued quality in fiction is what she calls 'distance', which she believes unites the eighteenth century with Firbank (skipping over, implicitly, the 'naturalism' occupying both the Victorian realist novel and the modernist psychological one). She explains 'distance' in psychoanalytic terms:

> Distance belongs par excellence to classical fiction, of the kind written by Jane Austen and Ronald Firbank. It takes place because the novelist has withdrawn some of his own wishes from the happiness of the hero and directed them toward the felicity of the design; and it is in classical fictions that the designs are at their most formal.[17]

'Distance', then, means that identification with character has been sublimated into a cathexis of form. Its tendency is anti-psychological, insofar as the novel as object of art takes precedence over the novel as vessel for subjectivities. But this does *not* entail coldness. As Brophy puts it of Firbank's 1915 novel *Vainglory*:

> What made it so modern, in 1915, as to be puzzling was that it did something that had scarcely been achieved in English fiction since the death of Jane Austen and, when it was attempted, had not been much appreciated: it sets the author (and the reader) at a distance from his material, without making him emotionally remote from it.[18]

Of course, *Vainglory* remains 'puzzling' and Firbank remains 'minor'. Brophy, here, has identified something like the formal-affective structure of camp. As a model for authorship, camp involves the *distanced deployment of emotional attachments*. As a mode of reception, camp involves appreciation, even to the point of over-identification, that nevertheless holds itself sceptically. As Allan Pero puts it, 'Camp does not perform the universal, nor is it the disintegration of the universal into the subject – instead, Camp opens up the anxiety, the laughter, the bathos of shame – the failure to perform the becoming subjective of the universal.'[19] The failure of the subjective and the universal to meet up is the social experience captured by camp art's insistent eccentricity and minorness. Brophy's contention that 'The three greatest novels of the twentieth century are *The Golden Bowl, A La Recherche Du Temps Perdu* and [Firbank's] *Concerning The Eccentricities of Cardinal Pirelli*' riffs on the disjunction between camp and aesthetic universality. A witty surprise, Firbank's inclusion in the list indicates Brophy's real conviction that a certain deliberate minorness is not at odds with 'greatness'.[20]

Brophy's own eschewal of the universal obtains in the extreme stylistic variety of her works, each of which can seem the product of a completely different author from the last. Her refusal to establish a consistent authorial voice is no doubt part of the reason that, less than twenty-five years after her death, she has all but fallen off the map of literary history.[21] Though her novels tend to share some common themes and a general resistance to the constraints of realism (or, her preferred term, 'naturalism'), they are sufficiently heterogenous such that it is hard to imagine what the adjective 'Brophyan' might denote.

Brophy's irreverence and resistance to 'naturalism' are evident from her two fifties novels, *Hackenfeller's Ape* (1953) and, especially, *The King of a Rainy Country* (1956), a camp riff on the courtship plot in which the young male and female principals are each more interested in an ageing American opera star than they are in each other. As Patricia Juliana Smith puts it in a formulation that has applicability across all of Brophy's work, this novel is:

> an early example of postmodernity, a metafiction that tries on and discards a variety of conventional generic plots which, because of their deeply ingrained heterosexual narrative ideologies, offer no viable solutions or means of closure to the protagonists. Ultimately, Brophy indicates, when all other plots fail there is always opera. And opera, not coincidentally, has long been one of the few 'respectable' art forms in which women *en travesti* can switch their gender and make love to other women with impunity.[22]

These preoccupations will return in *The Snow Ball* (1964) and, allied to a far more flagrant variety of metafiction, in *In Transit*.

Flesh

But in *Flesh* (1962), her first novel of the sixties, Brophy would seem to be trying her hand at exactly the kind of 'naturalism' she elsewhere rejected. I believe, however, that *Flesh* offers something like a very skilful forgery, a sort of imitation realism whose major themes – connoisseurship, aestheticism and identity – will inform the more obviously campy novels that follow.

Flesh, which Brophy called 'an almost distressingly cold-blooded little story',[23] tells of the courtship and marriage of a pair of Jewish North Londoners; it is on one level a realist account of minority experience, focused on the ambivalence with which modern, young English Jews see their parents' old-world folkways. It is also a tale of sexual awakening. Marcus is an awkward, odd youth brought out of his shell by Nancy, who unexpectedly picks him for marriage and thereby initiates him into sex and into a new vision of himself and the world. Marcus gets a job restoring antiques; Marcus and Nancy have a child; Marcus grows fat and has an affair with the German au pair. All the characters are described with icy detachment and none is favoured or sympathised with: this is a kind of *nouveau roman* in a pseudo-ethnographical mode. The novel's 'Jewishness', for instance, is grotesquely overdone. 'We belong', Marcus implausibly says, when he and Nancy conceive a child on their first try, 'to a philoprogenitive race.'[24] The echo of T. S. Eliot's 'Mr. Eliot's Sunday Morning Service' (in which Jews are 'Polyphiloprogenitive / The sapient sutlers of the lord') is not so much clueless as knowingly absurd.

Despite its icy remoteness, *Flesh*, like Wilde's *The Picture of Dorian Gray*, is really a novel about aestheticism as obsession. Brophy has written a decadent fable but she has chastened the fabular element with the trappings of realism, which she applies with a parodically heavy hand. The Jewishness of *Flesh*'s milieu is Brophy's way of estranging her own preoccupation with aestheticism, which is arguably the novel's main focus. Early on, she establishes a continuity between Jewishness and aestheticism:

> There was a place reserved in the tradition for Marcus as the unworldly and dreamy one, and they [his parents] were quite prepared to keep his place open for him while suffering it to be secularized. Obviously, he was not going to be a rabbi. But he could be an artist, a scholar, an aesthete, a connoisseur – he could be anything he wanted, with their solemn, traditional blessing and their help.[25]

Despite the special place supposedly held by Jewish convention for such impractical pursuits, *Flesh* figures the formation of taste (in the consciousness at least of its characters) as a kind of deracination, an emancipation from the constraints of ethnic belonging. *Bad* taste is identified by Marcus with the old-world Jewishness of his parents, specifically their habits in interior decoration: over-furnished, orange-coloured and marked by a peculiar smell. Marcus is at first impressed at the absence of such stigmatising marks of Jewishness in Nancy's parents' place but discovers a flaw – the paintings hanging on the wall are not good: 'After he had walked around and examined them all, he became aware that they showed the same predilection for orange as his parents' furnishings.'[26] What at first seemed like a home refreshingly free of the taint of Jewishness eventually fails altogether: 'One day, when sunshine was falling through the drawing-room windows and its warmth was perhaps bringing out the scents of the house, he actually detected the smell which permeated his parents' home [. . .]. "I think they must make a kosher furniture polish," he said.'[27]

For Marcus, a studied minimalism offers a way out of the threat that one's own living quarters might be in bad taste. In this respect, 'Jewishness' is a figure for all of the familiar, human *clutter* that cultivation hopes to allay. The asceticism implicit in so much aestheticism comes to the fore. Deracination means, almost, the elimination of all signs of inhabitation. No pictures at all hang in Marcus and Nancy's apartment:

> [T]hey themselves, who had picked out and revealed its beauty, were more than ever under a moral obligation not to desecrate the place. There was not a wall Marcus would besmirch . . . . The place *was*, like all eighteenth century buildings, a temple: a small and chaste one, where no blood sacrifice had been performed.[28]

With the ironic precision of a fairy tale, Marcus's aestheticism is its own undoing. He is offered a job in an antique shop run by one Polydore, a dealer in fake rare things who is himself Jewish ('Presently Marcus realized that there arose from the desk a slight smell of the same furniture polish'[29]). Nancy first suggests that Marcus take the job but then becomes reluctant: 'I suppose I'm afraid that you might pick up commercialism. Or dilettantism.'[30] Marcus proves an expert restorer: his job is to render faux-antiques more plausible, a task to which his broad aesthetic knowledge, innate taste and manual dexterity all suit him. Polydore, an echo of the Jewish shop-owner in *The Golden Bowl*, exerts a mysterious, seductive influence over Marcus. Just as Nancy fears, Marcus's earlier connoisseurship, so disdainful and aestheticist, is collapsed into its putative opposite, debased commercialism. He becomes a mere fetishist of his materials:

> His head was immersed. When he heard [Nancy] come in he – without looking up – held out a fold to her between his finger, like an Oriental offering a morsel from his own plate. 'Come and *feel* it, darling.'
> 'Get up,' she said, in the traditional manner of the Victorian lady receiving a proposal of marriage from a physically repugnant suitor, but adding, 'You look like an old Jew merchant.'
> 'I *am* an old Jew merchant.'[31]

The ironic reversal whereby Marcus's skill with *objets d'art* renders him personally vulgar is *Flesh*'s central joke. Marcus becomes a glutton. He has always reminded Nancy, to her discomfort, of his sister ('she looks so like you, darling, in some ways. And then I look at her and suddenly see she's got women's breasts, instead of nice flat strong ones, like yours'[32]), a confusion of gender which his growing obesity tends to increase: 'Just look at yourself . . . . Look at your thighs. Look at your flesh. You've got great pendulous breasts, like a woman.'[33] *Flesh* is a drama of connoisseurship in which, paradoxically, aestheticist achievement results in a commercialism figured as both gluttonous and androgynous.

'Distance', as we have seen, is for Brophy the most highly prized aspect of the novelist's art. She saw Firbank's excellence as inhering in a distance from his material that does not prevent his affection for it. *Flesh*'s parodic ethnography – and the fact that ethnic self-ambivalence is one of its themes – manifests distance at every turn. But, as Brophy's own description of the novel as 'cold-blooded' suggests, affection is in short supply.

The Finishing Touch and *The Snow Ball*

In *The Finishing Touch*, the elements of aestheticist delectation and androgyny, which figure in *Flesh* as potentially sinister, have been liberated entirely from the framework of moralising melodrama that *Flesh* had inherited from *Dorian Gray* and decadent literature more broadly. This novel is Brophy's way of working through her interest in Firbank with as much fidelity to the tradition as she can muster. It is a kind of exercise. Set in a girls' boarding school overseen by a lesbian couple, Antonia and Henrietta, its delicately artificial style – in which minute distinctions in aesthetic perception are delineated with fussy precision – hits every note in the repertoire. Here is Antonia having her nightcap: 'Her palate prickled in a response almost erotic to the madeira, that liquid neither male nor female or, rather, both, that part-deep, part treble *glow*, that viola among wines.'[34] While Henrietta is straightforwardly butch, Antonia has a preference for feminised borrowings from male military attire: 'an epaulette here, a high collar there? or merely a straight, a darkening line of braid? . . . Somehow, at least, in giving indulgence to the dandy in her soul, she achieved a firm definition, a distinction of upright outline.'[35] The broadly androgynous lesbianism represented in *The Finishing Touch*, then, has its idiom (high-dandiacal) and its canon: Colette's *Claudine à l'École*, Proust's *Albertine disparue* and, above all, Gautier's 1834 gender-bending novel *Mademoiselle de Maupin*, which, as one of her students remarks, is Antonia's reliable bedtime reading 'the night before an Occasion'.[36]

It is true that each of Brophy's books sounds very different from the one before it but it is nevertheless possible to perceive some continuities of voice and style – at least, usually. *The Finishing Touch* might be an exception: an imitation so thorough-going in its absorption by other periods and manners as to leave 'Brigid Brophy' almost entirely behind. (This is 'distance' practiced to the point of authorial self-oblivion!) Written, she says, 'in a superficially Firbankian idiom', it is almost too good a parody quite to work as anything else – pastiche this committed seems to admit that the novel really is exhausted, that it can be kept alive only on a kind of virtuosic revivalist life-support. In her next novel, *The Snow Ball*, the aestheticist emphases are retained but deployed in a less aggressively pastiched manner.

The Snow Ball is the story of a one-night stand at a New Year's Eve costume party. Its protagonist, Anna, is dressed as Donna Anna from *Don Giovanni*; after a series of intricate deliberations, she agrees to go home with a masked Don Giovanni. A slender enough thread to hang a novel on but, despite (or perhaps because of) its brevity and minimal action, *The Snow Ball* advances a great deal of Brophy's thinking about aestheticism and novel form. In the early part of the novel, Anna's application of make-up offers an occasion for a meditation on masquerade: 'she was in sympathy with her face when she made it up . . . with the virtuoso craftsman's sympathy with the organic nature, the grain, the accidents that could be turned to account, of his medium'.[37] In her minute attention to Anna's make-up, an attention inspiring long passages of rather difficult prose, Brophy's is a strategy of anti-naturalism. Her manner of describing human forms and faces reduces or raises them to a kind of non-conscious object-hood very much like that achieved in the *nouveau roman* of Robbe-Grillet:

> Anna ... saw herself, with her head and most of her legs chopped off, in her hostess's looking glass. A middle view of her own verticality, it shewed chiefly her black dress, though it included her pale upper arms, thin as the body of a stick insect, and the bare skeleton of her shoulders and collar bone, harnessed by the dress's two broad black straps. It made, in the whiteness, a photograph of too high contrast. Only the Siamese kitten on the bed behind mediated between the tones, a small tussock the colour of snow turned slushy in the street.[38]

This Siamese kitten (one of the 'snow balls' of the title) introduces a bit of camp playfulness into a description that otherwise achieves something of the stasis of the *nouveau roman*, that stifling objectivity imposed on people in novels such as Robbe-Grillet's *In the Labyrinth* (1960). Anna's toilette, Brophy continues, is performed 'almost without thoughts, in the craftsman's near-automatism'.[39]

The Don Giovanni character (never named) is, on inspection, less an eighteenth-century rake than a nineteenth-century dandy, nostalgic for and envious of an aristocratic power he is, in fact, cut off from by class: 'On nights like this, I hate the rich ... almost as much as I hate the poor.'[40] He longs for the 'aristocratic frame of mind'.[41] Anna meets this dandiacal nostalgia with her own aestheticist improvisations, in which she expresses her desire to be solid and inhuman, like an object of art: 'I rather like the inorganic. Or at least the not very highly organic. Ideally, I would live surrounded by very beautiful, highly coloured, fantastic reptiles or fish. Something cold-blooded, that had never been in a womb.'[42] There is a crucial continuity between nineteenth-century aestheticism and the anti-humanist imaginary of the modernist avant-garde – think of Wyndham Lewis's alter-ego Tarr on 'deadness', which he thinks 'the first condition of art. A hippopotamus's armoured hide, a turtle's shell, feathers or machinery ... [as] opposed to naked pulsing and moving of the soft inside of life.'[43] Brophy, in her postmodern moment, revives this cluster of associations. This revival is itself, though, a kind of camp pastiche: the intensities of avant-garde theorising are here redeployed as verbal foreplay at a costume party. As Anna goes on to say, 'I'd like to be attractive not as a person but as a thing. Not to be made use of – no monetary value: I'd like to be a useless thing. I'd like to be neither warm-blooded nor cold-blooded but just for there to be no question of blood at all.'[44]

The desire to be like a work of art is, perhaps, quite natural for these two cultivated people whose flirtation involves, for instance, quoting Walter Pater at one another.[45] But, as a seduction plot, *The Snow Ball* dramatises the need to overcome Anna's brand of aestheticism, whose anti-humanism risks sterility. As Don Giovanni puts it, 'I'm one of the people who do prefer life to perfection.'[46] If these two people are to manage to go to bed together – and they do – Anna's protective arch-aestheticism will need to give way. *The Snow Ball*, then, is a kind of allegory about the consequences of a tradition of aestheticism running from the nineteenth century into what Jessica Burstein calls 'cold modernism' and beyond.[47] Such allegories are, in fact, conventional from *Dorian Gray* onwards, though by the 1960s, they are also consciously anachronistic. Like *The Finishing Touch*, then, *The Snow Ball* is a 'revival' of an older problem and an older style.

In Transit

When Brophy is remembered today, it is usually for *In Transit*, a comic metafiction whose narrator, Pat, is of ambiguous gender: either Patrick or Patricia, sometimes both in double columns of prose unfolding simultaneously. Pat loses knowledge of their gender while in an airport, when some spilt coffee obliterates the sex designation on their passport.[48] As in *Flesh*, deracination is theme and cause, since Pat's ancestral Irishness – they were orphaned young, then raised in England – motivates the verbal and sexual indeterminacies that are the novel's major subject. 'Transplanted', Pat says, 'I had become derooted and derouted. You can send shamrocks over the sea, but they will not grow outside of Ireland.'[49] Irishness on the one hand and opera on the other are the forces behind androgyny – 'o Irish O'Pera, who initially set this sexchange in train'.[50] Irishness entails an estrangement from one's mother tongue ('Imperialism gave us Irish/Indians/West Indians its vocabulary, but the idiom wouldn't travel'[51]) but opera (or 'O'Pera') promises to make good this estrangement, since, in opera, 'There is nothing so recuperative to the personality as that it should for a space impersonate someone else.'[52] Opera, Pat says, is 'the Amphisbaena (trans. colloqu. The push-and-pull or the have-it-both-ways)'.[53] But the operatic libretto is only one of *In Transit*'s parodied modes; others include the detective novel, the pornographic novel and the revolutionary tract. Like 'The Winds of Aeolus' in *Ulysses*, *In Transit* is a virtuosic grab-bag of literary genres and styles.

One of these styles is metafiction itself, whose experimental conventions Brophy gleefully exaggerates:

> I've muttered to you, my dear Reader, several asides on the subject of the technique of fiction, including some about alienation effects – one of which I am indeed practising on you now [. . .]. I have invited you to inspect and (I hope) concur in the machinery of my narration. And now I want to urge your attention towards one particular and cardinal cog. Has it occurred to you there may be a specific determining reason why this narrative should be in the first person? [. . .] Yours to the end of alienation.[54]

The answer, of course, is that 'I' has no gender in English. *In Transit*, as Frank Kermode noted in his review in *The Listener*, is 'a *nouveau roman* insofar as it pretends to accept the view that older styles of fiction are discredited'; but, since it is in English and not French, this 'antinovel's antinovel' is still 'allowed to be funny'.[55] This is a more profound observation than it might at first seem. Brophy's disintegration of the codes of realism shares nothing of the grim seriousness of, say, Robbe-Grillet but that background grimness, the grimness of the continental anti-novel, is assumed, so that part of *In Transit*'s effect involves the pastiche of the *nouveau roman*. This is one of its camp features: high aesthetic difficulty (and *In Transit* is 'difficult' by any measure) need not preclude a kind of playfulness that (unlike the merely nominal playfulness of the 'play of the signifier') is actually funny. Indeed, if you do not enjoy *In Transit*, it is probably because you find its playfulness manic or antic – closer to what Sianne Ngai calls 'zaniness' than to the celebratory affirmations of camp.[56]

In Transit announces at its outset that it is a tale of verbal disintegration, of 'linguistic leprosy', and the body of the novel pursues this disintegration with zest.[57] There are, though, two organising principles, like bones or support beams over which this leprous, unravelling text has been, however provisionally or inadequately, draped. The first is the literature of aestheticism proper, which, as in all of Brophy, figures in *In Transit* quite explicitly as a literary ancestor. The second is opera, or theatrical performance more broadly. In the appreciation of opera, the narrator says, 'I am free of self.'[58]

'Fly with me', our narrator says, 'but do not decamp.'[59] To decamp, here, would be to demand the narrative satisfactions of realism, to reject as too arbitrary or unweighty these metafictional experiments in which 'my thoughts got gautier and gautier'.[60] (Recall Antonia's special love for Gautier, original novelist of androgyny.)

From Gautier to the 1890s is but a short distance in the history of aestheticism and decadence, so it should come as no surprise that the airport's 'Poets' Corner' consists only, as a version of the narrator reports, of 'Nineties poets'.[61] And from the 1890s it is no distance at all to Aubrey Beardsley, whose name appears in graffiti on the airport wall towards the novel's end: 'DON'T FORCIBLY SHAVE ME NURSE – I'M TRYING TO GROW A BEARDSLEY!'[62] These allusions are more than just the reflexes of Brophy's interest in aestheticism. They indicate that aestheticism and decadence underwrite in important ways the extreme experimentation with novel form of which *In Transit* is an example.

The most specific way this ancestry emerges is the androgyny topos itself, a topos whose decadent form can involve an almost surgical emphasis on interiority-as-physiology. As Pat says of their ambiguous (sexually and otherwise) subjectivity, 'It's like showing you a constant dissection, with a square of skin cut, folded back and pinned down in order to display the sinews.'[63] But more generally and perhaps more importantly here, aestheticism's pressure on subjectivity informs the anti-novel's analogous scepticism about the coherence of the self. As Pater puts it in the conclusion to *The Renaissance*, 'It is . . . with the passage and dissolution of impressions, images, sensations, that analysis leaves off – that continual vanishing away, that strange, perpetual weaving and unweaving of ourselves.'[64] Pat's own version of this subjective dissolution goes a long way – as does Pater himself – towards considering identity dispersal its own reward, even its own species of identity:

> But in my case I can feel no sympathy with supposed loss of identity. I can conceive of losing many things [. . .]. Memory, even, I can imagine blotted out [. . .]. Identity, however, is unloseable. That which feels the loss [. . .] that is your identity. I have doubted often what I am, but never who.[65]

In this fascinating formulation, the experience of subjective dissolution is itself predicated, logically, on the possession of an 'identity', no matter how inchoate, changeable or temporary the content of that identity might be. Metafictive self-reflexivity of the kind made popular in the 1960s and 1970s is here overtly identified with gender ambiguity. Even before the narrator's indeterminate gender is revealed, Brophy has already executed some virtuoso verbal manœuvres on the theme of linguistic gender. The narrator especially loves the Italian 'lei' form for polite second-person address, in which an excess of good manners is displayed by a language that renders 'you (sing.) are' by 'she is' [. . .]. And this Italian does, povero innocente, without a clue how camp it's being. Poveri inno-gents politely addressing one another as she. Is She satisfied, sir?[66]

In Transit's narrator finds in opera the most aesthetically rewarding species of mutable identity: the '[s]weet monster opera' has 'drawn me down into identifications with your characters by your sheer liquid expressiveness of their emotions': '[I am] delivered from what seems the sinfulness but not from the delights of selfishness.'[67] Opera, as the 'have-it-both-ways' monster,[68] permits one to suspend one's 'own' identity in the affective solution of a fictional other.

As Susan Sontag famously said, 'Camp sees everything in quotation marks,'[69] an insight powering *In Transit*'s many parodic riffs – on opera, on detective fiction and on pornography, in the internal narrative 'L'histoire de Langue d'Oc'. The subjunctivity Brophy associates with opera receives its most extreme treatment:

> Applying the bows with 'His' right hand, 'He' he continued to 'stop the strings' with 'His' left.
> Even through the 'mute', Oc gave a cry of delight, which was almost drowned by the thunder of the audience's applause.[70]

In an interpretive gloss on this text-within-a-text, the narrator insists that 'that enigmatic inverted-comma'd He' is '[t]he clue to it all': moreover, 'I am (déchirez whatever does not apply) a he/a she/a "he"/a "she".'[71] Camp's signature quotation marks are here tethered explicitly to gender ambiguity and, implicitly, to the novel's more general metafictional tactics. Gender, like genre, is shown to be a performance involving transient emotional cathexes.

But, while this variety of aestheticist subjunctivity is obviously approved of by Brophy, *In Transit*'s dénouement presents an at best ambivalent vision of 1960s dissolution. As a committed revivalist, Brophy is a conservative, in the sense that she is committed to conserving past modes and styles, which can be harvested for their potency in the present. When, therefore, she depicts a kind of sixties-ish 'revolution' in the airport – the events of the novel's last section – she cannot lend her full approval because she sees the revolutionaries as culpably ignorant about the reservoir of culture. As Brooke Horvath correctly observes, Brophy's depiction of the revolution amounts to a set of 'charges against the sixties'.[72] As catastrophe unfolds, Brophy unleashes some of her most gloriously camp sentences, no quotation marks required: 'The mannerist angel of panic passed with his lovely, long, nervous, affected and invisible strides over the Transit Lounge.'[73] Pat or Patricia falls to his or her death – alternative narratives are offered but both end badly ('entrails were too distorted to be of any use for transplants') – and the narrator provides this gloss:

> In the truth of baroque metaphor, Bernini's Saint Teresa reclined and expired in a smile of orgasmic ecstasy, while her honey-tongued, artificial-shepherd-cheeked seraph, in an act of inspired and transcendent bad taste, pierced and pierced her with his phallic spear, wearing on his honeysweet and musical lips a silly sexy simper.[74]

'Inspired and transcendent bad taste' might be a motto for camp itself. In the figure of the mannerist angel astride the wreckage of the present, shoring up fragments against the ruins of the era, Brophy's radical revivalism finds its most eloquent, and most ridiculous, expression. And the Berniniesque death scene lodges an ironic protest against the hostility towards the past which Brophy finds in the counterculture.

Such mannerist 'bad taste' relies on a combination of stylistic difficulty and potential triviality which will always be 'minor' – and Brophy preferred it this way. An artistic and social radical who is nevertheless committed to the conservation of past modes; a champion of emotional 'distance' who nevertheless loves form itself with high aestheticist intensity; a passionate advocate of experiential dissolution who nevertheless believed subjective identity to be a logically predicated fact – Brophy in her sixties fiction unites the avant-garde and the literary past in a manner uniquely, inimitably, her own. Fly with her but do not deCamp.

Notes

1. Besides a 1995 issue of *The Review of Contemporary Fiction* partially devoted to her work, Brophy also makes an appearance in Patricia Juliana Smith's *Lesbian Panic: Homoeroticism in the Modern British Novel* (New York: Columbia University Press, 1997). Additionally, Leslie Dock published a rich interview with Brophy in 'An Interview with Brigid Brophy', *Contemporary Literature*, 17:2 (1976), pp. 151–70. There are not, to my knowledge, any monographs devoted exclusively to Brophy.

2. Brophy, *Black Ship to Hell* (New York: Harcourt, Brace and World, 1963), p. 13.
3. Brophy, *Prancing Novelist: A Defence of Fiction in the Form of a Critical Biography in Praise of Ronald Firbank* (New York: Barnes and Noble, 1973), p. 42.
4. Susan Sontag's 'Notes on Camp' is, of course, the major statement on camp aesthetics from the 1960s. In *Reading Innovative American Fiction* (Cambridge: Cambridge University Press, 1995), Richard Walsh observes a general confluence between Sontag's 'celebration of form' in 'Notes on Camp' and the experimental American fiction of the 1960s. In the American case, a broad range of the most 'experimental' fiction of the period can be productively analysed under the rubric of 'camp', including works by John Barth, Gilbert Sorrentino, Robert Coover and, perhaps especially, William S. Burroughs.
5. Brophy, *Prancing Novelist*, p. 77.
6. See my 'Muriel Spark's Camp Metafiction', *Contemporary Literature*, 58:1 (Spring 2017), pp. 53–81.
7. Brophy, *In Transit* [1969] (Chicago: Dalkey Archive Press, 2002), pp. 177, 184.
8. Brophy, *Black Ship to Hell*, pp. 133–4.
9. Ibid. p. 343.
10. I am using the term in a broad way, to refer to loosely affiliated developments in Victorian art and culture from, say, the publication of *Les Fleurs du Mal* to the end of the century.
11. Brophy, *Black Ship to Hell*, pp. 326–7.
12. Ibid. p. 326.
13. Eve Kosofsky Sedgwick, *Epistemology of the Closet* (Berkeley: University of California Press, 1990), p. 74.
14. Brophy, *Prancing Novelist*, p. xiv.
15. Ibid. p. 76.
16. Ibid. p. 6.
17. Ibid. p. 56.
18. Ibid. p. 83.
19. Allan Pero, 'Camp: Kant's Unwritten Fourth Critique', *The Word Hoard*, 1:3 (2015), pp. 7–18, p. 15.
20. 'Firbank', in Brophy, *Don't Never Forget* (London: Jonathan Cape, 1962), pp. 243–8, p. 243.
21. See Chris Hopkins, 'On the Neglect of Brigid Brophy', *Review of Contemporary Fiction*, 15:3 (1995), pp. 12–17, p. 12.
22. Patricia Juliana Smith, 'Desperately Seeking Susan[na]: Closeted Quests and Mozartean Gender Bending in Brigid Brophy's *The King of a Rainy Country*', *Review of Contemporary Fiction*, 15:3 (1995), pp. 23–31, p. 23.
23. Quoted in Sarah Lyall, 'Brigid Brophy is Dead at 66; Novelist, Critic, and Crusader', *The New York Times*, 9 August 1995.

24. Brophy, *Flesh* (Cleveland and New York: The World Publishing Company, 1962), p. 131.
25. Ibid. p. 34.
26. Ibid. p. 40.
27. Ibid. pp. 34–44.
28. Ibid. p. 82.
29. Ibid. pp. 90–1.
30. Ibid. p. 84.
31. Ibid. pp. 113–14.
32. Ibid. pp. 112–13.
33. Ibid. p. 157.
34. Brophy, *The Finishing Touch* (London: Secker and Warburg, 1963), p. 38.
35. Ibid. p. 45.
36. Ibid. p. 40.
37. Brophy, *The Snow Ball* (London: Secker and Warburg, 1964), p. 21.
38. Ibid. pp. 26–7.
39. Ibid. p. 28.
40. Ibid. p. 111.
41. Ibid.
42. Ibid. p. 116.
43. Wyndham Lewis, *Tarr: The 1918 Version* (Santa Rosa: Black Sparrow Press, 1990), p. 299.
44. Brophy, *The Snow Ball*, p. 120.
45. Ibid. p. 115.
46. Ibid. p. 193.
47. Jessica Burstein, *Cold Modernism: Literature, Fashion, Art* (University Park: Penn State University Press, 2012), p. 2.
48. For convenience I will use 'they' throughout.
49. Brophy, *In Transit*, p. 29.
50. Ibid. p. 145.
51. Ibid. p. 35.
52. Ibid. p. 54.
53. Ibid. p. 55.
54. Ibid. p. 66.
55. Frank Kermode, 'Sterne Measures', *The Listener*, 25 September 1969, p. 413.
56. See Sianne Ngai, *Our Aesthetic Categories: Zany, Cute, Interesting* (Cambridge, MA: Harvard University Press, 2012), pp. 174–232.
57. Brophy, *In Transit*, p. 11.
58. Ibid. p. 54.
59. Ibid. p. 47.
60. Ibid. p. 37.
61. Ibid. p. 116.
62. Ibid. p. 209.

63. Ibid. p. 86.
64. Walter Pater, *The Renaissance*, available at <http://www.gutenberg.org/files/2398/2398-h/2398-h.htm> (accessed 6 November 2017), n.p.
65. Brophy, *In Transit*, p. 44.
66. Ibid. p. 43.
67. Ibid. p. 54.
68. Ibid. p. 55.
69. Susan Sontag, 'Notes on Camp', *Against Interpretation and Other Essays* (New York: Farrar, Straus and Giroux, 1966), p. 280.
70. Brophy, *In Transit*, p. 147.
71. Ibid. p. 143.
72. Brooke Horvath, 'Brigid Brophy's It's-All-Right-I'm-Only-Dying Comedy of Modern Manners: Notes on *In Transit*', *Review of Contemporary Fiction*, 15:3 (1995), pp. 46–53, p. 53.
73. Brophy, *In Transit*, p. 227.
74. Ibid. p. 236.

Chapter 5

Alexander Trocchi: Man at Leisure
Christopher Webb

> I must have talked incessantly about myself, about how I didn't really want to do anything, about how, even if I still wrote, and used to think of myself as a writer, I didn't any longer, how I thought of myself as a man with nothing to do in the world ever, except to remain conscious, and that was what the writing was for, for my own use and the use of my friends. I told her that the great urgency for literature was that it should for once and for all accomplish its dying, that it wasn't that writing shouldn't be written, but that a man should annihilate prescriptions of all past form in his own soul, refuse to consider what he wrote in terms of literature, judge it solely in terms of his living.[1]
> Alexander Trocchi, *Cain's Book*

If these look like the words of a writer who wished to give up novel writing, then perhaps that is because they are. After *Cain's Book* (1960) – which was an immense struggle to complete – Trocchi never attempted to write another novel (at least not in the conventional understanding of the term). Much has been made of Trocchi's 'failure' to do so. Many of his friends and contemporaries put it down to his heroin addiction, which began just before he started writing *Cain's Book* in Paris during the mid-1950s and lasted until his death in 1984. But, as this survey of his work questions, what if this failure was, in fact, a refusal? What if Trocchi's addiction was itself only a symptom of a much deeper conviction he had, one that had hardened long before he started using drugs? This conviction, I argue, was directly related to ideas to do with work and leisure, two subjects Trocchi never ceased thinking and writing about throughout his career, two subjects – or issues – that were continually discussed across the media and amongst artists and writers throughout the 1960s and 1970s.

Trocchi's outlook on work and leisure shaped his writing in a fundamental way, and in a way that differentiates it from other avant-garde writing of the period. This is significant because if we understand that this preoccupation with work and leisure is something that informs Trocchi's entire œuvre, then we might begin to see his choice to abandon fiction as part of a purposeful artistic trajectory. It will be argued here that we can trace a correlation between Trocchi's increasingly critical stance against work and the formal aspects of his writing. The more critical Trocchi became of the traditional ideas surrounding work, the more fragmented and broken his texts became, ending with *The Long Book* (1963 to c. 1973), a group of texts and ephemera that has been considered – when considered at all – an embarrassment.[2] In this sense, then, novel writing was only the starting point within a much larger personal project. Understanding him from this perspective is vital because it goes against the grain of the dominant narrative that has Trocchi's 'ability to write' simply 'paralysed' by drug abuse; this, it will be suggested, is part of a broader (and problematic) impulse to mythologise the Scottish artist as a failed 'junky writer', whose life and works, when judged solely in terms of literature, become little more than a parable on the hazardous effects of drugs on creativity and natural literary talent.[3]

*

In 1991, Trocchi's UK publisher, John Calder, summarised Trocchi's 'legacy', and in doing so reinforced the dominant narrative that surrounds his life and career:

> What I think of when Alex Trocchi crosses my mind is the immense waste that his life represents. He started with every advantage that the welfare state and his natural talent could give him, went to the country [France] that has traditionally been most promising for such talent, made an instant impact on the arts scene in Paris, and then frittered it all away. He leaves a small legacy: a promising first novel *Young Adam*; an erratic but brilliant second one, *Cain's Book*; a few poems and stories; aside from this there are the erotic novels he wrote for [Maurice] Girodias, patchy, wonderful in parts, yet often no more than exercises in commercial pornography that nevertheless rise well above their peers.[4]

Perhaps it is unsurprising that Calder is unable to comprehend his 'legacy' in any other way: that is, in terms of what he had published. Based on these standards, Trocchi does come off as a failure. Yet, it does not seem fair to judge him using Calder's criteria because, by the late 1950s, Trocchi no longer saw himself as exclusively a writer, since such classifications, he would tell Alex Neish in a 1962 *Guardian* interview, are 'meaningless' and 'literature [...] is not what I'm interested in. It's merely one of the several disciplines I have specialised in.'[5] He went on to say:

> [t]o become a writer is to become a falsity. You get caught up in the straitjacket of meaningless classifications. I don't think of myself as a writer or a novelist or anything else so much as an intelligent man. I believe you've got to be artistic about everything, whether it's painting, love, homosexuality, or just living, and it's not success which is important so much as trying spontaneously to do something. Spontaneously – that's the crucial word there, meaning that at any particular moment in time it seems right for you to do something.[6]

In other words, Trocchi refused to define himself in terms of his occupation. It is our tacit acceptance of *being* what we do, he suggests, which ultimately limits us. It is the little, day-to-day questions – 'what do you do?' – and the impulse to judge others based on arbitrary definitions of success – what one does, what one achieves – that cause us to think more narrowly about ourselves and others.[7]

It is precisely this way of thinking which the eponymous narrator of Trocchi's first (and commercially popular) pornographic novella *Helen and Desire* (1953) rails against. The novella – one of Trocchi's first pieces of published fiction – contains within it some of the most scathing critiques of the western work ethic in all of his œuvre. Towards the end of the text, there is a withering assessment of 'stupid westerners [...] geared towards industry'.[8] Helen describes a dystopic western landscape, where '[m]ountains of industry [and] seas of commerce come into being', and where '[e]verything' is nightmarishly 'computed in terms of time', which 'must not be "wasted"'.[9] She complains that 'in the west everybody is busy because his neighbour is', that everybody is obsessed only by end results, causing them to lose sight of the present moment:

> Art, the aesthetic of the flesh, the cultivation of leisure, are despised, tolerated, perhaps but basically thought of as not quite respectable. [...] Geared for industry, those stupid westerners never pause to analyse the word 'waste'. Time is accepted without question as valuable; like money or land or food, it must not be 'wasted'; at the end of one hour one must have something to show for it. The question for them is: What 'excuse' for passing the hour in such and such a way? If one can produce riches at the end of the hour, then time has not been 'wasted'. But if one has merely derived pleasure from living? If one considers living important – in itself?[10]

Despite it being a pornographic novella with a basic, straightforward plot, Trocchi still manages to incorporate many of the major themes that are discussed in his later novels. This specific theme – the impossibility of wasting time within western society – is a prominent one that runs throughout Trocchi's fiction and one that, by the time he writes *Cain's Book*, is distilled into a single sentence: 'man should be able to waste time without being seized with anxiety'.[11] In fact, Trocchi would later write, it was the inability to do this that caused him to leave Glasgow for Paris in the first place.

Born in 1925, Trocchi grew up in Glasgow but left his native city for Paris in 1952, after graduating. In Paris, he founded and edited the avant-garde magazine *Merlin*, which was responsible for publishing the works of several major postwar writers, including Samuel Beckett, Eugène Ionesco and Jean Genet, introducing their work to English audiences for the first time.[12] Trocchi himself was writing at this point, producing several erotic novellas (known as 'd.b.s' or 'dirty books') for Maurice Girodias, who would pay him a lump sum up front on the condition the books would be completed quickly, often within a matter of weeks.[13] And it was in Paris that the Scottish writer met and became friends with Guy Debord, leader of the Situationist International, which Trocchi joined before departing for New York. Debord's theories would exert a major influence on Trocchi's writing and, later on, inspire him to start a similar movement in London, called project sigma, the principal aim of which was to 'prepare' people for an oncoming leisure society. He also met Jean-Paul Sartre in Paris, who allowed him to reproduce some of his essays for *Merlin*. This period was a formative one for Trocchi and many of the ideas in circulation on the Left Bank would go on to define his career in both New York and London. It was also in Paris that Trocchi's first 'serious' novel, *Young Adam* (1954), was published, which bears traces of his interest in many of the philosophical debates of 1950s Paris.

Young Adam is an existentialist novel about the moral dilemma of not owning up to your own actions. The protagonist, Joe Taylor, is disgusted by the society he finds himself in, which he complains is mostly made up of 'representative[s] of the industrious working classes',[14] the 'good people', as he ironically describes them, of 'the Presbyterian city of Glasgow',[15] who he regards as his 'enem[ies]'.[16] The problem with these people, he tells us in no uncertain terms, is their tendency to make a virtue of work – 'I dislike people who make a virtue of their work'[17] – an attitude that goes hand in hand with the impulse to conform, to accept a society or 'impersonal machine', as he puts it, whose function is 'to maintain order, to explain the presence of an ambiguous thing like a corpse, to see that, if foul play was deduced, someone atoned for it so that the moral structure of this system might be preserved – that was horrifying'.[18] It turns out Joe is involved in the death of his former girlfriend but when another (innocent) man is sentenced for her murder, he cannot decide whether he should go forward with the information he withholds. He knows that if he does, the 'impersonal machine' will eliminate him, too.

Not long after *Young Adam* was published, Trocchi began writing *Cain's Book*. He left Paris for New York in 1955 to get a job on the Hudson River as a scowman: essentially a live-in caretaker of a barge that carried materials up and down the water, tugged along by a tow-boat. By this stage Trocchi had started using heroin on a frequent basis and *Cain's Book* is a largely autobiographical document about his experiences on the scow. It is important, however, to remember that it is not entirely autobiographical, as Trocchi himself noted in a BBC Radio Scotland interview: '[*Cain's Book*] is not absolutely coincident with myself. But nevertheless, there is a great deal of me in it.'[19] At the beginning, we might wonder why *Cain's Book* is so incongruous and uneven in its narrative disclosure. But we are soon told the reason for its peculiar form: the text is a compilation of notes consisting of old memories and past thoughts. Written by the narrator Joe Necchi, these notes repeatedly take us out of the frame narrative, which is set in the present time of writing, on board a scow on the Hudson River, as Necchi attempts to finish writing a book about his experiences in New York as a junky, which is provisionally entitled 'Cain's Book'. From its very beginning, *Cain's Book* demonstrates its intention to meander, to segue fluidly from episode to episode without any pretension to more logical and perhaps more familiar modes of narrative progression. And if we forget that this is how *Cain's Book* works, or begin to wait with the vain hope that eventually there will be some kind of narrative 'pay-off', then Joe seems ready to remind us at various points that this will not be the case, that '[t]here is no story to tell',[20] and that he is 'unfortunately not concerned with the events which led up to this or that'.[21]

As a writer, Necchi finds himself in a strange and unsettling position, one that is explored in the following note: 'To lose my identity as a writer is to lose all social identity. I can choose no other any more than I can seriously sustain that.'[22] Necchi has come to doubt his occupation and is caught between two impulses: he can try to continue being the writer everyone knows him to be, an identity he does not believe in any longer, or he can give up his role as writer but 'lose all social identity'. He wants to write in the way he used to but has little faith in novel-writing, so ends up writing to keep up appearances, so to speak: 'I wrote for example: "If I write: it is important to keep writing, it is to keep me writing. It is as though I find myself on a new planet, without a map, and having everything to learn. I have unlearnt. I have become a stranger."'[23] Necchi is trapped in a cycle, reflected in the entirely circular logic of this line. He is stuck – or, rather, suspended – as a writer. This sense of being caught or stuck is also central to the formal organisation of the narrative: *Cain's Book* refuses to 'go' anywhere. It drifts and meanders, and never quite gets to the point, which again is something that Necchi himself points out when he says:

> Reading what I have written, now, then, I have a familiar feeling that everything I say is somehow beside the point. I am of course incapable of sustaining a simple narrative . . . with no fixed valid categories . . . not so much a line of thought as an area of experience . . . [. . .]. Moreover, what's not beside the point is false.[24]

The narrative is, to use a word that is repeated throughout the novel, in 'abeyance'.[25] This word, abeyance – 'a state of temporary disuse or suspension' – perfectly encapsulates the twin impulses of both Necchi's experience and narrative direction. Abeyance, from Old French *abeyance*, meaning 'aspiration, desire', takes its root from *abeer*, meaning 'to aspire' but derived from the Latin *batare* – 'to yawn, gape'.[26] We might sense a contradictory movement here, in the etymology of the word, which at once 'yawns' and stands still with its many images of boredom and inertia whilst also wanting, desiring to move forward, to 'aspire' towards something.

At times, *Cain's Book* reads like an anti-work treatise, a document about not only the virtues of drugs and their effects (which prevents most of the characters from working), but also the virtues and importance of play, a concept that becomes increasingly associated with the idea of leisure in Trocchi's later (and mostly unpublished) work. Waiting around, writing and 'fixing' (injecting heroin) assume a form of protest, a way of distancing oneself from the society that proselytises the 'sanctity of hard work'[27] and relentlessly impinges on the individual's freedom. *Cain's Book* contains within it many of the seeds of Trocchi's later non-literary activity (that is, project sigma) and argues for a society where one can 'be alone and play',[28] to enjoy leisure without having to work in the conventional sense. The text is obviously preoccupied with drugs. Yet, if we look more closely, the use of drugs, which is almost always taken as the principal concern of *Cain's Book*, is, in fact, the corollary of the narrator's intransigent will not to work. 'Fixing' is an important pastime (and a way of halting time) and this is what makes the novel so controversial. Taking drugs is often seen as an unproductive activity but to use them consciously as a form of protest, as a way of gratuitously wasting or killing time – this is a more serious matter altogether. As Trocchi himself said in 1962, 'for some people, using narcotics comes to be a form of protest against their society, and there were times in New York when I just wouldn't trust any creative person who wasn't on them'.[29] To retreat from society, from 'the city with its complicated relations, its plexus of outrageous purpose',[30] is to become a deadweight on a society that has no desire to support those who do not subscribe to its values. This is especially pronounced in a welfare state. Just one year before the UK publication of *Cain's Book*, Trocchi provocatively gestured to this idea of the state supporting his leisurely lifestyle:

> Narcotics bring about a state of mind so that automatically you find creative ways of using leisure. [. . .] I know that junk made it possible for me to approach a life in which I will never take a job, where I shall always do what I want to do, where I will never have to be entertained from the outside. [. . .] With junk I wish there were 96 hours in every day, and so long as I had enough wits to be able to experience [it,] I would sign on for eternity right now.[31]

Cain's Book caused a great deal of controversy in the UK. The book was seized in a bookshop raid in Sheffield and Calder was charged on account of it being 'obscene'. The 1964 trial of Trocchi's text introduced a new precedent in UK law, as John Sutherland points out. Lord Chief Justice Parker's decision, Sutherland writes, 'was highly significant', as it 'marked a new phase of obscenity-hunting in which the primary target would not be the work's text (for instance its incidence of four-letter words) but the *lifestyle* it advocated, or that was associated with its author or even its readership'.[32] If we do not take into account Trocchi's growing interest in leisure and his absolute rejection of conventional societal views and morality surrounding work, then we lose sight of what made him such a radical – and threatening – figure.

*

Shortly after Trocchi had written *Cain's Book*, he was arrested and charged with selling heroin to a minor. He was released on bail and managed (illegally) to cross the US border to Canada. From there, he eventually made it to London. Many critics and friends of Trocchi agree that, after *Cain's Book*, his writing career was more or less over. He engaged himself in other non-literary activities, the most famous of which was the formation of project sigma. The idea for sigma started to crystallise in Trocchi's mind as he was writing *Cain's Book* but it was only formally announced when Trocchi published an essay entitled 'Invisible Insurrection of a Million Minds' in 1964.[33] The premise behind this essay–manifesto was that approximately one million likeminded 'creative' intellectuals and dissidents would instigate a 'cultural revolt'.[34] It was an instance of '[p]rotest phenomena' of the 1960s and 1970s, which, as Detlef Siegfried writes, did not aim to 'achieve [an] impact just by contributing to a generalized mood of upheaval, but by focusing on the creation of new lifestyles and cultural norms with profound political implications'.[35] Trocchi believed that, with the right people (and the right amount of funding), sigma would provide the impetus to shatter the ossified and anachronistic social values that surrounded the contemporary notions of work and leisure. One of the main premises upon which sigma was founded was that automation of the central industries would all but do away with the problem of production, the idea being that human labour would no longer be needed and that the time normally spent dedicated to working would open up and become free time. In just one of many similar statements Trocchi made at this time, he warned about the threat this posed:

> I think leisure is going to be possibly our greatest problem. Right now we are sedulously training people not to be able to use it – give it to people now and they would either go insane or go back to work.[36]

His ideas did not belong in a vacuum, of course. Numerous writers, theorists and sociologists at this point were writing about what they saw as the almost inevitable outcome of a society in which the social need for work would be diminished.[37] Leisure became an extremely popular topic for debate at this time. Without considering this context, Trocchi's ideas come off as politically naïve.[38] This ambitious and wide-ranging project, which for a brief period drew much public support from intellectuals and artists across the UK and the USA, has mostly been viewed as Trocchi's 'excuse' for not writing another novel after *Cain's Book*. Calder made this claim in the *Edinburgh Review* one year after Trocchi's death:

> What sigma was really about was unclear to all except a few devotees, but it gave Trocchi an excuse to avoid getting on with a sequel to *Cain's Book*. After 1962 his literary work consisted only of articles and translations

together with a small collection of poems. He was an excellent translator and his ability to catch in English a French writer's style gave a good indication of the talent he had wasted. Although he drifted into relative obscurity in Britain and the United States, he has remained a literary hero to the dissident young men in many parts of Europe while Cain's Book remains the prime example of British Beat writing.[39]

Calder published most of Trocchi's work in the UK and played a substantial role in Trocchi's career as a writer. While Calder is right (again) to assert that Trocchi's output after *Cain's Book* consisted only of some articles, translations and a collection of poetry, this just takes into account his *published* output. Even during the composition of *Cain's Book*, Trocchi became far more interested in merging literature and art with everyday existence. This was one of sigma's main aims: to encourage a 'living art', to break what he saw as the artificial categorisations and boundaries between art and everyday life, boundaries that were in his mind perpetuated by publishing houses, museums, galleries and other institutions. The 'Wholly Communion' poetry event held at the Royal Albert Hall in 1965, which Trocchi orchestrated, was a classic example of a 1960s 'happening' where art and life were temporarily bridged and where, for Trocchi up on stage, it must have seemed as if the 'million minds' had assembled.

To bypass the traditional institutions that published or curated literature and art, Trocchi set up the sigma portfolio, which would collect all the contributions of those involved and then disseminate these works to every subscriber to the project. The sigma portfolio was set up and a number of articles, fiction and essays were distributed but, in the end, the portfolio, like the project itself, lost its initial impetus and by the early 1970s was effectively over.[40] This might suggest that Calder's claims were justified. But if we consider Trocchi's unpublished writings during this period, we begin to see that he was very resistant to the idea of writing another novel – regardless of whether he *could* write another or not. As he mentions in one of the notes in *The Long Book*:

> I didn't say anything about novels. I tried to make that clear in my last book. At least I thought I made it clear to myself. And if this book is written to kill, it is to kill me. Scourge, plague and fire is my business. I am a fireman, and like Pepys or Sir Thomas Browne, I keep a log.[41]

'[I]f this book is written to kill me' echoes Joe Necchi's declaration in *Cain's Book* (that is, 'my last book') that all literature should accomplish its own death. And by framing himself as both 'fireman' and 'Pepys', Trocchi implies that *The Long Book* is for him and him alone. As creator and extinguisher of the fire, he retains full control over the text and he can choose what to burn and destroy (no editor required). *The Long Book* was conceived along with project sigma, as a 'log' about Trocchi's present circumstances (similar in the sense to Joe Necchi's notes in *Cain's Book* about logging and inventorying the here-and-now) and as a work that would eventually be included in the sigma portfolio, as and when it was written. Much of the material related to *The Long Book* concerned project sigma's ideas, such as '[s]ubversion' on a global scale, which would change public attitudes towards work and leisure:

> Subversion. Of course, that is precisely what we are about ... what we must inspire (and, on a global scale,) is a structural change in men's attitude towards, for example, 'work'. That old adage about the right to work, the correlative crap about the nobility of work, etc., all this is anachronism ... the complex moral buffering of the economy of scarcity: 'to eat you must work ... '. Such old prejudices get in the way of an intelligent exploitation of automation. The problem of today and tomorrow is that men should learn to cope creatively with leisure; we must think now of the nobility of non-employment.[42]

The Long Book was a site for Trocchi to exercise his ideas freely without having even to think about what others, who he saw as external to the writing process, might demand from him. It was a way for Trocchi to write without the composition process feeling like work, and it was a means to refine his views on various topics (mainly ideas related to work and leisure), a place to jot down new ideas he came into contact with concerning the future of work. As shown in the passage above, Trocchi wrote at length about an oncoming leisure society, in which automation would eradicate human labour.

While many of the sentiments Trocchi expresses in *The Long Book* also feature in *Cain's Book*, they are written in a far more explicit and spontaneous way, as if he is celebrating the fact that he is not writing for anyone other than himself. This is demonstrated most clearly when he writes about how he could use *The Long Book* to 'coax' money from his publishers. The only condition was that he told them it is a novel, which it clearly is not:

> What this book is about is the making of itself [. . .]. And it would probably never have occurred to me to call it 'a novel' were it not for the fact that by doing so, and only by doing so, was i [sic] able to coax an advance royalty from my publishers, English & American, monies i had to have if the work was to be done at all.[43]

As Trocchi writes, *The Long Book* is about the 'making of itself'. In other words, it is an *act* of pure gratuitousness but one that, once in the process of being made, serves a financial purpose.[44] It is Trocchi's critique of those 'contemporary industrial writers' who write stories to make money. But *The Long Book* is only masquerading as a novel. In reality, it is a text made up of fragments, most of which are quite clearly written without any commercial consideration. It was a space for Trocchi to write about Necchi (who had long outlived his purpose) when he wanted, to write about the banning of *Cain's Book*, to write poetry and essays, and even to include and rework old material – old drafts of *Cain's Book*, for example – and all the commercially unviable material that contained personal significance for him. Perhaps most usefully, it was a means to write about his publisher in less than friendly terms, whilst using it as a kind of bait with which to 'coax' money, as he writes and as Calder has frequently noted, from those asking for another commercial novel.

*

There is something very beautiful about *The Long Book* as a material object. It consists of material housed in folders (loose sheets, typescripts) and books (which are literally long, about half the width of A4 but of longer length); it has no defined form. *The Long Book* highlights its own fragmentary nature and the pieces appear almost deliberately partial. Sometimes there are duplicates or passages that are similar but not precisely the same. Many pages contain multiple errors: some revised, others not. Most of the material, apparently irrelevant and useless, is kept. There are drawings in the books and the books themselves are painted. These physical attributes point to and raise questions about many of the themes discussed in Trocchi's earlier fiction (waste, obsolescence, utility, incompletion and so on). As a physical object, *The Long Book* can claim thematic synthesis with the other (literary) works Trocchi produced (albeit in a different form). Critics have paid scant attention to *The Long Book* because it resembles an incomplete manuscript of the sequel to *Cain's Book* (parts of the text are titled '*Cain's Book pt. II*'). Yet, *The Long Book* resembles an object, a piece of visual art in keeping with Trocchi's sculptures of the time, which he termed 'futiques'.[45] It is the logical extension of *Cain's Book*'s fragmentation and its refusal to call itself a novel.

The traditional notion of 'work', treated as both a noun (the activity of work) and a verb (to describe whether something works or not), is deeply and deliberately problematised by many of the experimental writers of the time (such as B. S. Johnson and Eva Figes). Indeed, it is part of their very enterprise – as 'experimental' writers – to question these notions surrounding work and what works, and equally, to test what works as writing. For many of them, this translated into exposing the limits of storytelling, attempting to subvert or undo narrative, and to try to write or represent experience truthfully. This was certainly the case with *The Long Book*, as Trocchi began eventually to conceive it as something much grander: a large 'multi-dimensional canvas of his life'.[46] Scrawled in Trocchi's hand on one of the folders of part of *The Long Book* manuscript collection is a tentative plan:

Volume 1 up to 1950
Volume 2 1950 to Cain's Book
Volume 3 Cain's Book
Volume 4 New York (to supplement and continue Cain's Book)
Volume 5 London[47]

This volume plan is significant because it shows Trocchi curating his life and works, arranging his life as one might edit or order a work of art. Trocchi's life, this plan implies, is an unfinished text, a living art, which was exactly what he advocated in his essays related to project sigma. As Edwin Morgan has put it, Trocchi 'himself wanted all his writing to be seen as a continuum of communication, of self-definition, of modes of consciousness, rather than as a sculpture part of "novels" or "short stories" or "poems" or "essays"'.[48]

The Long Book is an anti-work document, a work that refuses to finish, which refuses to conform to any kind of categorical definition. As already mentioned, the Necchi–Trocchi figure claims that *The Long Book* is all about 'kill[ing]': 'this book is written to kill, it is to kill me'. And in a way it does just that: it kills Necchi as a delineated character or narrator. It marks the end of Trocchi's status as a novelist who uses the typical props and apparatuses. Trocchi's 'Joes', like Beckett's 'brandips' (Murphy, Molloy, Malone and Mahood), have been exhausted, have worked for long enough, and now, in *The Long Book*, have been dispensed with. But, from the perspective of the Joe Necchi in *Cain's Book*, this is a positive thing; he suggests that all literature should 'accomplish its dying'.[49] While many critics have chosen to ignore the significance of *The Long Book*, this chapter understands it as an extension of Trocchi's artistic development after *Cain's Book*, after he had supposedly frittered away his talent. *The Long Book* is a rude gesture towards those traditional and conventional values that Trocchi had opposed throughout the whole of his writing career, towards that value system that he criticised from the start of his career, and the novel form itself, which stood as a symbol for him of what Joe in *Young Adam* calls 'literature, false'.[50] And in this respect, *The Long Book* could also be interpreted as something else: as a reaction against the marketplace and his various publishers (or *'the brokers'*, as he refers to them in 'Invisible Insurrection'[51]).

Trocchi himself vehemently opposed the western work ethic and believed that work ought to be a choice rather than an obligation. In an undated journal written sometime after the publication of *Cain's Book*, Trocchi writes of his own 'underprivileged' status of having been born into a society that refuses him the liberty and freedom he desired. In the short piece, he writes that he is constantly 'run[ning]' as he attempts to 'board a train' that promises to take him where he wants to go (his 'personal play garden'):

> Sometimes i [sic] scare myself. It is as though i am frantically trying to board a train which always goes just one mile an hour faster than i can run, stiffer in the knees now i am thirty-eight and not twenty-eight. i cannot live in the present because i am always anxious about the future because i tell myself i am. i am always going to do something – tomorrow. There are certain technical difficulties, of course. i want to be able to use this world as my personal play garden. All the time. Meanwhile, i am still nailed to the economic rack. That is the big game into which i was born underprivileged.[52]

The passage evokes a restlessness, an attempt to get the 'ungettable', which characterises Trocchi's entire œuvre. From the early pornographic novellas to *The Long Book*, Trocchi's writing contains characters and narrators who desire what they cannot have. Trocchi gestures to this in the passage above: the long, running sentences and the exaggerated use of the infantilised 'i's contribute to the sense of frantic restlessness, of being in the wrong place at the wrong time ('i cannot live in the present') and knowing that one can never catch up. The combination of the simple language, the uneven pace and the self-absorption suggests childishness but, more specifically, a self-conscious childishness, which recalls Joe Necchi's anxiety in *Cain's Book*, in which Joe desires to write, be alone and play, but knows that he will be accused of being childish for wanting this. In line with most of Trocchi's work, this passage is primarily about being caught in between desperately wanting something and being unable to have it, which is made only more painful by the proximity of the desired object (in this case, the train that runs only one mile an hour faster).

In *The Long Book*, there are two lines that capture this tantalising situation most effectively. 'Over the years', Trocchi writes:

> i have had sight of great continents of experience just beyond human-reach. I was up, down, here, there, back, through, round, high, & clear into what a generation now thinks of as inner space, and, when i could, i took notes all the way.[53]

Trocchi describes himself as constantly on the go and, much like the narrators of *Young Adam* and *Cain's Book*, he is never content to remain still. While this anthropological impulse might allow one to go everywhere ('up, down, here, there [. . .] high & clear'), it also presents an unsettling proposition: one is unable to *be* anywhere. Each deictic reference (often used to indicate presence) only gestures to where Trocchi 'was' or has been – but no longer is. This incapacity to be present ('i cannot live in the present because i am always anxious about the future because i tell myself i am') is a hallmark of what constitutes leisure within an advanced capitalist society, as Trocchi saw it. In such a society, leisure is always about distracting oneself from work (before busily returning to it). Leisure is rarely about being at leisure. His work is a continual and dogged exploration of this grey zone of everyday life. While he is often perceived as a decadent product of 1960s hedonism, his work interrogates some of the most fundamental and profound issues of his time, issues that continue to have relevance today: how to be and how to employ or unemploy oneself within a relentlessly restless society geared towards industry and productivity.

Notes

1. Alexander Trocchi, *Cain's Book* (London: Oneworld Classics, 2011), pp. 106–7.
2. See, for instance, Andrew Murray Scott, *Alexander Trocchi: The Making of a Monster* (Kilkerran: Kennedy & Boyd, 2012), p. 175.
3. Allan Campbell, 'Shooting Star', *Scotland on Sunday*, 28 January 1996. Campbell co-edited with Tim Niel *A Life in Pieces: Reflection on Alexander Trocchi* (Edinburgh: Canongate, 1997), in which you can find many interviews with Trocchi's contemporaries who express the same sentiment: Trocchi's writing career was ended earlier than it should have been due to his addiction.
4. John Calder, 'An Iconoclast Programmed to Self-Destruct', *The Scotsman*, 8 June 1991. Found in the Edwin Morgan archive at University of Glasgow. No page number was identified; the material was a paper clipping.

5. Trocchi, 'Bold Testament', interview with Alex Neish, *The Guardian*, 24 January 1962, p. 9.
6. Ibid.
7. The question, 'what do you do?', certainly troubled other avant-garde writers like B. S. Johnson, who wrote in his poem, 'Hafod a Hendref': 'In London if you should (unwary) / call yourself a writer they mostly / say: *Yes, but what do you really do?*' This theme was also given poetic expression by Basil Bunting in his poem, 'What the Chairman Told Tom'. Many writers of the time, especially those funded by the Arts Council, were criticised by the media for essentially not doing anything.
8. Trocchi, *Helen and Desire* (Edinburgh: Canongate, 2012), p. 117.
9. Ibid.
10. Ibid.
11. Trocchi, *Cain's Book* (London: Oneworld Classics, 2011), p. 155.
12. The editors of Beckett's letters, for instance, recognise that Trocchi 'was essentially responsible for introducing [Beckett's] post-War novels to the English-language literary world'. See George Craig, Martha Dow Fehsenfeld, Dan Gunn and Lois More Overbeck, *The Letters of Samuel Beckett, Volume II: 1941–1956* (Cambridge: Cambridge University Press, 2011), p. 721.
13. Along with *Helen and Desire*, Trocchi also published *The Carnal Days of Helen Seferis* (1954), *Frank Harris: My Life and Loves, Volume 5* (1954), *School for Sin* (1955), *White Thighs* (1955), *Thongs* (1956) and *Sappho of Lesbos* (1960). All of these, with the exception of the last one, were published by Olympia Press.
14. Trocchi, *Young Adam* (London: Oneworld Classics, 2008), p. 98.
15. Ibid. p. 101.
16. Ibid. p. 98.
17. Ibid.
18. Ibid. p. 99.
19. Trocchi, as quoted in Campbell and Niel, *A Life in Pieces*, p. 148.
20. Trocchi, *Cain's Book*, p. 121.
21. Ibid. p. 123.
22. Ibid. p. 180.
23. Ibid. p. 94.
24. Ibid. p. 192.
25. Ibid.: for example, pp. 5, 6, 93, 94.
26. 'abeyance, n.', *OED Online*, available at <www.oed.com/view/Entry/268> (accessed 3 March 2018).
27. Trocchi, *Cain's Book*, p. 205.
28. Ibid. p. 56.
29. 'Bold Testament', p. 9.
30. Trocchi, *Cain's Book*, p. 5.
31. Ibid. p. 9.
32. John Sutherland, *Offensive Literature: Decensorship in Britain, 1960–1982* (Totowa, NJ: Barnes & Noble Books, 1983), p. 46.

33. Trocchi insisted on the non-capitalisation of project sigma.
34. Trocchi, 'Invisible Insurrection of a Million Minds', in Campbell and Niel, *A Life in Pieces*, pp. 164–76, p. 164.
35. Detlef Siegfried, 'Foreword', in *Between the Avant-Garde and the Everyday: Subversive Politics in Europe from 1957 to the Present*, ed. Timothy Brown and Lorena Anton (Oxford: Berghahn, 2011), p. ix.
36. 'Bold Testament', p. 9.
37. Of course, leisure had been analysed by theorists like Thorstein Veblen in his *The Theory of the Leisure Class* (New York: Macmillan, 1899) but it was only during the 1950s and 1960s that it became a widely discussed subject. See David Riesman, *The Lonely Crowd* (New Haven, CT: Yale University Press, 1950) and 'Leisure and Work in Post-Industrial Society' (1958), in *Abundance for What? And Other Essays* (New York: Doubleday, 1964); John Kenneth Galbraith's *The Affluent Society* (Boston: Houghton Mifflin, 1958); and Clement Greenberg, 'The Plight of Culture' (1953), in *Art and Culture: Critical Essays* (Boston: Beacon Press, 1989). Debord and other Situationist International members were highly critical of leisure within a capitalist society throughout the 1960s, and later, Jean Baudrillard would go on to write about leisure in *The Consumer Society* (1970).
38. For more recent discussions on leisure and automation, see Nick Srnicek and Alex Williams, *Inventing the Future: Postcapitalism and a World Without Work* (London: Verso, 2015).
39. John Calder, 'Alexander Trocchi', *Edinburgh Review*, 70 (1985), pp. 32–5, pp. 34–5. The link between Trocchi and the Beats is an obvious one. After all, he collaborated frequently with William Burroughs, kept in regular contact with Allen Ginsberg, and compèred the International Poetry Incarnation at the Royal Albert Hall on 11 June 1965 (a Beat poetry event that gained a great deal of media attention).
40. Contributors included William Burroughs, Stan Brakhage, Michael McClure, R. D. Laing and Trocchi himself. It is worth adding at this point that project sigma still continued to make an impact elsewhere, outside the UK. In Amsterdam, for example, Trocchi's ideas were built upon and taken more seriously than they were in the UK. For a detailed analysis of this, see Niek Pas's essay, 'In Pursuit of the Invisible Revolution: Sigma in the Netherlands, 1966–68', in Brown and Anton, *Between the Avant-Garde and the Everyday*, pp. 31–43.
41. Trocchi archive, Washington University in St Louis, Box 33, Folder 4.
42. Ibid.
43. Ibid.
44. Even the title of *The Long Book* gestures towards its own gratuitousness. As Andrew Murray Scott, Trocchi's biographer, mentions, 'The title was itself the result of a misunderstanding between author and publisher; asked what he was working on, Trocchi replied "a long book", and didn't bother to correct the assumption that this was the title.' See Scott, *Alexander Trocchi: The Making of a Monster*, p. 175.

45. These were bits of driftwood that Trocchi collected, which he would paint over in an assortment of colours. The name is a portmanteau of 'future' and 'antique', the reason being that Trocchi believed that they would gain value in the future in spite of their immediate worthlessness.
46. Trocchi archive, Box 33, Folder 4.
47. Ibid.
48. Edwin Morgan, 'Alexander Trocchi: A Survey', *Edinburgh Review*, 70 (1985), pp. 48–58, p. 49.
49. Trocchi, *Cain's Book*, pp. 106–7.
50. Trocchi, *Young Adam*, p. 129.
51. Trocchi, 'Invisible Insurrection', in *A Life in Pieces*, p. 172.
52. Trocchi archive, Box 33, Folder 4.
53. Ibid.

Chapter 6

Anna Kavan: Pursuing the 'in-between reality' Hidden by the 'ordinary surface of things'

Hannah Van Hove

'Haven't we had enough of realistic descriptions by now?', Anna Kavan wrote, frustrated, in a letter to her friend Raymond Marriott in 1964.[1] Her conviction that '[i]t certainly seems time for a movement away from realism' was one she had already been declaring twenty years earlier whilst writing for Cyril Connolly's *Horizon*.[2] In a review entitled 'Back to Victoria' (1946), Kavan had bemoaned the lack of experimental fiction published after wartime paper restrictions had been lifted. Wondering why the novels and novelists of the past, especially of the Victorian age, were in such high demand, Kavan concluded:

> Chaos and uncertainty outside must be compensated by a solid stability within. Hence the extraordinary favour shown to the Victorians who, while somewhat lacking in gracious qualities, certainly possessed another characteristic typical of a safe and leisurely existence – an unshakeable assurance, victorious over everything but the grave.[3]

After the 'enormous chaotic shambles' of the end of the Second World War, the threat of nuclear warfare meant the human race was now 'facing its most fearful predicament'.[4] For Kavan, then, the proliferation of nineteenth-century forms in the mid-1940s literary landscape was due to 'a childish reaction of flight' in the face of such a catastrophic world situation.[5] In her eyes, however, literature should confront this situation rather than turn away from it, and she would therefore have expected postwar publishing preferences 'to go to new names and experimental forms', more 'appropriate to the inchoate fluidity of a time when culture as previously known is almost certainly ending'.[6]

Her letter to Marriott illustrates that, in Kavan's view, the British literary landscape had generally not moved on from the 1940s. She continues to be exasperated by the dominance of 'realistic descriptions' in contemporary writing, which, in her eyes, have 'been done so well as they can be done over and over again, and as long ago as Zola'.[7] As she elaborates:

> I find it hard to make out a convincing case for the continuance of factual writing, when the microphone catches reality and transmits it to millions, who thus acquire their facts far more easily and quickly than by reading the shortest book or seeing a one act play.[8]

Instead, Kavan expresses an interest in exploring 'the in-between reality hidden by the ordinary "surface of things"', elaborating,

> You know I'm very interested in this reality thing – in the changes that continually shatter the seemingly objective world, which only our mental and physical health hold together in some sort of equilibrium, and which the least indisposition causes to slip and dissolve in confusion.[9]

Kavan's body of work written between 1940 and her death in 1968 can be understood as working to deconstruct what she termed the 'seemingly objective world'. Moving away from conventional forms and modes, which were predicated on the idea of attempting to represent an objective reality, her œuvre instead aims to go beyond the ordinary 'surface of things' in order to represent subjective experience in innovative ways. Whilst the six novels she wrote between 1929 and 1937 under the name Helen Ferguson had already illustrated an interest in exploring the inner thoughts and emotions of their characters, they operated in a largely conventional realist framework. When, in 1940, *Asylum Piece* appeared under her newly adopted name, 'Anna Kavan', it announced a move away from a more conventional mode of writing to one that she herself called 'experimental'.[10]

The fact that Kavan assumed the name of one of her fictional characters has been taken as licence to conflate fact and fiction by biographers, who perpetuate the myth of Kavan's name change as signalling the radical transformation from so-called 'home counties novelist' to 'avant-garde fiction writer',[11] aptly summarised by Kate Zambreno:

> [I]t's almost imperative to speak of Helen Ferguson and Anna Kavan as two different writers. Part of the fascination of the Helen Ferguson years is in the break that occurs along with her assumption of a new identity

and style. Like Sylvia Plath's Lady Lazarus, Kavan rose as if from the dead, specter thin because of hospitalization and narcosis. But instead of rising with the red hair of the poem, the former hearty bulldog breeder and brunette girl-nextdoor bleached hers movie-star blonde to mirror the fragile waif, the 'glass girl' that would become the nameless heroine in her later works.[12]

Critics such as Victoria Walker and Jennifer Sturm have successfully unpicked the fictional aspects of this 'Kavan myth' and argue that 'the metamorphosis of the woman born Helen Woods into the writer Anna Kavan was not as sudden and dramatic as it has been represented'.[13] Yet Zambreno's portrait of Kavan is illustrative of the ways in which critics have considered Kavan's work, often focusing on the writer herself, as Jane Garrity has pointed out, as 'a literary curiosity, driven by a raving solipsism'.[14] This approach to Kavan's fiction has no doubt been encouraged by the fact that it has consistently been introduced, posthumously, as the work of someone who was addicted to heroin throughout her life, who died with 'a syringe poised in her hand' and enough heroin in the house 'to kill a whole street'.[15]

With Kavan having become something of a cult figure since her death in 1968, critical attention devoted to her work has nevertheless been sparse, and until recently she had been largely forgotten in academic circles. What is particularly striking is that she has generally remained absent from studies which aimed to recuperate lost women writers of the twentieth century. As Garrity has rightly pointed out, 'despite the critical attention feminist theorists have paid both to redefining the boundaries of modernism and to recuperating "lost" twentieth-century women writers, there remains a conspicuous neglect of British experimentalists, among them, Anna Kavan'.[16] Walker has suggested that Kavan's 'reputation of hostility towards other women and a troubled relationship to feminist politics' are possibly to blame for this, with her work having been, to some extent, perceived 'as inimical to, or wary of, second-wave feminism', despite the fact that her 'representations of women's lived reality emphasize a critique of sexual inequality inherent in [her] fiction'.[17]

Much more recently however, there has been a renewed surge of interest in her work and this chapter aims to contribute to this scholarship by situating Kavan within a 1960s avant-garde tradition, whilst illustrating how a consideration of her work blurs boundaries between so-called 'late-modernist' works and sixties 'avant-garde' literature.[18] By focusing on the representation of psychic decentredness in her last novel, *Ice*, and reading it in conversation with R. D. Laing's thoughts on the schizophrenic experience, I argue both that *Ice* can be considered 'a classic 1960s' work in its exploration of fragmentary identity and alignment with anti-psychiatry theory, and that it equally highlights key concerns and influences throughout Kavan's work more generally. Concluding with a brief consideration of *Asylum Piece*, the first work of fiction to appear under the name 'Anna Kavan' in 1940, this chapter illustrates how Kavan's wartime experimentalism in fact prefigures and anticipates countercultural concerns of the sixties in its exploration of the osmotic relationship between interiority and external reality.

Ice: Reality Happening in a Different Way

Ice was published in 1967, the year before Anna Kavan died, and garnered her, belatedly, a modicum of success and acclaim. Whilst her short story collections published in the 1940s, *Asylum Piece* (1940) and *I am Lazarus* (1945) had been well received in both the UK and USA, Kavan had struggled in the postwar publishing climate since the critical and commercial failure of her experimental novel *Sleep Has His House* (1948). She had nevertheless continued to write and publish fiction during the 1950s and 1960s, but it was only when Brian Aldiss drew attention to *Ice*, calling it the 'best science fiction novel' of 1967, that Kavan's work once again enjoyed some brief recognition.[19]

Ice charts an unnamed narrator's attempts to find and dominate a helpless, elusive being called 'the girl', against the backdrop of a post-apocalyptic world which is in the process of being enveloped by snow and ice. Early on in the novel, the reader is told that the narrator used to be infatuated with this girl and had intended to marry her. Represented as being vulnerable and scared, she had apparently learned to trust him over time, before unexpectedly leaving him for another man. This male rival appears in various guises throughout the novel and is most frequently referred to as 'the warden'. Very little is known about these three principal characters (narrator, girl and warden) but they are at all points engaged in a peculiar *ménage à trois*; the narrator crosses war-torn countries and landscapes in his obsessive search for the girl, locked in a continuous relationship of rivalry and identification with the warden over their shared objective to possess and dominate the young woman. At one point the narrator reflects:

> It was clear that he [the warden] regarded her [the girl] as his property. I considered that she belonged to me. Between the two of us she was reduced to nothing; her only function might have been to link us together.[20]

It is clear from the start of the novel that the narrative voice of *Ice* is unstable; as the narrator says in the first few pages of the novel, 'Reality had always been something of an unknown quantity to me.'[21] Not long after this acknowledgement, we are presented with the first of many fantastical visions which involve the girl:

> An unearthly whiteness began to bloom on the hedges. I passed a gap and glanced through. For a moment, my lights picked out like searchlights the girl's naked body, slight as a child's, ivory white against the dead white of the snow, her hair bright as spun glass. She did not look in my direction. Motionless, she kept her eyes fixed on the walls moving slowly towards her, a glassy, glittering circle of solid ice, of which she was the centre. Dazzling flashes came from the ice-cliffs far over her head; below, the outermost fringes of ice had already reached her, immobilized her, set hard as concrete over her feet and ankles.[22]

This passage exemplifies how the narrator relates his experiences in a continual stream of information with a disregard for, or indeed an inability to distinguish between, fantasy and reality, between dream, past and present. As such, time in *Ice* does not appear to submit to the rules of chronological, teleological time. Rather, past and present become blurred; there is no clear demarcation between them. When analepses occur, as they do quite frequently, it is not at all clear where these start or end. As readers, we thus experience a similar feeling of disorientation to the narrator when he says 'I felt I had moved out of ordinary life into an area of total strangeness.'[23] Yet, as he goes on to say, 'All this was real, it was really happening, but with a quality of the unreal; it was reality happening in quite a different way.'[24] All of these events befall the narrator, whether they belong to the 'real', tangible world or to the realm of the mind, and they are communicated thus to the reader.

The text's experimentalism stems from its portrayal of this 'unreal reality'. As the narrator puts it, 'the unreality of the outer world' appears to be 'an extension of [his] own disturbed state of mind'.[25] There is very little in the way of conventional plot or characterisation. The main plot line itself, concerning the narrator's quest for the girl, can be considered as no more than a mere façade; some semblance that its events can be positioned within an interrelated sequence is nevertheless undermined by the text itself. Thus, when the narrator does finally succeed in finding the girl and they escape to a country which is not yet in the throes of destruction, he quickly tires of her and abandons her in favour of returning to the world of warfare and ice. Yet as soon as he gets there, he becomes obsessed with her once again and reignites his efforts to track her down, thereby inevitably re-engaging with the warden. The form and structure of the novel thus rely heavily on repetitive events. Whilst specific events are not repeated, every situation has, in a sense, happened before: the narrator is constantly looking for the girl, finding her, being eluded by her, at which point the process starts all over again. Certain phrases are repeated within the novel, emphasising how everything ultimately stays the same (or worsens). Thus, at one point, the narrator reflects, 'I was aware of an uncertainty of the real, in my surroundings and in myself. What I saw had no solidity, it was all made of mist and nylon, with nothing behind.'[26] Thirty pages later, the same image reappears when the narrator describes another town he finds himself in: 'a scene made of nylon with nothing behind'.[27] The phrase '[t]hings had turned out very much better than I had expected'[28] also makes more than one appearance in the novel as the same situations keep recurring. But, though the narrator is constantly moving, nothing is ever very different; on arrival in yet another town, he states: 'It could have been any town, in any country.'[29] Descriptions of places and characters remain minimal throughout the novel; self-consciously flimsy, they draw attention to their insubstantial and vaporous nature, imbuing everything with a sense of unreality.

A Classic 1960s Novel?

Doris Lessing stated that '[h]owever we class the book, there is nothing else like it'.[30] After selecting *Ice* as 'best science fiction novel' of 1967, Aldiss later admitted that he had chosen it 'less from any firm conviction that it was science fiction [. . .] than to draw attention to a splendid piece of writing'.[31] This uncertainty regarding how to label the novel is illustrative of the problem of categorisation throughout Kavan's œuvre. Her works of fiction, appearing between 1929 and 1967 during her lifetime, have attracted a wide variety of labels: the works she published as 'Helen Ferguson' have often (quite dismissively) been referred to as 'Home Counties novels',[32] and are generally seen to be relatively conventional in style and radically different from her later works, which have variously been called '(late-)modernist', 'literary slipstream', 'experimental', 'surrealist', 'symbolist' and 'science-fiction'.[33] Spanning several decades and seemingly overlapping with several movements and genres, Kavan's œuvre resists being comfortably placed within any definitive category, a hallmark of her fiction which has no doubt contributed to her neglect.[34]

Retrospectively, however, *Ice* has been hailed as a product of the sixties *Zeitgeist*, most recently by Penguin Press; reissuing a fiftieth anniversary edition of *Ice*, it described the novel as a 'classic 1960s novel of J. G. Ballard-ian strangeness'.[35] The implication here is that *Ice* is representative of a 1960s literary 'avant-garde' movement, one which evidently includes Ballard, along with other writers considered in the pages of this collection. With increasing attention justly focused on experimental British sixties writers, it is tempting to conceive of the sixties as a decade which embraced and championed experimentalism once again. Yet, as Julia Jordan has pointed out, this way of viewing the era 'remains a way of seeing the past that is itself a product of its time, indeed a product of a specific critical reassessment – and perhaps of no small amount of wishful thinking'.[36] Jordan draws attention to Patricia Waugh's perceptive warning about hasty judgement in the mid-1990s that 'we cannot entirely bring [the sixties'] meaning or significance to conscious articulation'.[37] At the time Waugh was writing this, sixties avant-garde experiments were hardly paid any attention at all and the decade was, for many years, 'subject to a critical consensus that labelled the British fiction of the period in particular as parochial, nostalgic and insular'.[38]

Reviews of Kavan's *Ice* upon its initial publication further caution against viewing the sixties as a decade which generally celebrated experimental fiction, and are representative of how Kavan's work had often been received since the 1940s. Whilst the novel enjoyed a few complimentary reviews, a number of publications were resolutely dismissive of the work. In the latter, it is possible to trace a common frustration at what was perceived to be a lack of engagement with external reality in favour of a style which was deemed too heavily influenced by the avant-garde. Thus, Irving Wardle in *The Observer*, interpreting the novel as 'a series of linked nightmares featuring standard dream situations', wrote that *Ice* 'is written compulsively enough to take you inside the dream, if not to relate it to the outer world'.[39] The implied critique here is one which was regularly directed at Kavan's fiction; *Sleep Has His House* had, for example, attracted harsh criticism from Diana Trilling, who interpreted the novel as 'carefully avoid[ing] reality' and adding nothing to 'our information about the world of consciousness'.⁴⁰ Kavan's stories in *A Bright Green Field* (1958), divided into 'realistic' and 'allegorical' ones by the reviewer, were respectively deemed as meaning 'a little less than they say' and having 'no real application, so far as I can see, to anything at all'.⁴¹ *London Magazine*'s review of *Ice* situated the novel within a consideration of 'avant-garde' fiction (also reviewing work by Wilson Harris, Gil Orlovitz and Peter Weiss) and its introductory paragraph was representative of a particular postwar critical attitude towards avant-garde fiction (and, often, towards Kavan's writing):

> As if Beckett had cut up Henry James, as if Kerouac had written Ulysses, as if Kafka had scripted Marienbad: immersion in the avant-garde stimulates such phrases as a hysterical recoil; and also as a register of the derivativeness, the determined literariness, of the productions, words nurtured on words, silences bred of libraries. At least to recognize sources is, like finding a square inch of newsprint on a deserted tropical beach, some indication that a world of communication does exist elsewhere. For the rest, one is left with hard objects like pebbles or shells, that are in fact words, to sift through and from which to try to assemble a meaning, a pattern, a diagram, anything.⁴²

The implication here is that avant-garde fiction purposely sets out to be 'difficult', to make one look for 'some indication' that 'meaning' does exist somewhere. This exemplifies a dominant trend in postwar criticism, which often all too easily equated formal inventiveness with a forfeiting or obfuscation of meaning. Thus, Kavan's other sixties work, *Who Are You?* (1963), a novel divided into two main parts with the second representing a more concise and subtly different version of events to the first, was called 'a kinky experimental work rather than a novel' due to the fact that its author 'unfortunately [. . .] wishes to show the relativeness of reality'.⁴³ This kind of criticism relies on the idea that novels should portray an objective and recognisable reality, thereby positing the existence of precisely such a universally experienced 'reality', which the work of fiction should reflect. Kavan's œuvre, however, troubles such a notion of 'the real'; as she states in some notes which date from the sixties, 'The increasing materialistic pressures of our times have made even the word "reality" come to mean the reality of the concrete world, as if there were no other. But [. . .] there is no "absolute" reality.'⁴⁴ Yet the rejection of an absolute reality does not necessarily refute a relationship between subjectivity and the external environment, as some of the more hostile contemporary reviews appeared to imply. Indeed, this chapter proposes that *Ice*, whilst predicated on what might be termed 'absolute subjectivity', nevertheless draws attention to the influence of the external environment on the fragmentary subject. Multiplying and destabilising meanings, *Ice* can be understood as a text concerned with the schizophrenic experience, thereby challenging the idea of selfhood as an ordered narrative. In order to explore this idea further, the next part of the chapter will look at the novel's representation of this, reading *Ice* in the context of 1960s anti-psychiatry.

The Divided Self

As *Ice* unfolds, the identity of the narrator, through whom the narrative is mainly focalised, is repeatedly called into question. To understand the narrating voice as a complete and distinct persona appears misleading; such a reading throws up numerous inconsistencies. How, for example, can the narrator be aware of what is happening or has happened between the girl and the warden in his absence? At different points throughout the novel, the narrative switches focalisation and the reader is suddenly granted access to the mind of the girl or the warden, yet the text nevertheless remains narrated by the same voice. The explanation that these episodes are simply fantastical projections of the narrator's mind does not quite go far enough, considering the text consistently suggests that one could interpret the three principal characters (the narrator, the girl and the warden) as different personas of one individual. At one point, for example, the narrator, reflecting on his obsession with the girl, states:

> When I considered that imperative need I felt for her, as for a missing part of myself, it appeared less like love than an inexplicable aberration, the sign of some character-flaw I ought to eradicate, instead of letting it dominate me.[45]

There are numerous instances throughout the novel in which the warden and the narrator seem to be merging into one person, or when the warden seems to be a reflection of the narrator himself. These suspicions are formulated quite readily by the narrator himself: 'I suddenly felt an indescribable affinity with him, a sort of blood-contact, generating confusion, so that I began to wonder if there *were* two of us.'[46] In moments of brutality when dealing with the girl, the narrator's voice becomes, as it were, that of the warden's. As the narrator states earlier on in the novel, 'I had a curious feeling that I was living on several planes simultaneously; the overlapping of these planes was confusing.'⁴⁷

Whilst various reviewers and critics have noted the text's suggestion that the three main protagonists can be interpreted as different embodiments of a single self, the implications of a psychoanalytical reading, and in particular an anti-psychiatric reading, of *Ice* have not yet been fully explored.⁴⁸ And yet the consistent emphasis on the fluidity and interchangeability of the novel's three principal characters strongly encourages such a reading. Indeed, *Ice* can be understood as engaging with a key concern of sixties culture in its exploration and depiction of the fragmented subject: namely, the schizophrenic experience as theorised by R. D. Laing in *The Divided Self* (1960).

In his influential study, Laing set out his phenomenological and existential theory, in which he insists that the schizophrenic person must be understood within a social context, suggesting that the thought patterns and behaviour of the schizophrenic are reasonable and understandable when viewed in such a context. Laing points out that a schizophrenic individual experiences himself or herself not as a complete person 'but rather as "split" in various ways, perhaps as a mind more or less tenuously linked to a body, as two or more selves, and so on',⁴⁹ and goes on to give an example of a schizophrenic's experience of this phenomenon:

> One of the fragments of the self generally seems to retain the sense of 'I'. The other 'self' might then be called 'her'. But this 'her' is still 'me'. Rose [a patient] says, '*She*'s *me*, and I'm *her* all the time'. One schizophrenic told me: '*She*'s an *I* looking for a *me*'.⁵⁰

In *Ice*, the narrator's confused sense of self similarly appears to deconstruct binary oppositions of self and other, entertaining a plurality of possible precarious selves which refuse to be contained within one single representation of the ego. According to a Laingian reading of *Ice*, the narrator could be understood as suffering from 'ontological insecurity', a concept Laing interprets as lying at the root of schizophrenic behaviour. To be ontologically insecure is to have a threatened and precarious sense of existence, to 'feel more unreal than real' and, often, to lack any experience of temporal continuity.⁵¹ This appears to encapsulate the experience of the narrator in *Ice* and offers an explanation of the temporal discontinuity of the novel. As Laing explains concerning the ontologically insecure individual:

> It is, of course, inevitable that an individual whose experience of himself is of this order can no more live in a 'secure' world than he can be secure

'in himself'. The whole 'physiognomy' of his world will be correspondingly different from that of the individual whose sense of self is securely established in its health and validity.⁵²

Laing here points to the osmotic relationship between interiority and the external world. As he states earlier on in his study, 'We all know from our personal experience that we can be ourselves only in and through our world and there is a sense in which "our" world will die with us although "the" world will go on without us.'⁵³ The narrative in *Ice* has been called 'deceptively objective' for it is, in fact, completely and utterly subjective, presenting the worldview of an individual experiencing their sense of self as irrevocably split, rooted in the phenomenological approach to the depiction and understanding of being in the world, which it shares with Laing's theory in *The Divided Self*.⁵⁴

It is important here to point out that Laing often employed the term 'schizophrenia' in a much broader way than is customary today. In *The Politics of Experience* (1967), Laing suggests, for example, that in order to understand schizophrenia we should read into it 'its etymological meaning: *Schiz* – "broken"; *Phrenos* – "soul or heart"'.⁵⁵ As he makes explicit, 'schizophrenia', 'in this existential sense, has little to do with the clinical examination, diagnosis, prognosis and prescriptions for therapy of "schizophrenia"'.⁵⁶ 'Schizophrenia' in this much broader Laingian sense, then, denotes the alienation of an individual in the modern world, a condition caused by the pressures of an external environment and interpersonal experiences on an individual.

As Waugh has pointed out, Laing's ideas, formulated in *The Divided Self*, amounted to 'one of the most influential theses to come out of the radical movements of the sixties'.⁵⁷ Michel Foucault's *Madness and Civilization* had also been translated in 1966 and further fostered the idea that 'madness is only what the ideology of a particular age defines as madness', a notion which resonated in the countercultural circles of the sixties.⁵⁸ *Ice* can be situated in a particular strand of sixties literature which explores the concept of divided selves and / or madness, including Doris Lessing's *The Golden Notebook* (1962), Angela Carter's *Several Perceptions* (1968), Ann Quin's *Passages* (1969) and Margaret Drabble's *The Waterfall* (1969). As such, it forms part of a group of novels which can be considered 'inner space fiction', occupying the zone that Ballard identified as 'inner space', in which 'the dream worlds, synthetic landscapes and plasticity of visual forms' are 'external equivalents of the inner world of the psyche'.⁵⁹ Like other works of fiction of the period which explored altered states of cognisance,

Ice's concern with notions of consciousness and its focus on the divided self can be construed as a countercultural critique of the functionalist rationality of the postwar era. As Waugh has commented in her study of the British sixties:

> Literary culture was rife with disaffection at the inadequacies of the Welfare State, the contradictions of a sagging liberalism, the apocalyptic legacy of Hiroshima, the evil incarnate of Auschwitz and Belsen, the perceived threat from technologized mass cultures. Both traditional religion and rationalized secular culture appeared to have failed to provide a foundational value-system which could anchor a fragmenting society whose new technologies had unleashed unprecedented horrors and thrown up unresolvable ethical dilemmas.[60]

Ice can be understood both as sketching the effects of a fragmenting society on the individual, and as tracing such a search for a foundational value-system. Thus, the narrator's fascination with the Indris, the almost extinct mysterious singing lemurs that he loves to study, is rooted in the fact that they become, for him, a 'symbol of life as it could be on earth, if man's destructiveness, violence and cruelty were eliminated'.[61] For life on this planet, however, it is too late: 'The ultimate achievement of mankind would be, not just self-destruction, but the destruction of all life; the transformation of the living world into a dead planet.'[62] Ruminating on humanity's role in the end of the world, the narrator is oppressed by 'the enormity of what had been done, the weight of collective guilt': 'A frightful crime had been committed, against nature, against the universe, against life. By rejecting life, man had destroyed the immemorial order, destroyed the world; now everything was about to crash down in ruins.'[63]

A Laingian reading of *Ice*, then, illustrates how the novel explores the psychic borderline landscape of the schizophrenic as theorised in Laing's influential study, as its three main protagonists merge into one another, ultimately resulting in their destruction as the girl and narrator's (literal) death drive mirrors the planet's road to extinction. Engaging with the 1960s notion of the divided self, fragmented by the pressures and violences of an exploitative and competitive society, *Ice* can be construed as advancing a critique of postwar society through a focus on the inner workings of the mind, and thus highlighting the relationship between interior and exterior reality. The final part of this chapter aims to illustrate that this emphasis on the osmotic relationship between self and world is a key concern of Kavan's œuvre more generally, by showing how a work of fiction published twenty-seven years earlier foreshadows this central concern of *Ice*.

Asylum Piece: Prefiguring the Anti-Psychiatry Movement

Whilst I have not come across archival evidence to suggest that Kavan had read Laing's *The Divided Self*, it is highly likely she would have been aware of his theory, considering her life-long interest in psychoanalytical thought. Her surviving diaries, notes and correspondence make clear that she kept abreast of the latest thoughts and theories in the field of psychoanalysis. She herself had experiences both of being an in-patient at different psychiatric institutions and of working with patients suffering from mental health issues during the Second World War; in the 1940s she worked at the Mill Hill Emergency Hospital in London with Dr Maxwell Jones, who was then pioneering the method of community therapy; and in the late forties, Kavan underwent treatment with the existential psychoanalyst Ludwig Binswanger.[64] Both Jones and Binswanger would come to influence Laing's thought. Nevertheless, *Asylum Piece* predates this contact, and shows Kavan prefiguring Laing's popularised idea of human madness as a perfectly rational response to an insane world.

Published at the outbreak of war in 1940, *Asylum Piece* can be read either as a collection of distinct short stories or as a work which traces one single individual's experiences from the subtle onset of paranoia to madness to asylum internment. Consisting of fourteen short prose pieces, its fragmented form and its suggestion that the different stories can be read as significant moments in the development of a psyche are firmly grounded in an interest in human psychology. With this first work published under her newly adopted name, Kavan can be understood as critiquing the practices and so-called 'treatments' of the world of the asylum, portraying life in the institution through the eyes of its inmates. In doing so, Kavan not only succeeds in rendering the narrator's 'madness' understandable, but also makes the reader aware of the senselessness and inherent irrationality of society itself. Thus, in 'The Enemy', the narrator muses:

> Perhaps I am the victim of some mysterious political, religious or financial machination – some vast and shadowy plot, whose ramifications are so obscure as to appear to the uninitiated to be quite outside reason, requiring, for instance, something as apparently senseless as the destruction of everybody with red hair or with a mole on his left leg.[65]

This idea of a spectre of violence 'quite outside reason', of the 'senseless' destruction of a whole group of people on the illogical basis of some physical characteristic, is eerily prescient of the atrocities which were to be committed in the Second World War and renders the presumed paranoia of the narrator not so irrational after all. This ambiguity, the question of whether the persecution mania and paranoia present throughout *Asylum Piece* have any grounds for believability, or whether these can merely be reduced to the symptoms of a deluded mind, is in part what is so striking and radical about the collection. By refusing to settle the question, the text encourages the reader to consider another interpretation: what if the narrator *is* being persecuted? Would this be so baffling in an age set on destruction, which arbitrarily singles people out according to their beliefs? By privileging the voice of an asylum inmate, one deemed insane in the eyes of society, Kavan encourages the reader to suspend their judgement and view society through someone else's eyes. From this liminal position, society itself often appears insane and thus it is not without reason that, in the last story, 'There is No End', the narrator muses:

> And of late the idea has come to me – fantastic enough, I admit – that possibly after all he [her persecutor] is not my personal enemy, but a sort of projection of myself, an identification of myself with the cruelty and destructiveness of the world. On a planet where there is so much natural conflict may there not very well exist in certain individuals an overwhelming affinity with frustration and death? And may this not result in an actual materialization, a sort of eidolon moving about the world?[66]

Asylum Piece here foreshadows the split selves of *Ice*: a split caused by an identification with the world's destructive urges, thereby drawing attention to the osmotic relationship between the individual and society around them. This is a central idea in understanding Kavan's protagonists throughout her œuvre: to write of the self is also always to write of the world. Indeed, writing in *Horizon* in July 1945, Kavan makes it clear that, in her view, the work of fiction writers should demonstrate 'by means of individual types the sociological and psychological structure of the collective scene'.[67] As this chapter suggests, Kavan's focus on the inner life of the individual throughout her œuvre reflects this view, and her experimentations with form, grounded in a study of the workings of the human mind, can be understood as contributing to her engagement with and reflection on society at large.

In conclusion, this chapter has proposed that *Ice*'s fragmentary subject(s), and Kavan's experimentations with form more generally, are concerned with exploring the dissonances of the human psyche, thereby tracing the relationship between interiority and exteriority. As such, Kavan's last novel can be situated within a particular 1960s literary and psychoanalytical context in its concern with portraying and exploring the experiences of the fragmentary subject, and can be construed as a direct response to the instabilities of the external environment. Whilst this notion gained increased traction in British 1960s society, Kavan's fiction had prefigured this idea since 1940. A study of Kavan's writings, spanning several decades and culminating in the sixties, thus allows us to trace a continuity between pre- and postwar experimentation, encouraging us to view the sixties not as a sudden break from what went before, but as a period in which complex, interweaving trajectories and influences culminate.

Notes

1. Letter from Anna Kavan to Raymond Marriot, 20 September 1964, Series II, Box 2, Folder 12, Anna Kavan Papers, McFarlin Library, University of Tulsa.
2. Ibid.
3. Kavan, 'Back to Victoria', *Horizon*, XIII:73 (1946), pp. 61–6, p. 62.
4. Kavan, 'Selected Notices', *Horizon*, XII:67 (1945), pp. 63–9, p. 63; Kavan, 'Back to Victoria', p. 63.
5. Kavan, 'Back to Victoria', p. 63.
6. Ibid. p. 62.
7. Kavan to Marriott, 20 September 1964.
8. Ibid.
9. Ibid.
10. Letter from Kavan to Ian Hamilton, 6 February 1943, Walter Ian Hamilton Papers, Alexander Turnbull Library, National Library of New Zealand, Wellington.
11. Anna Kavan had been the name of the protagonist of the Ferguson novel *Let Me Alone* (1930) and also made an appearance in Ferguson's *A Stranger Still* (1935).
12. Kate Zambreno, 'Afterword', in Anna Kavan, *Ice* (Penguin: New York, 2017), pp. 183–93, p. 186.
13. Victoria Walker, *The Fiction of Anna Kavan (1901–1968)* (Doctoral Thesis, Queen Mary, University of London, 2012), p. 13; Jennifer Sturm, *Fictionalising the Facts: An Exploration of the 'Place' of Aotearoa / New Zealand in the Post-War Autobiographical Fiction of Anna Kavan* (Doctoral Thesis, University of Auckland, 2006) and *Anna Kavan's New Zealand: A Pacific Interlude in a Turbulent Life*, ed. Jennifer Sturm (Auckland: Vintage, Random House New Zealand, 2009).

14. Jane Garrity, 'Nocturnal Transgressions in *The House of Sleep*: Anna Kavan's Maternal Registers', *Modern Fiction Studies*, 40:2 (1994), pp. 253–77, p. 253.
15. Quoted in Clive Jordan, 'Among the Lost Things', *Daily Telegraph Magazine*, 25 February 1972. For an examination of how Kavan has been constructed as an 'addict writer' and how this designation has influenced critical readings of her work, see Carole Sweeney, '"Keeping the Ruins Private": Anna Kavan and Heroin Addiction', *Women: A Cultural Review*, 28:4 (2017), pp. 312–26.
16. Garrity, 'Nocturnal Transgressions', p. 253.
17. Victoria Walker, 'Ornithology and Ontology: The Existential Birdcall in Jean Rhys's *Wide Sargasso Sea* and Anna Kavan's *Who Are You?*', *Women: A Cultural Review*, 23:4 (2012), pp. 490–509, pp. 504–5.
18. See, for example, *Anna Kavan: New Readings*, Special Issue of *Women: A Cultural Review*, 28:4 (2017).
19. Brian Aldiss, 'Kafka's Sister', in *My Madness: The Selected Writings of Anna Kavan*, ed. Brian Aldiss (London: Picador, 1990), p. xi.
20. Kavan, *Ice* [1967] (London: Peter Owen, 2006), pp. 76–7.
21. Ibid. p. 6.
22. Ibid. p. 7.
23. Ibid. p. 146.
24. Ibid.
25. Ibid. pp. 60–1.
26. Ibid. p. 31.
27. Ibid. p. 60.
28. Ibid. p. 108.
29. Ibid. p. 104.
30. Doris Lessing, 'Anna Kavan', in *Time Bites* (London: Fourth Estate, 2004), pp. 142–4, pp. 143–4.
31. Brian Aldiss, 'Kafka's Sister', p. xi.
32. Rhys Davies first referred to the Helen Ferguson works as 'Home Counties novels' in a review of her posthumously published collection of short stories *Julia and the Bazooka*. See Davies, 'The Bazooka Girl: A Note on Anna Kavan', *London Magazine* (February 1970), pp. 13–16, p. 16.
33. For these appellations, see Garrity, 'Nocturnal Transgressions', p. 254; Christopher Priest, 'Foreword', in Kavan, *Ice* (London: Peter Owen, 2006), n.p.; Davies, 'The Bazooka Girl', p. 14; Francis Booth, *Amongst Those Left: The British Experimental Novel, 1940–1980* (Lulu Press, Inc., 2012); Lee Rourke, 'Found Guilty: Anna Kavan's Latest Novel', *The Guardian*, 28 June 2007, available at <https://www.theguardian.com/books/booksblog/2007/jun/28/foundguilty> (last accessed 1 December 2017).
34. Leigh Wilson has pointed out how problematic assessments of Kavan's work as *sui generis* are 'because they are so often linked with the assumption that the social and psychological isolation of the last

decades of her life was matched by a literary isolation, and that, indeed, her experimental achievements are those of a kind of idiot savant, the result of serendipity rather than any critical engagement with literary tradition and debate'. Wilson, 'Anna Kavan's *Ice* and Alan Burns' *Europe After the Rain*: Repetition with a Difference', *Women: A Cultural Review*, 28:4 (2017), pp. 327–42, p. 328.
35. Penguin Press, Autumn 2017 Catalogue, p. 81, available at <https://www.penguinrandomhouse.co.uk/content/dam/prh-corporate/penguin-random-house/catalogue/penguin-press/Penguin_Press_Autumn_2017_as_at_29_Sept.pdf> (last accessed 27 November 2017).
36. Julia Jordan, 'Introduction: Avant-Garde Possibilities – B. S. Johnson and the Sixties Generation', in *B. S. Johnson and Post-War Literature*, ed. Julia Jordan and Martin Ryle (Basingstoke: Palgrave Macmillan, 2014), pp. 1–13, p. 2.
37. Patricia Waugh, *The Harvest of the Sixties: English Literature and Its Background, 1960–1990* (Oxford: Oxford University Press, 1995), pp. 1–2.
38. Jordan, 'Introduction', p. 2.
39. Irving Wardle, 'Twilight in St Petersburg', *The Observer*, 3 September 1967, p. 23.
40. Diana Trilling, *Reviewing the Forties* (New York: Harcourt Brace Jovanovich, 1978), pp. 218, 220.
41. John Mortimer, 'Camus, Durrell, Wain, and Kavan', *Encounter*, June 1958, pp. 83–6, p. 86.
42. Michael Wilding, 'Selected Books', *London Magazine*, 1 August 1967, pp. 95–7, p. 95.
43. Venetia Pollock, 'New Novels', *Punch*, 21 August 1963, pp. 285–6.
44. Series II, Box 2, Folder 12, Anna Kavan Papers.
45. Kavan, *Ice* (London: Peter Owen, 2006), p. 24.
46. Ibid. pp. 76–7.
47. Ibid. p. 52.
48. Thus *The Spectator* interpreted the novel as a 'quest for identity' (Kay Dick, 'Paradox and Poetry', *The Spectator*, 15 September 1967, pp. 303–4, p. 304), whilst *The Listener* stated that 'it needs no great sophistication to perceive that Miss Kavan is truly dealing with a single, undivided consciousness' (F. W. J. Hemmings, 'Robbing Grillet', *The Listener*, 7 September 1967). Critics since then have equally suggested such a reading of the novel; see, for example, Janet Byrne, 'Moving toward Entropy: Anna Kavan's Science Fiction Mentality', *Extrapolation*, 23:1 (1982); and Gregory Stephenson, 'An Inward Ice-Age: A Reading of Anna Kavan's *Ice*', *Foundation*, 40:113 (2011), pp. 20–8.
49. R. D. Laing, *The Divided Self* [1960] (London: Penguin, 1990), p. 17.
50. Ibid. p. 158.
51. Ibid. p. 42.
52. Ibid.
53. Ibid. p. 20.

54. Hemmings, 'Robbing Grillet'.
55. Laing, *The Politics of Experience: And, The Bird of Paradise* (Harmondsworth: Penguin, 1972), p. 106.
56. Ibid.
57. Waugh, *The Harvest of the Sixties*, pp. 6–7.
58. Arthur Marwick, *The Sixties: Cultural Revolution in Britain, France, Italy, and the United States, c.1958–c.1974* (London: Bloomsbury, 2012).
59. J. G. Ballard, 'Time, Memory and Inner Space', in *The Women's Journalist* (1963), available at <http://www.jgballard.ca/non_fiction/jgb_time_memory_innerspace.html> (last accessed 3 December 2017).
60. Waugh, *The Harvest of the Sixties*, pp. 7–8.
61. Kavan, *Ice* (London: Peter Owen, 2006), p. 57.
62. Ibid. p. 142.
63. Ibid.
64. For a detailed discussion of Kavan's time working at the hospital and its influence on her writing, see Victoria Walker, 'Heart and Minds: War Neurosis and the Politics of Madness in Anna Kavan's *I Am Lazarus*', *Women: A Cultural Review*, 28:4 (2017), pp. 375–90.
65. Anna Kavan, *Asylum Piece* [1940] (London: Peter Owen, 2001), pp. 32–3.
66. Ibid. pp. 210–11.
67. Anna Kavan, 'Selected Notices', *Horizon*, XII:67 (1945), pp. 63–9, p.64. For an analysis of Kavan's *Sleep Has His House* in light of this statement, see my 'Exploring the Realm of the Unconscious in Anna Kavan's *Sleep Has His House*', *Women: A Cultural Review*, 28:4 (2017), pp. 358–74.

Chapter 7

J. G. Ballard: Visuality and the Novels of the Near Future

Natalie Ferris

The growing dominance of the visual in twentieth-century culture is magnified in the writings of J. G. Ballard. His fiction communicates, with greater lucidity than many of his peers, the social realm as spectacle: a landscape invaded and sustained by surveillance cameras, urban signage, communications networks. Arguably, this was an approach founded in 1956, a singularly formative year that witnessed both the publication of his first stories and the opening of an exhibition that was of 'revolutionary' significance for Ballard.[1] 'This is Tomorrow', held in August and September at the Whitechapel Gallery in London, was a provocative staging of multimedia installations that challenged the divisions between 'high' and 'low' art enforced by contemporary critics such as Herbert Read and Clement Greenberg. 'Purity of media, golden proportions, unambiguous iconologies, have been so powerful', Lawrence Alloway argued in his introduction to the exhibition, 'that we have contracted art and architecture down to very narrow fields.'[2] The twelve 'display stands of ideas' were devised by twelve different 'groups' of three participants, notionally a painter, a sculptor and an architect, to throw the perimeters of those disciplines wide open and to embody visions of the immediate future.[3] Each stand, devoid of interpretation panels but rich in signification, was an immersive scenario or 'total environment' that made sensual and physical demands upon spectators.[4] Cutting across a spectrum of representational modes of the period, such as abstraction, advertising and documentary, the exhibits ranged from sandy plots scattered with arcane symbols, to zones of 'dynamic equivalence' between static structural planes, illusory patterning and kinetic mobiles, to interactive tackboards and montages of commercial slogans or pop cultural icons, such as Robbie the Robot from *The Forbidden Planet* (1956).[5] In this 'playground of Modern Art', the overall effect was to give viewers a sense of what it meant to experience competing, and even antagonistic, visual and spatial environments.[6]

Ballard recognised 'This is Tomorrow' as a cultural watershed moment, 'among the most radical statements of the human imagination ever made'.[7] The participants counted among their number members of the Independent Group (IG), a loosely affiliated collective of artists, architects and critics connected to the Institute of Contemporary Arts (ICA), whose one unifying conviction was that all visual communication demanded the same degree of scrutiny as that awarded to 'high' art.[8] This was a posture partly inherited from Marshall McLuhan's *The Mechanical Bride: Folklore of Industrial Man* (1951), a subject of discussion at early IG meetings, which had set a precedent for the renewed critical appreciation of the imagery of modern mass media.[9] Reyner Banham later referred to the practices of the IG as 'cultural tilth', describing the levelling of the visual landscape in their use of collage, photography, installation and found material.[10] By employing this anti-hierarchical, non-linear approach, Banham noted, 'art and life alike are instantly made into a common order'.[11] It was this objective that made the greatest lasting impression on Ballard, noting in 1971: 'to see my experience of the real world being commented upon, played back to me with all kinds of ironic gestures, that was tremendously exciting'.[12] As a lesson in spectatorship, Ballard surmised, the exhibition would also have powerful implications for contemporary writing. This chapter will contend that Ballard's most innovative works of the 1960s were built upon such deliberate cultural interventions and informed by their experiments with visual design. It will trace a line of graphic experimentation throughout the decade to suggest that closer contact with the textual surface became a defining ambition in Ballard's fiction.

Author as Designer: Envisaging the 'New Novel'

The exhibition proposed an acutely visual future, informing Ballard's presentiment that the twentieth century would be defined by an engagement with the visual:

> I sensed way back in the late fifties when I started that the tide was running away from the written word towards the visual mode of expression and therefore one couldn't any more rely on the reader, you couldn't expect him to meet you any more than half way.[13]

The understanding early in his career of the growing dominance of the visual prompted Ballard to explore means of meeting the reader 'half way', pushing his writing increasingly in the direction of design. As recounted by Martin Bax, 'What he said was – what people read nowadays is advertising, so if you want to have novels that people read, you should publish them as advertisements!'[14] The most striking instance of this, as precursor to his fascination with the designed text, is his sequence of graphically experimental text collages produced in 1958, later titled *Project for a New Novel*. Letters, symbols, headlines, tables and paragraphs were cut from a variety of print sources, primarily Society of Chemical Industry journals, and arranged on to backing sheets with glue, forming the double spreads of the 'novel'.[15] Each black and white page announces mysterious developments in plot through the arrangement of textual snippets, which do not directly correspond to or follow a coherent chain of events. Divested of all the imagery, colour and instruction of modern publicity spreads, the collage sequence placed power back in the hands of the viewer, requiring them to piece together the fragments imaginatively.

A wilfully inscrutable work of fiction, *Project* operates a signifying loop all of its own. Containing what Ballard called the 'chromosomes' for his later work, tropes such as scientific discovery, consumerism and psychological landscapes, the pages are also populated by enigmatic figures, phrases and objects that return and repeat over the course of his career: 'mr f. is mr. f', 'the terminal beach', 'intertime', Kline, Coma and Zero.[16] Ballard explained in a 1984 interview that he intended *Project* to be a 'deliberately meaningless text', one informed by the desire to create 'a new kind of novel, entirely consisting of magazine style headlines and layouts'.[17] He was so taken with the potential of the *Project* to disrupt the communications landscape that he even considered mounting the collages onto advertisement billboards for display throughout London, predating Daniel Buren's anarchistic striped posters by more than a decade.[18] This was not financially possible but he did mount the collages in a continuous sequence on a long horizontal board in his garden.[19] Much of the lettering below the headlines is small and dense, and appears to be slightly blurred, so as to confer that sense of pedestrian attention to large advertisements, reading the headlines and paying little attention to the small print. The pages were not published until two decades after their creation, in which they are described as 'displays'.[20] Riveted throughout with affirmative colons, *Project* fashions an aura of scientific certainty that is diffused by the persistent ellipses and indecipherable text. The aim was that 'the imaginative content could be carried by the headlines and overall design', making 'obsolete the need for traditional text except for virtually decorative purposes'.[21] Therefore, 'far from being meaningless, the science news stories somehow became fictionalised by the headings around them', proposing a reading experience determined not by content but by format.[22]

It is worth noting that 1958 also marked the year Ballard was appointed assistant editor to the scientific journal *Chemistry & Industry*. The work undertaken during his tenure at the magazine (1958–1962) was evidently key to his development as a novelist, nurturing his scientific interests and sharpening his approach to the selection and display of information. Ballard was responsible not only for content, overseeing features and writing reviews of scientific books, but also for production: 'all the basic subbing, marking copy up for the typesetter, dealing with the printer, doing make-up and paste-up, dealing with the artists who drew the scientific formulae'.[23] The *Project* took root in this assembly of journal copy, designing the reading experience of research findings, data sets and laboratory reports between the full-page advertisements taken by chemical companies. The welcome challenge posed by his editorial role was also to be 'at the centre of a huge information flow':

> I feasted on all this material [Ballard later recalled], conference reports, annual bulletins from leading research laboratories around the world and publications put out by UN scientific bodies and organisations such as Atoms for Peace [. . .] the accounts of psychoactive drugs, nuclear weapons research, the applications of the latest-generation computers.[24]

Project demonstrates 'a prescient instance not of "the designer as author", but of the author as designer'.[25] The original collages reveal the precision with which they were constructed: single letters have been meticulously clipped from their source; sections of body copy are tessellated to read as one block; grids and ellipses have been built from carefully trimmed dots, lines and dashes.[26] Many letters have been cut as squares and thickly pasted, indicating Ballard's designer's grasp that only the letters would remain in Xerox replication. Each sheet in *Project* displays his sensitivity to the nature of media copy, deploying the same arresting presentational strategies – such as display type, kerning, body copy, legibility, exclamations, spatial hierarchies, negative space – in order to subvert them.[27] While the media relied upon quickfire bursts of information, colourful imagery and memorable slogans, Ballard stripped these pages of images in favour of a cryptic textual field. It is as if he is disorienting and deconditioning his readers, turning their heads from the striking use of imagery that would come to define the material culture of the 1960s.

'a whole multiplex of contacts': The Novel Meets Collage

In the wake of 'This is Tomorrow', Ballard had cultivated a commitment to fictional work that would align itself as closely as possible to the contemporary visual continuum. At a moment in which contemporary art had 'opened all the doors and windows onto the street', Ballard felt that literature too had a responsibility to create new pathways of signification that would stretch between the street and the page.[28] The compositional technique of Ballard's *Project* was reminiscent of the *papiers collés* of the Cubists, the *poèmes–découpages* and *ciné-poèmes* of the Surrealists, the seamless overlays of the vernacular in Pop, and the 'cut-up', 'fold-in' and collage methods later made notorious by William S. Burroughs and Brion Gysin. Raising the ephemeral to the status of art, these practitioners extended a modernist line of experimentation that drew on urban detritus in order to be critical of the cultural economy and its persuasive rhetoric. By virtue of reproducing the language and projecting the fantasies generated by consumer culture, textual collages could be both compelled by and resistant to a society increasingly saturated by slogans, soundbites, captions, speeches, instructions, platitudes, commentaries and product descriptions. Language could be extracted, transformed and 'sprayed back' into the media atmosphere.[29] Where Ballard differed in approach from several of these antecedents and contemporaries is that in his work, the word and the syntactical unit remained intact. Ballard was not seeking to atomise the word, but to atomise the inner landscape of the postwar world by using its own language, images, idioms, fantasies, fears and folklore. Although he never again produced a 'novel' of such typographically inventive design, *Project* awakened Ballard to the possibilities of non-linear narratives, chance connectives, media spectacle, and the blurring of distinctions between the real and the imagined. The ability to discern one's relationship to a concatenation of disparate elements, whether environmental, physical or psychological, was essential to survival in the modern world, and therefore essential to representations of the modern world. How could writing, and the novel, more authentically represent the flickering, overlapping, transient nature of lived experience?

A number of Ballard's contemporaries had, in the early 1960s, come to similar conclusions about the promise of collage-like practices for the novel. Threatened by the notion that the novel had been 'in eclipse' in Britain since the late 1940s, leading to a fashion for announcing its obsolescence, 'exhaustion' and 'death', writers such as Alan Burns, Rayner Heppenstall and Ann Quin sought a solution to this impasse outside of the conventions promoted by the popular novel.[30] Among them, B. S. Johnson was the most virulent in his dedication to finding a form that would be faithful to 'the moment-to-moment fragmentariness of life'. This novel of the future would be compendious yet unsystematic, a 'collage made of the fragments of my own life, the poor odds and sods, the bric-à-brac', and would remain attentive to the material fact of the book.[31] There was a growing sense, one which Ballard shared, that writing, and the novel in particular, had fallen behind conceptual leaps made by the visual arts.[32] Publications such as Martin Bax's *Ambit*, Jeff Nuttall's *My Own Mag*, Ralph Rumney's *Other Voices* and the Royal College of Art's *ARK* sought to remedy this as testbeds for new fusions of art, literature and activism. The chaotic nature of life could be echoed in the technique of the telling, as explored and lampooned by new wave cinema, assemblage, auto-destructive art and happenings. For Ballard, the only literary form that was equipped to face this challenge was science fiction, maligned by the literary establishment as a pulp phenomenon. In the first few years of the new decade, Ballard penned articles for publications as varied as *New Worlds*, *The Woman Journalist* and *The Guardian*, arguing for the importance of science fiction to the evolution of the contemporary novel. Ballard contended that it was 'the only medium with an adequate vocabulary' of concepts and imagery to confront the perceptual challenges posed by an accelerated visual and technological culture.[33] In 'Which Way to Inner Space?' (1962), Ballard proposed that science fiction 'turn its back on space, interstellar travel, extraterrestrial life forms, galactic wars' to focus inward, on 'inner space', to account for aspects that make Earth and the human race 'alien'.[34] What are 'the interrelationships between space and time'? How does 'inner space' skew perspective? How do new technologies intrude upon human expression and selfhood?[35]

'living inside an enormous novel': Radical Realities and Invisible Literatures

As the new decade began and Ballard embarked upon his career as a novelist, penning four dystopian novels – *The Wind From Nowhere* (1961), *The Drowned World* (1962), *The Burning World* (1964) and *The Crystal World* (1966), these questions rose in volume.[36] Although radical in subject matter, portraying worlds ravaged by human and environmental catastrophe, these novels largely followed the linear conventions of narrative. As a self-proclaimed 'frustrated painter', Ballard's allegiance to the visual realm provided critical tools to challenge modes of representation in his writing and found expression in the inclusion of artworks within the narratives.[37] Paintings take on a totemic significance in these books, adopting what Ballard referred to as the 'logic of the visible at the service of the invisible'.[38] Immersing the characters within their visual frame of reference, paintings operate as keys to the workings of the territory and, as a consequence, to a protagonist's psyche. In *The Drowned World*, Kerans gazes at the 'spectral, bone-like' paintings of Paul Delvaux and at the 'self-devouring phantasmagoric' jungle-scapes of Max Ernst; in *The Burning World*, Ransom recalls the strange 'drained' beaches of Yves Tanguy's 'Jours de Lenteur' (1937); at the opening of *The Crystal World*, Father Balthus likens Port Matarre to Arnold Böcklin's foreboding 'Isle of the Dead' (1880).[39] As the characters spend periods of time looking at and living with these pictures, they begin to embrace submersion beneath their surfaces. The imagery penetrates their dreams and their territories as the 'outer world of reality and [. . .] the inner world of the mind meet and merge', with often disquieting dénouements.[40] These novels were all directed by the notion communicated in these Surrealist artworks that an individual is 'largely ruled by the laws of fictions, by one's dreams, visions, impressions' and by the narrative power of the unconscious.[41] By the mid-1960s, however, Ballard had reached a terminal moment:

> I think the assassination of Kennedy acted as a kind of catalyst. It seemed to me that by that point the fictional elements of reality had begun to overwhelm the so-called 'realistic' ones [. . .] I thought that the balance between reality and fiction had tilted by the mid-sixties so we were living inside an enormous novel.[42]

The Surrealist position had been 'reversed': 'It's the external world which is now the realm, the paramount realm of fantasy. And it's the internal world of the mind which is the one node of reality that most of us have. The fiction is all out there.'[43]

The dream, which had proven so potent for Freud and the Surrealists, was broadening into a 'dream machine' of fictions produced by television, advertising, politics, the press and radio.[44] The killing of the American President had coincided with the sudden death of Ballard's young wife, moments of rupture that pressured Ballard's ability to make sense of the world. The 'kinship' between the two tragedies had given rise to a 'nightmare logic' in his writing, by which the extremity of present-day realities and the stylised nature of human reactions necessitated 'a kit of desperate measures, desperate devices'.[45] For Ballard, Pop Art, running in tandem with science fiction, was the present endpoint in a tradition of imaginative responses to science and technology, one that reached back to H. G. Wells and Aldous Huxley.[46] The seamless nature of pop collages, such as Richard Hamilton's 'Just what is it that makes today's homes so different, so appealing?' (1956), splicing together the domestic realm and popular advertising, proved that 'science fiction was far closer to reality than the conventional realist novel of the day'.[47] Science fiction was 'close to the world of the Pop painters and sculptors, Paolozzi, Hamilton', as it also took inspiration from unexpected encounters between the ideas, images and situations of everyday life:

> the gleam on refrigerator cabinets, the contours of a wife's or husband's thighs passing the newsreel images on a colour TV set, the conjunction of musculature and chromium artefact within an automobile interior, the unique postures of passengers on an airport escalator.[48]

The challenge for contemporary writing, Ballard noted, was to 'add one unique ingredient to this hot mix – words'.[49]

Intriguingly, in answer to his own proposition, Ballard appears to have paid less attention to the activities of his fellow wordsmiths in favour of forging his closest working alliance of the decade with the artist Eduardo Paolozzi. Although the two did not meet until 1966, they had operated in each other's orbit for some time and 'long shared many of the same interests, obsessions and themes'.[50] Both identified with the work of the Surrealists, both were fascinated by scientific discovery, both recognised the mystery and symbolism of technology, both accepted the purgative power of violence. Above all, both understood the intrinsic power of popular imagery to provide clues to contemporary society. The sixties heralded increased print activity across the cultural and countercultural spectrum, which can be attributed in part to technological advances such as the invention of the mimeograph machine, offset lithography and laser printing.[51] It was not the effects of the underground press, however, that fuelled their imaginations, but the documents of administration, industry, publicity, the laboratory. Ballard came to call this source material, donated by friends, received through the letterbox or obtained from every corner of the city, 'invisible literatures'.[52] These were texts marginal to the literary mainstream, rarely seen, let alone read, by the majority of the population, 'scientific journals, technical manuals, pharmaceutical company brochures, think-tank internal documents, PR company position papers'.[53] Destined for obsolescence, they were 'part of the comedy of waste, a central figure in the life of our time'.[54] Where use of the media in Surrealism tended to be 'a salvage operation, rescuing unique and choice bits', here 'topical relics' rose above the tumult.[55] The 'tools' of their undertaking were their 'own hands and eyes', and although Ballard later considered this to be one of the 'clumsiest' ways of collating information, there was an especial exhilaration reserved for this 'incredibly primitive' contact with the written word.[56] The act of 'filtering', as Ballard described it, had become central to the craft of the writer.[57] As noted by critics such as David Brittain and Andrzej Gąsiorek, Ballard's aleatory practice chimed with the way Paolozzi described his creative process: 'Assembly decided on the floor of the workshop; creative decision on several levels. Spontaneity meets discipline and so these simple objects grew in assembly into positive forms.'[58] This was an aesthetic approach first made conspicuous by Paolozzi's *Bunk* collages, a prototypical work of Pop Art created between 1947 and 1952, which culminated in the groundbreaking projection of his collages and 'tearsheets', postcards, diagrams and magazine clippings in April 1952 at the ICA.[59] A decade later, in Paolozzi's first artists' book, *Metafisikal Translations* (1962), text stood in for images and objects, stamped, shaped and juxtaposed to elicit serendipitous connections. In the same way that the source images of Pop were repeatedly tested, processed, reshot, fading their potency until a new, polished identity emerged, so too could language be excised, recontextualised and heightened in exposure to the progressive technical discourses of the age.

From 1966 onwards, Ballard became 'much more radical' in literary content and style, in 'a desperate attempt to prove that black was white, that two and two made five in the moral arithmetic of the 1960s'.[60] It was a time of 'revolutionary' societal change, in which 'Pop music and the space age, drugs and Vietnam, fashion and consumerism merged together into an exhilarating and volatile mix'.[61] All of this contributed to a long pause in the writing of novels that stretched until 1973, in which Ballard effectively abandoned the form to write shorter, more 'experimental' stories and to craft a small number of mixed media works that found audiences in publications such as *Ambit* and *New Worlds*.[62] In editorial roles at both publications, Ballard was able to lodge his 'more experimental stories' alongside the work of artists, poets and critics such as Alan Brownjohn, B. S. Johnson, David Hockney, Michael Moorcock, Eduardo Paolozzi and

Stevie Smith.[63] The progressive attitude of editor Martin Bax at *Ambit* towards experiments in word and image allowed Ballard to commission and oversee the development of Paolozzi's 'visual literatures', and to contribute four of his own full-page back cover 'Advertiser's Announcements'. These visual riddles, published between 1967 and 1970, used enigmatic captions and provocative found imagery to promote concepts central to Ballard's ideology: geometry, 'inner space'; the body as landscape; neurological glitches, sex, memory and desire. The advertisements distilled his ambitions for fiction:

> I had a number of ideas which I could fit into my short stories, my fiction in general, but they would be better presented directly [...]. I'm advertising extremely abstract ideas in these advertisements, and this is a very effective way of putting them over.[64]

The copy is cryptic: the enumeration of topical references results in no one obvious message and the tone is equivocal about the associated imagery. Ballard's language resists the easy transactional relationship assumed of publicity campaigns, acting instead as a 'delivery system' to intimate his unease about the exploitative nature of such commercial material.[65] A fifth 'advertisement', 'J. G. Ballard's Court Circular', printed within *Ambit* no. 37 (1968) as opposed to the back cover, pushed his experimentation with printed language to its furthest point.[66] Contemporaneous with experiments in concrete and sound poetry, the columns of monosyllabic words recall the work of Bob Cobbing or Edwin Morgan. Evocative of regurgitated reams of computing processing data, the words themselves, such as 'LOVE', 'FUCK', 'GIRL', 'HAIR', 'WIFE', 'SUCK', are ecstatic in their capitalised repetition and deliberate in their downward direction to images of alluring female bodies. Language itself is eroticised, actions and exclamations marshalled behind a stylised printed façade much like the seductive postures below. Noting in 1969 that 'advertising was an unknown continent as far as the writer was concerned', Ballard had clearly begun to make its central tenets more manifest in his fiction.[67]

In the closing years of the 1960s, Ballard's writing took on an increasingly excisional, 'non-linear' and 'quantified' style.[68] The only work Ballard published as a book during this time was *The Atrocity Exhibition* (1970), written between 1967 and 1969. Ballard had conceived of *Atrocity* as a large-format graphic book and experimented with pictorial interjections in several earlier versions of the stories.[69] Described variously as 'a literary collage', 'prose blocks' and an 'elaborate collage novel', *Atrocity* is the most complete expression of Ballard's iconoclastic 'speculative fiction' of the 1960s.[70] It was 'not a novel', nor was it 'just a collection of stories', but rather an incendiary sequence of 'condensed' passages, subdivided into subtitled paragraphs reminiscent of newspaper articles, which imagine asylums, wreckages, warfare, sexual unions with politicians, the deaths of starlets, bodies as geometric planes, and the speed of newsreels. Designed from the material 'of years of thinking, imagining, living', 'evolving in a random sense' from lived experience and the media environment, 'Very important events were contracted' into its fifteen sections.[71] In a manner evocative of *Project for a New Novel*, these succinct titles are often enigmatic, obscure or incidental to the narrative that follows, complicating their status as prescriptive. Everything is suggestion, echoes, repetition, accrual: the 'modern mind is used to cutting', Ballard suggested in an interview with Alan Burns, adept at gleaning, skimming and extracting the details necessary to constitute an impression of the whole.[72] Relayed by the splintering personalities of the central character, Ballard fragmented the stories into subtitled paragraphs and frequently partitioned sentences into numbered or punctuated sections, so that each instant can be 'examined from a number of angles'.[73] This technique had made a debut of sorts in his first 'Advertiser's Announcement', 'Homage to Claire Churchill', itemising unrelated timely references in relation to the face of Claire Walsh, providing 'a set of operating formulae for their passage through consciousness'.[74] The female body appears to be particularly susceptible to this kind of disintegration or reassembly, terraced across the urban landscape or reconstituted from a 'Sex Kit':

> (1) Pad of pubic hair, (2) a latex face mask, (3) six detachable mouths, (4) a set of smiles, (5) a pair of breasts, left nipple marked by a small ulcer, (6) a set of non-chafe orifices, (7) photo cut-outs of a number of narrative situations – the girl doing this and that, (8) a list of dialogue samples, of inane chatter, (9) a set of noise levels, (10) descriptive techniques for a variety of sex acts, (11) a torn anal detrusor muscle, (12) a glossary of idioms and catchphrases, (13) an analysis of odour traces (from various vents), mostly purines etc., (14) a chart of body temperatures (axillary, buccal, rectal), (15) slides of vaginal smears, chiefly Ortho-Gynol jelly, (16) a set of blood pressures, systolic 120, diastolic 70 rising to 200/150 at onset of orgasm. . . .[75]

The clinical indexicality of lists such as the above, with their telescopic zooms into detail and the self-consciousness of their enumeration, are exercises in 'free association' that swell in the scrutiny of them. The lists are not always numbered, more frequently finding expression through the punctuation of colons, semicolons and dashes, with vignettes construed from these accretions of interlocking postures, settings, citations. Ballard suggested in his 'Author's Note' that the reader should 'simply turn the pages until a paragraph catches your eye. If the ideas or images seem interesting, scan the nearby paragraphs for anything that resonates in an intriguing way,'[76] in much the same way as 'This is Tomorrow' encouraged viewers to 'play with signs' and engage in the 'multi-channelled activity' of their environment. Ballard's language is overwhelmed by the attempt to keep pace with the rate of development, new lexical collisions wrought by words such as 'Neoplasm', 'Autogeddon', 'Cinecity'. As noted by one of the book's most perceptive interlocutors, William Burroughs, the 'magnification of image to the point where it becomes unrecognisable is a key note of *The Atrocity Exhibition*'.[77] *Atrocity* compels the reader to look into the 'fog' of reality, to bear witness to the 'multiple images ... that swamp our retinas', poorly prepared though that look might be.[78] By '*blowing up* the image', as Burroughs mentions, in the same way as 'combines' artist Robert Rauschenberg, or the dramatic expansion of vision signalled by the Cinemascope camera and the roadside billboard, Ballard frustrates the ability of the reader to see easily or fully, in order to exceed the illusion of experience, and the novel, as a totalising whole.[79] Where did this deliberate frustration of the gaze leave Ballard's fiction at the close of the decade?

'remorselessly visual': Designing Stupefaction at the End of the 1960s[80]

Beginning the decade with stories such as 'The Overloaded Man' (1961), in which the protagonist cultivates a 'talent' to blur and 'obliterate' the appliances, billboards, consumer goods and 'over-associated' status symbols from his visual field, Ballard, by the end of the decade, had acquired an uncompromising vision, one that sought to overwhelm and to confound the eye.[81] Visual intractability was a tendency that Ballard and Paolozzi shared, a thread common in their attempts to broaden the scope of visual and literary representation. As Paolozzi noted in 1971 of their common objectives, 'We're both involved with forcing people to look and with preventing them from escaping from certain facts.'[82] In 1969, Paolozzi had been commissioned by Ballard and Bax to perform his own experiments with the form of the novel: 'WHY WE ARE IN VIETNAM: A Novel' and 'THINGS: A Novel', published in two consecutive issues of *Ambit* (40, 41). The two volumes of the 'planned long novel sequence' were more didactic and solemn in tone in comparison to the playful layouts, journalese and nostalgic turns of his first collage work for *Ambit*, 'MOONSTRIPS– GENERAL DYNAMIMC F.U.N.'[83] The novels are visual essays, assembling photographs, advertisements, columns of text, newspaper cartoons, statistics of youth satisfaction and articulation defects, to build a nexus of impressions that, primarily, criticise the bellicosity of American culture and its willingness to believe in its own frontier myth.[84] Their explicit nature – depictions of rape, waste, weaponry, devastation, hospital beds, grinning politicians, all establishing their own plot lines – elicits the eye of the reader, but also acknowledges the surface tension presented by the revelation of discomforting realities. More than this, in a mode comparable to *Atrocity*, they convey a world of accelerated perception: the transportability of the items and the sudden shifts in ocular register create a dynamic, flickering impermanence.

In this way, by the close of the 1960s, Ballard had anticipated Fredric Jameson's discussion of video, which he considered to have instigated an epistemic break with modernism to produce the consummate postmodernist 'text', the 'video-text', as a 'sign flow which resists meaning'.[85] 'What happens if you regard the whole of reality as a vast video game?' Ballard asked himself in an undated note, answering, you get the 'overheated realm' of *The Atrocity Exhibition*.[86] Considered by critics to be the termination point of the twentieth-century late modernist novel, video was considered by Fredric Jameson to be the 'artform [. . .] *par excellence*' of late capitalism.[87] *Atrocity* foretold the discursive chaos of the information age. Increased exposure to moving image, to television, film, newsreels, heralded a 'death of affect', an alienation from direct experience, a hypothesis that continued to steer his work into radical new forms in the ensuing years.[88] At the close of the decade, Ballard had not yet adopted the unblinking stare redolent of his novels of the 1970s, nor the stunned gaze that characterised a collaborative sequence of 'apocalyptic texts' published in *Ambit* from 1976 to 1979: 'The Invisible Years', in which the interminable matrices of modern architecture mirrored the futile quest to fix meaning.[89] However, his fiction was on the cusp of making one of its most radical leaps, from the printed page to the sculptural form. In his 1970 exhibition of 'new sculptures' at the New Arts Lab, 'Crashed Cars', Ballard found the ultimate contraction of his fictional concepts, into the buckled bodywork of a Mini, Pontiac and A40.

In the same way that *Project for a New Novel* was a typographical testbed, training the eye of its author in the manipulation of information and his reader, so too was the exhibition a space of trial, to witness psychological responses when confronted by the spectacular. Inside the 'enormous novel' of the mid-sixties, visual modes of storytelling, 'cassette and videotape fictions', had acquired an ever more aggressive visible presence.[90] All writing could do now was to continue to probe these new ways of seeing, to provide new methodologies for the discovery of contemporary reality.

Notes

1. J. G. Ballard, 'Speculative Illustrations: Eduardo Paolozzi in Conversation with J. G. Ballard', *Studio International*, 183:937 (1971), pp. 136–43, p. 141. Ballard published 'Prima Belladonna', *Science Fantasy* (December 1956), and 'Escapement', *New Worlds* (December 1956).
2. Lawrence Alloway, 'Design as a Human Activity', *This is Tomorrow*, ed. Theo Crosby (London: Whitechapel Art Gallery, 1956), n.p.
3. Ibid.
4. See Catherine Spencer, 'The Independent Group's "Anthropology of Ourselves"', *British Art in the Cultural Field 1939–1969*, ed. Lisa Tickner and David Peters Corbett (Oxford: Blackwell, 2012), pp. 117–37.
5. Kenneth Martin discusses 'dynamic equivalence' in 'Architecture, Machine and Mobile', *Arts and Architecture*, 73 (1956), p. 34. See Alastair Grieve, '"This is Tomorrow", a Remarkable Exhibition Born from Contention', *The Burlington Magazine*, 136:1093 (1994), pp. 225–32.
6. Lawrence Alloway, 'The Robot and the Arts', *Art News and Review*, 8:16 (1 September 1956).
7. Ballard, 'Nothing is Real, Everything is Fake: Interview with Hans Ulrich Obrist', *Extreme Metaphors: Collected Interviews* (London: Fourth Estate, 2014), pp. 383–95, p. 385.
8. See Anne Massey, *The Independent Group: Modernism and Mass Culture in Britain 1945–1959* (Manchester: Manchester University Press, 1995).
9. Mark Wigley, 'Network Fever', *Grey Room*, 4 (2001), pp. 82–122, p. 107.
10. Reyner Banham, 'The Gutenberg Backlash', *New Society*, 10 July 1969, p. 63.
11. Ibid.
12. Ballard, 'Speculative Illustrations', p. 141.
13. Ballard, 'J. G. Ballard', *The Imagination on Trial*, ed. Alan Burns and Charles Sugnet (London: Allison and Busby, 1981), pp. 15–30, p. 30.

14. Martin Bax, 'Interview with Martin Bax', *RE/Search: JG Ballard*, 8/9 (San Francisco: V/Search Publications, 1984), pp. 36–9, p. 39.
15. Five of these double-page spreads remain, four of which are in the Papers of James Graham Ballard 1931–2010, Western Manuscripts, British Library, Add. MS. 88938/3/3, sheets A–D. In 2008, Ballard revealed that 'there were originally many more pages than seem to have survived'. Rick McGrath, 'J. G. Ballard's Graphic Experiments', available at <http://www.jgballard.ca/criticism/experimental_fiction.html> (last accessed 18 July 2018).
16. Ballard, 'From Shanghai to Shepperton', *The Profession of Science Fiction*, ed. Maxim Jakubowski and Edward James (London: Macmillan, 1992), pp. 44–72, p. 65.
17. Ballard, quoted in 'Martin Bax', p. 38.
18. Daniel Buren's 'affichage sauvage' was mounted at 53 Shaftesbury Avenue in 1972.
19. An author photograph dated 1960 shows Ballard standing before the *Project* displays in his garden.
20. J. G. Ballard, 'Project for a New Novel', *New Worlds*, 213 (1978).
21. Ballard, quoted in 'Martin Bax', p. 38.
22. Ibid.
23. Ballard, 'From Shanghai to Shepperton', p. 62.
24. Ballard, *Miracles of Life: An Autobiography* (London: Harper Perennial, 2008), p. 190.
25. Rick Poynor, 'Project for a New Novel', *Eye*, 23:6 (1996), n.p.
26. Ballard, *Project for a New Novel* (c.1958), Add. MS. 88938/3/3, sheets A–D.
27. Ibid.
28. Ballard, *Miracles of Life*, p. 185.
29. Terry Wilson, 'Brion Gysin', *RE/Search*, 4/5 (San Francisco: V/Search Publications, 1982), pp. 39–43, p. 41.
30. Anon., 'Novels in Eclipse', *The Times*, 22 August 1950, p. 5.
31. B. S. Johnson, *Albert Angelo* (London: Constable, 1964), p. 169.
32. In 1959, Brion Gysin announced 'Writing is 50 years behind painting.' See William Burroughs and Brion Gysin, *The Third Mind* (New York: Viking Press, 1978), p. 34.
33. Ballard, 'Which Way to Inner Space?', *A User's Guide to the Millennium: Essays and Reviews* (London: Flamingo, 1997), pp. 195–8, p. 197.
34. Ibid.
35. Ibid.
36. Ballard often omitted *The Wind From Nowhere* from lists of published works. See David Pringle, 'Interviews Part 2', 4 January 1975, available at <http://www.solaris-books.co.uk/Ballard/Pages/Miscpages/interview4b.htm> (last accessed 18 July 2018).
37. Ballard, 'An Interview with J. G. Ballard', *J. G. Ballard, The First 20 Years*, ed. J. Goddard and D. Pringle (Middlesex: Bran's Head, 1976), pp. 5–35, p. 9.

38. Ballard, 'The Coming of the Unconscious', *A User's Guide*, pp. 84–8, p. 84.
39. Ballard, *The Drowned World* (London: Victor Gollancz, 1962), p. 29; *The Crystal World* (London: Jonathan Cape, 1966), p. 13; *The Drought* (London: Jonathan Cape, 1965), p. 147.
40. Dan O'Hara, 'Interview with J. G. Ballard', *Munich Round-Up*, 100 (1968), pp. 104–6, p. 104.
41. Ballard, 'Speculative Illustrations', p. 136.
42. Ballard, 'J. G. Ballard', *The Imagination on Trial*, p. 20.
43. Ballard, 'Speculative Illustrations', p. 136.
44. J. G. Ballard, 'Fictions of Every Kind', *Books and Bookmen*, 16:5 (1971), pp. 11, 64, 11.
45. Ballard, 'J. G. Ballard', *The Imagination on Trial*, p. 22.
46. See Ballard, 'Which Way to Inner Space?', *New Worlds*, 40:118 (1962), pp. 2–3, pp. 116–88; and Lynn Barber, 'Sci-fi Seer', *Penthouse*, 5:5 (1970), pp. 26–30.
47. Ballard, *Miracles of Life*, p. 189.
48. Ballard, 'Fictions of Every Kind', p. 64.
49. Ibid.
50. David Brittain, 'Introduction', *The Jet Age Compendium: Paolozzi at Ambit* (London: Four Corners Books, 2009), pp. 1–23, p. 9.
51. See Malcolm Bradbury, *The Social Context of Modern English Literature* (Oxford: Blackwell, 1971).
52. See Elizabeth Stainforth, '"The Logic of the Visible at the Service of the Invisible": Reading Invisible Literature in *The Atrocity Exhibition*', in *J. G. Ballard: Landscapes of Tomorrow*, ed. Richard Brown, Christopher Duffy and Elizabeth Stainforth (London: Brill, 2016), pp. 99–111.
53. Ballard, *The Pleasure of Reading*, ed. Antonia Fraser (London: Bloomsbury, 2015), pp. 88–95, p. 94.
54. Lawrence Alloway, 'Paolozzi and the Comedy of Waste', *Cimaise*, 7:4 (1960), p. 122.
55. Ibid.
56. Ballard, 'Speculative Illustrations', p. 143.
57. J. G. Ballard, *'Shanghai Jim'* (BBC documentary, dir. James Runcie, 1990).
58. Eduardo Paolozzi, *The Metallization of a Dream* (London: John Munday, 1963), p. 5.
59. John-Paul Stonard, 'The "Bunk" Collages of Eduardo Paolozzi', *The Burlington Magazine* (2008), pp. 238–49. See Rosemary Miles, *The Complete Prints of Eduardo Paolozzi: Prints, Drawings, Collages 1944–77* (London: Victoria and Albert Museum, 1977), and Hal Foster on the meaning of 'bunk' in *The First Pop Age* (Princeton: Princeton University Press, 2014), p. 261.
60. Ballard, *Miracles of Life*, p. 189.

61. Ibid. p. 208.
62. Ibid. p. 209.
63. Ibid.
64. Ballard, 'An Interview with J. G. Ballard', *Speculation*, 21 (1969), pp. 4–8, p. 5.
65. Rick Poynor, 'The Conceptual Advertising of J. G. Ballard', *Design Observer*, 14 April 2014, available at <https://designobserver.com/feature/the-conceptual-advertising-of-jg-ballard/38432> (last accessed 18 July 2018).
66. Referred to as an 'advertisement' in *Ambit*, 37 (1968).
67. Ballard, 'An Interview with J. G. Ballard', p. 5.
68. J. G. Ballard and George MacBeth, 'The New Science Fiction', *The New SF*, ed. Langdon Jones (London: Hutchinson, 1969), pp. 46–54, pp. 46–7.
69. See 'The Summer Cannibals', *New Worlds*, 186 (1969).
70. Andrzej Gąsiorek, *J. G. Ballard* (Manchester: Manchester University Press, 2005), p. 58; Roger Luckhurst, *Science Fiction* (Cambridge: Polity, 2005), p. 150; Jeannette Baxter, *J. G. Ballard's Surrealist Imagination* (London: Routledge, 2006), p. 69.
71. Ballard, 'J. G. Ballard', *The Imagination on Trial*, p. 21.
72. Ibid. p. 24.
73. Ballard, 'The New Science Fiction', p. 53.
74. Ballard, *The Atrocity Exhibition* (London: Harper Perennial, 2006), p. 13.
75. Ibid. p. 84.
76. Ballard, 'Author's Note', *The Atrocity Exhibition*.
77. William Burroughs, 'Preface', *The Atrocity Exhibition*, rev. edn (San Francisco: RE/Search Publications, 1990), p. 7.
78. Ballard, 'Walt Disney on Dope', *The Guardian*, 23 June 1989, p. 27.
79. Burroughs, 'Preface', p. 7.
80. Martin Amis, 'JG Ballard: From Outer Space to Inner Space', *The Guardian*, 25 April 2009, available at <https://www.theguardian.com/books/2009/apr/25/jg-ballard-martin-amis> (last accessed 18 July 2018).
81. J. G. Ballard, 'The Overloaded Man', *New Worlds*, 36:108 (1961), pp. 28–40.
82. Paolozzi, 'Speculative Illustrations', p. 142.
83. Brittain, 'Introduction', p. 16.
84. Ibid.
85. Fredric Jameson, 'Reading Without Interpretation: Postmodernism and the Video-Text', *The Linguistics of Writing: Arguments Between Language and Literature*, ed. Nigel Fabb, Derek Attridge, Alan Durant and Colin McCabe (Manchester: Manchester University Press, 1987), pp. 199–223, p. 223.
86. Ballard, Add. MS. 88938/3/7/2, ff. 3, n.d.
87. Patricia Waugh, *Metafiction* (London: Routledge, 1984), pp. 147–8.

88. Ballard, 'Speculative Illustrations', p. 137.
89. One of 'The Invisible Years' images, by the artist Ron Sandford, adorns the cover of this very book.
90. Ballard, 'Fictions of Every Kind', p. 205.

Chapter 8

Ann Quin: 'infuriating' Experiments?
Nonia Williams

Response to the publication of Quin's *The Unmapped Country: Stories & Fragments* (2018) has rightly aimed to bring about a renaissance of interest in her work, as well as in that of other British avant-garde writers of the 1960s (such as those included in this collection).[1] While this chapter participates in and contributes to such recuperation, in terms of renewed positive critical attention, I also want to take seriously some of the contemporaneous, more negative responses to the work – such as the claim (cited above) that Quin's writing might be considered 'infuriating'.[2] Rather than rejecting or overwriting such criticism, this chapter considers how instead it might help us towards a useful critical terminology for thinking about Quin. My aim is not to deny or obscure the achievements of her writing, or the pleasures of reading it, but to read against the grain of a solely celebratory response, in order to insist on the importance of attending to its more 'negative' effects and affects: boredom, frustration and infuriation. In this, my work draws on Sianne Ngai's *Ugly Feelings* (2005), in particular her aim to, as Ngai puts it, recuperate 'dysphoric' or 'negative affects for their *critical* productivity', without either romanticising them or denying their radical potential.[3] Thus, my readings of *Berg* (1964), *Three* (1966) and *Passages* (1969) below attend to Quin's writing's potentially aggravated, impatient and tiresome reading effects and affects, to argue that acknowledging the reader's dysphoria has the potential to complicate and nuance our critical responses to her work.

While her first book, *Berg*, was hailed as '[m]urkily original and menacing', 'promis[ing] a talent likely to develop in strength',[4] *Passages*, Quin's own favourite, took the experimentation in a direction many readers and reviewers found hard to follow. 'I gave up halfway through', 'a short discouraging book, which is almost certainly important, and just the thing for the French', one wrote.[5] In such responses, Quin is being criticised, on the one hand, for pursuing formal novelty, and on the other, for being piecemeal, inauthentic, derivative of the 'new-wavers its author had obviously read in her own publisher's translations' and 'self-indulgent' directors such as Antonioni.[6] At the same time, her debt to literary and cinematic movements such as the *nouveau roman*, *nouvelle vague* and American experimentalism gained her a place among 1960s British avant-garde writers, evidenced, for example, by her membership of the 'Writers Reading' 'collective'.[7] Although diverse, this group were united by 'a profound interest in prose as a form of expression and not simply as a medium for storytelling'.[8] In 1973, shortly before both of their premature deaths, B. S. Johnson named Quin as among those 'writing as though it mattered, as though they meant it, as though they meant it to matter'.[9] Such writers, he said, refused the 'stultifyingly philistine [. . .] general book culture of this country' and sought refuge in the imaginary of the continental avant-garde.[10] Similarly, Giles Gordon put Quin in the same category as 'Beckett, Burroughs, Creeley, Duras, Claude Mauriac, Henry Miller, Pinget, Robbe-Grillet, Sarraute'.[11] However, like many of her milieu, Quin's escalating desire to test the possibilities of 'prose as a form of expression' increasingly distanced her from the 'general book culture' of 1960s Britain. Indeed, Johnson rightly observed that '"Experimental" to most reviewers is almost always a synonym for "unsuccessful".'[12]

However, while Johnson himself, among many others, rejected the term, my reading finds 'experimental' more useful for describing the techniques and aesthetics of Quin's writing than 'avant-garde', particularly in light of John Cage's emphasis on process: 'the word "experimental" is apt [when] understood not as descriptive of an act to be later judged in terms of success and failure, but simply as of an act the outcome of which is unknown'.[13] It seems to me that Quin's intertextual and reiterative prose is deliberately risky and provocatively eclectic; like Cage's, her process is 'inclusive rather than exclusive', encompassing a wide range of source materials and textual forms, the patterns and connections between them sometimes haphazard and incidental, the effects unknown.[14] In 1972, Alan Burns described Quin's methods thus:

> Ann's writing contains areas of shadow, inhabited by shadow images, areas of association, which slip further and further away from the text. She has this talent for throwing off ripples of association, and that's very fine, it's her best quality, her subconscious quality.[15]

Here, Burns identifies the elusive, slippery, slipping-away property of the writing, which works both to include and to throw off ripples of association. Indeed, the letters, short stories and books of the 1960s are crafted out of numerous and divergent repetitions within and outside of themselves. For example, the word 'shadowing' itself ripples across the writing – in 'Never Trust a Man who Bathes with His Finger Nails' (1968), 'cloud shadows [gather] speed across the valley';[16] in *Passages*, the '[r]ain walked designing its own shadow'.[17] In turn, this echoes a phrase from one of Quin's letters to her then lover Robert Sward: '[s]ometimes it is enough to watch the rain walk designing its own shadow'.[18] This is writing where intra- and intertextuality are deliberately evident, which is 'experimental' precisely because the connections and ripples of association are in flux and the outcome(s), or effects, are necessarily unknown, created by a play of associations and part-repetitions that the reader may or may not 'get'.

My readings of Quin in this chapter are particularly interested in this *inclusive* experimental quality of the writing, in its processes of setting-associations-in-motion or, as Deleuze and Guattari put it, of what they call 'Strange Anglo-American literature'[19], this 'tracing flows and causing them to circulate'.[20] My analyses of *Berg*, *Three* and *Passages* therefore consider the effects of the inclusion of intertexts, in order to show how source materials work both to place limits on and to energise the writing, sitting sometimes ironically, uncomfortably or seemingly undigested within Quin's prose. Such intertexts work to create the potential difficulty and unease of the reading process by frustrating expectations of progression, linearity, originality, coherence, closure and so on. In *Passages* in particular, such material often works to infuriate, rather than orientate, the reader. My readings suggest that taking such dysphoric responses seriously might help us to navigate and articulate the experience of reading Quin in such a way that works with, rather than denies, some of the difficult, and perhaps problematic, elements of the writing. In this way, I argue for the critical energy and usefulness of declaring Quin's inclusive intertextual experiments dysphoric and 'infuriating'.

Berg

Although it is a text whose dark comedy of procrastination and agonised existential angst were directly influenced by Quin's reading of Beckett and Sartre, the most explicit intertext in *Berg* is the Oedipus myth: 'A man called Berg, who changed his name to Greb, came to a seaside town intending to kill his father . . . .'[21] So *Berg* opens on a separate page before the narrative begins, and in the narrative that follows, the protagonist, a man called Alistair Berg but posing as one named Greb, does indeed go to a seaside town apparently intending to find and kill his father, Nathaniel. This parricidal drive, motivated by the desire to please or win his mother, Edith, deliberately repeats and parodies the basics of, for example, Sophocles' *Oedipus Rex*. Oedipus echoes elsewhere in Quin's work: 'At eighteen I went up to London to spend Saturdays with my father (he had left my mother when I was ten) and pretended he was my lover,' she writes in 'Leaving School' (1966);[22] and the story 'Every Cripple Has His Own Way of Walking' (1966) figures both the repulsion towards and longing for the father.[23] In *Berg*, the Oedipal quest is characterised by a longing not only to kill, but also somehow to have – and even to become – the father. Having arrived at the seaside town, the disguised 'Aly Greb' finds himself an attic room (next door to, and divided by only a thin partition from, his father and his father's lover, Judith, it emerges). Here, living in squalor and on a pittance, he procrastinates with an ultimately unrealised plan to kill his father; in place of Nathaniel's death are a series of hesitant, agonised parricidal failures, where Berg instead kills Judith's cat, Seby, possibly strangles Nathaniel's budgie, Berty, and actually does 'strangle' his father's ventriloquist's dummy in a farcical case of presumed mistaken identity.

While, in *Oedipus Rex*, Oedipus' ignorance is juxtaposed with the audience's knowledge, in *Berg* familiarity with Oedipus not only is assumed in the reader, it is made explicit by the protagonist himself:

> Such an absurd, fantastic idea: To take his father's corpse back home to Edith – the trophy of his triumphant love for her! In a Greek play they'd have thought nothing of it, considered to have been a duty, the final act of what the gods expected from their chosen hero.[24]

Yes, Berg apparently desires his father's corpse to demonstrate triumphant love for his mother and thereby become the hero of his own life but, the narrative implies, while supposedly in 'a Greek play they'd have thought nothing of it', here the idea cannot be taken seriously. The protagonist is aware of the temptation to interpret, to psychoanalyse even, his own 'story' in terms of Oedipus, but at the same time such a reading is exposed as 'absurd, fantastic'. In this, the narrative simultaneously 'speaks' and denies the legitimacy of its appropriation of Oedipus: Berg himself, as much as the reader, recognises and appreciates the Oedipal 'joke'. This joke comes from the refusal of Oedipus as the norm, concurrent with the inability to escape from it. In this way, the myth, as a knowing re-enactment of a re-enactment, is offered as a frame for reading at the same time as this is exposed as a limited interpretative tool. For some, such as Dulan Barber, Quin's editor, 'the Oedipal bones of *Berg*' were 'set together with such astonishing individuality that they positively rattle for attention'.[25] For other readers, it may be that the endless deferral of Oedipal action, together with how the Oedipal frame seems to structure and guide but actually frustrates and ironises the possibility of narrative progression and readerly interpretation, is an infuriating rather than (or even as well as) an enjoyable, humorous experience. As I demonstrate below in my more extended reading of *Passages*, such an experimental technique, which explicitly includes intertextual material but without giving a clear sense of its role or significance (or not), or the relationship between source texts and Quin's own writing, has the effect of interrupting and frustrating the reading process. But first I turn my attention to *Three*, in order to consider further how Quin's inclusive experimental techniques might work to resist and interrupt, or even halt, narrative progression.

Three

A man fell to his death from a sixth-floor window of Peskett House, an office-block in Sellway square today.
He was a messenger employed by a soap manufacturing firm.

Ruth startled from the newspaper by Leonard framed in the doorway. Against the white-washed wall. A wicker arm-chair opposite the Japanese table. Screen. Sliding doors. Rush matting. A mirror extended the window. Gardens. A bronzed cockerel faced the house.
What's the latest then? Fellow thrown himself out of a window. Ghastly way to choose. But Leon hers wasn't like that – I mean we can't really be sure could so easily have been an accident the note just a melodramatic touch. No one can be blamed Ruth we must understand that least of all ourselves.[26]

Three begins with the fragment of a newspaper report about an unnamed 'man [who] fell to his death from a sixth-floor window'. The fragment itself seems alternately shocking – 'fell to his death' – and absurd – 'employed by a soap manufacturing firm', in its mixture of specific and incongruous detail. This is juxtaposed with a narrative giving precise and vivid but isolated physical details of the domestic space that the book's protagonists Ruth and Leonard are in, before it slips – without speech markers, qualifiers or conventional punctuation – into their interpretation of the man's death as suicide: 'Fellow thrown himself out of a window. Ghastly way to choose.' From discussion of this death, conversation moves on to 'hers' which 'wasn't like that'. This other death, of an unnamed woman who nevertheless seems significant due to the intimacy implied by the non-specific pronoun, also 'could so easily have been an accident'. Yet the fact of the 'note' and the anxiety about blame imply it was not. Further, the absence of commas in the phrase 'we must understand that least of all ourselves' interrupts comprehension as to whether it is the blame that can be attributed to them least of all or the understanding. Like *Berg*, then, this book's opening seems to offer clues about the narrative to come, but instead of the structuring frame of a mythic intertext (however much of a red herring that storyline turns out to be), here uncertainty and death are announced as the destabilising core of the text, as well as the key problem of interpretation: 'I mean we can't really be sure'.

The disorientated and unresolved effect outlined above is an example of the wider experience of reading *Three*, where the process of attempting to navigate the text is continually disrupted and complicated by an overlapping, composite collage of different narrative forms. As well as the evasive form of the third-person narrative sections, to read *Three* is to read the three (Leonard, Ruth and the missing dead woman, 'S') protagonists' written diaries and 'listen' to the free verse of a diary transcript. The resulting combination of poetry, prose and lists makes the form of this book even more consciously 'experimental' than *Berg*, in which the majority of the narrative is told through free indirect slippage between first- and third-person perspectives. The narratives of both books refuse the possibility of closure, play with questions of narrative perspective and include multiple voices, but in *Three* questions of perspective and narrative progress are further complicated and frustrated by the juxtaposition of and movement between distinctly different textual forms. The narrative moves between unconventional third-person free indirect narrative, such as that evidenced in the example above, and journal sections including small excerpts from Leonard's diary – in the form of a minimalist record of 'facts' – and a page or so of Ruth's anxious prose, as well as large sections of S's journals which appear as free verse on the page. Although the journal texts are presented one after the other across the book, and so are read in series, the partial repetition and overlap across different journal sections interrupt and resist any sense of chronology or progression, and instead the reader is presented with a collection of multiple and sometimes contradictory versions of the same events without a steer as to which, if any, might be the more 'reliable'.²⁷

The experimental collage method of *Three* thus results in a kind of circling and interrupted reading process. This refusal of progression and the frustration of attempts at interpretation and understanding at work in Quin's text can, it seems to me, usefully be thought about further by considering *Three*'s inclusive experimental collage form in light of one of its key intertexts, the *nouvelle vague* film *Last Year in Marienbad* (1960), written by Alain Robbe-Grillet and directed by Alain Resnais.²⁸ The film contains performances that are so slowed and stylised as to become fetishised: similarly, in the book there is a particular emphasis on the visual, on scenes which appear as frozen images rather than dynamic spaces. Both narratives are told through highly ambiguous flashbacks or versions of events and disorientating shifts of time and location: in both, different characters' versions of events are irreconcilable, and these competing imaginaries and voices deliberately complicate and frustrate the desire for understanding. As I have suggested above, this effect is evoked in the book by the plurality of written forms, which actively prohibit the creation of a coherent or master narrative of events. In both film and book, the confused and resistant aesthetic effects are exacerbated by the ways that characterisation is excluded in favour of performance and how conversation is staged. In *Three*, this is particularly visible in the narrative's strange momentum and uncanny characterisation. In the third-person narrative sections – as with the party or group scenes in the film – domestic scenes between Leonard and Ruth are strangely still and unreal. This is contrasted and made more noticeable by the interruptions of erratic acceleration. Often, a slow and dreamy scene-setting – 'Each held a corner of the room, cigarette smoke formed a screen between them' – is interrupted by mania:

> They brought their chairs together when the television programmes started. She commented on women announcers' clothes. He shifted around into more uncomfortable positions, hugged his knees, burst into sudden loud laughter. She knitted faster, dropped several stitches. There look what you've made me do I don't see anything very funny in that. For a time he froze into one position, the flash of television and candles darted over him.²⁹

The composition of such scenes is strange and unsettling. The dead-pan and 'neutral' narration – 'they brought', 'she commented', 'he shifted', 'she knitted' and so on – renders the characters' actions mechanical and almost meaningless. They are dehumanised: still lives frozen and devoid of life one minute, barking out meaningless sound the next. The action in the scene – Leonard's shifting into uncomfortable positions and Ruth's accelerated knitting – is jerky; their 'noise' – his 'sudden loud laughter', her bitchy commentary – frenetic. Here, specifically with the knitting, where Ruth speeds up and drops several stitches, the form, textuality and crafting of the writing process, as well as the slippery knottiness of the reading and interpreting experience, are dramatised. Reduced, as they are, to caricatures or automata, it is impossible to forget that Leonard and Ruth are unreal. (Their representation here bears striking similarities to the dream-like appearance and automatic motions of the guests at the hotel in *Marienbad*.) The knitting and automata both write the constructedness of the narrative large, and, as a result, infuriate and refuse an affective engagement that feels satisfying because it has the illusion of feeling 'positive' or 'deep'. In this way, the multiple textual forms and emphasis on surface in *Three* create an unease that precisely comes about from the dissatisfaction of reading impenetrable surfaces and irreconcilable narratives. Thus, the intra- and intertextual inclusive experimentation of *Three* works to disorientate and frustrate – or infuriate – the reading process in a way that is more complex and dysphoric than *Berg*. At the same time, as I have shown, such a response is critically productive because it enables us to attend to the text's difficulty and complexity without feeling the need to suppress, overwrite or feel comfortable with it.

Passages

Saturday
So let us begin another journey. Change the setting. Everything is changing, the country, the climate. There is no compromise now. No country we can return to. She still has her obsession to follow through and her fantasies to live out. For myself there is less of an argument. I am for the moment committed to this moment. This train. The distance behind and ahead. And the sea that soon perhaps we will cross.[30]

Quin's third and final book of the 1960s, *Passages*, ends with a 'distance behind and ahead' to 'begin another journey'. However, this is both provisional – 'I am for the moment committed to this moment' – and uncertain – 'the sea that soon perhaps we will cross'. *Passages* is a narrative always in transit across and through different passages of text and this journeying leads the writing (and reader) on towards an endpoint or resolution ever absent and deferred. Its storyline follows a woman and man's quest onward and across a Mediterranean landscape, in a search of her lost brother. The book is divided into four sections, which shift alternately between two perspectives: broadly, those of the woman and man. Her narrative is an impressionistic account of the sensory experiences along the way, his an annotated journal. The woman's sections are formed of an interconnected chain of transitional passages that mimic, but are often in fact not, paragraphs; the material in them is not necessarily coherent or connected, and they are markedly incomplete, often broken off mid-sentence, to be continued in the passage below. This episodic form creates a simultaneous stasis and momentum, a stop–start from one arbitrary place or point in the narrative to another. In contrast, the man's journal sections do not so much narrate the passing of time as cross and mediate between different viewpoints and ideas. Notes, reported speech, recorded dreams, cut-up techniques, sections taken from source material and diary entries are placed in parallel, side by side in columns on the page. The result is that various types of text are co-present on the page, in parataxis and without clear interconnection. Such a layout means that the possibility is denied not only for a coherent, stable narrative perspective, but also for a familiar or linear reading action. Instead, the eye must track back and forth between the columns of text, to try to work out possible relationships between them, while the very format of placing texts side by side means that the possibilities for multiple meanings are always explicitly present. While the momentum of the book's title, together with the search storyline, seems to connect disparate ideas or pieces of text, what exactly that connection is remains deliberately and frustratingly unresolved.

The writing in the woman's sections of *Passages* is characterised by slippage and continuity across the line of words:

> His hands round the glass, veins pressed under hairs, lighter from cuffs to knuckles. Hands above his head, marking the design of some unfamiliar birds. Slant of wings to the slant of their bodies under, caught the light of falling. They turned from a straight course into a curved one, remained at the same height, wings on the convex side of their curving movements, moved in line. Lines
>
>   under his eyes, mouth. His mouth betrayed the eyes' attention on the play we saw that night.[31]

This section moves around, under, above, under, between man and birds. Across the trajectory of the words the two become closely associated, the line(s) slanting, falling, straight, curved, moving together.

The connecting instance, when the man's action mimics the movement of the birds, is proliferated by repetitions and patterns in the language. However, the seemingly chance gesture that connects them – 'hands above his head, marking the design of some familiar birds' – is also one which marks and declares the text's design and fabrication. The birds move in an ordered chain, they turn and slant; so too does the line of words that moves with and weaves around them. Furthermore, this focus on the particular shapes of the birds' movement – 'slant of wings to the slant of their bodies' – announces a source text. In his notebooks, Leonardo da Vinci describes the structure of birds' wings in detail in terms of their anatomy and function during flight. He observes the 'lines of movements made by birds', saying that 'they enter the wind with a slanting movement from below and then place themselves slantwise upon the course of the wind'.[32] Quin herself said of da Vinci's notebooks:

> God wot fine things these are: beautiful descriptions [. . .]. Have actually taken notes down and used some of his descriptions in my own work, juxtapositioning the words (shhhhh you'll be the only ONE who'll know what a 'fraud' I really am!).[33]

Here, Quin admits to the eclectic inclusiveness of her experimental technique; sometimes patterning in her writing which might seem intratextual – where here the line of words coincides with and energises the line of the birds' flight, for example – is also, in fact, intertextual, borrowed from the words and images of another writer and artist. Unlike the overt and explicit presence of other intertexts in *Passages*, the inclusion of da Vinci is private, an intertext that Quin's reader may be aware of only if she chooses to share it. This insight not only gestures towards the sheer range of inclusive experimental processes, but also is, it seems to me, particularly useful for considering the reader's potential unease and infuriation when reading Quin's texts. It connects to Burns's remarks about the way ripples of association slip and echo across the writing. Perhaps, when some of the unexplained connections between texts or inconclusive and unresolved storylines *feel* excluding, when they snag and trouble the reading process, their dysphoric affect is because of our not being (or at least not feeling) party to the intertextual intimacy or in-joke.

However, at the same time, the detail of the description of man and birds in the extract above simultaneously seems transparent, as if communicating acute observation. Its *Times Literary Supplement* review praised *Passages* for precisely this kind of mimetic effect. For that reader, the 'juxtaposition of precisely caught experiences', together with 'the confused overall shape of the story', 'suggest exactly the reactions of the traveller whose senses acquire a new responsiveness to detail'.[34] And the woman's sections do primarily seem to be concerned with communicating observational detail. Out of a train window, she sees 'valleys grown wider, deeper, where rivers continually change their position. Bases of the hills bent back towards the course of the river. Lights, signs from cities, villages, towns I know only from maps, brochures'.[35] The resulting accumulation of minutiae seems to mimic the wide-eyed observations of a traveller, to be observant and descriptive of the detail of the outside world; at the same time, this apparent transparency is troubled and complicated – these hills are 'bent back'. To the attentive reader familiar with Quin, the crafting of the imagery is even more obvious. The woman also supposedly sees the '[r]ain walked designing its own shadow' out of the train window.[36] Moreover, the image of a shadow almost immediately then repeats: 'Shadow thrown on a long wall'.[37] As I mention in my introductory section, this phrase haunts Quin's letters and writing of the later 1960s – however, as with the da Vinci above, there is a sense in which such repetitions are for those 'in the know', rather than openly declared. The inclusion of these less visible intra- and intertexts may not interfere with a reading which, as in the review above, is struck by the vividness of Quin's acute details, but at the same time, this layering makes the writing uneven and imbues certain images or figures with apparent significance, as if aiding an interpretation and comfortable grasp of the text which is nevertheless never quite in sight.

Furthermore, the contrasting form of the man's diary requires a different reading direction; rather than following the line of words, the reader's eye must sidestep to and fro across, as well as down, the page. The structuring of these sections makes them ideal for considering questions of sequential readability and simultaneity.[38] The reading process here, then, is always necessarily frustrating / frustrated and difficult because of how the material resists familiar reading directions and processes (Fig. 8.1). As the eye passes to and fro, there are plenty of what seem to be connections between the two columns of text in this extract.[39] The annotations on the left do appear to comment on and give meaning to the memories narrated on the right, where the Jewish man recounts the experience of watching his mother dying. The accompanying notes in the margin include a description of a drawing which illustrates the sightless eye of a third siren, as well as the narrator's self-identification with the image of Bar-Lgura, an occult Semitic demon. In this way, the content of the parallels and sequencing

Drawing of third Siren's eye by two strokes only, without the pupil: the sightless eye, eye in death/sleep/blindness.	Sometimes she talks in her sleep. Names I don't know. Some secret language. She says I talk Hebrew in my sleep, yet I only know a few words in that language. There are moments when she looks at me startled, not really seeing me, perhaps thinking I am someone else. The walls shift in patterns, colour, shapes behind her head, and I think I am somewhere else. At home perhaps, when the murmurs are Mother's, made from her bed, the light shining from the kitchen, stopping in a blade of light at the foot
Image of myself as Bar-Lgura, the Semetic demon sitting on the roof and leaping down on them all.	of the bed. How I hated Mother then. Day after day (and nights, long nights) of pain. Windows closed, curtains pulled, thin-walled box rooms. Death, the smell of it, of sickness permeated everything. Nurses, doctors came and went, she thought were the family. I made her hot drinks, and thought of pissing in them. I wanted to

Figure 8.1 Ann Quin, *Passages* [1969] (Chicago: Dalkey Archive Press, 2003), p. 37.

here imply connections between, for example, the 'Drawing of a third Siren's eye', taken from a description in Jane Ellen Harrison's *Prolegomena to the Study of Greek Religion* (1903), and the mother's death.[40] Thus, we read the imagery and connotations of 'eye', 'sleep', 'blindness' and 'death' as if there are connections with the marginal notes and the journal text. But it remains unclear what the relationship between the marginal notes and journal entry here is meant to be, whether interpretative and meaningful, or randomly inclusive and incidental. Consequently, the reading processes, in terms of both the physical movements of the eye across the page and the desire to understand the text, remain frustrated and uncertain.

In addition, for some readers, the fact that many of the myths in the margins are comprised of close and unacknowledged paraphrasing of *Prolegomena* rendered *Passages* particularly derivative and problematic. Robert Nye, for example, objected that the book is 'too rigorously informed by' this source text, 'choice bits of which', he says, 'float about undigested in [Quin's] text'.[41] While this is an exaggeration, Nye's objection here perhaps has a point in terms of how Harrison's descriptions and interpretations of ancient Greek artefacts are indeed often taken out of context, and are always without the photographs and illustrations included in the source text. Instead, in *Passages*, the excerpts are placed side by side or one after the other alongside the man's journal entries, without their relevance, if there is any, being made clear. The reader is faced with texts which seem unrelated, and the simultaneity of the layout on the page demands that we 'improvise an order of reading' because we cannot ascertain one.[42] But even once the reader has improvised an order for reading these fragments of text, the narrative remains resistant and the reading is always an ambivalent one, where the possibility of unreadability remains present. A coincidence of ideas does not necessarily illuminate the content of either parallel text, and there are differences and irresolvable tensions which remind the reader that seeming connections may be nothing more than incidental juxtaposition. Indeed, throughout the man's journal sections the marginal notes tend to problematise, rather than aid, desire for narrative comprehension. And for many of the book's contemporaneous reviewers, such resistance – the book's 'parade of mystification' – was infuriating and discouraging, closing down the possibilities of reading and enjoyment.[43] One of these describes Quin as a writer who 'dearly loves obscurity': 'I was left here muddling through annotated diary passages, dream sequences, split paragraphs and all sorts of stylistic mannerisms. Miss Quin is a pioneer, but no clear trail is made for the reader to follow her.'[44] For others, negotiating the difficulties created by the man's journal sections was seen to result in a more energised reading experience. For one such reviewer, while the book is 'irritatingly opaque and elliptical', and the 'connexion between these [margin notes] and the entries themselves is often tenuous and unilluminating', 'the effect of the diary sections – even where it fails to explain motive or predicament in the ordinary sense – does suggest a different order of experience'.[45] This response to the man's journal sections of *Passages* expresses the frustrating and yet perhaps creative energy of attempting to read a text that resists the reader's desire for comprehensibility and instead demands a different order of reading that remains open and ambiguous. Even more so than the collage of texts across *Three*, *Passages* refuses the notion of a dominant narrative.

Furthermore, the inclusion of undigested source material from the most overt of *Passages*' intertexts, the *Prolegomena*, which by turns affronts, frustrates and energises the readers in the reviews above, is arguably a paramount and necessary element in Quin's development of her inclusive experimental processes, as well as for her writing's particular infuriating and dysphoric affects and effects. More so than in *Berg* or *Three*, the unresolved tensions of the appropriation, reiteration and incorporation of source texts in *Passages* are central to the book's method. On one hand, by incorporating and recontextualising

Harrison's own rereading of Greek myth, *Passages* seems to engage in ongoing traditions of rereading and reinterpretation. Harrison wrote the *Prolegomena* to redress 'a fundamental error in method'.[46] Her writing offered the first anthropological interpretation of Greek mythology, based on a search for the (hidden) patterns and meaning of artefacts, and in turn the practices and beliefs they delineate. As a result, the *Prolegomena* participates in a reinterpretation of Greek myths as 'modern' developments of older beliefs. Quin had also read H.D.'s *Helen in Egypt*, an avant-garde appropriation of a mythic story.[47] *Helen in Egypt* has an experimental paratactic structure somewhat similar to *Passages*: the sections of the book intersperse illustrative reasoning about Helen's situation with passages of poetry. These sections act in tension with each other: although there are similarities, they are also highly different in both content and form, and the relationship between the two remains unexplained.[48] However, while the *Prolegomena*, *Helen in Egypt* and *Passages* all work to free up source texts from static meaning, arguably in *Helen in Egypt* and *Passages* the inclusion of mythic source texts is not so much a retelling as a repositioning. According to Bruce Morrissette, the *nouveau roman* – of which Quin was an avid reader – appropriated mythic parallelism precisely to draw attention to processes of transition, narrative evolution, counterpoint and difference, rather than for purposes of connection and continuity.[49] As my analyses here have shown, reading *Passages* is difficult and frustrating because of its covert and overt inclusion of intertexts in such a way that, rather than enabling us to navigate the text, particularly disrupts and resists the reader's desire for orientation.

Beyond the 1960s

In a discussion of David Foster Wallace that is germane to my analysis of Quin, James Wood claims that the 'risky tautology' of his writing is a willingness to mangle and debase itself for the sake of its project.[50] Wood claims that Wallace's fiction 'prosecutes an intense argument about the decomposition of language in America', through a method that degrades and discomposes his own style 'in the interests of making us live through this linguistic America with him'.[51] Similarly, Quin's final completed book, *Tripticks*, which draws on the excruciatingly familiar 'American road trip' storyline, enacts the œuvre's most frenetically inclusive, repetitive and unstable experimentation. *Tripticks* is precisely not original, not 'novel', but a collage of repetition, quotation and cliché. In this way, *Tripticks* is the most exaggerated and problematic example of the inclusive, 'derivative' experimental method that Quin developed in the 1960s, the text which tests and strains the reading process even further. I have argued throughout this chapter that rather than responding to such strain by either giving up on and dismissing the texts because of their 'difficulty' or, on the other hand, denying that such methods are problematic and frustrating by responding to Quin in a solely celebratory recuperative mode, we might instead begin to broaden and revitalise our recuperative work in order instead to admit, attend to and take seriously their discouraging, boring, frustrating and dysphoric effects and affects, and even, perhaps, to see the potential usefulness and critical productivity of describing Quin's writing as 'infuriating'.

Notes

1. Quin's *The Unmapped Country: Stories & Fragments* (Sheffield: And Other Stories, 2018) has been widely reviewed in the UK and USA. There have also been recent appraisals of the wider 1960s British avant-garde: for example, D. J. Taylor's 'From Blank Pages to 13,000 Word Sentences: A Brief History of British Avant Garde Writing', *The Guardian*, 5 March 2018, and BBC Radio 4's *The Advance Guard of the Avant-Garde*, 10 March 2018. See also, for example, Julia Jordan, 'Late Modernism and the Avant-Garde Renaissance', in *The Cambridge Companion to Post-1945 British Fiction*, ed. David James (Cambridge: Cambridge University Press, 2015), pp. 145–59.
2. Unsigned review of Quin's *Passages*, *The Sunday Times*, 30 March 1969.
3. Sianne Ngai, *Ugly Feelings* (Cambridge, MA: Harvard University Press, 2005), p. 3.
4. Elizabeth Harvey, 'New Fiction', *Daily Telegraph*, n.d.
5. David Benedictus, 'Books', *Queen*, 30 April 1969.
6. Respectively: Robert Nye, 'Against the Barbarians', *The Guardian*, 27 April 1972; Helen Lucy Burke, 'People Wandering', *The Irish Press*, 8 April 1969.
7. The collective included Paul Ableman, Alan Burns, Carol Burns, Barry Cole, Eva Figes, B. S. Johnson, Jeff Nuttall, Alan Sillitoe and Stefan Themerson.
8. Alan Burns and B. S. Johnson, Introduction, in *Writers Reading* (London: J & P Weldon, 1969), p. 1. Philip Stevick identifies this impulse as a rebellion 'against "story-ness"', Introduction, in *Anti-Story: An Anthology of Experimental Fiction* (New York: The Free Press, 1971), p. xv.

9. B. S. Johnson, *Aren't You Rather Young To Be Writing Your Memoirs?* (London: Hutchinson, 1973), p. 29. Johnson includes Samuel Beckett, John Berger, Christine Brooke-Rose, Brigid Brophy, Anthony Burgess, Alan Burns, Angela Carter, Eva Figes, Giles Gordon, Wilson Harris, Rayner Heppenstall, 'even hasty, muddled' Robert Nye, Ann Quin, Penelope Shuttle, Alan Sillitoe – 'for his last book only, Raw Material indeed' – and Stefan Themerson, pp. 29–30.
10. Ibid. p. 29.
11. Giles Gordon, Introduction, in *Berg* (Chicago: Dalkey Archive Press, 2001), p. ix.
12. Johnson, *Aren't You Rather Young To Be Writing Your Memoirs?*, p. 19. He adds: 'I object to the word *experimental* being applied to my own work. Certainly I make experiments, but the unsuccessful ones are hidden away.'
13. John Cage, *Silence: Lectures and Writings* (London: Calder and Boyars, 1968), p. 13. Marion Boyars claimed that 'if any influences are to be found in her [Quin's] later work, it seems [. . .] appropriate to name Robert Creeley and John Cage'. Giles Gordon (ed.), *Beyond the Words: Eleven Writers in Search of a New Fiction* (London: Hutchinson, 1975), p. 251.
14. Cage, *Silence: Lectures and Writings*, p. 13.
15. Alan Burns, 'Blending Words with Pictures', *Books and Bookmen*, 17:10 (July 1972), n.p.
16. Quin, 'Never Trust a Man who Bathes with His Finger Nails', *El Corno Emplumado*, 27 (July 1968), pp. 8–16, p. 8; republished in *The Unmapped Country*, pp. 95–107, p. 96.
17. Quin, *Passages* (Chicago: Dalkey Archive Press, 2003), p. 7.
18. Letter: Quin to Robert Sward, 18 July 1968. Olin Library Collection: Robert Sward Papers, Series 1.1, Box 10.
19. Gilles Deleuze and Felix Guattari, *Anti-Oedipus: Capitalism and Schizophrenia*, trans. Robert Hurley, Mark Seem and Helen Lane (London: Continuum, 2011), p. 145.
20. Ibid. p. 144.
21. Quin, *Berg* (Chicago: Dalkey Archive Press, 2001), prologue, unnumbered page.
22. Quin, 'Leaving School', *London Magazine*, July 1966, pp. 63–8, p. 64; republished in *The Unmapped Country*, pp. 15–24, p. 17.
23. Quin, 'Every Cripple Has His Own Way of Walking', *Nova*, December 1966, pp. 127–35; republished in *The Unmapped Country*, pp. 51–64.
24. Quin, *Berg*, p. 106.
25. Barber's afterword to an edition of *Berg* (London: Quartet Books, 1977), p. 170.
26. Quin, *Three* (Chicago: Dalkey Archive Press, 2001), p. 1.
27. A more thorough examination of the dispersive and disruptive effects and effectiveness of the various journal forms of *Three* can be found in Andrew Hassam's *Writing and Reality: A Study of Modern British*

Diary Fiction (London and Westport, CT: Greenwood Press, 1993), pp. 132–7. In particular, Hassam reminds us that written journals always foreground the writtenness of the writing.
28. The film is named as a key influence – 'wouldn't you know it "Last Year at Marienbad"' – in John Hall, 'The Mighty Quin', *The Guardian*, 29 April 1972, p. 8.
29. Quin, *Three*, p. 50.
30. Quin, *Passages*, p. 112.
31. Ibid. p. 16.
32. Leonardo da Vinci, *Notebooks*, ed. Irma Richter (Oxford: Oxford University Press, 1952), pp. 97, 101.
33. Letter: Quin to Sward, 21 September 1966. Robert Sward Papers, Series 1.1, Box 8.
34. Unsigned review, 'Lovers', *Times Literary Supplement*, 3 April 1969.
35. Quin, *Passages*, p. 7
36. Ibid.
37. Ibid. p. 8.
38. For Glyn White, parallel columns of text serve to present simultaneity in narrative. He notes, in Johnson's *Albert Angelo*, 'the specific graphic device of parallel lineation in which space *equals* time', *Reading the Graphic Surface: The Presence of the Book in Prose Fiction* (Manchester: Manchester University Press, 2005), p. 98.
39. Quin, *Passages*, p. 37.
40. Jane Ellen Harrison, *Prolegomena to the Study of Greek Religion* (Cambridge: Cambridge University Press, 1903), p. 201. In the relief under discussion – a photograph of which is included in Harrison's book – the third siren throws herself to her death in despair at the fortitude of Odysseus.
41. Nye, 'Against the Barbarians'.
42. White, *Reading the Graphic Surface*, p. 97.
43. Unsigned review, *The Sunday Times*, 30 March 1969.
44. David Haworth's review, *New Statesman*, 21 March 1969.
45. 'Lovers', *Times Literary Supplement*, 3 April 1969.
46. Harrison, Introduction, in *Prolegomena*, p. vii.
47. Letter: Quin to Sward, 10 August 1966, Robert Sward Papers, Series 1.1, Box 8.
48. See H.D., *Helen in Egypt* (New York: New Directions Books, 1961).
49. Bruce Morrissette, 'International Aspects of the "Nouveau Roman" Author(s)', *Contemporary Literature*, 11:2 (Spring 1970), pp. 155–68.
50. James Wood, *How Fiction Works* (London: Jonathan Cape, 2008), p. 27.
51. Ibid.

Chapter 9

Contradiction, Incongruity and Fragmentation: Political and Avant-Garde Compromise in the Work of Alan Burns

Kieran Devaney

Charles Sugnet writes that Alan Burns has 'always been uncompromisingly political and uncompromisingly avant-garde at the same time; the work demonstrates at the sentence level Burns' conviction that these two positions are inseparable'.[1] In this chapter I will examine Burns's relationship to the avant-garde, as evidenced in his texts of the 1960s, to ask whether Sugnet's contention is fundamentally correct. I will consider how Burns's work plays into debates about the relationship of the avant-garde to political practice. Sugnet proposes an uncomplicated relationship between the avant-garde and politics; in his essay he argues that Burns is able to occupy both simultaneously. However, a great deal of the theory concerned with such a relationship, particularly the work of Peter Bürger, deals with the complexities of that relation. Bürger's book, *Theory of the Avant-Garde*, argues that the political function of the classical avant-garde of the early twentieth century (a function he claims cannot be recuperated by artists and writers after that period) was the integration of life with the praxis of art as a means to critique the status of art as institution. Bürger defines the purpose of the avant-garde as a process of unveiling, whereby 'the weight that art as an institution has in determining the real social effect of individual works [becomes] recognisable'.[2] It is not, he contends, that the avant-garde destroys art as an institution, but rather that the way in which that institution mediates between the work and the public becomes more visible through the integration of life and art. The work of art itself is unable, in Bürger's view, to overcome bourgeois art without bourgeois society first being overcome. If we follow Bürger's theory, the attempts of artists and writers in the 1960s to create new forms of, and spaces for, art are inextricably tied to the power structures they seek to critique. As such, the attempts made by experimental writers and artists in the postwar period, including Burns, by reusing or updating the techniques and political impetus of the classical avant-garde, are condemned to replicate the political failure of the classical avant-garde. This chapter will argue that Sugnet's contention that Burns is both uncompromisingly political and uncompromisingly avant-garde presents an unrealistically simplistic version of what Burns attempts to achieve through his fiction. I will use Bürger's two fundamental categorisations of avant-garde practice to examine this: firstly, that the avant-garde aims to critique art as an institution; and secondly, that it seeks to reintegrate everyday life into the praxis of art. I will focus in particular on Burns's novels of the late 1960s and early 1970s: *Europe After the Rain* (1965), *Celebrations* (1967), *Babel* (1969) and *Dreamerika!* (1972).

Burns's Novels of the 1960s: An Overview

Buster, Burns's debut novel, was published by John Calder in 1961. Largely autobiographical and written in a realist mode, it recounts a middle-class childhood spent during the Second World War and an adolescence and young adulthood in its aftermath. The protagonist, Dan Graveson, shares many of the qualities of the Angry Young Men of the fifties and early sixties – a loss of purpose, a disenfranchisement, even an emasculation. There is a particular sense in the novel of the imbrication of personal trauma experienced during the course of the war, and Dan's inability to find his way in life or to form relationships. Dan, afforded various opportunities as a result of his class and upbringing, finds himself unable to take advantage of any of them and ends the novel virtually destitute, forced to return to the care of his family. Early in *Buster*, Burns recounts the death of Dan's mother and his older brother during the Second World War, but also shows that these traumatic events can be moments of politicisation, moments during which the implicit violence that underpins relations in society is briefly and decisively revealed. Dan's left-wing consciousness emerges during those moments, and it is this traumatic relation that informs his reluctance to engage with society.

With his second novel, *Europe After the Rain*, titled after the Max Ernst painting, Burns begins to use collage techniques and cut-ups, drawing on material he collected from a range of sources and largely abandoning drawing directly from his own experiences (although elements of his life emerge in how he selects and puts together that material). By retaining the syntax of found material, and juxtaposing phrases and sentences from a disparate range of origins, the novel loses the sense of having a coherent authority at its centre. The reader encounters a multiplicity of voices and discourses which Burns has meshed together. The novel recounts the movements of an anonymous narrator moving through an unnamed but ruined country during a war which several, also anonymous, characters say has ended but whose violence persists so that the distinction between wartime and peacetime is blurred. Burns seems to suggest that the wartime situation intensifies these everyday activities without fundamentally changing the relations that construct them, but makes those relations – of power, money, authority – more visible, less able to conceal themselves.

Celebrations transposes the techniques of *Europe After the Rain* into the workplace where the violence persists but is more concealed, occluded by family hierarchies and arcane legal structures. The novel is again composed of a range of source material, cut up and put together by Burns, and structured around a series of set-piece rituals (the 'celebrations' of the title), legal proceedings, marriages, funerals, parties. Burns's focus seems narrower than previously, the narrative concentrating on a factory-owning family, particularly the patriarch, Williams, and his son, Michael. After Williams's other son, Phillip, is killed, either by his brother Michael or as the result of an industrial accident (the text vacillates between these two explanations), Williams and Michael compete for the attention of Phillip's widow, Jacqueline. By limiting his scope in this way, Burns is able to show the way in which the workplace replicates and extends the ideological work of the family. The novel's characters are ciphers, described in ways which are often contradictory, most clearly in the description of Williams at the beginning of the novel which first has: 'He turned the wheel slowly, his temperature and the machine's were taken, his serious brown eyes apart, reading the faintest movement of the quivering needle.'[3] This is then followed a few lines later by: 'His buttons still glinted in a neat row, his eyes very blue, there was no point in measuring them, the ruptured middle ear caused tears to run down the cheeks, crystals on wheels.'[4] This deliberate contradiction emphasises the elision in the description between Williams and the machine, which is a large component of these early passages. In being machinic, Williams is made to be a component in the industrial system that Burns portrays, and by so explicitly assigning him these contradictory details, he is made less human in the eyes of the reader. This reveals the arbitrary and constructed nature of the character.

Following *Celebrations*, Burns published *Babel*, stylistically his most radical work and the high point of his experimental phase. Babel has no narrative, a huge cast of characters including politicians and celebrities of the time, and short sections of highly condensed, often grammatically difficult prose. Again, Burns's targets in the novel are the state, violence and power. The novel deals repeatedly with the Vietnam war, the effects of colonialism, religion, the amorality of the political class, the workplace, the violence inherent within the family, with the movement of money and state-sanctioned violence. But more than its explicit content, Burns's novel deals, on a structural level, with the increasing fragmentation of the society it depicts. Burns understood and anticipated the rapid social changes that were occurring, and the novel deals with the emergence of new technology and media, as well as the increasing role of mass media, the influence of new art forms alongside new political and artistic voices, and the coming to prominence of the counterculture, all of which he shows as complicating the staid, monadic left-wing consensus of the time. Consider this in the context of *Babel*:

> CRYSTALLISED BLACK DELIRIUM, metal-white terror, singular stone mania, mineral illness, inexplicable earth, hills of stone, changed leper, green sun, dense bright green swollen bodies, pulverised heart, heart thump, illness, science at each step, give oxygen, horizon on the margin of a strange thing, the use of the knife.[5]

Burns's novel emphasises the enmeshment of the individual in a wider politics and the way in which inorganic objects, institutions and discourses impinge upon the individual. The quotation from *Babel* above conjoins hard, tangible materials with evocations of fear, illness and extreme emotional states. The hardness and impregnability of crystal, metal and stone – cold and implacable materials – are contrasted with the 'dense bright green swollen' diseased body, which is porous, mutable, the 'changed leper' suggesting a body which is contaminated, possibly disfigured, but also one which has succumbed to contagion. The 'horizon on the margin of a strange thing, the use of the knife', appears to bring that hardness into confluence with the soft and fragile body at the point of the surgical incision. Burns's style here, collapsing images on top of each other, gives the reader a sense of simultaneous action, of the body being 'full', swollen and dense, and it is possible to see this fullness as a consequence of a range of discourses – of violence, of power, of the media – acting upon it, *and* to see the surgeon's knife as both an interruption of that acting and another instantiation, another discourse, with its own violence and forms of control.

Babel received mixed reviews, even from those, like Robert Nye, who Burns saw as supporters of his work, and sold relatively poorly. But Burns continued his commitment to its style in *Dreamerika!* (1972), which traces a fictional history of the Kennedy family in America, seeing them as exemplars of the insidious movement of money and power, and of the relationship between politics and money. In the novel, the Kennedys become mythical figures, but incredible wealth and influence cannot shield them from an essentially tragic character.

As these summaries show, Sugnet's notion of Burns's fiction as uncompromising does not account for the dense, complex way in which his way of writing and his politics are imbricated. As I will show in the next section, this complexity is the logical result of the way in which Burns conceived of the interrelation between aesthetics and politics in his work.

Political and Aesthetic Uses of Collage and Montage

In the summary of his work that appears in the short story anthology, *Beyond the Words* (1973, ed. Giles Gordon), Burns mentions that even his earliest works began with an image or images, something external to him that he then built around, constructing the narrative from these sources. For *Buster* it was a photograph of a young couple, on to which Burns projected the image of his parents.[6] As a starting point, this is concise, personal, even sentimental, reflecting the autobiographical content of that novel. In contrast, *Europe After the Rain* draws on a wider and more disparate set of sources: namely, the transcript of the Nuremberg Trials and an unnamed book about postwar Poland, both of which Burns found by chance. Burns's use of the Nuremberg Trials transcript reflects his continuing interest in the law and the incorporation of the legal profession into his fiction,[7] as well as his interest in transcribed speech, which came to greater prominence with the publication of *The Angry Brigade* (1975) and subsequent works. Compared to Burns's wide-ranging and indiscriminate accumulation of material for his later projects – drawing on any printed material that he could find – the source material for *Europe After the Rain* is focused and narrow, albeit used in much the same way as in later works: that is, as an accumulation of fragments that Burns draws from to form his text. Both the book about postwar Poland and the Nuremberg Trials transcripts are used by Burns to form a collage text in which the sources exist as traces. That is, the texts that Burns drew on are not immediately discernible in the novel but can be felt in its evocation of violence. Bürger's analysis of the function of the collage as a major constituent part of the avant-garde is instructive here. Burns's choice of materials recalls Bürger's comments concerning the role of chance in the production of avant-garde artwork: 'Objective chance', he writes, speaking of the chance encounter depicted at the beginning of André Breton's *Nadja*, 'rests on the selection of congruent semantic elements [. . .] in unrelated events.'[8] His use of the word 'selection' is significant here because, for Bürger, the specific role of chance in the avant-garde, as exemplified by the Surrealists, is not to reveal something free from bias or ideology, but is rather the construction of meaning through the 'painstaking calculation' of scenarios, events or sources.[9] In the selection of source material for *Europe After the Rain*, no matter how much the discovery of the books was apparently unplanned, and regardless of how random and scattershot his use of them is in the construction of the novel, Burns's practice exemplifies what Bürger describes as 'the attempt to gain control of the extraordinary'.[10] That is, any reading of production through chance must take into account the methods employed to produce that apparently chance scenario, an important factor to consider regarding Burns's literary technique, particularly as it grows more fragmentary in his novels of the late 1960s.

The choice of the Nuremberg Trials transcript, as well as showing Burns's abiding interest in the functioning of the legal system, is also a document of great historical significance and authority. Burns's use of it is provocative. By dismantling the text, cutting it up and attributing fragments of it to his anonymous characters, Burns profanes the text and reimmerses the finality and closure of its legal discourse into the murky and uncertain networks of power and violence presented by the novel, a novel which, rather than attributing blame to individuals, instead seeks to widen the scope of attribution to something more structural or cultural. For Bürger, the desire to present fragments is central to the practice of the avant-garde, a desire which presupposes the absence of a totality or 'organic whole'.[11] Bürger also draws on Walter Benjamin to elucidate the role of the fragment and the way in which the assembling of various fragments in a work creates meaning which 'does not derive from the original contents of the fragments' but is instead mutable and unstable, lacking coherence and inviting a variety of perceptions and interpretations.[12] Such effects are evident in *Europe After the Rain*, where the fragmentation of the trial transcript contributes to the lack of centre in the novel. In addition, as *Europe After the Rain* progresses, the two sides of the conflict are shown to be almost indistinguishable from each other and intertwined at every level, so that the political landscape of the novel is incoherent and the only real powers that remain are violence and money.

Burns's collage process is illuminated by Sugnet's discussion of Burns's methodology with him in their interview in *The Imagination on Trial* (1982). Sugnet asks Burns:

> When you talk of organizing your work you mention photographs, table tops – what you're describing is spatial rather than temporal. It doesn't consist of putting material in time sequence, the way some novelists might do. You're talking of the kind of inspiration that comes by juxtaposing things in space?[13]

Sugnet's characterisation of Burns as a novelist who arranges material in space rather than in time seems apposite when considering *Europe After the Rain*, given the novel's arrangement and rearrangement of grids, networks, maps, frontiers and scenes of violence to form a system which, in the space of the novel, is resistant to the conventional movement of narrative. Part of this resistance stems from Burns's use of the cut-up, a device which he employs, as William Burroughs does, as a means of dismantling language's power.

Babel moves beyond the practices of *Europe After the Rain* and is a true montage text, drawing on a far wider and more extensive range of sources. The novel is made up of short, abrupt paragraphs whose narrative style often presents its surreal content in the form of straight-faced reportage:

> THE SUBURBAN CINEMA CHRIST WAS THERE, spending a week in Britain, preaching at the Albert Hall because Billy Graham was in bed with 'flu. They were boys together, they fell in love, pointing his finger at Mary, going bang bang, it's war. The spiritual scum lead others to the Lord while Billy and Mary spent six months in the States. Then he rang up from Birmingham and asked the people to go on a crusade. He decided he needed an organisation in October, professionals to work at it. Billy was looking for businessmen, (his chunky cardigan cost four

hundred pounds), his relations were scattered round the country working for the Lord at reduced rate. The Lord told him to marry a young American girl, and he went away on a youth night with Betty Lou and her psychedelic rhythm while his transcendental wife was missing.[14]

This passage, which appears as a discrete unit in *Babel* among other similarly narrated passages, is typical of the way that Burns both frustrates the reader with his use of odd syntax and non sequitur, and also understands how a reader can move through a passage like this, using familiar reference points (well-known people and places, familiar objects) as handholds. This combination of the familiar and the alienating creates the particular sense of dislocation that characterises the experience of reading Burns's avant-garde work. In this quotation, individual actions and circumstances (which, on their own are straightforward) accumulate, and through their juxtaposition, the text creates a series of images whose specific meaning may be obscure, but the effect of which has a direct impact upon the reader. The words in capitals, which Burns uses to begin almost every section in *Babel*, function like headlines, drawing the eye towards them and giving them emphasis. In this particular section, 'SUBURBAN CINEMA CHRIST' introduces the paragraph with an image of conservatism and inauthenticity, an ersatz Christ filtered through the lens of cinematic representation (which can be contrasted with the 'missing' transcendental wife at the close of the passage). These factors are highlighted and they set the tenor of the entire paragraph, in terms of both the type of imagery and the rhythmic quality of the passage, the short clauses which stack together, and the repeated names, details and actions. This sense of rhythm, alongside the repeated motifs of movement and relocation, mitigate the difficulty of comprehending what is going on in this passage. Meaning, in Burns's avant-garde work, emerges from this precise combination of form and content.

As well as this rhythmic quality to the prose, Burns makes use of real names, positioning the narrative within its contemporary situation and within a specific history in a way that his previous works had been unable to. The evocation of Billy Graham and the hints about his infidelity and religious hypocrisy evince a fascination with and repulsion from a media-saturated, celebrity culture. In Burns's novel, the celebrities become fragments, components of a work which functions allegorically. Montage, as Bürger suggests, 'presupposes the fragmentation of reality and describes the phase of its constitution of the work'.[15] The way in which Burns depicts Billy Graham is not to tell in detail the story of his life and to find some coherence in it, some reason for it, but rather simply to present a few details and then move on to the next thing. He is not interested in Billy Graham the person, but rather in what Billy Graham can stand for, what he can represent, how he can become a node in a system of representations within the novel. As such, Burns's focus is only partially a critique of celebrity culture – he is more interested, in passages like this one, in showing the way that celebrity culture intersects with other discourses, and how it can be used to create the specific sense of disorientation achieved in *Babel*. The real-life figures of *Babel* are not objects of fascination to be lingered over; they resemble more the red and grey ruins of *Europe After the Rain*, they are monuments in a petrified landscape, functioning as part of what Bürger calls a 'paradigmatic nexus'.[16] Writing about the construction of avant-garde texts, Bürger states that 'New events of the same type could be added, or some of those present could be omitted, and neither additions nor omissions would make a difference. A change in order would also be conceivable.'[17] These statements are certainly true of *Babel*. While an underlying structure can be discerned – consecutive sections will often feature similar themes and, occasionally, the same characters and motifs, particularly the role of the celebrity, the Vietnam war (as well as war and violence more generally), the media, religion and the hypocrisy of religious figures, the exploitation of women and class division – there is no move toward a cohesive whole in the novel; in fact, its emphasis is on disorder and fragmentation. Underlying the novel's construction is its commitment to a wide-ranging and voluminous sense of scale; at the back of the book, Burns lists a cast of more than 200 characters – some names of real contemporary celebrities and politicians, others invented – which makes this scale explicit.

Two of Burns's other works from this period also employ this extreme fragmentation by cutting up and splicing together different sources, but in different media: his play written in 1969, *Palach*, and Peter Whitehead's 1967 film, *Jeanette Cochrane*, for which Burns wrote the script and the subtitles. Whitehead's film is a montage of images of the emerging counterculture in London, including footage taken at the UFO Club and at the Slade School of Art. The film features brief shots of musician and actor Nico and is soundtracked by an early recording of Pink Floyd. Burns's intervention into this already hectic assemblage is to complicate it further. He writes subtitles which present questions and observations, such as 'How should I behave?', 'Should I talk to my daughter?' and so on.[18] On top of these, there is a voiceover, also written by Burns, which critiques and passes negative comment on both the subtitles and the images in a patrician tone, calling into question the ability of this kind of art to convey meaning. Here is an example from the voiceover: 'Try asking them what they mean by all this and of course the only answer you get is, Mean? Mean? We don't mean anything, it's art. Art. As soon as there's something any ordinary human being can't understand, that's art.'[19] The effect of this dual narration, alongside the constant stream of images and Whitehead's fluid camerawork, which zips around and changes focus, is one of disorientation, of too much information to take in and process.

Palach presents a highly stylised version of the story of Jan Palach, a Czech student who committed self-immolation in 1968 in protest against the Soviet occupation, which put an end to the events of the Prague Spring. The play was performed with the audience sitting at the centre of four stages, upon which the action often occurs simultaneously, the actors speaking over each other, or singing or performing actions, alongside blasts of music, recorded voices and televisions. Jinny Schiele, in her brief account of the play's first performance in 1970, directed by Charles Marowitz, suggests that Burns's aim was 'enveloping his audience in a total environment'.[20] Harold Hobson's review of the play (reprinted as an introduction in *Open Space Plays: Selected by Charles Marowitz*) emphasises the cacophonous nature of the first production of the play:

> I do not write this easily. The production employs means – simultaneous action on four separate stages, the blaring of loud-speakers drowning the voices of the players, the players themselves overlaying each other's speeches [. . .].[21]

Hobson concludes that Burns's and Marowitz's presentation 'establish[es] in beauty and vulgarity the extreme qualities of our civilization'.[22] The extremes of the total environment that Burns and Marowitz create are exemplified in the indifferent reactions of the cast to Palach's self-immolation. The act and its politics are lost among the accumulated voices, as indicated in the stage directions:

> *For the next sequence the page is divided into five columns, with characters' names placed at the head of each. Where, reading across, speeches overlap, this indicates that the actors speak simultaneously. A crescendo will thus be built up in which all five speak together, creating a noise reminiscent of the Prague Noise, in which individual speeches are incomprehensible. In particular, the BOY'S frantic attempts to communicate are frustrated.*[23]

What Burns is seeking in his work on *Palach* and *Jeanette Cochrane* (to which I would also add *Dreamerika!* with its emphasis on the materiality of the page) is a particular kind of affect which moves beyond mere recapitulation of the themes and techniques of the classical avant-garde: that is, a surfeit of information, a sense of excess, which the reader (or audience member or viewer) experiences and cannot fully comprehend or process in its entirety. In structural terms, this reconfiguring of strategies of representation leads to a focus on the fragment as the key component in Burns's 1960s experimental work. *Babel*'s short, cluttered paragraphs and cut-up sentences are a truer representation of the media culture of the late 1960s than conventional narrative techniques. By decoupling himself from those techniques, Burns creates a novel which, as with his work in film and the theatre, creates a total sensory environment, and he does this through his use of the fragment. In contrast to *Europe After the Rain*, these fragments emerge from an abundance of sources; there is no sense of the palimpsestic weight and authority of the Nuremberg Trials transcripts in the text of *Babel*. Instead, Burns sifts through material, picking out and putting together pieces of text in an assemblage. As Burns's work developed, he sought to incorporate a multiplicity of voices; on the page this cacophony is challenging for the reader to move through and, in abandoning traditional characters and protagonists, Burns aimed to represent the mass, rather than the individual.

Post-'68: *Dreamerika!* and Beyond

Dreamerika! is relevant to a discussion of Burns's 1960s work because it represents the culmination of his avant-garde period. The novel directly incorporates fragments of newspaper clippings, phrases from books and magazines, as images on the page, alongside blocks of equally fragmentary text. By focusing largely on the Kennedy family and using these techniques to depict them, the novel is Burns's most direct engagement with politics, and the endpoint of a particular style of writing. Burns writes of John F. Kennedy that:

> Jack was powered by quartz. He had been in existence for only a short time but had grown steadily. He was a piece of the mechanism of the world. He attended to the split second. He could say exactly when.[24]

Here Kennedy is described in terms which remove his personal agency and render him as a component of a larger system. Kennedy is, or perceives himself to be, a well-wrought mechanical element, essential to the functioning of a world which can be understood in simple, mechanical terms – each piece in its place, working in relation to the others around it. Just prior to this, while he is campaigning, another description of Kennedy is offered: 'Jack dressed in white in the park,' it reads, 'the marshmallow extended through the hotel lobby. The candidate seemed sweet, with a note of pleasure in his voice.'[25] The connotations are clear: the marshmallow is saccharine, shaped to be consumed – sweet, light, bland, attractive; it has a malleable quality, can be reshaped and manipulated. The description comes at a point when Burns is referring to Kennedy's appeal to female voters: 'Among his loveliest electorate he could claim girls with a special twist of sex across the heart.'[26] There is something gendered in the way that Kennedy is presented and something misogynistic in Burns's vocabulary here, in calling the female voters 'girls' and in the sense of their easy manipulation.[27] Kennedy's appeal to women softens him. Furthermore, Burns seems to be suggesting that there is something about this appeal which is not only gendered but also infantilising, rendering the would-be President bland and faceless.

By invoking the image of a marshmallow, Burns aims to say something about Kennedy but also to extend the understanding of the reader, to create a new image of the President, an extreme and dehumanising one with decidedly feminine connotations. It is also an image of commercial availability and readiness for consumption. As such, the metaphor shows Kennedy to be a convergence of a set of qualities that might be described as 'cute', a designation which Sianne Ngai writes about in her essay, 'The Cuteness of the Avant-Garde'. Ngai describes the confluence of high art and advertising that emerges in the post-Second World War period, in which 'corporate advocates of the industrialisation of modernist aesthetics sought to develop a new commodity aesthetic in the rapidly expanding fields of design and advertising'.[28] Ngai critiques a commonly held notion of the avant-garde, and the way in which certain accounts of its techniques divide along gender lines:

> [W]hile the avant-garde is conventionally imagined as sharp and pointy, as hard – or cutting-edge, cute objects have no edge to speak of, usually being soft, round and deeply associated with the infantile and the feminine.[29]

It is clear that these latter 'infantile and feminine' descriptions could be applied to Burns's marshmallow, and Ngai goes on to reference Adorno's discussion in *Aesthetic Theory* of art and the edible, which 'brings art into an uncomfortable proximity to "cuisine and pornography"'.[30] Given that Burns's marshmallow metaphor occurs as part of a discussion of Kennedy's appeal to women, there is a clear intermingling of sex and food in his portrayal, where Kennedy is reconstituted as cute, effeminate, pliable and edible.

Ngai, however, does not simply see the cute object as malleable. For her, the qualities of the cute object 'call forth specific affects: helplessness, pitifulness, and even despondency'.[31] And it is here that the image of the marshmallow takes on more sinister connotations. Ngai goes on to claim that 'the cute object is as often intended to excite a consumer's sadistic desires for mastery and control as much as his or her desire to cuddle'.[32] For Ngai, the helplessness of the cute object allows a kind of violence to be exerted upon it. By conceiving of Kennedy as a marshmallow, Burns not only prefigures the violence that Kennedy suffered later in his life, but also shows the underlying violence that comes with becoming a public political figure; Kennedy becomes the object of various desires and manipulations by submitting himself to the mass media. In this way, the two metaphors that Burns uses about Kennedy – the marshmallow and the component of a watch – which at first glance seem opposed to each other, are in fact related. The violence Kennedy suffered is presented in *Dreamerika!* as merely an extension of the media spectacle which he had become a part of, a spectacle in which the celebrity takes the position of the 'cute' object that Ngai identifies.

The Angry Brigade (1973) followed *Dreamerika!* and marked a turning away from the experimental by Burns, towards a simpler and more direct style which, he felt, would more effectively convey his political message. *The Angry Brigade*'s radical break from the style and form of Burns's 1960s work can only be seen as a repudiation of that style, a sense that it had failed in some way to address the issues Burns had wanted to address (as well as failing to meet his commercial expectations). In his interview with Sugnet, Burns is asked about the reason for his move 'towards a surface that appears simpler':

> You say I moved away, I think I have more of a sense that I was moved away. [. . .] I had fragmented myself out of existence, [. . .] I had to do something else. Secondly, I had driven myself into a certain corner in relation to the readers who were interested enough in my work to buy the books. There were not enough of them! That's the negative aspect, the place I was pushed out of. As to where I went, I was influenced by a speech made by Heinrich Böll on receiving the Nobel Prize for

Literature. He took a strong political line, saying there was no point in writing for the few, one had to find a language that was accessible, close to 'the language of the people'. In *The Angry Brigade* I tried to do something of that kind.[33]

This interview identifies three key components of Burns's change from the fragmentary, avant-garde style of his works up to *Dreamerika!* to the vernacular style of *The Angry Brigade*. What emerges from these motivations is a 'documentary' novel, which replaces the avant-garde style as Burns's chosen form for expressing his politics. Despite the failure of May '68 to produce a truly revolutionary moment, many felt that global revolution was imminent, pointing to worldwide protest movements, student movements, the growth of feminism, the emergence of the civil rights movement and third world revolutions. In addition, a key component of this activism was the sense of internationalism – that a coherent ideology ran through these disparate movements which could unite them. Jeremy Varon, who groups all these ideologies under the banner of the New Left, describes the 'consciously *internationalist*' thinking, whereby activists 'saw themselves waging a revolution which would overthrow both the US-led imperialism of the West and the ossified, bureaucratic communism of the East'.[34] The political violence of *The Angry Brigade* is predicated upon this kind of thinking: that small-scale, violent actions, largely directed at property, are steps towards that radical, revolutionary break, a process of unveiling that resembles Bürger's notion of the function of the avant-garde.

This chapter has made clear how Burns's work responded to the rapid political and societal changes that were occurring while he was writing. The surfeit of information, the variety of media, the splintering of political groups and interests, and the rise of a multifarious counterculture all contributed to a density and fragmentation of the way in which contemporary life was experienced, and Burns's fiction seeks not just to depict that experience, but also to replicate it, to produce in the reader the disorientating effect of being in that world. The political and the historical clearly informed Burns's approach to fiction and his desire to deploy a vast accumulation of voices, discourses and points of view in his work. At the height of his experimental phase, in the novel *Babel*, this reached a critical point in which the weight and density of the competing plurality of perspectives threatens to break down meaning and language itself, and erodes any sense of traditional notions of character or story. But this density also makes the work unpredictable and exciting to read.

I began with a discussion of Sugnet's claim that Burns's work is uncompromisingly political and uncompromisingly avant-garde. The idea of Burns as uncompromising in his fiction, as Sugnet suggests, is a provocative one, but it also places Burns on a somewhat lofty pedestal above the messy and difficult ideological negotiations and sacrifices that are part of being politically active. In fact, as I have shown in this chapter and as the position of Bürger makes clear, the relationship between the two is complex. Nevertheless, while Bürger sees any attempt to recuperate avant-garde techniques beyond the 'classical' avant-garde period as doomed to failure, we should see Burns's texts of the 1960s and beyond as an attempt to find a political and aesthetic response to his time which attempts to incorporate the messiness and incoherence that make up political activity. It is possible to see Burns's use of the fragment and of multiple discourses in his work as part of Bürger's notion of the reintegration of everyday life into the praxis of art – Burns's work teems with life in this sense – but we might also usefully see it as an attempt to represent the upheaval of the late 1960s and early 1970s. In this sense, Burns's work is not uncompromising, but rather consciously and deliberately contains contradiction, incongruity and fragmentation. That is, it is, in fact, deliberately *compromised*.

Notes

1. Charles Sugnet, 'Burns' Aleatoric *Celebrations*: Smashing Hegemony at the Sentence Level', *The Review of Contemporary Fiction*, 17:2 (Summer 1997), p. 193.
2. Peter Bürger, *Theory of the Avant-Garde*, trans. Michael Shaw (Manchester: Manchester University Press, 1984), p. 83.
3. Alan Burns, *Celebrations* (London: Calder and Boyars, 1967), p. 5.
4. Ibid. pp. 5–6.
5. Alan Burns, *Babel* [1969] (London: Marion Boyars, 2009), p. 145.
6. Alan Burns, 'Essay', in *Beyond the Words: Eleven Writers in Search of a New Fiction*, ed. Giles Gordon (London: Hutchinson, 1975), p. 64.
7. Burns studied law at university, and worked as a libel lawyer for Beaverbrook Newspapers in the late 1950s and early 1960s.
8. Bürger, *Theory of the Avant-Garde*, p. 65.
9. Ibid.
10. Ibid. p. 66.
11. Ibid. p. 70.
12. Ibid. p. 69.
13. Alan Burns and Charles Sugnet (eds), *The Imagination on Trial* (London: Allison and Busby, 1981), p. 163.

14. Burns, *Babel*, p. 16
15. Bürger, *Theory of the Avant-Garde*, p. 73.
16. Ibid. p. 80.
17. Ibid.
18. Peter Whitehead, *Jeanette Cochrane* (my transcription), in *Peter Whitehead and the Sixties* (DVD) (London: British Film Institute, 2007).
19. Ibid.
20. Jinny Schiele, *Off-Centre Stages: Fringe Theatre at the Open Space and the Round House 1968–1983* (Hatfield: University of Hertfordshire Press, 2005), p. 50.
21. Harold Hobson, 'Introduction', in *Open Space Plays: Selected by Charles Marowitz*, ed. Charles Marowitz (London: Penguin, 1974), p. 193.
22. Hobson in Marowitz, *Open Space Plays*, p. 194.
23. Alan Burns, *Palach*, in Marowitz, *Open Space Plays*, p. 236.
24. Alan Burns, *Dreamerika!* (London: Calder and Boyars, 1972), p. 22.
25. Ibid. p. 19.
26. Ibid.
27. The representations of women in Burns's work of this period are often misogynistic, which runs counter to the other progressive aspects of his politics at the time. Later works, particularly *The Day Daddy Died*, show Burns as having revised these views.
28. Sianne Ngai, 'The Cuteness of the Avant-Garde', *Critical Inquiry*, 31:4 (Summer 2005), p. 812.
29. Ibid. p. 814.
30. Ibid.
31. Ibid. p. 816.
32. Ibid.
33. Burns and Sugnet, *The Imagination on Trial*, p. 164.
34. Jeremy Varon, *Bringing the War Home: The Weather Underground, the Red Army Faction and Revolutionary Violence in the Sixties and Seventies* (Berkeley: University of California Press, 2004), p. 1.

Chapter 10

Eva Figes: Tracing the Survival of a 'Poetry of the Inarticulate'

Chris Clarke

Born in Berlin in 1932, Eva Figes and part of her Jewish family fled Germany for London in 1939, after her mother had to bribe a Wehrmacht officer to release Figes's father from Dachau concentration camp.[1] While the first rule of life in England was 'never speak German', Figes went on to work as a translator of modern German writers, having studied English literature at Queen Mary College.[2] Following her 'thinly disguised' autobiographical novel, *Equinox* (1966), Figes's experimental novels, *Winter Journey* (1967), *Konek Landing* (1969), *B* (1972) and *Days* (1974), were published by Faber and produced with financial support from the Arts Council.[3] In her 2012 obituary for Figes, Eva Tucker – a fellow Jewish refugee and innovative writer – suggests that Figes will be remembered for her 'ground-breaking experimental novels' and renowned feminist text, *Patriarchal Attitudes* (1970).[4]

However, in comparison to her well-recognised contribution to the second wave of feminism, 'Figes' reputation as a fiction writer has remained', as Anna Maria Stuby notes, 'somewhat obscured'.[5] The apparent obscurity of Figes's 1960s experimental novels stems partly from the disappointing reception of innovative fiction writers in postwar Britain, which Figes associates with the 'only' time in her life when she 'belonged to something which could be called a literary group'.[6] This avant-garde collective, Figes recalls, came to a sudden 'end with the death of B. S. Johnson' in November 1973:

> Ann Quin had killed herself by swimming out to sea only weeks before, and shortly after these two deaths Alan Burns, closer to both of them than I had ever been, chose to dig himself into an American university, and stayed there. Their loss still makes me feel solitary, and bereft.[7]

Writing in the *New Review* in 1978, Figes seems equally despondent when she reflects on this group's attempt to 'change the face of fiction' in the 1960s: 'we have failed to change the English literary scene, or it has failed us'.[8]

Figes's bleak assessment of the reception of these experimental fiction writers now appears somewhat premature, given the growing interest in what Julia Jordan has called the 'avant-garde renaissance' in 1960s Britain.[9] Cheryl Verdon's recent essay, for example, presents Figes as 'a writer of many concerns – Jewish, existential feminist' – and suggests that her experimental fiction 'was ahead of its time in its depiction of postmodern and post-Holocaust dilemmas of identity and knowledge'.[10] Similarly, Silvia Pellicer-Ortin's theoretical study claims that 'the evolution of the aesthetics employed by Figes' is 'paradigmatic of how human beings have dealt with trauma in the aftermath of the Holocaust'.[11] While the recuperation of Figes's experimental fiction through trauma and Holocaust studies has begun to compensate for its critical neglect, this chapter argues that we can deepen our understanding of the contemporary resonance of her experimental novels by reconsidering the sense of failure that marked their reception in the 1960s and early 1970s. In particular, I explore how the faltering reception of Figes's work has partially obscured the way in which she drew on the literary notion of failure outlined by Samuel Beckett. In her experimental mode of composition, Figes adopts this elusive and resistant sense of failure to respond to 'the harsher lessons of the twentieth century'.[12] In this, Figes's treatment of failure provides an alternative perspective on her refusal of 'the English conservatism and insularity' of the 1960s literary scene.[13] 'In England', she wrote in 1968, 'nobody really expects a writer to have the intellectual calibre of, say, a philosopher or a mathematician': 'people expect novelists and playwrights to entertain, not to tax their thinking powers overmuch'.[14] This chapter traces how a rhetoric of failure, or what Robert Nye called a 'poetry of the inarticulate', in *Winter Journey* and *Konek Landing*, articulates Figes's resistance to the limiting expectations of her literary scene and accentuates the unique demands of her early experimental novels.[15] My close readings of Figes's experimental fiction draw on the ethical philosophy of Emmanuel Levinas in order to suggest that Figes's rhetoric of failure acknowledges her responsibility for the other. In doing so, the chapter sheds light on how Figes's experimental novels, as Pellicer-Ortin proposes, would come to anticipate the 'ethical turn in literary criticism and philosophy'.[16] The lasting legacy of Figes's early experimental fiction lies, I hope to show, in how its treatment of failure continues to call for a responsible response from its reader.

Figes's Rhetoric of Failure and the English Literary Scene

In 1978, Figes suggested that 'mainstream English fiction is locked in the social realist tradition'.[17] While this claim identifies limited characterisations of the period as a 'conflict between experimental writers and realists', scholars since have increasingly sought to revise this version of literary history by attending to the legacy of 1960s literary innovators.[18] Peter Boxall, for example, suggests that the 'experiments in realism undertaken' by writers such as Ann Quin, Muriel Spark and, we might add, Figes register 'that the foundations upon which the human rested had been eroded', and that there was 'no revolutionary epistemology available with which to repoint or reconstruct the alienated subject'.[19] Boxall analyses this 'lapsing of the human' as an effect of 'the development of new technologies for the surveillance and reproduction of culture',[20] a point Figes recognises, writing in 1968: 'modern communications and mass media have accentuated the personality cult'.[21] Figes, however, roots her scepticism towards this technological displacement and refashioning of the human subject in a pressing crisis of representation entangled with recent history: 'the English social realist tradition cannot contain the realities of my own lifetime, horrors which one might have called surreal if they had not actually happened'.[22]

One can align Figes's concern for the limits of extant modes of representation and the difficulties of responding to recent atrocities with the work of Beckett, a critical influence on Figes and her contemporaries: 'for my generation Beckett was God, but he created a problem because it seemed he had gone as far as anyone could go'.[23] Though Beckett proved a tricky act to follow, the 'sense of failure' outlined by Beckett in his dialogues with Georges Duthuit nevertheless provided Figes and her fellow experimental writers with a kind of aesthetic anti-model through which to negotiate their paradoxical status as late modernists.[24] Beckett observes that 'relations between representer and representee' appear 'shadowed more and more darkly by a sense of invalidity'.[25] Yet, while 'this submission, this admission, this fidelity to failure' enables a critique of traditional modes of representation, Beckett calls attention to how the very attempt to capture its critical force is liable to be misrecognised as a theme of representation: 'a new occasion, a new term of relation'.[26] In a necessarily difficult articulation of this sense of failure, Beckett notes that one unavoidably makes 'an expressive act, even if only of itself, of its impossibility, of its obligation'.²⁷ 'This fidelity to failure' ultimately impresses, as Ewa Ziarek highlights, 'a sense of obligation beyond desire, knowledge, or aesthetic pleasure', an obligation to which Figes and her contemporaries were particularly attuned.²⁸ In an interview from 1999, for instance, Figes suggests that writers 'from the same generation', such as her 'personal friend', Günter Grass, who had 'witnessed what happened in Europe', share similar views regarding the writer's 'particular position in society'.²⁹ While 'every citizen has a duty to stand up for certain rights and certain values', a writer, Figes contends, 'not only has a duty as a human being but has the opportunity to express it [. . .]. I think it [the writer's work] is lacking in responsibility if they don't.'³⁰

In a short essay from 1975, Figes elaborates on the relationship between her experimental fiction and her sense of responsibility. Responding to the way in which 'old modes' of representation 'seem hopelessly inadequate', Figes's experimental novels try to 'find [. . .] some way of expressing the peculiarities, awfulness and seemingly ungraspable qualities of life itself'.³¹ Echoing Beckett, Figes acknowledges that her attempt to express the 'ungraspable' aspects of existence 'inevitably involves [her] in constant literary innovation'³² – a mode of composition through a 'painful process of trial and error'³³ – before reflecting on the reasons why her work refuses to 'engage in the trade of reassurance'³⁴:

> The price of survival is eternal vigilance. I am less concerned now with creating beautiful artefacts and more with the problem of going on, of survival, of grasping where I am and coming to terms with it. For me, now, each book is a life saving act on which my personal survival as a whole human being depends. If I succeed in fashioning structures which can contain the anxieties, the difficulties, the insights which beset me and which I regard as general rather than private to me I am not reassuring anybody, on the contrary, I am being highly subversive, painful, disturbing, but ultimately constructive.³⁵

Figes claims that her 'survival' 'as a whole human being' depends on the way in which her experimental texts are 'highly subversive, painful, disturbing' and refuse 'to reassur[e] anybody'.³⁶ Figes's experimental mode of composition thus welcomes failure ('trial and error') in order to acknowledge her acute sense of responsibility; her very 'survival' as a 'human being' rests on how her experimental novels – 'life saving acts' – take on the other's needs. I argue that Figes's poetics insinuates a responsibility *for* the other (as distinct from a responsibility *to* the other). Derek Attridge highlights that 'being responsible for the other involves assuming the other's needs (if only the need to exist)', and if I am responsible to the other, 'the other calls me to account, I answer to it as best I can'.[37] Figes acknowledges her responsibility for the other by entwining her own 'survival' with saving the lives of others – one cannot exist without the other.

We can formulate a way to read the inordinate responsibility that Figes entwines with her work's experimental poetics by turning to Levinas's ethics of alterity. Levinas's reconceptualisation of ethics in the aftermath of the catastrophes of the twentieth century offers a pertinent way to attend to the responsibility that Figes's rhetoric of failure insinuates. If theories of ethics have traditionally derived their notions of the good from the true, Levinas presents an ethical relation to the other person as the unfounded foundation of such theories. Levinas argues that subjectivity primarily rests on an 'inescapable and incontrovertible' responsibility for an unthematisable other, and consequently, in Levinas's unique sense, ethics underlies conventional moral, political or legal systems.[38] In contrast to how modern western philosophy has represented the other to itself, and thereby dissolved their alterity, Levinas suggests that the otherness of the other person always already withdraws from attempts to think or appropriate it. The ethical relation to what Levinas calls the 'face' of the other rests on no prior ground:

> [T]he person with whom one is in a relationship through the face [. . .] does not appear as belonging to an order which can be 'embraced', or 'grasped'. The other, in this relationship of responsibility, is, as it were, unique: 'unique' meaning without genre.[39]

Levinas's contention that one is always already responsible for the irreducible alterity of the other person underpins the reconsideration of failure that he presents in his reading of Marcel Proust's *In Search of Lost Time* (1913–27): 'the failure of communication is the failure of knowledge. One does not see that the success of knowledge would in fact destroy the nearness, the proximity, of the other.'[40] Moreover, Levinas suggests that 'the best thing about philosophy is that it fails [to totalise the alterity of meaning]' because it thereby remains open to the ethical claims of the other.[41] Levinas's reappraisal of failure is symptomatic, as Ewa Ziarek has argued, of how, in his revision of scepticism ('usually understood as a negative or critical attitude questioning the possibility of knowledge and truth'), 'failure functions not only as a theme but also as a rhetoric', 'implying a model of language transgressing the bounds of the philosophy of the subject'.[42] This rhetorical turn in Levinas's work,

Ziarek elucidates, 'shifts the entire paradigm of language: from the one based on the centrality of the speaking subject to the one based on "the search for the other and the other of language"'.[43]

Following Ziarek's contention that Levinas's rereading of failure also provides a way to intervene in the tendency to misread modernist experimentation as apolitical or detached from social concerns, my analysis of Figes's experimental novels traces the ethical dimension of the sense of failure that informs her poetics. In particular, my reading of Figes's rhetoric of failure illustrates what Boxall has recently argued is one of the novel's 'greatest gifts, and a source of its own ethical thinking': its 'particular resistance to reading, its perennial refusal of the conventions within which we might seek to evaluate it'.[44] It thereby proposes another way to understand the faltering reception of Figes's early experimental fiction.

Winter Journey

Winter Journey presents Janus Stobbs, an elderly person not far from death and all but deaf, as he survives a day in London; he visits a library and his daughter (Nan), before returning to his rented room. Though Figes states that she chose 'to work with an old person, because everyone who survives becomes old', survival, as we have seen, is an important term in her poetics, entwined with her work's treatment of failure.[45] In a review of the novel, Nye points towards this sense of failure by noting how 'all the odds and sods of Janus's pointless existence are drawn together in a jerky, rambling style that is [. . .] reminiscent of Beckett in that it makes a kind of poetry of the inarticulate'.[46] We can explore *Winter Journey*'s 'poetry of the inarticulate' by considering Figes's comment that 'reading [William] Faulkner's *The Sound and the Fury* [(1929)]' prompted her desire 'to write a book about being old, the defective human being'.[47] While composing the novel, Figes suffered from an 'abscess in one ear', an experience that accentuated her sensitivity to the limits of one's senses as well as the alterity of others: 'we live in different worlds. The child's perceptions are so fantastically different from the adult's, the sick person's from the healthy.'[48] Figes's recognition that 'we are all defective though we don't think we are' is reflected in her novel's sound texture, which resounds with cracks and stutters.[49] The text's opening onomatopoeic lines are indicative of how Figes attempts to 'make a direct emotional impact through prose, to break through the rational prose structures':[50] 'Numm bll num mun ssooo sss tck. I dreamt, that was it. Not a soul about.'[51]

My analysis of *Winter Journey* supplements Pellicer-Ortín's Levinasian reading of the novel by stressing how Figes's 'poetry of the inarticulate' disrupts rational prose structures through its presentation of Janus's hearing.[52] In a sleepless early morning, we listen to 'that train, I couldn't have heard that train, not without my aid on. And yet I always hear it, I always have heard it, every night in the small hours.'[53] The text impresses what Janus will 'hear' even if there is nothing to be heard, since Janus's hearing does and does not depend on whether he has turned on his hearing aid. Moreover, Figes emphasises how, for Janus, 'reason comes to a stop, isn't a straight line, is so far, then it ties itself in knots, no one could disentangle them again'.[54] Janus's hearing aid symbolises his vulnerability to being lost in misconceptions of the welfare state, a vulnerability reiterated by his despairing question, 'What happened to the care? No one left over to. Throw out and start again, that's their motto. They.'[55] Where the hearing aid may resound with the idea that the reader could be here to aid Janus, the uncertainties that resound through the text disturb the reader's exposure to his hearing (or trial of conscience) with the alterity of the other.

The ambiguities that reverberate through *Winter Journey* are evident in the text's presentation of the persistence of missing voices. When we first encounter Nora, Janus's partner, it seems as though she is present beside Janus: 'Nora stirring by now, grumbling about me having to get up, awake anyway, but grumbling.'[56] The present continuous 'stirring', 'grumbling' and the immediacy announced by 'now' give the impression that Nora is with Janus in his room. It is only when we hear Janus's landlady complaining through a wall that we are informed of Nora's absence: 'should have given the old codger notice, he's no use to himself or anyone else. [. . .] Should have tied his notice to quit on Nora Stobb's wreath.'[57] Janus, alone, is left with an echo of Nora's view of 'who is to blame for hard times': 'Men, she'd say in her rock bottom voice, all you can do is kill each other and then come home and give us more kids to fill the gap. Women.'[58] Reverberations of Nora's voice trouble Janus's hearing, highlighting his part in the violence and self-interest of men. Janus's son Ted is said to have had 'no time for' the former's interest in clock mechanics, the 'precision, care involved', as the latter moved to Australia to 'sell fast'.[59] However, Janus's bitterness towards his son wavers as Nora's voice resurfaces: 'You drove him, she said, you drove him as far as he could go.'[60] Janus's guilt at driving people away is compounded by his anonymity in the speed and cacophony of London's traffic. With 'noise coming from all directions', the city is 'all too fast for' Janus as he finds himself 'only half-way across' the road, while the lights have already sped through 'green and then amber to red'.[61] When someone helps him across the road, Janus repeats his plea, 'What happened to the care?', but receives little support in the words that meet him: 'Come on, Dad, let's get across, shall we? Haven't got all day. All day.'[62] That the passer-by addresses Janus as 'Dad' augments how the pressure of the traffic's noise drives his growing sense of guilt through voices from missing times (they do not have 'all day' for him). Janus's relationship with his son impinges again when Nora's earlier rebuttal, 'You drove him',[63] works its way into the re-emergence of how 'Ted drove him to it': '[Ted's] face so stark white and I could hear him say Dad Hit Me Mum when Nora got in. And he didn't.'[64] The clash and collision of the sounds of lost voices and 'boom[ing]' traffic driving into Janus makes the text tremble, as it barely holds together the 'pressure of noise in the head',[65] a 'frail wall between two seas of sound'.[66]

Where Janus's relation to Ted tremors with the return of words heard and not said, and which typify Nora's claim that men 'kill each other', Janus's relationship with his daughter, Nan, echoes Nora's image of women as posited in the 'gap' to which men 'come home'.[67] Unnerved that Janus's parcel of washing includes Nora's skirt, Nan exclaims '"Are you out of your mind?"', before questioning Janus further: '"You didn't expect me to wash it, did you?".'[68] The questions strike Janus with the 'gap',[69] the emptiness of the domestic role limiting his relation to his daughter; Janus 'can't let her in, not that she wants. But when people say that they mean: my own daughter. The shame.'[70] What follows is another desperate, unvoiced statement: 'I'm your father.'[71] The fact that what Janus would say he cannot say, and that this unsaid reverberates in his hearing, insinuates the appeal of another time dislocating his own: 'Janus did not answer, he could not answer. He stared at the red and white pattern on the table and weak tears ran down his face. Now there was no shame left.'[72] *Winter Journey* closes with the acknowledgement, 'Yes, but I hear her now and she can't hear me answer', as though its broken hearing admits it is overwhelmed by being out of time with a responsibility for other persons.[73] Figes's rhetoric of failure demands, as W. L. Webb put it in his commendation of the novel after it won the 1967 Guardian Fiction Prize, that readers 'feel the stammer of that old heart [. . .] as if we had inherited it, the pain of all his experience, and the pulse of will that keeps him going'.[74]

184   Chris Clarke

Konek Landing

Where *Winter Journey*'s poetry of the inarticulate asks the reader to listen in on an increasingly vulnerable mishearing, in her next experimental novel, *Konek Landing*, Figes heightens her work's rhetoric of failure. Figes recalls how John Berger felt that the '"book makes a physical impact on you"', which was 'what [Figes] was trying to do' by 'push[ing] language to its limits' and emphasising its 'sound texture'.[75] This intensification of Figes's aesthetic radicalism could be read as a repercussion of the historical subject to which her novel responds. 'On a personal level', Figes states in an interview with Alan Burns, *Konek Landing* 'dealt with the extermination of the Jews', and she admits that she 'never thought about [her] German–Jewish past again in the way [she] did before [she] wrote that book'.[76] Figes's later accounts of her early life – her family's escape from Nazi Germany (*Little Eden* (1978) and *Tales of Innocence and Experience* (2003)), and their housemaid's survival there (*Journey to Nowhere* (2008)) – elucidate the historical context of *Konek Landing*. In her memoirs, Figes reveals how, when she was twelve going on thirteen, her Jewish identity became 'less [of] a mystery and [more of a] terrible reality', having viewed the newsreel of Belsen concentration camp and the images of 'dazed survivors with huge haunted eyes'[77]:

> I had lost my tongue. I could not speak a word of the language I had learnt so assiduously. I felt it was a lie, the bank on the corner, the municipal flowerbed, the bus stop opposite the haberdasher. What had I to do with this pretence of normality?[78]

Where Figes renders this moment in her memoirs as a linguistic and epistemological impasse – 'I had lost my tongue. I could not speak' – it foregrounds how her experimental fiction employs a similar rhetoric of failure to impress the ethical dimension of its representation of survival.

Konek Landing concerns Stefan Konek, who, in Figes's words, as 'a survivor of the ghetto and an orphan, [eventually] finds himself in a veterans' home for German soldiers'.[79] *Konek Landing* evokes the fractured time experienced by German–Jewish refugees – what Figes notes as an apparent inability to 'live in the real world' because of being 'stuck in the past' – through the contrast between the open-ended 'landing' of the text's title and the finality of the 'landed' presented at the end of the novel.[80] In a care home for soldiers, who murmur, 'nobody cares about us', one voice is deliberately 'drowned' out, as he jeers, 'They all piled on top of one another, fighting for the last bit of air, so the kids and women landed down at the bottom.'[81] Figes reiterates the text's stutter between times, evoked by the difference between 'landing' and 'landed', when she describes the novel as pointing towards 'things in one's past that are like a thorn in one's flesh, and [how] they irritate'.[82] We can read Figes's text's representation of the past as a persistent interruption of oneself through Levinas's conception of one's ethical exposure to the other as a form of unsettled embodiment; Levinas also calls upon the image of 'a thorn burning the flesh' in order to impress how the responsibility for the other, or ethical subjectivity, is a 'living human corporeality'.[83]

Figes's rhetoric of failure in *Konek Landing* presents and formally enacts a body continually being undone by the appeal from persons beyond its own time. The novel oscillates between Stefan's attempts to evade recognising his status as a deserter somewhere in postwar Europe and recollections of the places he fled as a child. The text's lack of punctuation gives the prose a breathlessness, as is evident in the following excerpt, which describes Stefan hiding from the police who wear 'uniform tunics':

> Legs beginning to prickle, back aching, feet dead how did I pass the time wriggling toes pee-ed into my pants once sniffing dipped fingers into the warm trickle licked at it how did I ever get through the first I was a caveman she suggested that so I wouldn't make a sound because the lion was prowling about outside in the forest waiting to get his jaws into me gobble me all up so I sat there very quiet for what must have been hours holding my breath listening men's voices once I heard them then I was really frightened they were shouting so I thought if they take her away who is going to let me out no one.[84]

Stefan's attempt to fictionalise his situation as a 'caveman' hiding from 'the lion' struggles to hold together because the very recollection of these events continues to be unsettled by the overwhelming nature of the experience. Fictions tenuously enable Stefan's survival and pierce him with loss, as, finding himself without his mother and father, he is told 'of course mother or father will come back, but just for now you are going to have a nice holiday with auntie, and just for a game you are going to have a new name. You are now Pavel Zuck.'[85] The story's urgency and cautionary tone betray its collapse: 'Now, she warned your name is Pavel, remember, your father is dead, your mother has gone away to nurse her sister your aunt. Repeat that, let me hear you say it now.'[86] The iteration of 'now' that begins and ends the attempt to pin down Stefan's new identity draws attention to its dislocation by the passing of other times, obliquely acknowledged in the withdrawal of his mother and father.

Stefan's grounding in the space and time of the text is repeatedly unsettled by his encounter with women suffering the loss and ruin of men. In search of shelter, Stefan happens to mention his name to an elderly woman, Nelly, who lost a son of his name 'many years ago now' and insists that he 'must come back with her'.[87] Stefan wakes in an 'airless room, push[ing] back the too hot feather quilt', and is told by Nelly that she has kept his 'butterfly collection'.[88] The suffocating domesticity – 'net curtains across the windows, stuffy, radiators full on'[89] – escalates as Nelly places under Stefan's eyes 'his' butterflies, 'each creature the rusted pin stuck through its dry back, one wing dropped off, dust obscured, Latin label':

> Afraid to breathe fearing that the expelled air the breath coming out of him would send the dusty grubs to their final disintegration him held with lungs caught holding the foul air pinned there the pin itself crusted with rust: pain through nerve ends, recognition, a collection of trivia uglier than old leaves, the last ray of a bygone summer it was better not to remember, light photons dead, the eye having seen nothing, a distant agony perpetuate.[90]

The withdrawal of air seems to tighten the text; its syntax almost 'faints' in the juddering 'him held lungs caught holding', before hinting towards a painful memory 'it was better not to remember'.[91] Stefan confronts his will to forget when he happens upon a notebook of the man who has left Nelly and her daughter, Lili, reiterating his own restless condition: '*But there is no one, nowhere to turn [. . .]. Why should I waste my last breath in struggling to mitigate their guilt?*'[92] The notebook, whose pages 'dropped off at the spine' and which Stefan has to hold 'carefully to stop them disintegrating, falling away from the central thread', anticipates the collapse of the text's body in its attempt to respond for others.[93]

Konek Landing heightens its rhetoric of failure through the fragmentation that accompanies Stefan's arrest and imprisonment for deserting the navy. A 'number among other numbers',[94] Stefan becomes subject to unsound sounds that unravel the saying offered at the beginning of the novel: 'mens sana in corpore' [sic] (a sound mind in a sound body).[95] The gaps in the text emphasise Stefan's faltering sensibility, which stages the limits of hearing:

> Ears unstoppered now, the flaw in the cracked pot traced with one forefinger, soothing eyepads re-moved for dust, inflammatory, to irritate, scratch,
>
> and if rubbed

Now the ship has arrived I am reluctant to leave,

am in no condition for leaving

How to

Imagine I was not born.[96]

'Doubly aware of sounds' and with an ear for hearing what goes missing, Stefan seems to go on in a 'halt' as though he were 'a heart missing a beat I have not heard before'.[97] Extending the exploration of the limits of the audible presented in *Winter Journey*, the passage underscores Figes's concern for the paradoxical interdependence between language and the body: 'somehow you have to have an ear for it [language]'.[98] The novel intensifies its representation of an unsettled sensibility, as Stefan attempts to catch 'a wisp of sound blown away, impossible to say', and falls overboard the ship that he had abandoned:

> coughing dark drops choking on his own blood now ribs broken still breathing though harshly now fighting punctured agonies invading black perhaps tasting thick black oil spitting salt swallowing blood sobbing mother hold me tight screaming in the dark.[99]

The text's faltering form – a collapsing body – insinuates how one must fail again and fail better in being responsible for the other person. In this way, *Konek Landing* adopts a rhetoric of failure to evoke the difficulties of acknowledging unaccountable losses puncturing the postwar world. *Konek Landing* underlines how Figes's work, like that of her contemporaries, responds, in Jordan's words, 'to a genuinely felt crisis of representation that followed modernism and the Second World War', drawing on a sense of failure to impress one's ethical responsibility for the other.[100]

After the Sixties

One could consider Figes's unravelling of male subjectivity and limiting domestic spaces in *Winter Journey* and *Konek Landing* as literary precursors to her feminist treatise, *Patriarchal Attitudes*, which dissects the different ways in which 'women have been largely man-made'.[101] While a fuller illustration of this argument is beyond the scope of this chapter, the experimental novels that Figes produced following *Winter Journey* and *Konek Landing* reflect her contention that 'things that [she] was repressing or keeping in the background in order to keep them under control were [. . .] able to come out' after the publication of *Patriarchal Attitudes*.[102] *Days* (1974) and *Nelly's Version* (1977) explore female subjectivities, presenting what we might call 'limit experiences' to challenge constructions of gender. *Days* focuses on the immobility of an unnamed narrator as she lies in a hospital bed reflecting upon her relationships to her mother and daughter. Similarly, *Nelly's Version* offers a direct subversion of how, in Figes's view, 'self-consciously feminist fiction [was] hampering itself by taking off, being propagandist'.[103] In the novel, Figes plays on the protagonist's amnesia to critique how reified notions of femininity were taking form through 'realist' texts and 'limit[ing] the imagination'.[104]

Yet, despite Figes's later texts' exploration of new subjects, her early experimental fiction's acute concern with the problems of surviving underpins the legacy of her work. In response to a question about how she felt being viewed as 'one of the last survivors of the experimentalist tradition' during an interview from 1999, Figes spoke of how:

> I do feel alone [. . .]. I always thought that one of the good things about my situation is I'm ahead of my time, therefore when I get older I will come into my time, but that hasn't quite happened.[105]

This enquiry into the 'survival' of Figes's early experimental fiction has shown how our recovery of her work in the contemporary is problematic, as whichever way we address and characterise it, we risk, as Figes put it, making her fiction part of a 'trade of reassurance': discourses that encourage us to forget that a 'statement is being made'.[106] However, I would argue that this very difficulty is another trace of the ethical dimension of Figes's early experimental fiction. It intimates how her novels' fragmented forms and admission of failure continue to encumber their reader with a responsibility for the other, in much the same way as Figes acknowledges, in a comment from late in her career, 'that a subject matter for a book is not the one that you choose but one that chooses you. You know, it's an idea that will not go away.'[107]

Notes

1. Eva Figes, 'Authors' Lives', interviewed by Sarah O'Reilly, The British Library, 2010. *Konek Landing* is dedicated to 'Emil Cohen and his wife Ella', Figes's maternal grandparents, who died during the Second World War, having been imprisoned in a concentration camp in Poland.

2. Eva Figes, *Little Eden: A Child at War* (London: Faber and Faber, 1978), p. 19. Figes translated, amongst other texts, *The Gadarene Club* by Martin Walser for Longmans in 1960.
3. Eva Figes, interviewed by Alan Burns, in *The Imagination on Trial: British and American Writers Discuss their Working Methods*, ed. Alan Burns and Charles Sugnet (London: Allison and Busby, 1981), p. 34.
4. Eva Tucker, 'Eva Figes Obituary', *The Guardian*, 7 September 2012, available at <http://www.guardian.co.uk/books/2012/sep/07/eva-figes> (last accessed 18 July 2018).
5. Anna Maria Stuby, 'Eva Figes's Novels', in *Engendering Realism and Postmodernism: Contemporary Writers in Britain*, ed. Neumeier Beate (Amsterdam: Rodopi, 2001), pp. 105–16, p. 105.
6. Eva Figes, 'B. S. Johnson', *Review of Contemporary Fiction*, 5:2 (1985), pp. 70–1, p. 70.
7. Ibid. p. 70.
8. Eva Figes, 'The State of Fiction: A Symposium', *New Review*, 5:1 (1978), pp. 38–9, p. 38.
9. Julia Jordan, 'Late Modernism and the Avant-Garde Renaissance', in *The Cambridge Companion to British Fiction since 1945*, ed. David James (New York: Cambridge University Press 2015), pp. 145–59.
10. Cheryl Verdon, 'Forgotten Words: Trauma, Memory, and Herstory in Eva Figes's Fiction', *Jewish Women Writers in Britain*, ed. Nadia Valman (Detroit: Wayne State University Press, 2014), pp. 116–34, p. 118.
11. Silvia Pellicer-Ortin, *Eva Figes' Writings: A Journey through Trauma* (Newcastle-upon-Tyne: Cambridge Scholars, 2015), pp. 4, 8.
12. Figes, 'The State of Fiction', p. 39.
13. Figes, 'B. S. Johnson', p. 70.
14. Eva Figes, 'The Writer's Dilemma', *The Guardian*, 17 June 1968, p. 7.
15. Robert Nye, 'A Dull Head Among Windy Spaces', *The Guardian*, 7 April 1967, p. 7.
16. Silvia Pellicer-Ortin, 'The Ethical Clock of Trauma in Eva Figes's *Winter Journey*', in *Ethics and Trauma in Contemporary British Fiction* (New York: Rodopi, 2011), pp. 37–60, p. 37.
17. Figes, 'The State of Fiction', p. 39.
18. Andrzej Gąsiorek, *Post-War British Fiction: Realism and After* (London: Edward Arnold, 1995), p. 2.
19. Peter Boxall, 'Science, Technology, and the Posthuman', in *The Cambridge Companion to British Fiction since 1945*, ed. David James (Cambridge: Cambridge University Press, 2015), pp. 127–42, p. 134.
20. Ibid. p. 132.
21. Figes, 'The Writer's Dilemma', p. 7.
22. Figes, 'The State of Fiction', p. 39.
23. Eva Figes, 'Eva Figes: An Interview', interviewed by Manuel Almagro and Carolina Sánchez-Palencia, *Atlantis*, 22:1 (2000), pp. 177–86, p. 185. Figes also suggests that she is 'a much more local writer than [Beckett] is, and the fact that I am a woman makes a difference' (p. 185). Other

important influences on Figes's work include Virginia Woolf, Franz Kafka and T. S. Eliot.
24. Jordan suggests that Figes and her contemporaries' relationship to modernism is paradoxical because 'to be an experimental writer after modernism is to inherit something defined by its resistance to tradition' (p. 145).
25. Samuel Beckett and Georges Duthuit, *Proust and Three Dialogues* (London: Calder & Boyars, 1965), pp. 124–5.
26. Ibid.
27. Ibid. p. 125.
28. Ewa Ziarek, *The Rhetoric of Failure: Deconstruction of Scepticism, Reinvention of Modernism* (Albany: SUNY Press, 1996), p. 170.
29. Figes, 'Eva Figes', p. 182.
30. Ibid. p. 182. Figes's and Grass's 'affection for each other', Tucker notes, survived the confessions Grass made in 2006 about his membership of the Waffen-SS, available at <http://www.oxforddnb.com/view/10.1093/ref:odnb/9780198614128.001.0001/odnb-9780198614128-e-105542?rskey=whRGsO&result=6> (last accessed 18 July 2018).
31. Eva Figes, 'Note', in *Beyond the Words: Eleven Writers in Search of a New Fiction*, ed. Giles Gordon (London: Hutchinson, 1975), pp. 113–14, p. 113.
32. Ibid. p. 113.
33. Ibid. p. 114.
34. Ibid. p. 113.
35. Ibid. p. 114.
36. Ibid.
37. Derek Attridge, *The Singularity of Literature* (London: Routledge, 2004), p. 124, pp. 123–4.
38. Emmanuel Levinas, 'Ethics of the Infinite', interviewed by Richard Kearney, in *States of Mind: Dialogues with Contemporary Thinkers on the European Mind* (Manchester: Manchester University Press, 1997), pp. 177–99, p. 192.
39. Emmanuel Levinas, interviewed by Raoul Mortley, in *French Philosophers in Conversation: Levinas, Schneider, Serres, Irigaray, Le Dœuff, Derrida* (London: Routledge, 1991), pp. 10–23, p. 16.
40. Emmanuel Levinas, 'The Other in Proust', in *Proper Names*, trans. Michael B. Smith (Stanford: Stanford University Press, 1996), pp. 99–105, p. 104.
41. Levinas, 'Ethics of the Infinite', p. 188.
42. Ziarek, *Rhetoric of Failure*, pp. 5, 82.
43. Ibid. p. 80.
44. Peter Boxall, *The Value of the Novel* (Cambridge: Cambridge University Press, 2015), p. 10.
45. Figes, *Imagination on Trial*, p. 35.
46. Nye, 'A Dull Head', p. 7.

47. Figes, *Imagination on Trial*, p. 34, p. 35.
48. Ibid. p. 36.
49. Ibid.
50. Ibid. pp. 36, 35.
51. Eva Figes, *Winter Journey* (London: Faber, 1967), p. 9.
52. Drawing a parallel between Dominick LaCapra's 'concept of empathic unsettlement' and Levinas's 'ethics of alterity', Pellicer-Ortin suggests that the text 'establishes a Levinasian "face-to-face relationship" between readers and characters' (Pellicer-Ortin, 'Ethical Clock', pp. 59–60).
53. Figes, *Winter Journey*, p. 11.
54. Ibid. p. 15.
55. Ibid. p. 47. Hearing aids were offered by the National Health Service up until the 1970s.
56. Ibid. p. 12.
57. Ibid. pp. 17–18.
58. Ibid. p. 25.
59. Ibid. p. 64.
60. Ibid.
61. Ibid. p. 46.
62. Ibid. p. 63.
63. Ibid. p. 64.
64. Ibid. p. 81.
65. Ibid. p. 59.
66. Ibid. p. 42.
67. Ibid. p. 25.
68. Ibid. pp. 70, 71.
69. Ibid. p. 25.
70. Ibid. p. 71.
71. Ibid.
72. Ibid.
73. Ibid. p. 118.
74. 'Winning Work of Fiction', *The Guardian*, 25 November 1967, p. 3.
75. Figes, *Imagination on Trial*, pp. 36–7.
76. Ibid. p. 37.
77. Figes, *Little Eden*, pp. 129, 131.
78. Eva Figes, *Tales of Innocence and Experience: An Exploration* (Rothley: W. F. Howes, 2003), pp. 122–3.
79. Figes, *Imagination on Trial*, p. 37.
80. Eva Figes, *Journey to Nowhere: One Woman Looks for the Promised Land* (London: Granta, 2008), p. 106.
81. Eva Figes, *Konek Landing* (London: Faber, 1969), pp. 168, 170, 169.
82. Figes, *Imagination on Trial*, p. 38.
83. Emmanuel Levinas, *Otherwise than Being, or, Beyond Essence*, trans. Alphonso Lingis (Pittsburgh: Duquesne University Press, 1981), pp. 50, 51.

84. Figes, *Konek Landing*, pp. 17–18.
85. Ibid. p. 27.
86. Ibid. p. 29.
87. Ibid. p. 69.
88. Ibid. p. 72.
89. Ibid. p. 71.
90. Ibid. pp. 72–3.
91. Ibid.
92. Ibid. p. 79.
93. Ibid. pp. 78, 79.
94. Ibid. p. 128.
95. Ibid. p. 20.
96. Ibid. p. 135.
97. Ibid. p. 136.
98. Figes, 'Eva Figes', p. 184.
99. Figes, *Konek Landing*, pp. 156, 164.
100. Jordan, 'Late Modernism', p. 150.
101. Eva Figes, *Patriarchal Attitudes: Women in Society* (London: Faber, 1970), p. 33.
102. Eva Figes, interviewed by Olga Kenyon, in *Women Writers Talk: Interviews with Ten Women Writers*, ed. Olga Kenyon (Oxford: Lennard, 1989), pp. 69–90, p. 76.
103. Ibid. p. 77.
104. Ibid. p. 77.
105. Figes, 'Eva Figes', p. 182.
106. Figes, 'Note', p. 113.
107. Figes, 'Eva Figes', p. 182.

Chapter 11

Christine Brooke-Rose: The Development of Experiment

Stephanie Jones

> Have you ever tried to do something very difficult as well as you can, over a long period, and found that nobody notices? That's what I've been doing for over thirty years.
> Christine Brooke-Rose[1]

From the early 1960s, Christine Brooke-Rose positioned herself as one of the most 'vociferous innovators' of British experimental literature by writing self-reflexive novels that interrogate the nature, structure and form of the text.[2] In the preceding years (1957–61), Brooke-Rose had produced four early novels largely concerned with social satire, along with some poetry including *Gold* (1955), a long poem with metaphysical and religious tones, based on the anonymous fourteenth-century poem *Pearl*. While her novels had been fairly successful and she had received some popularity for her poetry, shorter examples of which appeared in publications such as *Truth* (and later the *Times Literary Supplement*), in the early 1960s Brooke-Rose became considerably more experimental in her writing.[3] Her desire to interrogate and develop the novel form in bold, imaginative ways has challenged her readers and compounded her reputation as being an author of 'difficult' texts. This reputation has historically haunted her work, although, in recent years, there has been somewhat of an upsurge in published critical studies of her œuvre,[4] including a special issue of *Textual Practice* published in 2018 (ed. Ferris and Jones), collecting together critical and creative pieces dedicated to her life and work. Additionally, her name often appears in overviews of postwar literature as part of a list of writers who rejected the traditional constraints of the novel form, but these are rarely accompanied by a rigorous investigation of her techniques.[5]

This chapter will present a detailed analysis of the first three decidedly experimental novels written by Brooke-Rose – those published during the 1960s: *Out* (1964), *Such* (1966) and *Between* (1968).

It will investigate how Brooke-Rose borrows and experiments with different techniques, themes and language in these earlier novels to forge her own attempt at a new direction for the novel. It will argue that this period of experimentation is concluded not in the 1960s, but in the 1970s with Brooke-Rose's most eclectic, arguably most innovative novel *Thru* (1975). This novel is a culmination of the experimental techniques that Brooke-Rose 'tried out' during the 1960s in her earlier novels, and it has become the pinnacle of her experiment in the minds of her readers and her critics alike. This early period of experimentation presents a narrative of development and growth in Brooke-Rose as an experimenter; each text tests the reader in a different way, challenging them with increasingly more elaborate practices. Although her later novels (after *Thru*) continued to challenge and experiment with language and form, this chapter argues that it is in this early period that she is at her most voracious and her most 'difficult'. In *Metafiction* (1984), Patricia Waugh claims that *Thru* fails to provide sufficient direction for the novel, but that lessons learned from its complexity and its 'difficulty' may lead to a transformation in the novel genre as a whole:

> *Thru* fails to provide, beyond itself, sufficient direction for the novel genre as a whole. In my opinion, the future of the novel will depend upon a *transformation*, not an *abandonment*, of the traditional conventions of fiction, though it may well be a transformation based on lessons learned from radical texts like *Thru*.[6]

While the experiments that Brooke-Rose orchestrates in *Out*, *Such* and *Between* make each of these novels appear to be in opposition to the traditional novel form, they also incorporate traditional features including plot progression, characterisation and narrative voice. In this sense, Waugh's demands for a 'transformation' over 'abandonment' of traditional conventions is fulfilled by these earlier novels while *Thru* can be regarded as a line in the sand.

While Brooke-Rose identified with various authors throughout her career (Samuel Beckett, Alain Robbe-Grillet, Ezra Pound, Muriel Spark and Brigid Brophy, to name only a few), she remained reluctant to be part of any defined 'group'. Although her literary friends would often champion her work at any given opportunity (especially Frank Kermode, whose reviews of her work were always particularly admiring), it remained on the periphery of the mainstream literary scene, never being entirely absorbed or rejected by British culture. The reasons for this peripheral existence will be investigated in this chapter and, in turn, it will seek to reclaim these early experimental novels as significant contributions to the direction of the novel as a genre during this period.

Early Experiments

Brooke-Rose began writing *Out* during her convalescence after an emergency operation while visiting her aunt in France. Hailing originally from Geneva, the second daughter of a Swiss–American mother and an English father, Brooke-Rose was an accomplished polyglot, able to speak German, English and French fluently. She originally moved to England when she was thirteen to attend high school in Folkestone. Eventually, after having spent a short time in Liverpool, a while in Gloucestershire (working as a Women's Auxiliary Air Force (WAAF) officer at Bletchley Park) and three years studying for her undergraduate degree at Somerville College, Oxford (1946–49), Brooke-Rose studied for her PhD at University College London. She was settled in London until 1968, when she permanently relocated to France – originally Paris – to take up a teaching post at the Université de Paris VIII, then later to Gordes in Provence, where she eventually retired. This brief biographical history poses yet another obstacle to including Brooke-Rose in the British literary landscape of the twentieth century: just how British is Christine Brooke-Rose? Indeed, after 1968, Brooke-Rose never permanently relocated to Britain. There is a sense that Brooke-Rose's dual nationality and polyglottism allowed her access to experiences beyond any one culture, while simultaneously barring her from truly belonging anywhere.

When reading *Out* it seems impossible to ignore the author's heritage and long-term residence in France, as this novel, more than any of her others, is clearly influenced by the work of the *nouveau roman*, specifically the work of Alain Robbe-Grillet. Brooke-Rose admits this influence as a source of inspiration in her collection *Invisible Author: Last Essays* (2002), where she states that she uses 'the present tense in a specific, paradoxical way I owe to the French writer Alain Robbe-Grillet'.[7] She continues by asserting that:

> In 1953 Robbe-Grillet used the present tense throughout *Les Gommes*, as did Beckett in *Molloy* (original French version, 1950), and Sarraute in *Le Planétarium* (1959). [. . .] By 1963, in *Pour un nouveau roman* [. . .] Robbe-Grillet was naming the use of the past tense as the distinguishing mark of the traditional novel.[8]

Here, Brooke-Rose identifies the characteristic of the traditional novel to which she is reacting with her own writing. She claims that the 'very difficult' thing that she has been doing for 'over thirty years' is to write in a sustained present tense.[9] In fact, this is only one of the grammatical constraints that Brooke-Rose uses when writing her novels and, as this chapter will reveal, formal and grammatical constraints are frequently the focus of her experiments. She describes this particular experiment as a lipogram, an entire omission or 'refusal of the narrative past tense, replaced by a simultaneous present tense'.[10] By conducting this experiment, Brooke-Rose actively and deliberately refuses to be confined by the structure and expectations of the traditional novel. Nevertheless, there are aspects of the traditional novel that appear in *Out* and in Brooke-Rose's work more generally (for example, plot progression, characterisation), and the relationship between the experimental elements and the traditional aspects of the novels is worth investigating in more detail. While Brooke-Rose clearly and openly identified with the writers of the *nouveau roman* and Beckett – writers who had been interrogating the constraints of the traditional novel for some time – she did not consider that the same challenges to the novel form were taking place in Britain. Instead, to gain momentum and inspiration for her writing, Brooke-Rose frequently tapped sources from abroad, with little consideration for the experiments taking place at home in Britain.

However, in challenging the restrictions and boundaries of the traditional novel, Brooke-Rose was not alone amongst her British contemporaries. B. S. Johnson also took a stand against traditionalism, rather famously declaring that 'telling stories really is telling lies', thereby demanding a truth that had not existed within the realist novel of the nineteenth century.[11] Julia Jordan admits that Johnson's avant-gardism 'was in many ways [. . .] odd' essentially because of this 'old-fashioned sounding' concept of 'truth'.[12] Johnson's search for the truth can be seen in his semi-autobiographical novel *Trawl* (1966), which is both a 'novel about fishing as well as being a fishing expedition in its own right, allowing the author to rummage around the bed of his own mind in search of past memories and experiences'.[13] Jordan asserts that Johnson's 'aim is to collect the "accumulated guts, debris, starfish . . . rejectamenta" as he calls them – the stuff that other novelists would leave behind [. . .]. However, even with this compulsive trawl "truth" can slip through the net.'[14] In a sense, Johnson's striving for truth expresses his exhaustion and ultimate dissatisfaction with the novel as a form. Indeed, later Johnson's frustration with the confines of the traditional novel becomes physical with the publication of *The Unfortunates* (1969), which contains twenty-seven individually bound sections, twenty-five of which the reader is encouraged to shuffle and read in the order of their choosing. Brooke-Rose's expression of dissatisfaction with the novel form stays rigidly within the confines of the book's binding; however, her desire to present accurate, unbiased detail in *Out* is comparable to Johnson's insistent demand for 'truth' in the novel form: 'The left foot treads the length of the cement line. Between the tiles, the right foot carefully selects another line of cement parallel with the edge of the path.'[15] Each author regards their own method of experiment as the definitive direction for the transformation of the novel, and each ultimately fails in achieving their own goals. Jordan states that 'Despite the capaciousness of [Johnson's] inclusive method, we are often left with the feeling that something has been left out, that something has not been captured, that the truth has proved elusive.'[16] In the same respect, the details of the scenes in *Out* can never be entirely accurate or objective because language consistently creates meaning through its associations and through the creation of metaphors. This is evidenced by moments when the description becomes unavoidably metaphorical but still tries to retain an element of objectivity by using accurate description: 'The green thermoplastic snake lies along the inside of the right-hand flower-bed.'[17]

The desire to focus upon minute detail, thereby making the scene depicted within the novel hyperrealistic, is in part due to the influence of Robbe-Grillet, Beckett and the *nouveau roman*. Further to this, scenes are depicted with very few adjectives, making the narration seem cold and specific, as if reported by a camera lens – a technique typical of Robbe-Grillet, whose own novels are similarly concerned with voyeurism, looking and framing:

> A fly straddles another fly on the faded denim stretched over the knee. Sooner or later the knee will have to make a move, but now it is immobilised by the two flies, the lower of which is so still that it seems dead [. . .].[18]

This quotation is taken from the first paragraph of *Out* and the image is returned to throughout the novel. By pausing on this ordinary, mundane moment, Brooke-Rose collects for herself some 'stuff that other novelists would leave behind'.[19] In its reclamation, the knee becomes entirely defamiliarised to the reader, existing only as an object, a disembodied platform for the copulative performance of the flies. The description of the knee as 'immobilised' and the lower fly's appearing 'dead' imbue this passage with a stillness; the moment is held in suspension, paused so that the narrator can describe it in practical detail without poetic implication. This aspect is reminiscent of Beckett's style in *Molloy* where the protagonist's pebble-sucking habit is described at length in the form of a list. Beckett's use of lists allows for the formulation of various possibilities for actions and thoughts, blurring the lines between the hypothetical or the imagined, and the real. This line continues to be negotiated in *Out*, where the contrast between how things really are and how they are perceived comes into question:

> To live the gesture in immobility is to evoke and therefore to have observed the gesture. But imagination is not an imaged projection of observed phenomena. Sometimes it is sufficient to imagine an episode for the episode to occur, and that is the terrifying thing, though not necessarily in that precise form.[20]

The preoccupation with perception and creating through imagining occurs in Robbe-Grillet's work, particularly in the novels *The Voyeur* (*Le Voyeur*, 1955) and *Jealousy* (*La Jalousie*, 1957). In *The Voyeur*, Matthias's narrative is recounted through first-person perspective but told through third-person narration, which has the effect of creating an event from a distanced perspective.[21] In *Jealousy*, the observer is convinced that A. . . is having an affair with the neighbour, Franck, and, as Roch C. Smith notes, 'the narrator's descriptions allow for the possibility that things should merely be taken at face value or, alternatively, that they should be read as signs of a hidden reality'.[22] The indeterminacy and possibilities created by the transformation of narration in these novels are comparable to Brooke-Rose's engagement with the concept of perception. The closer the description moves to being accurate, the further away the reality becomes due to the altered perception of that reality through language. When discussing Robbe-Grillet's technique, Brooke-Rose asserts that he 'has undertaken nothing less than to cleanse objects of all the significance (moral, psychological, social, metaphysical, etc.) with which humanism has invested them [. . .]. The world is neither significant nor absurd, he says, it merely is.'[23] This undertaking is unrealistic because, although objects might appear to be cleansed, the observer / reader imbues these objects with significance and, as such, it becomes impossible to tell how 'clean' these objects are before their perception.

While Brooke-Rose continues to privilege ordinary moments and elongate them through long passages of seemingly objective description, she does so against an extraordinary plot concerned with the reversal of racial hegemony. The reader is confronted with the aftermath of 'the displacement', a possible nuclear event which has resulted in the white people, or the 'Colourless', suffering with a sickness similar in description to radiation poisoning. The 'Melanesian' races are immune to the sickness and have prospered. The unnamed, unemployed male protagonist is 'Colourless' and throughout the course of the novel his physical and psychological states deteriorate. He attends the Labour Exchange to look for employment every day and eventually is employed for a short time as a gardener by a wealthy 'Melanesian' woman, Mrs Mgulu. However, due to the sickness and the deterioration of his psychological state, he loses his job and has to be cared for by his wife. Throughout the novel, various different images are invoked and repeat, creating a call-back rhythm which continues throughout the text. For instance, Sarah Birch notes that the repetition of the image of the copulating flies, mirrored in the copulation of the humans, connects to the concept of the Labour Exchange as an example of Brooke-Rose's larger interest in converging different metaphors and meanings of words:

> This image of copulation serves as a linguistic act of 'insemination' which initiates a period of gestation and provokes a reference to giving birth towards the end of the chapter. In an imagined interview at the Labour Exchange, the protagonist claims that he has only been 'spasmodically in labour', then immediately corrects himself by rephrasing the slip as 'employed intermittently'.[24]

Birch goes on to explain that the metaphor is created by the pun on the word 'labour' and that these types of metaphor 'play on the identity of signifiers to highlight the multiplicity of signification and its discourse-dependence. They serve as prisms or refracting lenses which multiply meaning.'[25]

Another prevalent recurring image is that of the 'scope', which appears as part of the words 'gastroscope', 'microscope' and 'psychoscope' on multiple occasions. This repetition has the effect of reinforcing the focus on looking at the minute details in a sustained and examining way, as well as suggesting an invasive viewing of the individual's interior space. The repetition of 'scope' on so many occasions reinforces the idea not just of *looking* or *viewing* but of *finding* (scoping) something out as a result of this process. 'Scope', also meaning 'range', provides the repeated images with multiple possibilities in terms of what the reader will glean from looking at the novel in different ways, through different lenses: for example, on a micro-level (semiotic), at a psycho-level (psychoanalytical) and so on. Further to this, the repeated grey colour and 'pimpled', 'flaccid' texture of the gruel against the recurring image of the 'marble slab' / 'pink veined marble' / 'pink marble' provoke a cumulative image of a dead, white body in a morgue. The thread of sickness that runs throughout the novel reinforces this image and is juxtaposed with the 'rebirthing' at the Labour Exchange. These are only a few examples of Brooke-Rose's comparing of images by playing upon double meanings and metaphors. Significantly, this technique is not in keeping with Robbe-Grillet's 'cleansing' philosophy, as this language game hinges entirely upon the significance attributed to 'objects' and the duplicity of language and its ability to create metaphor.

Drawing from Brooke-Rose's own analysis of metaphor as used by the metaphysical poets, and the comparison that she makes between them and Robbe-Grillet, Karen Lawrence has argued that there is something 'baroque' about Brooke-Rose's style in *Out* which 'yokes together by violence disparate things'.[26] While Brooke-Rose's style is sometimes muted or overshadowed by her mimicry of Robbe-Grillet's style, the extraordinary juxtaposition (in the sense that the relationships between these images and their meanings are challenged by the comparative nature of the juxtaposition) of ordinary images in her writing makes it distinctive. *Out* draws upon much from Brooke-Rose's sources of inspiration but nevertheless finds contained ways to express her own experiment. Her later writing shows much more extravagant uses of metaphor and imagery, illustrating that *Out* is simply the beginning of her experiment.

Such: Life-After-Life and the Great Beyond

Published only two years after *Out*, *Such* can be regarded as a marked progression in terms of Brooke-Rose's ability to invoke disparate and contradictory discourses. The text is presented in two parts. Part I is the larger section and begins with the protagonist narrating the opening of his coffin lid: 'Someone creaks, levelling out nails perhaps with the prolonged side of a hammer. The coffin lid creaks open.'[27] The language used in this section of the novel rapidly launches into a discourse of astrophysics and psychoanalysis, betraying the specialisms of the protagonist during his life. There is also an early introduction of multiple narrators who jostle for prominence and power. One of the voices takes on a male identity; the other defines itself as a 'girl-spy'. The girl-spy becomes known as 'Something' due to the male 'Someone's' desire to name things. While Someone seems unfamiliar with the world in which he exists, Something has an intrinsic knowledge of her surroundings and becomes Someone's guide to this strange, astronomical space. Through the discourse between Someone and Something, it becomes apparent that the protagonist Larry or Lazarus is existing between life and death. Having earlier died and been buried, he is now physically immobilised, awaiting his resurrection, but psychologically he seems free, dispersed or diffused across space and time. Lawrence recognises that multiple previous critical analyses of *Such*, and, indeed, Brooke-Rose herself, have recognised that 'the novel relies on a fundamental analogy between inner and outer space'.[28] While Larry's body is lifeless in the outer space of the hospital room, the reader is taken on interior adventures within his unconscious mind.

These adventures include Something's 'children', who exist as planets stretched out along her left arm:

> On her left spiral arm she carries a row of quintuplets.
> They opened up my knee, and found a hard-boiled egg inside. I scooped it out, it hurt, and I flung the slices away like discs, but they came back in their orbits and now I have to carry them.[29]

The creation of Something's children appears as a strange, almost childlike take on the Dogon creation myth, in which the non- or dual-gendered Amma created an egg which, upon its spontaneous explosion, released the cosmological components of the universe. This creation myth continues when Something's children become 'baptised' by being placed on the end of the musician, Jonas's, trumpet when he ceremoniously plays a different style of blues to each planet:

> He places the first planet on the end of his trumpet, lifts the instrument to his big mauve lips and sobs out Gut Bucket Blues to the rhythmic counterpoint of clarinet, bass sax, trombone and drums. Gut Bucket moves off into his orbit. Jonas places the second planet on the end of his trumpet and plays Potato Head Blues, then, with the third, Tin Roof Blues, then Dippermouth Blues with the fourth and finally, to change the style, Really the Blues. Really follows his brothers into orbit.[30]

'Blues' becomes a shared surname between Something's children and, indeed, later in the novel, Someone is referred to as 'Mister Blues'.[31] This family connection is only further evidenced by Gut Bucket and Tin Roof repeatedly referring to Someone as 'dad'. Although Someone claims that naming and 'baptising' 'gets rid of the original cause', the familial connections created by the surname and the affectionate 'dad' allow the reader to trace the origins of these strange beings.[32] While Brooke-Rose presents us with a seemingly impenetrable narrative of astronomical proportions by setting the novel in the subconscious mind of a dying man, she juxtaposes this with the simultaneous presentation of the recognisable tropes of creation and family. The presence of multiple narrators who engage with each other in long passages of referential dialogue adds to the disorientation of the reader, and at times the novel feels like a second-person narrative. The appearance of these recognisable tropes comes as both a surprise and something of a relief to the reader.

These tropes are continued in Part II of the novel, when Larry wakes up from his unconscious state and is reborn. However, Larry's wife and two children have become distant to him, as he has found it increasingly hard to connect with them and the world around him since his death and resurrection. Larry's son Martin goes to visit his father to connect with him but finds it difficult to keep Larry's attention on one topic as he tends to jump between different conversations and recall various stages of Martin's childhood. Although Martin is disappointed, there seems to be an inevitability to Larry's state: 'Mother warned me I'd find it difficult to get through to you.'[33] Since Larry's resurrection, he has become absorbed in astronomical discourse and, frequently, can view the world only through this lens, unable to distinguish individual physical features. Birch describes this characteristic by asserting that '[Larry's] eyes resemble dish-telescopes that seem to look right through his friends and he sees the psychic energy people emit as an astrophysicist's radio-telescope "sees" sounds bounced off distant galaxies.'[34] Despite his newfound perspective, Larry longs to return to the interior world and exist in the space 'between'. His death has impacted upon his life-after-life in ways that cannot be measured or accounted for in the exterior or 'outer space' of the reality to which he returns. In this sense, Brooke-Rose inverts the concepts of 'interior' and 'exterior', 'inner' and 'outer', by playing with the dimensions of inner / interior and outer / exterior space.

In an interview with Lawrence, Brooke-Rose admitted that she was a 'Freudian' in the sense that she frequently privileged the 'individual stages of identity formation' over the formation of group identity in her fiction.[35] However, Larry's reconstituted identity is not fully reformed and so he is not able to reconnect himself with society. Consequently, he remains isolated and alienated from the world around him. The fragmentation of Larry's psyche, the isolation from the world around him and his inability to recognise himself within the fragments of his psyche can perhaps more usefully be compared to the anti-psychiatry of R. D. Laing in *The Divided Self* (1960). Laing asserts that 'schizoid':

> refers to an individual the totality of whose experience is split in two main ways: in the first place there is a rent in his relation with his world and, in the second, there is a disruption in the relation with himself. Such a person is not able to experience himself 'together with' others or 'at home in' the world, but, on the contrary, he experiences himself in despairing aloneness and isolation; moreover, he does not experience himself as a complete person but rather as 'split' in various ways, perhaps as a mind more or less tenuously linked to a body, as two or more selves, and so on.[36]

Lawrence gestures towards this connection, but never affirms it when she recognises that Something's children each represent a stage of Larry's own psychological development:

> Three-year-old Dippermouth (who has a clock face, tells time and occasionally, screams in alarm) [. . .] is the first basic indicator of Larry's flawed 'means of communication' [. . .], Gut Bucket, with the deeper and more contained emotional life of a six-year-old, and then Potato Head, the more opaque twelve-year-old girl (Brooke-Rose has called her the 'the opposite sex aspect of any psyche at that age, very affectionate but dumb, i.e., not really recognized' [Brooke-Rose email, 10 February 2003]). Tin Roof the outspoken and 'unscreened' twenty-four-year-old, is next, and, finally, the adult reality (Really) of the psychiatrist at forty-eight.[37]

The children represent the fragments of Larry's broken psyche as well as significant milestones in the development of a child. These small fragments are drawn together by the larger 'split selves': Someone and, in particular, Something, whose arm seems to anchor these floating fragments and stop them from drifting away. Significantly, while these 'children' or small fragments seem to have relationships with their 'parents', they do not tend to interact independently with each other; each fragment is isolated in its own orbit. Laing's definition of the schizoid personality seems to be encapsulated by Larry, who experiences himself as two adult entities (Someone and Something), as well as experiencing his childhood in fragments of isolated characteristics. Furthermore, Larry's mind is only 'tenuously' linked to his body as he continues to occupy this indeterminate space between life and death.

Laing's ideas were adopted by a number of authors during the 1960s (such as Ann Quin and Anna Kavan) and were often used to convey the internal disruption or social isolation of an individual. This idea of fragmentation, particularly of the self, illustrates the overlapping of modernist and postmodernist tropes in the experimental novels of this era. By showcasing the individual's experiences of fragmentation and isolation, these authors undertake the essential task of developing and transforming 'character' in the novel. This is most often portrayed through self-conscious, self-reflective narration (for example, Johnson's *Trawl*), as well as through non-linear narrative 'telling' (for example, Quin's *Berg*, Brooke-Rose's *Out*, Johnson's *The Unfortunates* (1969)). In this sense, *Such* directly engages with contemporary culture and literary trends of the period. However, Brooke-Rose's presentation of this trend is significantly unorthodox because of the way in which she systematically confronts parts of Larry's psyche with fragments of itself, focusing on specific detail in the examination of his internal space. This allows her to manipulate and stretch this trend to the point where it becomes an invasive, microscopic examination of the construction of identity. Her contribution to this trend, with her unnamed, dislocated, disenfranchised protagonist in *Out* and with Larry in *Such*, is essential to the development of character in the novel, and it is a theme that continues in *Between*.

The Space *Between*

While *Out* and *Such* are driven by male protagonists, the unnamed protagonist in *Between* is female. Although she remains anonymous, it is revealed through the narrative that the protagonist is a translator / interpreter who travels around the world attending conferences, helping to convey complex ideas in various languages. In *Stories, Theories & Things* (1991), Brooke-Rose justifies her decision to make the protagonist a woman, claiming that 'simultaneous interpretation is a passive activity, that of translating the ideas of others but giving voice to none of one's own, and therefore a feminine experience'.[38]

With *Between*, Brooke-Rose begins to interrogate the relationship between gender and language, and the influence of gender *upon* language, using the translator / interpreter role as a metaphor. The protagonist in *Between* is always bound to ideas that are not her own, responsible only for relaying information, not for making any original contribution. In this sense, she is imprisoned by the language used to describe these ideas, restricted by the language of the speaker who colonises her thoughts. As well as abiding by Brooke-Rose's self-claimed 'very difficult' style of writing in the sustained present tense, *Between* harbours a further lipogrammatic constraint: the omission of the verb 'to be'. The lipogram adds to the sense of indeterminacy that the protagonist experiences: she is constantly in a state of in-betweenness.

The novel achieves a sense of indeterminacy by having the protagonist in a constant state of transition. This perpetual state of movement is conveyed not only by the physical demands of the protagonist but also by the frequent use of metaphor in the novel, which makes demands upon the reader to see things in other ways. For instance, throughout the text there is a preoccupation with the body, often in the form of imbuing the fuselage of the aeroplane with anatomical characteristics:

> [T]he sheeted puffed up eiderdown that causes sweat and falls off causing coolness indicates an outside temperature of minus forty-two degrees perhaps although the body stretches out its many ribs in a pressurised comfort as if inside a giant centipede. Or else inside the whale [. . .]. Between sleeping and not sleeping the body floats.[39]

This repeated imagery forces the reader to contemplate the comparison between the mechanical shell of the aeroplane and the human body. The clear biblical reference to Jonah inside the whale reveals the novel's preoccupation with Catholic themes. Nevertheless, the disembodiment of the ribcage and the idea of being 'inside' it gives the metaphor a gory twist, which, in turn, dehumanises the image, as well as having the effect of humanising the machine.

Indeterminacy is also created at a narrative level through the exposure of the protagonist's past through flashback passages. The reader learns that, while on vacation visiting her aunt in Germany, she becomes trapped there due to the outbreak of the Second World War. She finds herself translating French for the Nazis. This act becomes a significant moment for the protagonist in terms of establishing / losing her own identity. As I have written elsewhere:

> The political and ethical implications of the protagonist's collaboration with the Nazis are that she has betrayed her mother country (France), and become morally bankrupted by her linguistic capability. Language is inextricably tied to the formation of a national identity and, by agreeing to translate for the Nazis, the protagonist disowns her national identity and, furthermore, allows the enemy access to previously protected information.[40]

In this respect, the translation process literally overwrites her sense of self and her concept of origin. The protagonist is interrogated as part of her questioning by the Nazi soldier who is trying to verify her claims of origin, identity and agenda. He states:

> You must excuse these questions Fraulein but in view of your French upbringing we must make sure of your undivided loyalty let us see now until the age of Herr Oberstleutnant at that age one has no loyalties.[41]

By being forced to disown her loyalties to her country of origin and, indeed, her mother tongue, the protagonist too becomes disowned, disenfranchised and dispossessed. These moments are seen only in brief flashbacks. For the most part, the novel is set in the present when the protagonist, no longer restricted to living in Germany, is constantly travelling, changing and adapting to her surroundings. Mineral bottle labels in different languages become a regular leitmotif scattered throughout the text, indicating to the reader the location of each moment. Nevertheless, loyalty continues to play a significant role in the protagonist's world. Despite Brooke-Rose's own assertion that the role of the interpreter is a 'passive one', the protagonist in *Between* does not entirely adhere to her role. Birch has recognised that:

> Though her job is to translate as faithfully as possible, this process is replicated in her mind by 'bad copies' in which analogous discursive systems are conjoined in such a way as to emphasize disparities between them or unexpected parallels. Very often her ludic manipulation of language takes the form of intentional 'errors'. Multilingual puns are a favourite plaything of both her and her friend Siegfried.[42]

On closer inspection, however, Brooke-Rose's protagonist is not the passive translator that we might first assume. Indeed, she seems to have little linguistic loyalty to the 'original idea' and uses signifiers creatively, alongside puns, to transform the meaning of the language into something beyond its original intended sentiment. For instance, after the war, the protagonist has to obtain 'a Persil-Schein certificate denatzifying us whiter than white' in order to work again.[43] The aural parity created by the German word 'Schein' meaning 'bill' and 'shine', and the reference to Persil washing-powder indicates a process of cleaning the war from the protagonist's identity.[44] In this respect, the protagonist exposes the fragmented nature of the relationship between the signifier, the signified and the sign by colliding different languages and discourses for her own pleasure. She is a linguistic deviant who is free to manipulate languages for her own ends and amusement, subverting the reader's expectations of her role and, indeed, her gender. This ability to deviate is created by the absence of loyalty to a particular language and, indeed, to language itself, and is perpetuated by her dispossession from her national origin. In this deviation, Brooke-Rose allows her protagonist to reclaim some agency and power over language.

Brigid Brophy's novel *In Transit* (1969), published only one year after *Between*, continues to negotiate the boundaries between language and gender. It is set in the similar location of an airport, where the novel's protagonist, Evelyn Hillary O'Rooley, experiences feelings of indeterminacy about his / her gender and consequently performs a string of tests upon his / her body in an attempt to define himself / herself. Like *Between*, *In Transit* is preoccupied with the physical body as well as the interior self and is scattered with language puns, which further develop the sense of uncertainty of meaning in the novel: 'There you are: fixed in your high (by several thousand feet) or wedged into your push (by jet engine) chair, dependent on h{a/u}rried n{u/a}nny's finding a moment to play attendant to you.'[45] Brooke-Rose's and Brophy's investigations into the relationship between language, gender and the self contribute to the trend of articulating indeterminacy in the experimental novel of the 1960s. This trend is a continuation of the expression of the self as being incomplete, disparate and isolated.

While Brooke-Rose's novels remain 'difficult' for readers to penetrate, there is evidence that her early work engages with contemporary literary developments. These early experimental novels reflect upon historical origins and trends, challenging and simultaneously preserving traditional narrative techniques in an attempt to build something new out of old materials. With these texts, Brooke-Rose, like her contemporaries, is searching for a new direction for the novel, exploring routes of possible transformation including character, form and plot. This search to save the novel continues in her magnum opus, *Thru*, which presents itself on first reading as a solid, almost impenetrable fortress of *bricolage*. *Thru* replicates the techniques trialled in these earlier novels (the repetition of key focal images, the inclusion of multiple languages, the tension between interior and exterior space) and stretches them to their extreme. If *Thru* is indeed a line in the sand, *Out*, *Such* and *Between* (with other texts considered in this collection) are located at the outer limits. They reside in the Badlands, in the wilderness of the landscape of the novel genre in the twentieth century, and their purpose is to map out a trajectory for discovery. These three novels are key texts in Brooke-Rose's œuvre not just because they are individually significant experimental novels, but also because, when read together, they reveal a development of radical experimental practice.

Notes

1. Christine Brooke-Rose, *Invisible Author* (Columbus: Ohio State University Press, 2002), p. 1.
2. Dominic Head, *The Cambridge Introduction to Modern British Fiction, 1950–2000* (Cambridge: Cambridge University Press, 2002), p. 225.
3. 'Once Upon a Time' (27 April 1956), 'Responses' (18 October 1957) and 'Mourning' (6 December 1957) all appeared in *Truth*. 'Today the Acupuncturist' (25 January 1963) appeared in the *Times Literary Supplement*. The Harry Ransom Center archive at the University of Texas contains pages from *Botteghe Oscura* of poetry by Brooke-Rose, including 'Asperges Me' (no dates).
4. See, for example: Michela Canepari-Labib, *Word-Worlds: Language, Identity and Reality in the Work of Christine Brooke-Rose* (London: Peter Lang, 2002); Karen E. Lawrence, *Techniques for Living: Fiction and Theory in the Work of Christine Brooke-Rose* (Columbus: Ohio State University Press, 2010); Noemi Alice Bartha, *Christine Brooke-Rose: The Chameleonic Text Between Self-Reflexivity and Narrative Experiment* (Newcastle: Cambridge Scholars, 2014).
5. See, for example: Andrzej Gąsiorek, *Post-War British Fiction: Realism and After* (London: Edward Arnold, 1995), and Head, *The Cambridge Introduction*.
6. Patricia Waugh, *Metafiction* [1984] (London: Routledge, 2013), p. 148.
7. Brooke-Rose, *Invisible Author*, p. 2.
8. Ibid. p. 132.
9. Ibid. p. 1
10. Ibid. p. 2.
11. B. S. Johnson, 'Introduction' to *Aren't You Rather Young to Be Writing Your Memoirs?*, in *The Novel Today: Contemporary Writers on Modern Fiction*, ed. M. Bradbury (Manchester: Manchester University Press, 1977), pp. 151–68, p. 153.
12. Julia Jordan, 'Introduction', in *B. S Johnson and Post-War Literature: Possibilities of the Avant-Garde*, ed. Martin Ryle and Julia Jordan (Basingstoke: Palgrave Macmillan, 2014), pp. 1–13, p. 4.
13. Stephanie Jones, '"The Immensity of Confrontable Selves": The "Split Subject" and "Multiple Identities" in the work of Christine Brooke-Rose' (unpublished PhD Thesis: Aberystwyth University, 2016), pp. 27–8.
14. Jordan, 'Introduction', p. 5.

15. Christine Brooke-Rose, *The Christine Brooke-Rose Omnibus: Out, Such, Between, Thru* (Manchester: Carcanet, 2006), p. 39. All page references for the novels *Out, Such, Between* and *Thru* refer to this edition but are abbreviated to the title of the particular novel being quoted.
16. Jordan, 'Introduction', p. 6.
17. Brooke-Rose, *Out*, p. 39.
18. Ibid. p. 11.
19. Jordan, 'Introduction', p. 5.
20. Brooke-Rose, *Out*, p. 175.
21. Roch C. Smith, *Understanding Alain Robbe-Grillet* (Columbia: University of South Carolina Press, 2000), p. 31.
22. Ibid. p. 45.
23. Christine Brooke-Rose, 'The Vanishing Author', *The Observer*, 1961. Accessed through the Harry Ransom Research Center Library (2014).
24. Sarah Birch, *Christine Brooke-Rose and Contemporary Fiction* (Oxford: Clarendon Press, 1991), p. 57.
25. Ibid.
26. Lawrence, *Techniques for Living*, p. 30.
27. Brooke-Rose, *Such*, p. 203.
28. Lawrence, *Techniques for Living*, p. 41.
29. Brooke-Rose, *Such*, p. 204.
30. Ibid. p. 206.
31. Ibid. p. 233.
32. Ibid. p. 207.
33. Ibid. p. 347.
34. Birch, *Christine Brooke-Rose*, p. 64.
35. Lawrence, *Techniques for Living*, p. 203.
36. R. D. Laing, *The Divided Self* [1960] (London: Penguin, 2010), p. 17.
37. Lawrence, *Techniques for Living*, p. 46.
38. Christine Brooke-Rose, *Stories, Theories & Things* (Cambridge: Cambridge University Press, 1991), p. 7.
39. Brooke-Rose, *Between*, p. 398.
40. Jones, '"The Immensity of Confrontable Selves"', p. 105.
41. Brooke-Rose, *Between*, p. 444.
42. Birch, *Christine Brooke-Rose*, pp. 84–5.
43. Brooke-Rose, *Between*, p. 473.
44. Sarah Birch writes about comparative coding systems in more detail in *Christine Brooke-Rose and Contemporary Fiction*, pp. 82–9.
45. Brigid Brophy, *In Transit* (London: MacDonald, 1969), p. 19.

Chapter 12

Aspirations Inevitably Failing: Hope and Negativity in Rayner Heppenstall's Experimental Fiction of the 1960s

Philip Tew

The following chapter revisits and reassesses Rayner Heppenstall's *The Connecting Door* (1962), *The Woodshed* (1962) and *The Shearers* (1969), three intriguing but now largely forgotten novels published in the sixties by an established writer with an avant-garde pedigree.[1] Before the end of the Second World War their author had been, variously: a working class graduate of Leeds, his local university; a quintessential Fitzrovian; (briefly) a Catholic convert in the late 1930s; and an experimental novelist. An avid Francophile, postwar Heppenstall was also regarded by many – including Hélène Cixous, who expressed her opinion in *Le Monde* in May 1967[2] – to have been the founding father of the French *nouveau roman*.[3] In line with that movement's emphasis on objective concretion, Heppenstall mirrored its aesthetic mistrust of realism, even influencing a group of mainly London-based novelists, detailed below, who became committed to furthering Britain's developing literary avant-garde, the significance of which is often critically underplayed. According to G. J. Buckell in 'Rayner Heppenstall', such writers were 'loosely unified around a shared opposition to literary conservatism more than a dedication to any defined set of aesthetic principles'.[4]

In contrast, more establishment figures such as William Cooper dismissed, simultaneously, both the French and the British experimental movements, rejecting literary experiment as a 'superannuated art'[5] and declaring that, in the postwar years, 'We meant to write a different kind of novel from that of the thirties and we saw that the thirties novel, the Experimental Novel, had got to be brushed out of the way [. . .].'[6] More specifically, Cooper condemned the 'imbecility' of

Michel Butor and described Alain Robbe-Grillet's *The Voyeur* (1955) as 'tedious and arid' and his aesthetic ideas as 'metaphysical gobbledegook'.[7] Heppenstall reflected on such British parochialism concerning experimental writing practices in *The Fourfold Tradition* (1961): 'In this country, there has been a strong reaction against all varieties of interior-monologue, stream-of-consciousness writing.'[8] With regard to Anglophone dismissiveness specifically of contemporaneous French writing practices and theories, he added, as a retort to those detractors such as Cooper, concerning Robbe-Grillet that 'The main plank in his platform is that we must avoid all complicity with things, that we must present things meticulously in all their alien thingness and not attempt to humanise them.'[9] Heppenstall knew such French figures personally, and there appears to have been mutual cross-cultural influence in matters of novelistic style and structure in particular. As Jonathan Goodman notes in *The Master Eccentric*, Butor 'had occasionally dined at the Heppenstalls',[10] and in *Rayner Heppenstall: A Critical Study* G. J. Buckell describes Heppenstall meeting Robbe-Grillet, a writer he admired, at the London première of the film version of *L'Année dernière à Marienbad* in 1961,[11] in which year John Calder published a translation of Robbe-Grillet's original novel from which the film derived.[12] In 'Rayner Heppenstall', Buckell alludes to a friendship that flourished with Nathalie Sarraute, 'who was impressed with [Heppenstall's] *The Greater Infortune*'.[13] As to the literary dynamics of the time, as Andrzej Gąsiorek concedes, 'while it might be argued that modernism was left behind by Assorted Angry Young Men and Movement writers, this judgment now seems premature, a glib refusal to think properly about the challenge modernism continues to pose'.[14] He includes Heppenstall among an extensive list of those extending that tradition, adding 'All these writers have in different ways seen that modernism both raised questions about representation that could not be ignored and opened up new possibilities for what writing could do that needed to be explored further.'[15] As will be detailed below, Heppenstall initiated ways of doing so by devising new perspectives and techniques that extend and challenge both modernist and more traditional techniques.

Part of this chapter's ensuing focus will be to offer more examples of such innovative aesthetic practices by Heppenstall to counter a popular critical metanarrative that reduces the postwar to simply the Angry Young Men and The Movement. In so doing, I intend to demonstrate that certain key stylistic and perspectival innovations in narrative incorporated in Heppenstall's fiction are sufficiently radical that they were to influence an often underrated, but in retrospect increasingly important, group of younger experimental writers, led from the very early 1960s by B. S. Johnson.[16] Heppenstall acted as a de facto mentor for this coterie, and in *The Master Eccentric* he recalls Ann Quin in the early 1960s:

> Her first novel, *Berg*, appeared in 1964. She first met B. S. Johnson at our flat, over a light, early dinner, after which Bryan drove us all to the shop called Better Books in Charing Cross Road, where Nathalie Sarraute was lecturing, with me as her chairman.[17]

However, on 31 July 1969, Heppenstall still refers to their faction with some caution as regards his own unequivocal commitment, since his own conservatism made him cautious about their passionate idealism, describing:

> *Avant-garde* novelists at the house of one of them, Alan Burns, off Portobello Road. They want to start public readings and discussion, under the name 'Writers Reading'. I was one of the two greybeards invited, the other Stefan Themerson. For some reason, Bryan Johnson seemed bent on needling me [. . .]. I don't think I'll go along with them. I don't think it [their project] will work.[18]

Heppenstall's caution was in part political, as many of these younger writers regarded themselves politically as radically left. And as Jeremy Green observes of them, it was precisely such an ideological commitment rather than an aesthetic one that was the foundation of the interplay of Alan Burns, Johnson, Eva Figes and Ann Quin: 'Although they were closely associated in the late sixties, devising ways to secure support and a readership for their work, they never succeeded in establishing a coherent identity as a literary movement.'[19] Nonetheless, friendship flourished, and on 22 May 1971 Heppenstall recorded of Johnson: 'Hospitable week. On Tuesday, we had Bryan and Virginia to dinner.'[20] Despite Heppenstall's wariness concerning the political radicalism of certain members of this grouping and their associates, such reflections contextualise the older writer's active contribution to their overall project, which included his chapter in *London Consequences* (1972), a collection of interlinked contributions by twenty writers, which served as a kind of heterogeneous novel. On 2 April Heppenstall noted: 'At Margaret Drabble's in Hampstead, to organise a composite novel which she and B. S. Johnson are editing for the Greater London Arts Association for next year's Festival of London and to which some twenty novelists are to contribute each a chapter.'[21]

Tragically, just over a year after this collection's appearance, Quin was to drown and Johnson was to commit suicide, the latter greatly mourned by Heppenstall, who wrote of his shock at the death, adding:

> For one thing, Bryan was the last person I should have expected to commit suicide. For another, as I have suddenly realised, he was my only friend of his generation. Indeed, I wonder whether, outside my family, he was not my only friend.[22]

Such long-neglected details indicate certain aspects of Heppenstall's role as an influential English experimentalist, and the analysis in this chapter seeks to recover his innovative voice, and the structures and approaches he developed in these novels, doing so through reconsidering his multiple elaborations on the lives of a full range of characters of all classes from northern England, the region of his own upbringing to which he remained committed. I will explore the insistent synthesis of pessimism and negativity in his fiction published in the 1960s.[23]

However, despite all of the above, for many, Heppenstall remains a figure remembered mainly for his closeness to George Orwell and for an often celebrated (although some argue infamous) incident when Orwell punched and set about a drunken Heppenstall late one Sunday evening in 1935 on his return to shared lodgings at 50 Lawford Road, Kentish Town. In 1960, the victim of the assault published an account, which supporters of Orwell, who regarded him to be a great humanist, found disturbing. Heppenstall wrote:

> There stood Orwell, armed with his shooting-stick. With this he pushed me back, poking the aluminium point into my stomach. I pushed it aside, and sprang at him. He fetched me a dreadful crack across the legs and then raised the shooting-stick over his head. I looked at his face. Through my private mist I saw in it a curious blend of fear and sadistic satisfaction.[24]

Despite this momentous incident, which seems to eclipse Heppenstall's own merits as a writer, as Gordon Bowker says, 'they remained friends throughout Orwell's lifetime'.[25]

Heppenstall was originally a supporter of the Labour Party but each of his novels published in the sixties serves as a testament to his growing social conservatism – which Green regards as precursor to 'the savagely reactionary flavour of his later views'.[26] I suggest here that this 'conservatism' instead represents an Augustinian ideology and aesthetics that is essentially pessimistic about human nature in an age where many intellectuals adopted an idealising Pelagianist optimism that purveyed a sense of innate human goodness, which in large part explains his rapid descent into obscurity after his death in 1981, during a period of continued left-liberal idealism amongst the artistic and intellectual classes. However, rather than further contextualise Heppenstall the man, I will attempt below to situate his own radical approach to the novel as an evolving genre.

Both *The Connecting Door* and *The Woodshed* are darkly autobiographical and, as Francis Booth observes, in them Heppenstall attempts 'to define himself in relation to his past experience (since other people are no more than shadows in either book) and, moreover, to recapture, Proust-like, his past life'.[27] Certainly, when both are considered with *The Shearers*, all three novels also offer coordinates in what Green describes as 'the survival of the modernist impulse after the war', although he adds saliently of their increasingly politically conservative author, 'What cannot be assumed in his case is any organic link between a progressive use of technique – fragmentation, collage, defamiliarization, play with conventions – and progressive politics.'[28]

Heppenstall further radicalises these aspects by tying his intensity of detail to a fundamental mundanity of perspective, resisting the aesthetic emphasis of much modernist writing, and shifting its perspective to the visceral explorations of writers seeking to develop an emergent style and perspective. As Buckell indicates, in 'Rayner Heppenstall: Context No 18', Heppenstall's initial prewar novel, *The Blaze of Noon* (1939), was received well, as was his fourth, in particular in avant-garde circles:

> This novel made a considerable critical impact, as did *The Connecting Door* (1962), which excited British avant-gardists seeking a domestic equivalent to the *école du regard* of Robbe-Grillet, Sarraute, Simon, Duras, and others in postwar France, being described by its publisher as an 'anti-novel to stand up to the performances of the Frenchmen'.[29]

The Connecting Door is a complex, cumulative and retrospective narrative that charts, in episodic and random episodes, successive visits to a city on the Rhine in Alsace by protagonist Harold Atha – who, aged nineteen in 1931, is referred to as 'Harold'; is called 'Atha' with attached pejorative descriptors, aged twenty-four in 1936; and is an unnamed narrator, aged thirty-six in 1948. The location is initially German territory but is French again following the

Second World War. The setting is Strasbourg – where, according to Juliet Jacques, Heppenstall lived as a student – which is confirmed by details in the novel: 'the Orangerie is a fair-sized park, and it contains a pavilion intended for residence by the empress Josephine'.[30] The last trip is for a brief journalistic project, marked by retrospective nostalgia, reminiscing about lost love. As Heppenstall indicated himself in *The Intellectual Part* (1963), his complex narrative strategy draws consciously upon Søren Kierkegaard's *Repetition* with his own intersection and interplay of different time periods, without a fixed or static point in time, the future and past challenging and defining the present.[31] Heppenstall's narrative progresses, without authorial contextualisation for its readers:

> THE DATE OF MY ARRIVAL WAS JUNE 1ST. YOUNG HAROLD (he is nineteen, rising twenty) arrived on 1st April, All Fools' Day, a Thursday at four o'clock in the afternoon. He felt a bit of a fool, but did not mind.[32]

Without direction or explication, the interrelationship of the characters (who are one and the same at different ages) in what proves to be multi-chronic fluctuations and interconnections remains initially challenging and puzzling.

The title of *The Connecting Door* suggests both a transition and interconnectedness, themes that emerge in the interrelatedness of its three narrative strands. The opening is dominated by the aural imprint on the consciousness of the protagonist, Atha, of an unnamed cityscape outside his hotel room: successive bells pealing, the sound of trams, voices and later children's voices, which, along with bombed spaces, confirm a postwar setting with their linguistic ignorance – 'They sing French folk-songs. Because their nursery background has not been French, they are learning the familiar ones.'[33] The last detail emphasises the political transition the city underwent after the war, whose aftermath is both culturally and visually evident, a change highlighted by the narrator's observation that 'Old St. Peter's stands, undamaged, sixty or seventy yards beyond St. John's.'[34] The focus then shifts to the initial journey of young Harold and his juvenile flirtation:

> On the boat, he took up with a girl who was going to Switzerland as a children's nurse. It was a night crossing. In adjacent deck-chairs, the two snuggled together under one hired rug, their foreheads and noses tormented by the same smuts. On the Bâle express, they had breakfast and luncheon together. At lunch they shared a bottle of sweet Muscat. Afterwards, they went on embracing in the compartment.[35]

The intensity and brevity of the intimacy variously evoke youth, libido and inexperience, as does his interrogation by police on arrival after 'the sleeve of his overcoat caught on the door handle'.[36] In effect, by retracing the past throughout the narrative, Heppenstall has Atha searching for memories and traces of Annelies, a lost love who married another, older man. As David Leon Higdon observes:

> Because the self is constantly in the process of becoming, it cannot truly look back and understand fully, but must look back hesitantly and uncertainly as does the narrator in *The Connecting Door*. Looking backwards is thus both an act of remembering and an act of forgetting.[37]

Heppenstall's intention is more radical and more complex. His synthesis of Kierkegaardian perspectives serves to introduce irresolution, a radical lack of fixity, which impermanence undermines the certainties of authorship and realism. Yet he sustains the everyday mundanity which enmeshes the individual, negating any potential resolution through aesthetic transcendence. According to Buckell in 'Rayner Heppenstall', 'a vital influence'[38] on this book was Alain Robbe-Grillet's *Jealousy*, a work that Tom McCarthy – in accounting for Robbe-Grillet's œuvre and its rejection by 'Anglo-American empiricism' – describes as being 'actually ultra-realist, shot through at every level with the sheer *quiddity* of the environments to which they attend so faithfully'.[39] Heppenstall's protagonist both exudes and encounters the obsessiveness McCarthy details as the central characteristic of such narratives. Atha's experience is evoked through multiple impressions and literalised objects imbued with suggestive intensity and clarity, such as his retrospective description of his journey in a Pullman carriage: 'A narrow road ran parallel with the railway. Along it moved an ox-cart. No doubt it creaked or rumbled, but, to me, shut in with the train noises, it was silent. The bullocks were long-horned, cream or pale buff, silky.'[40] The mood synthesises a touch of the elegiac with much nostalgia and even self-censure, an unusual narrative blend allowed by the multi-chronic amalgamation. The narrator seems sympathetic toward Harold but far less approving of Atha, finding him muddled, negative:

> I do not like him as well as I like young Harold, though Harold is a bit sorrowful at the moment. This is because of Annelies, the girl in the Orangerie.
> Atha's bad circumstances were financial, amatory and religious. His London address is a rather old-fashioned Bohemian one. When I get back, I ought to inspect it.

He is supposed to be in love with a dancer, a *ballerina*. His handwriting is pretty but illegible. One at first thought that he was in love 'with a *ballista*'. This seemed odd. One hoped that it was not *a tergo*. It is not.[41]

Despite such verbal playfulness, which effect is intensified by Heppenstall's oddly disjunctive rhythm, Atha's trauma revolves centripetally around the experience of ascending to the roof of the town's minster or cathedral, a potent symbol of both existential fear and desire, the chimes of its bell reminiscent of death.[42] The narrator says

That morning's Atha did not count the steps. He made angry fun of me for counting them this morning. It was, he gave me to understand, the kind of thing that only a journalist would do. As a matter of fact, he is right.[43]

Atop the building for the third time, recollecting the two other occasions he has visited, which coalesce, he peers down at the vertiginous view of the city from the south tower, a perspective viewed, as he observes, by Goethe, whose observations concerning his own explicit fears are quoted in a footnote at length. Heppenstall's narrator observes:

You can't climb beyond this point. There is an iron grating, how recent I don't know. Neither young Harold nor cold-weather Atha remembers it, but perhaps that isn't strange. In my journalist's rôle, I have a note here which clearly indicates that it wasn't here a hundred and fourteen years ago.[44]

The personal, political and historical in all three visits intersect, in disturbingly surreal fashion. As Jacques observes of the novel, 'It challenged the reader to disentangle three simultaneous planes of time, as well as which characters existed in present-day reality and which solely as the unnamed central figure's memories.'[45] The three periods at certain points appear to coalesce, at one point the narrator appearing to interrogate young Harold about Annelies,[46] although this may simply echo an inner debate about past motivations and contexts, and at other points memories are so vivid that they erupt into present consciousness from sleep:

There were the pale-cream, silky oxen along the road, the houses, the crops and the Minster spire, the grey station, the two of them there to meet me, young Harold and not-so-young Atha, then Anton Walbrook, my room, Jeanne, breakfast, the parallel sheets of light through the white iron blinds, the sounds from the next room, the telephones in the small hours. At whatever time I awake, bells are ringing.[47]

The repeated motif of the oxen and the bells, the rapid accumulation of detail blending visual and auditory images, serve to emphasise an intensely impressionistic sense of reality, a writerly consciousness, but the repeated bells add an overlapping sense of confusion, a presentiment of both celebration and mortality. Although on first reading, the different phases appear to overlap and merge, gradually the reader reconstructs an oblique cartography of the central romance and other key human interactions with friends and acquaintances which are present in fragmentary verbal sketches. Gradually, the impressions of the first-person narrator intensify, culminating in an enigmatic and open ending, with the forces of history an implicit influence in both, either driving the characters apart or drawing them together. The narrator is about to encounter a woman in her compartment on a train (returning to the mode of transport of his earlier arrivals, offering a perhaps illusory symmetry), uncertain if it is Annelies or Madame Zix, who in his mind resemble each other. Yet he concludes this moment would represent the seeking of pleasure rather than romance: 'That is all. I shall be granted no revelation about the long significance of my own life. No imaginative creation will be finished.'[48] Both teasingly and enigmatically, the narrative ends abruptly with him about to open the door before the identity of the woman can be revealed.

Incorporating self-reflexive elements and a diachronic structure, viewed through a determinedly stream-of-consciousness perspective responding to the minutiae of everyday life, *The Woodshed* offers another quasi-autobiographical account of Harold Atha and his return from Wales to the industrial West Riding in Yorkshire to visit his dying father, which pilgrimage initiates a series of recollections of his own, often tortuous path through education and his conflictual familial relations. The novel is essentially autobiographical, drawing on the past for what Jacques calls 'its tapestry of reflections',[49] and is prefigured by certain similar, if limited, memories and details included in *The Connecting Door*, which strategy serves to tie together this pair of fictions. First-person retrospection permeates the narrative and complicates its perspectives, which are those of a man estranged from his family while facing the myriad reminders of past familiarities when called back to visit his ailing father. As the reader discovers later, his father had ironically died even before his departure: 'He had been dead four hours when I got my sister's telegram this morning.'[50] And although its chronology is not linear, it is precise, for it concerns four days when the protagonist is present in his home town for his father's funeral, its intensity of emotion defining his four-day stay, enduring the loss of a parent, an experience commonly associated with retrospective impulses. Clearly a recurrent protagonist, Atha links this novel to the preceding one, a pairing confirmed by overlapping scenes and events, such as the father's death, which has been prefigured in *The Connecting Door*: 'A thing which the near future held in store for me was that my father died.'[51] Both texts are short, the narration in each case concerned with reconciling oneself as a thinking person, and writer, to the vertiginous momentum of one's life, with the perpetual loss of the present, and the necessary compulsion to account for a past which was at the time as ineffable and mysterious as the present itself, and as inscrutable as the future. Noting one major influence on these texts, Higdon concludes:

> What Heppenstall learned from Kierkegaard about narrative method and the dialogue between an individual's past, present and future states of being can be seen in *The Connecting Door*; however, I believe it is even more successfully assimilated into the companion novel, *The Woodshed*, also published in 1962.[52]

Such a method is fundamental to Heppenstall's practice in all three novels, yet its inclusion is not entirely progressive, as *The Connecting Door* and *The Shearers* are radical in their abutment of episodes concerning all three time frames with the absence of authorial guidance, thus serving as a challenge to the reader. Although still often only implicit, the interconnections between different periods in *The Woodshed* are far more self-evident, the elegiac act of mourning (as well as the autobiographical frame within clearly familiar surroundings) positioning them within his visceral response. Heppenstall, in all three time frames, synthesises the three phases of the character's life within a narrative that offers such implicit themes as multiplicities of correlated experiences and meanings across time, without having to state them directly, and therefore avoids an authorial didacticism. Clearly, if the past looms, so too does the future. In *The Woodshed*, the ultimate inevitability of anticipation is emphatically death (although it haunts the other two novels), which, as Higdon notes, impels Atha to think of the impending fate of his father and their conflicted relationship. He traces his father's failures and his own paternal relationship through a synthesis of personal recollections, inner reflections and outward observations, tinged by a sense of the pair's inability to communicate and evoking obliquely his father's many inadequacies. Even on the journey to see him, he imagines his father at home in the process of dying and regards him as inadequate: 'Through that rectangular hole in the wall, ventilating the box-room, failure, not a boggart, gibbers down onto his turning head. In every direction, his life stretches aridly about him.'[53]

Heppenstall refuses Atha any sentimentality, foregrounding the ongoing antipathy between son and father. The novel's opening typifies the apparent randomness of memory overlaid with current experience, with Atha, a writer, initially sharing a carriage with returning holidaymakers from Birmingham, his imagination retreating to the time spent at the seaside prior to his summons to his childhood home. Determinedly reflective, he encircles his narrative of current existence with fancies, projections and observations about the borrowed cottage where he is staying with his family and its owner, among other topics.

> Poor Gwladys. It is, I am sure, a good thing that her pottery fetches a high price in Chelsea and Wigmore Street. As to her pictures, it is simply that, once we had closed the door on Gwaelod, I, at least, would rather have had done for the day with lobster-pots, seagulls, lighthouses, upturned boats and drying nets. Those high-pitched colours and disarticulated forms suddenly gain intensity under an artificial light.[54]

The narrator's implicit critique of and objection to Gwladys's art is rendered subtly, as is an ironic sense of the location. After such ruminations concerning life at the coast, his focus returns reflexively to the journey to Hinderholme as part of a conscious narrative, his thoughts both incorporating and yet interrogating revealing formal literary issues such as stream of consciousness in comic, somewhat ironic fashion (thereby satirising modernist techniques):

> In a train, your consciousness streams like a cold. Mr A. regrets. Mr. A. is confined to his carriage with a streaming consciousness. If I had a secretary sitting opposite with a shorthand notebook, or a dictaphone, I could just talk like this. They reckon about ten thousand words to the hour. In a journey of eight hours, you could finish a book. Change the names, and you'd have a stream-of-consciousness novel. A man travelling somewhere for a purpose. What had led up to it, hopes and fears, retrospect and apprehension mingling, things noted as the landscape slid by. At the end, some kind of pay-off.[55]

Through such flippant self-parody, Heppenstall undercuts both his own narrative intentions and his status as a writer. He also foregrounds the artificiality of authorship, of the novel form, echoing Nathalie Sarraute's observations in 'Age of Suspicion':

Not only has the novelist ceased to believe in his characters, but the reader, too, is unable to believe in them; with the result that the characters, having lost the twofold support that the novelist's and the reader's faith afforded them, and which permitted them to stand upright with the burden of the entire story resting on their broad shoulders, may now seem to vacillate and fall apart.[56]

The holidaymakers are stereotypes more than individuals:

The men with their clean, open-necked, white shirts, the women in freshly ironed cotton frocks, one of the women really very handsome in a big, opulent way that reminded me of A'ntie Ada, all of them lobster-pink and smelling of sun and sea.[57]

And yet, however apparently stolid, still they vanish into an authorial negation, evoked and as quickly abandoned, their relevance subtly parodied and subsequently undermined.

Elsewhere, conscious meditation on the past becomes more extensive and foregrounded in the text. The apparently episodic and random nature of Atha's thoughts and memories continues but it offers both a literal and psychic journey, which involves, as Higdon notes, 'a metaphysical coming to terms with his past', with the retrospection stretching the narrative scope well beyond the four days of the short visit.[58] On the journey, Atha envisions his father at home approaching his death, and he recollects various unrelated aspects of the man's life and habits, followed by a comic episode concerning the delivery of an overly expensively and badly restored piano – once an aunt's – from Yorkshire to London, and a further episode when, during a trip to the Rhineland (from where he had recently returned) as a student, he had required money to return from Brussels and a fellow student had written to his father for funds, much to his father's annoyance. Such an intense cascade of intercalated quotidian and domestic memories (such as the ones analysed above) – ones that seem random, even discontinuous, apart from the vehemence of retrospective authorial reflection which provides a visceral framework – would prove an influential technique for younger writers such as Alan Burns in *Europe After the Rain* (1965) and *Celebrations* (1967), B. S. Johnson in *Trawl*, *The Unfortunates* and *See the Old Lady Decently* (1975), and Ann Quin in *Three* (1966) and *Passages* (1969), who developed their own versions in these fictions.

The day following his journey, Atha firstly retells the family history, particularly its association through work with the local Co-Op (in Britain a network of collectively oriented commercial enterprises owned by individual members and other co-ops), through photographs, detailing their contexts. Secondly, he recounts the sensations of the day, of the funeral, offsetting the personal with reflections on the wider political trajectory of the period that drew on the tenets of this institution, offering an opportunity to mock the nationalisation of parts of the economy: 'Perhaps it was industries like this which Mr Attlee and his colleagues should have nationalised in the first place. The *pompes funèbres*, some of the things solicitors do such as house-conveyancing, lotteries, pawnbroking.'[59] The narrative concerns a series of intimacies, traumas, disappointments and misunderstandings, many related to death and physical injury, which in combination offer a peculiarly negative or anti-Bildungsroman. Atha explores a homosexual fixation on him by another pupil at school, Peter Holmes – 'quiet, petal-skinned, unbroken-voiced, not good at games, lacking in physical boldness'[60] – and his own infatuation with 'Connie, a rosy, big-bosomed girl whose reputation was somewhat blown on, because she had been observed to go out driving with the son of the head of the engineering works, at which she worked as a clerk or secretary'.[61]

Death recurs emphatically in the narrative, which thereby echoes Georges Bataille's observation about contemporary philosophy, that 'Modern realism admits death, making human life, from the cradle onward, prey to an impossible nothingness.'[62] In June 1927, Atha recalls glimpsing from the woodshed in his newly married cousin's yard her husband, Gordon, seemingly enraged with him but, as he later reveals, in the process of hanging himself from a meat hook: 'He didn't shout at me, but clearly he was sending me away. In fact he seemed in a towering rage. He glared. His eyes almost popped with fury. His face was more darkly congested than ever.'[63] Another death follows when, 'on a hot afternoon, the Rev. Mr Allendale went down from the school-house to the Armoury and shot himself with one of the cavalry carbines we'd used for drilling with in the O.T.C.'[64] Heppenstall mocks any assumption of solemnity regarding death, but does concede its pervasiveness, to which Bataille alludes. Later, Atha reflects upon whether he might have saved his uncle 'if I had not so quickly been driven away by what I took for so improbable a bit of mere face-pulling', something he never reveals to his family. Gordon is implicated in a homosexual scandal related to the local football team.[65] Such a layering of detail suggests something of both the complexity and the inwardness of this community.

The novel ends with a 'Coda' in which Atha returns to Hinderholme, recollecting that he had sold his inherited piano for scrap (for less than the cost of restoration).⁶⁶ He considers returning more frequently, since 'My roots were there, after all. Roots. Another dead metaphor. Men are not plants,' again interrogating common literary procedures through quasi-parody.⁶⁷ His mother's decision to move severs his connection: 'And so I suppose I have finished with Hinderholme. It won't matter. This is not the centre of my life.'⁶⁸ The novel ends with the aftermath of the father's death, with Atha leaving associated memories and travelling back to the south. As Luce Irigaray says: 'Death's most terrible aspect lies in the charades you have invented to separate it from you,' but clearly any such barrier is breached in this narrative for Heppenstall.⁶⁹ Having successively rejected metaphors concerning the act of writing, he ends the novel with another striking one:

> If consciousness streams, it is backward. Or, rather, it is like the slack tide in an estuary. As I approach London, no doubt new urgencies will begin. At present, it is almost as though I were out at sea, glossily calm. If I again let down the deep trawl of memory, I should bring up dabs and elvers by the ton. The catch would be to throw back.⁷⁰

Symbolically, in the passage above, Heppenstall evokes enigmatically certain central themes of these paired books, in effect interrogating literary tradition and the supposedly universal perspective of the author and thereby foregrounding what Paul Ricœur describes as 'the equivocalness of the notion of author, the "narrative" incompleteness of life, the entanglement of life histories in a dialectic of remembrance and anticipation'.⁷¹ In *The Woodshed*, the implication of Heppenstall's ending and its tone is that it seems as if Atha has been suspended from his normal self, immersed in a past he has sought to avoid by the very fact of facing such paternal death despite his unwillingness to assess the equivocations of their relationship, which equivocations remain largely unresolved. He denies the reader any such convenient and balanced traditional resolution.

Juliet Jacques claims: 'Seven years elapsed between *The Woodshed* and his next novel, *The Shearers*, which uncharacteristically drew little directly from Heppenstall's life, its third-person narration and linear chronology representing his break with the *nouveau roman*.'⁷² I would argue that, both thematically and in terms of narrative perspective, elements of experimentalism do feature in this text, with seemingly random perspectives and events interrelated without any authorial explication, creating a sense of incongruence and heterogeneity. However, its chief focus is far more visibly coherent and familiar, revolving around criminal proceedings at Northallerton, the circumstances relevant to a murder trial, a traditional novelistic trope. In his journal on 24 July 1969, Heppenstall noted the novel's publication, reflected on some positive reviews and explained:

> The novel is dedicated to Pamela Snow. The ass in *The Times Literary Supplement* knows that she is also Pamela Hansford Johnson and that under this name published a book on the trial of Ian Brady and Myra Hindley three years ago. My novel [according to the reviewer] is therefore not a novel but a challenge to her theses in *On Iniquity*.[73]

Heppenstall demurred. Using a third-person narrative, Heppenstall's final novel of the decade is an eponymous family saga which depicts a group of eight working-class people blighted by poverty, ignorance and incest, belatedly on trial for killing two grandparents. The novel opens with arrests and concludes after the guilty verdicts, but the narrative veers off periodically to reflect on weather, national and global events, and the fears and vicissitudes facing people around the world, as if to offset the enormity of the supposed crimes:

> [Up] and down the sub-continent there had been rioting all day. The current Prime Minister of the United Kingdom of Great Britain and Northern Ireland knew what the West German government thought about the timing of an institution known as the Common Market. That morning, in London, a supposed Army deserter and a pregnant woman convicted of some motoring offence had been released from gaol.[74]

Heppenstall continually frames the conflicted tale of the Shearers, conveying it through a multiplicity of implied and explicit perspectives, of the family itself, the trial judge, lawyers and even a French journalist reporting the affair:

> He, the solitary judge, for a moment paid no attention to those in tailed wigs, but saw before him only eight faces in the dock, largely expressionless, the second obviously frightened. There were Andrew and Francis Shearer, Jacqueline Gledhill, *née* Shearer, then Jane Plews, *née* Shearer, then Lewis and Albert Shearer, then Jonathan Plews. All were on charges connected with the same crimes, some rather with the one than with the other.[75]

Certain interlocking strands of the novel consist variously of courtroom interrogations, narrative reflections on those proceedings, and descriptions of the impact upon the community and participants, with their responses either vocalised or interiorised in thought, including those of a nun, a member of the Shearer clan, Sister Mary-Oswald or May. Those around her ruminate on the scandal that threatens to engulf May, with the Mother Superior of her convent stating:

> You know, also, that, from the first moment of your novitiate here, I have been fully aware of certain, shall we say, oddities in your own family situation, which, indeed, you never tried to conceal either from me or, so far as I can have any knowledge of the matter, from your confessors. Your vocation appears to be a true one [. . .] you may leave us and travel to Northallerton tomorrow and stay there for two or three nights in a suitable residence, even if this means some form of hotel. I am deeply grieved for you, my child.[76]

Subsequently, she outlines the plight of her family to the unsuspecting May, revealing that 'seven members of your immediate family, together with a brother-in-law' have been accused of the murder of 'your maternal and paternal grandmothers'.[77] However, May rejects the offer to travel to the trial, the narrative reflecting in first person: 'I preferred not to go to Northallerton. At first, I think Mother Superior was pleased, though she said nothing.'[78] May later reflects on the Mother Superior's unspoken negativity after May presumes the verdict has been reached:

> I did not like the way Mother Superior was looking at me. It was not with sympathy. If she had spoken to me afterwards, there would have been no tears in her eyes this time. Perhaps I ought to have gone. I wish I had gone.[79]

Throughout the novel, such shifts in perspective, with each new focalisation, are rapid, unannounced, *in media res*, with the mundanity of the surroundings contrasting the seriousness of the charges and formality of the trial. Overall, centrally, the narrative elaborates the vicissitudes of working-class life in the north, a bleak landscape; however, since Heppenstall also incorporates a series of larger global coordinates, the effect is to dwarf the individuals under scrutiny, a new technique he appeared to be developing, for it is one that will feature far more extensively in *Two Moons* (1977). Toward the end, one learns, for instance, through facts plucked seemingly at random, from which one can infer a far wider world, of a plethora of other experiences:

> The Aleutian Islands and the Marquesas Island edged one by one into the cone of darkness. It was midnight in Toronto, Havana, Panama and Quito. Dakar and the Cape Verde Islands emerged into cloudless daylight

and drying dew. Peering with difficulty through so much humidity but possessed of strength to clear it later in the day, the sun, whose day it was, crept up Teesdale and beheld, under dripping eaves, the bottom half of a working sister pulling at a rope, but could not hear the bell.[80]

As Buckell says, 'Heppenstall interspersed his narrative with contemporary events, attempting to simultaneously present the trial as a microcosm of civilization, and civilization as coldly indifferent.'[81] Rendered powerless by such forces of nature, the Shearers (and even more generally humankind) are rendered hopeless, subject to larger forces. Such a diurnal rotation naturally leads ineluctably back to the location of the trial, and to May, who reflects upon the fate of her relatives: 'Our Mam will die in prison. Frankie will come out a crippled old man, and Janie will be thin and grey as a sheep lost in a quarry.'[82] The Shearers are doomed by fate, for, like humankind, they are always struggling against what Heppenstall describes as a constant 'battling against the earth's gravitational pull', wilfully unaware that inevitably 'Man's aspiration fails'.[83] Time is indifferent, for as the novel concludes, 'Throughout the United Kingdom, clocks with chimes began and finished chiming. A general consensus of watches and clocks agreed to call it a day.'[84]

Heppenstall's fiction remains intriguing as an avant-garde exploration of narrative intensity (at a time when supposedly there was little experimental impulse in Britain), conjoining a Kierkegaardian interplay of time sequences with random memories amidst a bleakly unsentimental rendering of ordinary, humdrum environments, where individual characters seek to contextualise some residual meaning in their lives and associated events. His model would be further developed by a range of writers such as Burns, Figes, Johnson, Quin and – arguably, to a degree – Spark. As demonstrated above, in many ways Heppenstall emerges aesthetically as both a literary conduit and a missing link between modernism and the postwar avant-garde.

Notes

1. And, as G. J. Buckell notes, the author's first novel made 'A considerable critical impact [. . .]. He was name-checked in B. S. Johnson's introduction to *Aren't You Rather Young to Be Writing Your Memoirs*, and, as Heppenstall recorded in his journals, Hélène Cixous stated that "*il* [Heppenstall] *a inauguré le nouveau roman dès 1939 avec* The Blaze of Noon" in an article for *Le Monde* on "*le roman expérimental*" in Britain, published in May 1967.' 'Rayner Heppenstall: Context No 18',

Champaign: Dalkey Archive Press, n.d., n.p., available at <http://www.dalkeyarchive.com/rayner-heppenstall/> (last accessed 19 July 2018).
2. Hélène Cixous, *Le Monde*, 18 May 1967, p. 16.
3. Cixous's statement is reported by Francis Booth and Jeremy Green, and by Buckell, who cites the influence of *The Blaze of Noon* (1939) as the reason for Cixous's claim. See Jeremy Green, 'Rayner Heppenstall and the Politics of Cultural Memory', *Hungarian Journal of English and American Studies (HJEAS)*, 5:2 (1999), pp. 95–108, p. 95; Buckell, p. 18; Francis Booth, *Amongst Those Left: The British Experimental Novel 1940–1980* (Lulu Press, Inc., 2012), p. 159. As Hannah Van Hove writes of that novel's protagonist, 'the heightened awareness of objects as necessitated by Louis' blindness, manifested in lengthy descriptions that emphasised their properties above any metaphysical "significance", strikingly prefigures the *choisisme* of the French new novel'. See Hannah Van Hove, '"I Have to Touch, As Another Man Will Look": The Unseeing Gaze in Rayner Heppenstall's *The Blaze of Noon*', in *We Speak a Different Tongue: Maverick Voices and Modernity 1890–1939*, ed. Anthony Patterson and Yoonjoung Choi (Newcastle upon Tyne: Cambridge Scholars, 2015), pp. 254–67, pp. 264–5.
4. Buckell, 'Rayner Heppenstall', n.p. It should be noted that G. J. Buckell is the preoperative nomenclature of Juliet Jacques, a transsexual writer. See Stephen Burt, '*Trans: A Memoir* by Juliet Jacques Review – An Honest Account of Gender Transition', *The Guardian*, 23 September 2015, n.p., available at <https://www.theguardian.com/books/2015/sep/23/trans-a-memoir-juliet-jacques-review-gender-transition> (last accessed 19 July 2018).
5. William Cooper, 'Reflections on Some Aspects of the Experimental Novel', in *International Literary Annual No 2*, ed. John Wain (New York: Criterion Books / John Calder, 1959), pp. 29–36, p. 32, accessible at <http://www.archive.org/stream/internationallit009773mbp/internationallit009773mbp_djvu.txt> (last accessed 19 July 2018).
6. Ibid. p. 29.
7. Ibid. pp. 30, 35.
8. Rayner Heppenstall, *The Fourfold Tradition: Notes on the French and English Literatures, with Some Ethnological and Historical Asides* (London: Barrie & Rockcliff, 1961), p. 157.
9. Cooper, 'Reflections on Some Aspects of the Experimental Novel', p. 191.
10. Rayner Heppenstall, *The Master Eccentric: The Journals of Rayner Heppenstall 1969–1981*, ed. Jonathan Goodman (London and New York: Allison and Busby, 1986), p. 72 n. 2.
11. G. J. Buckell, *Rayner Heppenstall: A Critical Study* (Champaign, IL, and London: Dalkey Archive Press, 2007) p. 58.
12. Alain Robbe-Grillet, *Last Year at Marienbad*, trans. Richard Howard (London: John Calder, 1961).
13. Buckell, 'Rayner Heppenstall', n.p.

14. Andrzej Gąsiorek, *A History of Modernist Literature* (Oxford: Wiley Blackwell, 2015), p. 565.
15. Ibid. pp. 565–6. Ihab Hassan lists Heppenstall's work as one example of 'a repertoire of procedures and attitudes' that Hassan groups together as postmodernism (p. 119) and he details key associated differences from modernism, including the following aspects, which may be found variously in Heppenstall's writing:
    Antiform (disjunctive, open)
    Play
    Chance [. . .]
    Absence
    Dispersal [. . .]
    Irony
    Indeterminacy.
    See Hassan, 'The Culture of Postmodernism', *Theory, Culture & Society*, 2:3 (1 November 1985), pp. 119–31, pp. 123–4.
16. Martin Stannard describes how the younger Scottish writer knew Heppenstall well, both professionally and personally. See Stannard, *Muriel Spark: The Biography* (London: Phoenix, 2010), pp. 180, 193. However, when Heppenstall made a pass on 31 May 1958 over lunch, Spark spurned him; Ibid. pp. 194, 198. Nevertheless, as Stannard details, she admired Heppenstall as 'a serious artist'; Ibid. p. 193.
17. Heppenstall, *The Master Eccentric*, p. 120 n. 1.
18. Ibid. p. 26.
19. Green, 'Rayner Heppenstall and the Politics of Cultural Memory', p. 96.
20. Heppenstall, *The Master Eccentric*, p. 70.
21. Ibid. pp. 67–8.
22. Ibid. p. 122.
23. Heppenstall's role as literary mentor is referred to in passing by both Buckell and Green, but the literary practices that drew younger writers to Heppenstall in the first instance are not considered in any detail.
24. Quoted in Gordon Bowker, *George Orwell* (London: Hachette Digital, 2003), n.p.
25. Ibid. n.p.
26. Green, 'Rayner Heppenstall and the Politics of Cultural Memory', p. 98.
27. Booth, *Amongst Those Left*, p. 187.
28. Green, 'Rayner Heppenstall and the Politics of Cultural Memory', p. 97.
29. Buckell, 'Rayner Heppenstall: Context No 18', n.p.
30. Rayner Heppenstall, *The Connecting Door* (Chester Springs: Dufour, 1968), p. 22. See Juliet Jacques, 'The Connecting Door', *3:AM Magazine*, 28 July 2011, n.p., accessible at <http://www.3ammagazine.com/3am/the-connecting-door/> (last accessed 19 July 2018).

31. Rayner Heppenstall, *The Intellectual Part: An Autobiography* (London: Barrie & Rockcliff, 1963), p. 215. David Leon Higdon argues that repetition is central to the influence and example Heppenstall found in Kierkegaard's writing, whereby 'the individual goes forward by going backwards in consciousness'. See David Leon Higdon, *Shadows of the Past in Contemporary British Fiction* (London: Macmillan, 1984), p. 53.
32. Heppenstall, *The Connecting Door*, p. 18.
33. Ibid. p. 10.
34. Ibid. p. 11.
35. Ibid. p. 18.
36. Ibid. p. 19.
37. Higdon, *Shadows of the Past*, p. 53.
38. Buckell, 'Rayner Heppenstall', n.p.
39. Tom McCarthy, 'Introduction: The Geometry of the Present', in Alain Robbe-Grillet, *Jealousy*, trans. Richard Howard (Richmond: Oneworld Classics, 2008), pp. i–vi, p. i.
40. Heppenstall, *The Connecting Door*, p. 13.
41. Ibid. p. 47.
42. Ibid. p. 77.
43. Ibid. p. 67.
44. Ibid. pp. 70–1.
45. Jacques, 'The Connecting Door', n.p.
46. Heppenstall, *The Connecting Door*, pp. 79–80.
47. Ibid. p. 97.
48. Ibid. p. 163.
49. Jacques, 'The Connecting Door', n.p.
50. Heppenstall, *The Woodshed*, p. 34.
51. Heppenstall, *The Connecting Door*, p. 133.
52. Higdon, *Shadows of the Past*, p. 54.
53. Heppenstall, *The Woodshed*, p. 29.
54. Ibid. p. 13.
55. Ibid. p. 18.
56. Nathalie Sarraute, *The Age of Suspicion: Essays on the Novel*, trans. Maria Jolas (New York: George Braziller, 1963), p. 55.
57. Heppenstall, *The Woodshed*, p. 10.
58. Higdon, *Shadows of the Past*, p. 55.
59. Heppenstall, *The Woodshed*, p. 43.
60. Ibid. p. 143.
61. Ibid. pp. 159–60.
62. Georges Bataille, *the unfinished system of non-knowledge*, trans. Michelle Kendall and Stuart Kendall (Minneapolis: University of Minnesota Press, 2001), p. 20.
63. Heppenstall, *The Woodshed*, p. 177.
64. Ibid. p. 179.
65. Ibid. p. 181.

66. Ibid. p. 185.
67. Ibid. p. 187.
68. Ibid. p. 188.
69. Luce Irigaray, *Elemental Passions*, trans. Joanne Collie and Judith Still (London: Athlone Press, 1992), p. 20.
70. Heppenstall, *The Woodshed*, p. 189.
71. Paul Ricœur, *Oneself as Another*, trans. Kathleen Blamey (Chicago: University of Chicago Press, 1992), p. 161.
72. Jacques, 'The Connecting Door', n.p.
73. Heppenstall, *The Master Eccentric*, p. 25.
74. Heppenstall, *The Shearers*, pp. 9–10.
75. Ibid. pp. 16–17.
76. Ibid. p. 134.
77. Ibid. p. 135.
78. Ibid. p. 136.
79. Ibid.
80. Ibid. p. 167.
81. G. J. Buckell, *Rayner Heppenstall: A Critical Study* (Champaign: Dalkey Archive Press, 2007), p. 76.
82. Heppenstall, *The Shearers*, p. 170.
83. Ibid. pp. 197, 199.
84. Ibid. p. 200.

Chapter 13

Maureen Duffy: The Politics of Experimental Fiction
Eveline Kilian

Maureen Duffy is not only a novelist (with almost twenty novels published to date) but also a poet, a dramatist, a writer of non-fiction books (such as biographies of Aphra Behn and Henry Purcell) and an activist (notably for authors' rights, gay rights and animal rights). Duffy's long-standing career as a novelist began in the 1960s with two comparatively conventionally structured narratives (*That's How It Was* in 1962 and *The Single Eye* in 1964), followed by *The Microcosm* in 1966, a much more radical generic experiment that set the agenda for a number of subsequent works probing and extending the boundaries of the novel. She particularly rejects a specific brand of realism governed by 'the tyranny of linear narrative' that links mainstream postwar fiction to the Victorian novel and that serves as a foil against which her literary experiments define themselves.[1] Instead of offering chronological developments and coherent plots, Duffy employs hybrid generic forms, collage, polyphony, parallel storylines, episodic structures, palimpsest visions and subjective temporalities. While her novels are firmly set within their own historical context, their intertextuality carries them beyond their contemporary framework and connects them with the literature of the past, notably modernist aesthetics and the classics. Duffy's literary experiments are coupled with a foregrounding of marginalised voices and a forward-looking discussion of political issues – for example around sexuality, gender, class and identity – which link her, at least in part, to critical engagements and theoretical positions commonly associated with postmodern thought.

In my chapter I will consider Duffy's literary experiments as a specific way of interlacing aesthetics and politics that rejects any dissociation between literary experiment and political investment. I will address this issue by concentrating on gender and sexuality, two areas explored in a number of Duffy's works, notably in *The Microcosm*, in *Love Child* (1971) and in the third part of her London trilogy, *Londoners* (1983). This focus will be used to locate Duffy's concerns in a network of discourses around gender and sexuality that looks back to modernist authors and forward to late twentieth-century gender queer theorists such as Judith Butler or J. Halberstam. It will be of particular interest how Duffy uses literary strategies and narrative experiments to intervene in gender and sexual politics by probing and destabilising established gender norms and expectations.

Leaving the Closet: *The Microcosm*[2]

The Microcosm, first published in 1966, is an apt example to begin a discussion of Duffy's experimental fiction. In her 1988 afterword to the book, she explains that the novel originated as a non-fiction project, an investigation into female homosexuality in the early 1960s, for which she conducted a number of interviews with women across the social spectrum. After being rejected by several publishers, she was persuaded to turn her findings into a novel, which not only prompted her 'to think more deeply about the nature and structure of novels themselves' but also to combine the radical subject matter, 'calculated then to make any publisher nervous', with 'an equivalent style and structure'.[3] In *The Microcosm*, Duffy not only shifts the focus to same-sex desire but also elides the conventions of the realist novel by establishing intertextual links to eighteenth-century narratives of gender transgression and to Greek mythology and, most importantly, by placing herself 'in the High Modernist tradition' and reviving an aesthetics successfully used by James Joyce and Virginia Woolf.[4] Similar to Woolf's intention to reinvent and reconfigure literary realism to correspond to a new vision of reality, Duffy set out to break with the conventions of mainstream postwar fiction and to produce what she called 'an energized realism'.[5] In *The Microcosm* she experiments with what one critic has called a 'decentered cross-section-of-society model'.[6] It is a kind of collage text using 'a mosaic style' that presents an ensemble of different voices and perspectives,[7] held together by associative links between the characters in the different narratives, by the overarching topic of lesbian existence in the early 1960s in London and by a central location frequented by most of the characters, a lesbian venue modelled on the legendary Gateways Club on the King's Road in Chelsea.[8]

The central location, the club, is a kind of sanctuary, a place where lesbians can meet their friends and lovers undisturbed. The central character, Matt, who acts as an observer of the scene, calls it 'The House of Shades',[9] a term that unfolds a number of connotations which significantly complicate the idea of an unproblematic comfort zone for lesbian socialising: 'Sometimes I think we're all dead down here, shadows, a house of shades, echoes of the world above.'[10] The club is situated in a basement, and to get to it the patrons have to climb down into a subterranean realm, 'down the stairway funnel into the gut of the earth'.[11] The reference is to the Shades, a synonym for Hades or the underworld, where the souls of the dead dwell; or, more specifically, to Dante's version of hell in *Inferno*,[12] the first part of his *Divine Comedy*.[13] The lesbians are separated from society and relegated to the underground, away from the eyes of the world. Outside of the club, they live a closeted life, seemingly in conformity with social norms and always in fear of being found out. Within the cultural system, they function as the dangerous 'other' that is 'best kept under severe check'.[14] Homosexuality is not to speak its name, not to spread its knowledge, not to disturb the boundaries of 'the normal subject': 'The strained silence that comes from things, which must never be said, never mentioned as if at the naming of them the whole order of society would crumble, the streets be filled with howling wolves welcoming the fall of civilisation.'[15]

Homosexuals are criminalised (that is, in the case of male homosexuals before the passing of the Sexual Offences Act in 1967), pathologised and reviled as morally corrupt and deviant.[16] As a silenced minority, they are in no position to speak for themselves and to make their own voices heard. They have no power of self-definition that would reach beyond the confines of their own circumscribed space. In this context, the former archaeology student Matt's final decision to leave hir[17] job at a garage and accept an offer to take part in an archaeological dig in Italy amounts to a refusal to content hirself with this self-contained subcultural existence hidden from the world, which also represents a kind of self-imposed exile: 'I'm just taking up my whole personality and walking quietly out into the world with it. We'll see what happens.'[18] It remains open whether this experiment will be successful but it must certainly be seen as a political act, a step towards a higher degree of self-determination and a claim to the right to become a fully integrated member of society. This form of agency is future-oriented and stands in marked contrast to the 'eternal present' of the club with its patrons being caught in a loop of constant repetition of their fixed patterns, just as the inhabitants of hell are condemned to reiterate their punishment without respite.[19] Matt finally breaks through this circle, steps out of the House of Shades, leaves the world of the dead and paralysis behind and (re)claims hir own future.

The notion of the House of Shades echoing the world above points not only to the lesbians' invisibility in the shadow of the heterosexual world, but also to their dependence on the codes and norms of the mainstream. This becomes particularly obvious in the butch / femme culture prevalent at the club, which reproduces a strictly binary gender order that operates according to many of the principles observable in straight couples of the time, from dress code, gestures of possessiveness and feelings of sexual jealousy to calling butch / femme couples 'husbands and wives'.[20] In that sense, the lesbian subculture establishes a code of conduct modelled on heteronormative structures that every newcomer has to conform to in order to be accepted by the community. This set-up implicitly raises the question of the status of butch / femme arrangements either as uncritical replicas of heterosexual power structures or as instruments of resistance and parodies of gender norms.[21] While always showing respect for the self-stylisations of the butches and femmes, *The Microcosm* offers two different perspectives on this issue. Matt repeatedly points out that the club's patrons wear masks, not only in their acts of conformity in the outside world, but also in their own cultural space: 'Come down the stairs slowly, adjusting your mask.'[22] There is a definite awareness of the constructedness of gender expression in *The Microcosm* that would support Judith Butler's claim that the 'replication of heterosexual constructs in non-heterosexual frames brings into relief the utterly constructed status of the so-called heterosexual original'.[23] Judy's elaborate grooming in the novel slowly turns her into a high femme, and the linguistic stylisation of the straight young women and men as 'girls [...] blown about the streets like flowers on long stalks and young men strut[ting] by on turkeycock legs thrusting against the March winds' stresses the idea of gender performance.[24] At the same time, the patrons of the club do not engage in conscious parodies of straight couples but mostly consider their self-presentation as an expression of their true selves and as a manifestation of a predominantly workingclass lesbian culture. For them, butch and femme are not drag acts but have become identity markers: 'the mask, once you've seen yourself in it, works inwardly upon the personality until in fact you become what you see yourself as'.[25]

There is another aspect, however, that reveals a more subversive streak, particularly in the figure of the butch, which is connected to Duffy's disorienting use of personal pronouns and names in the text. The butches in the novel are given male first names (Matt, Steve,

Carl) and are mostly referred to with male, or in some cases alternately with male and female personal pronouns, as in the following example where Matt is the subject of her lover Rae's defence: '"*she*'s only getting at the truth [. . .]." She turned towards *him*.'[26] This effectively challenges heteronormative structures, as well as the limitations of a language that reflects and is restricted by the binary gender norm. Butches like Matt or Stag do not consider themselves as women. Stag's comment, 'We wouldn't want to be women even if we could be rulers, generals. [. . .] I just can't think of myself in those terms,'[27] prefigures the transgender identities of the 1990s.[28] Thus *The Microcosm* also distances itself from a feminist agenda that relies on a clear boundary between women and men, a restriction that Duffy exposes in her 1969 play *Rites*, which is set in a women's public toilet and shows a group of women venting their feminist rage on and finally killing what they consider to be a male intruder, who, however, tragically turns out to be a butch that they mistook for a man. Politically, the conception of butchness in *The Microcosm* seems more compatible with Monique Wittig's dictum that '[l]esbians are not women' because the term 'woman' is bound to and derives its meaning from a heterosexual system of thought,[29] or, indeed, J. Halberstam's vision of butch as a queer appropriation of male prerogative, as 'masculinity without men'.[30]

As we have seen, the novel links social visibility with the politics of representation. In the end, Matt rejects the idea of the lesbian subculture as a microcosm separated from the rest of the world, 'the gay world as a universe in little', and suggests a more integrative model of society that consists of a plurality of ways of being.[31] In its historical context, Matt's position marks the transition in lesbian culture from a self-contained and isolated community to a more politically active presence fighting against the social marginalisation of homosexuals through organisations like Gay Liberation Front or the Campaign for Homosexual Equality, a shift that also affected the Gateways Club, causing a generational conflict, as Rebecca Jennings has shown.[32]

Duffy's narrative technique in *The Microcosm*, with its 'polyperspective, polyphonic' structure, reflects the idea of diversity as well as a commitment to giving lesbians across the social spectrum a voice of their own.[33] The book consists of different episodes highlighting slices of the various characters' lives in a mixture of mostly internally focalised homo- and heterodiegetic narratives. Their states of mind, thoughts and perceptions are presented in a seemingly unmediated way through the use of interior monologue, free indirect discourse and Joycean-style stream-of-consciousness, and they neither add up to a linear and coherent plot nor are synthesised by an omniscient or a central narrator. The privileging of marginalised subjects in the novel (mostly working-class lesbians) echoes feminist concerns to extend the cultural archive to include the submerged voices of women in history. Matt's telling of Boadicea's revolt against the Romans and the inclusion of Charlotte Charke's story of gender transgression make this point.[34] Moreover, *The Microcosm* proved to be an important intervention in the contemporary representation of homosexuals in literature and mainstream media by providing alternative narratives of lesbian lives. Duffy's kaleidoscopic take on the chequered experience of lesbians in the early 1960s registers the ups and downs of their lives, catching glimpses of their personal crises, successes and failures, but it never pathologises their experience; rather, it shows political awareness by linking salient instances of their suffering to the structural and discursive violence of a heteronormative society that stigmatises homosexuality to police its own borders. And Matt's story provides a window on the future that centres on participation rather than exclusion and a commitment to heterogeneity and to acknowledging that '[t]here are dozens of ways of being queer'.[35] This is a significant change to much of the mostly homophobic and sometimes sensationalist lesbian pulp fiction of the 1950s and 1960s with its stereotypical plots of misguided and ill-fated same-sex relationships shrouded in shame. Their logic required that redemption of the erring young woman could be achieved only through a timely return to the path of heterosexuality and that the depraved and inveterate lesbian invariably had to be punished with unhappiness and the loss of her beloved or worse – a fate that had already befallen the protagonist of Radclyffe Hall's 1928 novel *The Well of Loneliness*, a book still devoured by lesbians in the 1960s.[36] *The Microcosm* is also markedly different from Robert Aldrich's film *The Killing of Sister George* (USA, 1968), which depicts an equally stereotypical sick and destructive relationship between a domineering and abusive older woman and her naïve and dependent younger lover, which actually features one scene shot at the Gateways Club.[37] For many lesbians, Duffy's novel, in its variety, became an important landmark that provided more life-like portraits of same-sex love than the hackneyed clichés found in the scarce cultural narratives of the time.[38]

In a sense, the discussion around issues of segregation and inclusion in *The Microcosm* is mirrored by the marginal status of the novel itself and Duffy's strategies to connect it to the literary canon. While she writes about the lesbian subculture in 1960s London, she does not exclusively write for its members. Just as Matt considers hir way of life as a legitimate part of society at large, Duffy uses her specific material to engage with the literary tradition as a whole. She does so by reviving the literary experiments of high modernism, which, as in the case of Woolf's *Orlando*, also included critical investigations of hegemonic gender norms. Consequently, apart from Dante's *Inferno* and Charlotte Charke's autobiography, *The Microcosm* is pervaded by intertextual echoes of the modernist canon, which it seeks to continue. The different points of view and voices take up the multi-perspective structures of Woolf's *To the Lighthouse* or *The Waves*; Marie Pacey's thirty-two-page associative stream-of-consciousness ruminations in fragmented and erratically punctuated sentences are reminiscent of the Molly-Bloom episode in Joyce's *Ulysses*;[39] and the twilight, demi-monde atmosphere of the House of Shades evokes passages from Djuna Barnes's *Nightwood*, which also links the night with homosexuality. Duffy draws on the structural homology between subculture and avant-garde experimental writing – a subculture that refuses to comply with a certain set of values defined by the mainstream culture, and avant-garde writing that opposes the aesthetic principles of the dominant literary paradigm – to align herself with a high-profile art form with which she shares a common objective and to associate marginalised sexualities with the prestige and forward-looking nature of literary innovation.

Ungendered Narrators: *Londoners* and *Love Child*

Duffy continued her exploration of gender in narrative in two further novels which experiment with an ungendered narrator. *Londoners* (1983) bears the closest relationship to *The Microcosm*, in that it seems to follow Matt's integrative approach at the end of the novel by extending the horizon from the lesbian club to the sexual underworld of Earl's Court, which, moreover, forms part of and is affected by wider urban developments and politics.[40] It is the third novel of Duffy's so-called London trilogy, preceded by *Wounds* (1969) and *Capital* (1975), and is reminiscent of Patrick Hamilton's portrayal of 1930s seedy pub and bedsit land in *Hangover Square: A Story of Darkest Earl's Court* (1941). In contrast to Hamilton, Duffy focuses much more firmly on the variety of sexual outcasts frequenting the protagonist Al's two local pubs, the Nevern and the Knackers, however. *Londoners* shares a central intertextual reference with *The*

Microcosm, Dante's *Inferno*, but uses it in a much more systematic way, since it forms the underlying structural grid of the novel. The thirty-four cantos of the *Inferno* correspond to the thirty-four chapters of *Londoners*, with each taking up some often minor detail of Dante's poem and giving it a contemporary twist.[41] The image of the netherworld is now no longer restricted to the lesbian subculture but encompasses London in its entirety: '"Dis hellhole of a city," as the West Indian might say', the narrator comments with a pun on the city of Dis, whose gates Dante and Virgil enter in canto nine of *Inferno*.[42] Moreover, in Duffy's version of London, the marginalised take centre-stage, with the framework of Dante's *Inferno* linking 'high' art and 'low' culture, grand and small narratives.

The first-person narrator occupies a role similar to Matt's in that s_he acts as a self-appointed 'philosopher-in-residence for Earl's Court'.[43] More importantly, however, s_he is a writer working on a biography of François Villon and a translation of his poetry. The many references to authors such as Horace, Dante, Villon, Swift, Wilde, T. S. Eliot, Woolf, E. M. Forster, Orton, Halliwell and others highlight the fact that Al's vision of contemporary London is first and foremost a literary creation informed and inspired by a long line of pretexts, which, in turn, are also made to resonate with the perspective presented in Duffy's novel. This particular emphasis has repercussions for Duffy's treatment of the question of gender and narrative in *Londoners*, which goes beyond issues of gender and sexual identity to include reflections on literary creation.

Londoners follows the pattern of *The Microcosm*'s gender confusion in its description of the 'human kaleidoscope' the Nevern and the Knackers offer to the observer with its variety of homosexuals, male wives, drag queens and prostitutes of all genders.[44] In addition, it features an ungendered first-person narrator who defies deciphering. All we learn is that s_he is erotically attracted to women, but in the context of the novel this does not disambiguate hir gender. Moreover, Al's indefinite gender becomes an essential attribute of hir as a writer and an essential component of the creative process. Al's fluid gender is attuned to the protean nature of hir metropolitan surroundings: 'London is androgynous: all things to all men, and women too.'[45] To be receptive, and to respond adequately, to the city's openness, 'writers should be both, like oysters changing their sex every seven years'.[46] Similarly, Al's identification with Villon that helps hir to empathise with and recreate the object of hir biographical study and, in turn, impacts on hir own perception of reality, must not be hampered by a potential difference in sex and requires gender flexibility. This conception echoes Virginia Woolf's notion of androgyny as a combination of male and female powers in the creative soul that was inspired by Coleridge's dictum that 'a great mind is androgynous'.[47] The reference to Romanticism is relevant for Duffy's protagonist in that hir literary (re)creation of both London and Villon follows Coleridge's idea of the coincidence or 'reciprocal concurrence' of perceiving subject and object perceived that transforms the object into something new, a third thing.[48] Al's comment on the merging of hirself and Villon – 'making you in my own image or me in yours'[49] – reflects Wordsworth's concept of the synthetic mind, 'creator and receiver both'.[50] There is, however, a shift in Woolf's and Duffy's adaptation of Romantic theories of poetic creation. Whereas, for Coleridge and Wordsworth, androgyny is unquestionably the quality of the mind of a male poet, Woolf decouples creativity and biological sex, and Duffy seems to question the binary gender system and its limited options altogether.

In its mixture of foregrounding both non-heterosexual forms of existence and gender-bending as a poetic principle, *Londoners* draws not only on *The Microcosm* but also on *Love Child* (1971), an earlier text that is set in the world of the wealthy, untainted by social hardships and economic constraints. *Love Child* engages in the linguistic probing of gender norms and boundaries, and also strongly suggests that gender is limiting and inimical to the creative endeavour of the artist. Gender ambiguity in this novel is apparent not only in the first-person narrator Kit but also in hir father's new assistant, to whom Kit gives the name Ajax. The novel focuses on the adolescent protagonist's puberty and sexual awakening. The transition from adolescence to adulthood is marked for Kit by a profound insecurity about the emotional and erotic entanglements of hir parents and hir own relationship especially to hir mother, whose love s_he craves but is not sure about. The major part of the story and its tragic dénouement are set in Iticino, a small Italian holiday resort on the Mediterranean. While Kit's father diverts himself with their housekeeper's daughter, Renata, hir mother starts an affair with Ajax, and as their relationship deepens, Kit's sexual jealousy turns into an obsession. The crisis and subsequent dénouement are reached when Ajax, instigated by a letter faked by Kit, erupts in a bout of jealousy over hir lover's supposed infidelity during a party, leaves in a drunken rage, drives the car off the mole and dies.

The novel is highly intertextual and self-reflexive, interrogating the function of literature, specifically of myth and tragedy, to give meaning and depth to powerful emotions and to structure the protagonist's sense of reality. In *Love Child*, such pretexts become an integral part of Kit's own self-fashioning when s_he retrospectively casts the events at Iticino in the form of a tragedy inspired by world literature and brought about by hir own ingenuity. For Kit, the classics and myth are 'inflammatory, anarchic, and entirely seductive',[51] and s_he eclectically casts Ajax and hir mother as Venus and Adonis, Actaeon and Diana, or Venus and Mars, and hirself as Cupid.[52] Another obvious choice for hir mindset is Shakespeare's *Othello*, with hirself in the role of Iago and Ajax in that of Othello, or hirself as Othello and hir mother as Desdemona.

It becomes clear in the course of the novel that Kit uses the story s_he constructs to shield and compensate for hir emotional vulnerability and insecurity by wielding absolute power over hir own narrative, by assuming the role of puppet master, arranging hir characters 'as if they were waxworks in a tableau' and producing a 'shimmering myth of my own invention'.[53] Like Duffy, Kit disdains the conventions of realist writing and prefers to reflect the everyday existence of hir characters through the lens of 'the symbolic actions of mythical figures' for greater depth and dramatic effect.[54] Kit's conclusion of the episode after their return to London reads as follows: 'My mother's lover [that is, Kit!] has killed Ajax rather than live without the chrysolite. I have made my mythology.'[55] It is important to understand that *Love Child* is not a realist text that details Kit's actual implementation of an ingenious plot to kill off Ajax in order to remain the sole possessor of hir mother's love. Rather, it is first and foremost the narrative the 'precocious child' fabricates in order to navigate, give shape to and, indeed, contain hir own emotional turmoil and impotence in the face of the sexually charged events unfolding around hir.[56] Myth and tragedy serve a cathartic function, as Duffy explains in her afterword to *Rites*: 'The Greek gods and heroes form a huge family encompassing every human emotion [. . .]. There is no need for us to commit incest or murder: they have done it already. [. . .] somewhere there will be a story to embody our hopes and terrors.'[57] This argument is borne out by the ambiguity surrounding Kit's actual involvement in and precipitation of Ajax's 'accidental death' that, told from a different perspective, might have been purely incidental and much less significant than s_he makes out.[58]

The rich intertextuality of Duffy's novels, rather than being a 'burden' obliterating 'the original authenticity of her vision and voice', as one critic has claimed, is an integral part of the fabric and meaning of these texts and, in a more general sense, testifies to both the productivity and the inescapability of cultural narratives in our personal world-making.⁵⁹ In keeping with Kit's attempts to stay clear of limiting gender assignments, *Love Child* also foregrounds cultural texts that do not adhere to the contemporary fixity of gender and identity. One such model of permanent shapeshifting and transformation is provided by one of Kit's main intertextual sources: the mythological universe of Ovid's *Metamorphoses*, where men can be turned into women and vice versa (as in the case of Tiresias), and humans are transformed into animals or plants. The protean nature of art is also evoked by Ellie in the novel, who, as an opera singer, 'can be anything I want'.⁶⁰ This openness is set off against more narrow cultural models like the psychoanalytic gendering of sexual identifications embodied in the Oedipal situation that is echoed in the love triangle between Ajax, Kit and hir mother, as well as in Kit's excessive mother fixation, but frustrated on account of Kit's and Ajax's gender ambiguity. Gender fluidity in *Love Child* is just one aspect of Kit's 'polyglot, polygamous, polymorphous, and polysyllabic' family that seems to be free of any kind of social definition and that provides an ideal soil for Kit's creative ventures.⁶¹

Nevertheless there is a discrepancy between the unfettered freedom of the imagination and the demands of an inevitably gendered reality that is reflected in Kit's own transitional or 'chrysalis' stage between the free play of childhood and the more coercive demands of adulthood and heteronormativity, 'work and sex', to which Kit is reluctant to submit.⁶² There is a noticeable change in hir relationship to some of hir friends at Iticino, for example, who have entered adulthood and shifted their interest to the other sex. This makes it difficult for Kit, who 'had hoped to keep a precarious footing in a supposed childhood a little longer', to stick to the gender-indifferent world of hir family.⁶³ The only thing s_he can do is profess bisexual interests: 'My trouble is I can't choose between Gennaro and Gerry. I think basically I just think I want everybody and don't really want anybody.'⁶⁴

A similar tension becomes apparent on the textual level in the conflict between the author's design to create and explore a genderless or gender-neutral world in the virtual space of the literary text on the one hand and the linguistic constraints imposed on this project through the specific gendering of language itself. Gender ambiguity in a protagonist is only really narratable in the first person. This means that having another ungendered character in the homodiegetic narrative already poses problems because pronouns in the third person are gendered in English. Livia has pointed out that Duffy's avoidance of pronominal references for Ajax and the constant repetition of hir name derealise the character to a certain extent and distance the reader, which does not necessarily coincide with the intended effect.[65] This issue becomes even more obvious when we read *Love Child* in conjunction with fellow novelist Brigid Brophy's *In Transit*, which was published two years before *Love Child* and to which Duffy playfully and unobtrusively alludes in a number of instances.[66] *In Transit* is also a first-person narrative and is set in the transit lounge of an international airport, a space of symbolic significance for the protagonist Pat O'Rooley's predicament, who cannot remember hir sex and is unable to recover this lost detail. The fact that Pat is afflicted not only with 'sexual amnesia' but also with 'linguistic leprosy' indicates the close connection between gender and language.[67] And while Brophy uses a whole artillery of puns across different languages and creates a host of polysemies that explode any stable relationship between signifier and signified, and that expose and ridicule the arbitrariness of linguistic conventions and of gender categories, her protagonist remains caught in the transit lounge of the first person that s_he cannot leave without assuming a place in the binary gender order of the pronominal system. Given these limitations, it is not surprising that Kit in Duffy's *Love Child* recoils from the demands of the adult world and roams through the realm of myth and the imagination to engage critically with and erode a rigid gender system s_he is loath to embrace.

Coda

'I have no qualms at all about identifying myself as a political writer, as long as nobody thinks that this excludes my being an artist,' Duffy said in one of her interviews.[68] This chapter has demonstrated that it is precisely the use of specific experimental techniques that shapes the political issues of her books. In that sense, it can be said that Duffy is a political writer precisely because she is an artist.

Her work across more than five decades is far too varied to be subsumed under a single label. She is known to be a writer who never repeats herself, who tries something different with every new project.[69] Duffy saw herself as part of a group of avant-garde writers, including B. S. Johnson, Eva Figes, Christine Brooke-Rose and Brigid Brophy,[70] whose 'interruptions of given horizons'[71] were just as radical as the modernists' rejection of nineteenth-century models of realism. Her early work shows a clear indebtedness to modernist aesthetics but it also embodies tenets that are central to postmodernism. Linda Hutcheon has defended postmodern fiction against charges of random playfulness and narcissistic self-reflexivity by stressing that '[p]ostmodern art cannot but be political' in its aim 'to "de-doxify" our cultural representations' and to displace and decentre totalising master narratives in favour of a pluralisation of voices and views.[72] This is exactly what Duffy's novels achieve. Sexually marginalised characters already feature in her earliest novels: the homosexual language teacher Colin in *The Single Eye* and the adolescent protagonist Paddy in *That's How It Was*, who falls for her English teacher Miss Tyson in what is clearly more than a schoolgirl crush, as well as some further instances of lesbian coding in minor characters.[73] Sexual outcasts take centre-stage in *The Microcosm* and in *Londoners*, two texts that, together with *Love Child*, reconfigure and diversify the gender system by introducing cross-gender identifications and by exploring the linguistic possibilities of representing these new formations. Literature is one of the prime creative spaces to enact such revisions by probing the limits of language and narrative conventions, as well as the boundaries of cultural intelligibility. It is precisely through her formal experiments that Duffy intervenes in gender and sexual politics by denaturalising and destabilising established gender norms and expectations. The rich intertextual tapestry Duffy constructs in her novels not only bestows canonical weight upon her literary projects; it also multiplies significations by adding voices from the literary past with which her contemporary frameworks interact and which sometimes suggest new dimensions of thinking about gender and sexuality. Just as gender-variant characters and sexual minorities are part and parcel of the social fabric in Duffy's literary universe, the microcosm of the individual, historically specific text forms part of the macrocosm of the larger culture and literary heritage.

The novels discussed in this chapter were radical for their time, in terms of both literary experiment and sexual politics, anticipating later developments in gender theory such as Judith Butler's concept of gender performativity or J. Halberstam's discussion of female masculinity, as well as related issues that have become part of trans and queer studies.[74] With regard to contemporary fiction, obvious parallels exist between Duffy's *The Microcosm*, *Love Child* and *Londoners* and later novels such as Jeanette Winterson's *Written on the Body* (1992) or Leslie Feinberg's *Stone Butch Blues* (1993), which explore gendered discourses through an ungendered or transgendered narrator, respectively, although Duffy's literary experiments remain somewhat under-acknowledged in discussions of these more recent examples. Maureen Duffy is not a best-selling author, but she is undeniably one of the pioneers and an important voice in the reshaping of British postwar fiction.

Notes

1. Maureen Duffy, 'Afterword', in *The Microcosm* [1966] (London: Virago Press, 1989), p. 290.
2. My reading of *The Microcosm* draws on the chapter on Duffy in my book *GeschlechtSverkehrt: Theoretische und literarische Perspektiven des gender-bending* (Königstein: Helmer, 2004), pp. 238–49.
3. Duffy, 'Afterword', p. 291.
4. Maureen Duffy and Christoph Bode, 'Maureen Duffy, London, in Interview with Christoph Bode', *Anglistik*, 6:2 (1995), pp. 5–16, p. 9.
5. Duffy, 'Afterword', p. 290.
6. Patricia Juliana Smith, *Lesbian Panic: Homoeroticism in Modern British Women's Fiction* (New York: Columbia University Press, 1997), p. 152.
7. Duffy, 'Afterword', p. 290.
8. For a survey of the club's importance for lesbian life during the half-century of its existence, see Jill Gardiner's book *From the Closet to the Screen: Women at the Gateways Club, 1945–85* (London: Pandora, 2003).
9. Duffy, *The Microcosm*, p. 35.
10. Ibid. p. 5.
11. Ibid. p. 8.
12. Dante Alighieri, *The Divine Comedy*, I: *Inferno*, trans. and ed. Robin Kirkpatrick [c. 1307–20] (London: Penguin, 2006).
13. See Maureen Duffy and Dulan Barber, 'Maureen Duffy Talking to Dulan Barber', *Transatlantic Review*, 45 (Spring 1973), pp. 5–16, p. 7.
14. Duffy, *The Microcosm*, p. 23.
15. Ibid. p. 170.
16. For details on the Sexual Offences Act 1967 see Jeffrey Weeks, *Coming Out: Homosexual Politics in Britain, from the Nineteenth Century to the Present* [1977] (London: Quartet Books, 1979), pp. 168–82.
17. Because of Matt's incompatibility with the binary gender coding, I use the gender-neutral pronouns 'hir' and 's_he'.
18. Duffy, *The Microcosm*, p. 288.
19. Ibid. p. 24.
20. Ibid. p. 276.
21. For a historical survey of Anglo-American butch / femme culture in the 1950s and 1960s see Sheila Jeffreys, 'Butch and Femme: Now and Then', in *Not a Passing Phase: Reclaiming Lesbians in History 1840–1985*, ed. Lesbian History Group (London: The Women's Press, 1989), pp. 158–87; and Lillian Faderman, *Odd Girls and Twilight Lovers: A History of Lesbian Life in Twentieth-Century America* [1991] (New York: Penguin, 1992), pp. 159–87.
22. Duffy, *The Microcosm*, p. 7.
23. Judith Butler, *Gender Trouble: Feminism and the Subversion of Identity* (London: Routledge, 1990), p. 31.

24. Duffy, *The Microcosm*, p. 5.
25. Ibid. pp. 214f.
26. Ibid. p. 174 (my emphasis).
27. Ibid. p. 235.
28. The protagonist of Leslie Feinberg's novel *Stone Butch Blues* (Ithaca, NY: Firebrand Books, 1993), for example, similarly cannot classify herself as a woman: 'I'm a he–she. That's different. [. . .] It doesn't just mean we're [. . .] lesbians' (pp. 147f).
29. Monique Wittig, 'The Straight Mind', in *The Straight Mind and Other Essays* [1980] (Boston: Beacon Press, 1992), pp. 21–32, p. 32.
30. Judith Halberstam, *Female Masculinity* (Durham, NC: Duke University Press, 1998), p. 2.
31. Duffy, *The Microcosm*, p. 286.
32. Rebecca Jennings, 'The Gateways Club and the Emergence of a Post-Second World War Lesbian Subculture', *Social History*, 31:2 (2006), pp. 206–25; see also Gardiner, *From the Closet*, pp. 178–84.
33. Christoph Bode, 'Maureen Duffy: A Polyphonic Sub-version of Realism', *Anglistik & Englischunterricht*, 60 (1997), pp. 41–54, p. 44.
34. Duffy, *The Microcosm*, pp. 229–34, 70–97; Duffy paraphrases *A Narrative of the Life of Mrs. Charlotte Charke*, ed. Robert Rehder [1775] (London: Pickering & Chatto, 1999), pp. 82–138.
35. Ibid. p. 273.
36. See Kaye Mitchell, 'Popular Genres and Lesbian (Sub)Cultures: From Pulp to Crime, and Beyond', in *The Cambridge Companion to Lesbian Literature*, ed. Jodie Medd (Cambridge: Cambridge University Press, 2015), pp. 154–68; and Jaye Zimet, *Strange Sisters: The Art of Lesbian Pulp Fiction 1949–1969* (New York: Viking Studio, 1999), which provides a survey of the book covers of lesbian pulp with their sexy, enticing images and telling titles like *Degraded Women*, *Sin School*, *The Evil Friendship*, *The Damned One*, *The Odd Ones*, *Warped Women*, *Warped Desire* or *Unnatural*.
37. See Gardiner, *From the Closet*, pp. 132–55.
38. See Ibid. pp. 102–6.
39. Duffy, *The Microcosm*, pp. 99–133.
40. See also Sebastian Groes, *The Making of London: London in Contemporary Literature* (Basingstoke: Palgrave Macmillan, 2011), p. 34.
41. For a more detailed explanation of these references see Christine Wick Sizemore, *A Female Vision of the City: London in the Novels of Five British Women* (Knoxville: University of Tennessee, 1989), pp. 203–7.
42. Maureen Duffy, *Londoners* (London: Methuen, 1983), p. 85.
43. Ibid. p. 95.
44. Ibid. p. 43.
45. Ibid. p. 88.
46. Ibid. p. 115.

47. Virginia Woolf, *A Room of One's Own* [1929] (London: Panther, 1977), p. 94.
48. Samuel Taylor Coleridge, *Biographia Literaria or Biographical Sketches of My Literary Life and Opinions*, ed. George Watson [1817] (London and Melbourne: Dent, 1975), p. 145.
49. Duffy, *Londoners*, p. 196.
50. William Wordsworth, *The Prelude: A Parallel Text*, ed. J. C. Maxwell [1805 and 1850] (London: Penguin, 1986), p. 86.
51. Maureen Duffy, *Love Child* [1971] (London: Virago Press, 1994), p. 132.
52. Ibid. pp. 154–6, 72.
53. Ibid. pp. 202, 164.
54. Ibid. p. 66.
55. Ibid. p. 214.
56. Ibid. p. 3.
57. Maureen Duffy, *Rites* [1969], in *Plays by Women*, vol. II, ed. Michelene Wandor (London: Methuen, 1983), pp. 11–25, 'Afterword', pp. 26f.
58. Duffy, *Love Child*, p. 213.
59. Jane Rule, *Lesbian Images* (London: Peter Davies, 1976), p. 182.
60. Duffy, *Love Child*, p. 157.
61. Ibid. p. 6.
62. Ibid. p. 7.
63. Ibid. p. 78.
64. Ibid. p. 196.
65. Anna Livia, '"One Man in Two is a Woman": Linguistic Approaches to Gender in Literary Texts', in *The Handbook of Language and Gender*, ed. Janet Holmes and Miriam Meyerhoff (Chichester: John Wiley & Sons, 2008), pp. 142–58, p. 151.
66. Given the then close friendship between Duffy and Brophy, it would perhaps be more appropriate to speak of mutual inspiration. Kit's name and hir will to create hir own myth in *Love Child* seem to echo Brophy's pun 'Do it yourself Kid' (Brigid Brophy, *In Transit: A Heroi-Cyclic Novel* [1969] (Harmondsworth: Penguin, 1971), p. 14), which in the novel is the title of a postmodern book inviting the reader to participate in the fiction making; conversely, the term 'Microcosm' (Ibid. p. 183) is evoked by Brophy in connection with a lesbian guerrilla group. For an in-depth discussion of gender and language deconstruction in Brophy's *In Transit* see Kilian, *GeschlechtSverkehrt*, pp. 90–9, 174–85, as well as Eveline Kilian, 'Discourse Ethics and the Subversion of Gender Norms in Brigid Brophy's *In Transit*', in *The Ethical Component in Experimental British Fiction Since the 1960s*, ed. Susana Onega and Jean-Michel Ganteau (Newcastle: Cambridge Scholars, 2007), pp. 31–49.
67. Brophy, *In Transit*, pp. 79, 111.
68. Duffy / Bode, 'Interview', p. 14.

69. Ibid. p. 11; see also Duffy / Barber, 'Talking', p. 9.
70. Maureen Duffy and Melanie Seddon, 'B. S. Johnson and Maureen Duffy: Aspiring Writers. A Conversation with Maureen Duffy', *Writers in Conversation*, 2:1 (February 2015), available at <https://dspace.flinders.edu.au/xmlui/bitstream/handle/2328/35173/Duffy_Seddon.pdf?sequence=1&isAllowed=y> (last accessed 12 December 2017), p. 5.
71. Andrew Gibson, *Postmodernity, Ethics and the Novel: From Leavis to Levinas* (London: Routledge, 1999), p. 91.
72. Linda Hutcheon, *The Politics of Postmodernism* (London: Routledge, 1990), pp. 3, 62–6.
73. See Lyndie Brimstone, '"Keepers of History": The Novels of Maureen Duffy', in *Lesbian and Gay Writing: An Anthology of Critical Essays*, ed. Mark Lilly (Basingstoke and London: Macmillan, 1990), pp. 23–46, pp. 26f.
74. Butler, *Gender Trouble* and *Bodies That Matter: On the Discursive Limits of 'Sex'* (New York and London: Routledge, 1993).

Chapter 14

Not the Last Word on the Sixties Avant-Garde: An Afterword

Glyn White

This tail piece, bringing up the rear of the avant-garde, as it were, is a feather on the end of the spear headed by the Introduction. In it I will discuss questions raised for readers, writers, critics and our discipline as a whole through looking back at avant-garde sixties literature from a twenty-first-century vantage point. These questions include 'Why this interest now in writers of a distant period who were often dismissed at the time and have been marginalised or in danger of being forgotten ever since?', 'Why wasn't this all sorted out much earlier by previous generations of critics?' and 'What has happened in the mean time to justify revisiting this aspect of the period?' I suspect critically engaged readers will have started gnawing away at these questions for themselves long before now.

The Avant-Garde Versus the Literary Mainstream

The foregoing chapters present a gallery of 1960s British writers, from the relatively popular to the more obscure, all with a claim to belong to the avant-garde. These essays also start to redress a gender imbalance in awareness of such writers, and the cumulative effect, I hope, will be to change the perspective from which the field of British writing in this period has usually been seen. The term 'avant-garde' has proven extremely useful for capturing writers who are non-mainstream without necessarily falling under the 'experimental' label that was used to marginalise some of them at the time. Those labelled with it are well represented here and B. S. Johnson's identification of the term 'experimental' as one of opprobrium, reiterated by Giles Gordon, is noted in several essays in the collection (see Williams, Darlington and Hucklesby). The core of the experimentalist group (Johnson, Burns, Quin, Figes), to the extent it was a group, fell by the wayside by their own hands or self-exile in 1973, leaving Figes isolated. Some prior critical accounts have been tempted to add to their number, usually on the basis of Johnson's polemic 'Introduction' to *Aren't You Rather Young to be Writing Your Memoirs?*, which includes a list of writers he considers are 'writing as though it mattered, as though they meant it, as though they meant it to matter'.[1] This group goes far beyond his regular associates, even as it misses out other writers featured in the volume. Implying that chalk and cheese figures like Johnson, with his penchant for rude jokes if he suspected reader interest might be flagging, and Christine Brooke-Rose, multilingual theorist and academic whose *raison d'être* was rigorous technical challenges that were sometimes invisible to readers, actually met on a regular basis is counterfactual. Ongoing exclusion from mainstream literary notice did not belong exclusively to writers who were part of any inner circle of experimentalists: Anna Kavan died in 1968, unable to capitalise on the success of *Ice* (1967); Alexander Trocchi effectively stopped writing literature during the 1960s after the controversial *Cain's Book* (1960); Maureen Duffy was largely regarded as a playwright despite her groundbreaking *The Microcosm* (1966); and Brigid Brophy's varied novels of the sixties are matched in number by a diverse range of non-fiction publications. Better to consider the writers covered here as a British avant-garde and acknowledge their breadth of experiences.

The term avant-garde has the implication of going ahead, leading the main body into new territory and new conflicts, but for a considerable period within the late twentieth century it was considered that sixties avant-garde writers had not led anywhere and they were left missing in action. This account was significantly flawed, however. Primarily, it was based on the hegemony of realist writers in the 1950s and into the 1960s, jostling for canonical positions among themselves, occupying the conventional mainstream centre and able to define anything 'avant-garde' as beyond the mainstream taste (thus 'highbrow' and 'difficult'). This was far from accidental in terms of self-interest, class prejudice and also, as this collection illustrates, in terms of gender and sexuality.[2]

The accounts of the field in the 1980s and 1990s continued to position the experimentalists at the margins,[3] but literature is a long game and the sixties avant-garde work had taken hold with up-and-coming writers who could see the through-lines of influence from modernism to the 1960s and continued them into their present.[4] This is not to say that the sixties writers discussed here have now swept the field, or hubristically to imply that they will do so, but the fragmentation of the field of literary criticism away from monolithic notions such as the 'Great Tradition' allows them space to exist and be acknowledged. Local narratives and circuitous paths in literary production are now more fully mapped as an effect of postmodern rejections of grand narratives and rigid canons. Twenty-first-century readers are less likely to be influenced by the critical wisdom of the past and more likely to be swayed by the enthusiasm of avant-garde authors of the present (and their fans) on websites and blogs. Where the avant-garde of the past are in print, their texts can easily be found by this readership but, with internet sales and auctions, even out-of-print authors can be tracked down and read. Many of the so-called experimental writers of the 1960s discussed in this volume can now even be seen as accessible and engaging gateway texts to the more challenging avant-garde contemporary literature and practice (see Darlington's conclusion in this volume).

Critically speaking, Spark, Ballard, Johnson and increasingly Brooke-Rose are coordinates on the map. Other writers from the sixties avant-garde have made it by other means; Angela Carter was certainly an avant-garde writer of the 1960s, and so (I would argue) was Anthony Burgess in that period. The late Wilson Harris's Guyana Quartet, starting with *Palace of the Peacock* (1960), could be seen as sixties avant-garde but has been acknowledged as significant postcolonial writing. Others such as Kavan, Brophy, Robert Nye, Trocchi, Stefan Themerson, Zulfikar Ghose and 1930s holdover Rayner Heppenstall, many covered in this volume, are still making their way uncertainly along the path to greater recognition.

How does this work? If the avant-garde always challenges mainstream taste, being therefore 'highbrow' and 'difficult', how might its products migrate from the margins towards the centre, becoming 'accessible' and 'seminal'? How do sixties writers previously relegated to a forgotten avant-garde (such as B. S. Johnson) become better known than contemporaries who once outsold them?

The Times They Keep A-Changing

To state the obvious, over time cultures change and, consequently, readers change and the status of a book or author can change. Roughly twenty years ago, I was arguing that Brooke-Rose's *Thru* (1975) could yet find its audience and John Lanchester was making a parallel point in his Foreword to Picador's 2001 edition of Johnson's *Christie Malry's Own Double-Entry*: 'With good writers it can take some time for us to become their contemporaries.'[5] Catching up with the avant-garde writers of the 1960s has taken a while and I will suggest some reasons why.

As suggested above, the avant-garde's rejection of conventional form and style was identified as a stray trickle away from the mainstream, but this interpretation depends on a very particular and deeply entrenched conception of what the mainstream of literature should be: in short, realism. Rubin Rabinovitz surveys the period in 1967 and establishes that this attitude set in during the early fifties and had become pervasive to the extent that

> The greatest fear of the [conventional] English contemporary novelist is to commit a *faux pas*; every step taken is within prescribed limits; and the result is intelligent, technically competent, but ultimately mediocre. When a novelist goes outside the set limits, he [or she] can expect no help from the critics, no matter how good his [or her] work.[6]

This attitude of resisting all innovation endured in literature rather longer than in other forms and Johnson argued that 'the avant-garde of even ten years ago is now accepted in music and painting, is the establishment in these arts in some cases'.[7]

In 2014, Martin Ryle contrasted the approach of John Wain's *Hurry on Down* (1953) with B. S. Johnson's *Albert Angelo* (1964), two *Künstlerromane* published nearly a decade apart.[8] Wain's ideologically conservative neo-realism stands up poorly against Johnson's stylistic diversity and political engagement. Since, in their own ways, all avant-garde writers rebel against the prevailing conventions of their day, this is exactly what we would expect from two novels published a decade apart, whether or not they were concerned with the development of the artist figure. Yet, in a sense, the social realists, neo-realists like Wain, 'The Movement' and the so-called Angry Young Men were already playing this card with their aggressive anti-modernism.[9] Though they ostensibly drew on the Edwardian tradition, the neo-realist line was always to criticise avant-garde work as harking back to outmoded modernism.

Evidence that at least some avant-garde writers of the period looked back to modernism is very clear (Johnson admired James Joyce, Brooke-Rose worked on Ezra Pound) but they also looked sideways to the *nouveau roman* in France (Johnson cited Nathalie Sarraute, Brooke-Rose translated Alain Robbe-Grillet).[10] The writers in question were keen to claim legitimacy and an inheritance of cultural capital from wherever they could, in a literary environment that questioned their right to it. I want to suggest that the key reason for pointing in these directions in their critical pronouncements is to remind their readers that there has been and is avant-garde writing that does not follow a realist model. The case for such writers being neo-modernists, intermodernists or just late modernists can be argued on a case by case basis, though my feeling – strengthened in reading this collection – is that the sixties avant-garde's extreme self-reflexivity and fragmentation so far exceed the modernist model that it will not fit. Lynn Wells makes the following point in relation to B. S. Johnson, who 'seeks to go a step beyond the modernist paradigm, which remains, for him, a form of falsification, an aestheticization of the real'.[11] I agree that aestheticising the real is at least a plausible description of what Johnson thought the conventional novel did and therefore exactly what he thought needed resisting.

In Christopher Webb's chapter I was intrigued to read that Alexander Trocchi was working on *The Long Book* in tall, formatted parish record books, an apparently ubiquitous piece of sixties stationery also used by B. S. Johnson for the manuscript of *Trawl* (1966) and a format on which he sought to model the original hardback edition.[12] Given that the original use of parish records would be as permanent registers of human lives, the incongruous personal projects for which these authors used them are indicative of an appropriation of existing forms for their own purposes. Even though many of Johnson's attitudes about the role of a writer (conceived of as a job, a means of breadwinning and of social engagement) are almost diametrically opposed to Trocchi's, both saw the 'novel', as most people at the time understood it, as inauthentic and false.

The question for the avant-garde writer had become 'How can the novel be made relevant to the present?' And the immediate answer is to do something other than what the vast majority of contemporary writers were doing. These authors responded to the problem quite dramatically: Anna Kavan changed her name and set her subsequent novels apart from her earlier 1930s work; Christine Brooke-Rose radically changed style after her four more conventional 1950s novels; after several science fiction novels, J. G. Ballard produced material approaching conceptual art (see Ferris in this volume); while B. S. Johnson argued he was writing autobiography in the form of a novel.[13] Writers discussed in this collection have other things to say about identity, individuality, psychology, work, gender and sexuality. They were responding to a decade of particularly visible social flux and set off in a variety of directions. Their stylistic diversity and range of responses to those social changes are what make these authors fascinating.

Avant-garde writers who felt something very different was called for were searching for what that was without the benefit of theory.

Even in the late 1960s, common usage of postmodernism as a literary term was at least a decade away. Since they did not know what postmodernism was, their works were not intended as proto-postmodern texts, and have never convincingly been pressed into service as precursors of high postmodernism. Nor did they make an intuitive leap directly to that position. Precisely none of our examples fits Linda Hutcheon's central postmodern category of historiographic metafiction, while much iconic British fiction of the eighties does, such as Salman Rushdie's *Midnight's Children* (1981), D. M. Thomas's *The White Hotel* (1981), Graham Swift's *Waterland* (1983) and Angela Carter's *Nights at the Circus* (1984).[14]

When criticism was freed from the 'Great Tradition', the sixties avant-garde might have expected to benefit from postmodernism's incredulity towards grand narratives, yet because the works in question seldom conform fully to the much debated tropes of postmodern writing, it has required the theoretical dominance of postmodernism to be dislodged or set aside for these sixties texts to get a proper hearing within literary criticism.[15]

As the various foregoing chapters of this book show, the avant-garde authors were seldom making their lives easier by following their chosen paths, rather like the authorial narrator of Kurt Vonnegut's *Breakfast of Champions* (1973), who says 'This much I knew and know I was making myself hideously uncomfortable by not narrowing my attention to the details of life which were immediately important, and by refusing to believe what my neighbours believed.'[16] One could argue that these authors were internally compelled to write as they did, but in fact, there was support and encouragement for the choices they made. Several avant-garde authors were funded by the Arts Council in some of their endeavours, and there were publishers (such as John Calder and Marion Boyars) for their work who would also advance money, sometimes for little in return. The acknowledgement of Samuel Beckett's achievements in the decade (the Formentor International Prize for Literature shared with Jorge Luis Borges in 1961, and Nobel Prize for Literature in 1969) gave currency to avant-garde writing, even if it in some ways marked a limit, too, with Beckett's trilogy famously ending: 'it will be the silence, where I am, I don't know, I'll never know, in the silence you don't know, you must go on, I can't go on, I'll go on'.[17] And of course, not going on.

Though the currency of this idea of the inability to go on led to increasingly frequent suggestions that the end of the novel as a form had been reached in the period, the sixties avant-gardists, undaunted, were prepared to take significant risks in their writing.

The Value of the Unreadable

Like criticism, reading has changed since the 1960s. There remains a literary readership and a general readership (that is, a readership that values intellectual stimulation and cultural capital and a readership that seeks escapism and entertainment), and though the tolerances of both have, I think, been expanded since the 1960s, the points at which they diverge are instructive. Experiment does not have to be aggressively offered but it can still disproportionately trouble, offend or put off, as, for example, when George Saunders's 2017 Booker Prize winner *Lincoln in the Bardo* is given a grudging reception, which suggests he should go back to writing short stories since 'there is a feeling that we're being encouraged to lean back in our seat, impressed at the show rather than hunching forward eagerly to see what happens next'.[18] This is not quite the neo-realist harking back to the Victorian novel but it is an example of reviewer conservatism warning readers off from something they might find unfamiliar. B. S. Johnson might fulminate against the childish need for stories and the refusal to engage with different ways of telling them.[19]

The ideal reader for an avant-garde novel is one that approaches innovation with an open mind and a willingness to regard a novel as an experience rather than (just) a vehicle for a narrative. If novels are conceived of as blueprints for experiences, not to enter into the experience is to miss the point. To believe that reading a review substitutes for the experience is to be satisfied with the spoiler rather than the thing itself, and Johnson wholeheartedly disbelieved the reviewers' claims to be able to predict readers' interest better than he could as an author.[20]

Readers must be challenged. Johnson's *Albert Angelo* infamously casts aside its established narrative 163 pages in with 'OH, FUCK ALL THIS LYING!' But the authorial rant that follows acknowledges '– It is about frustration'.[21] Avant-garde writing is about the willingness to take the risk that there is no reader because the potential readers will be frustrated if they do not (or will not) get it. Johnson's determined search for engaged readers is encoded in his texts, which are artefacts designed to deliver experience (deliver in the sense of communicate) and very often it is *his* experience with little attempt at a 'convincing' fictional setting. As a result, Johnson's work might be described as postmodern in its fears and anxieties over the ability to communicate with readers and not at all postmodern in its desires to embody experience for the reader as effectively as possible.[22]

Most of the authors discussed in this book were willing to take the attitude 'fuck the general reader' and write something that did not cater to their expectations.[23] Spark, quoted by MacKay, is the writer here who best avoided any suspicion of doing so but the impulse to challenge readers is clearly there to be seen in her 1960s novels, too. It takes the form of a hyperconsciousness of the diverse discourses that surround us and, as a reader, with which we can be surrounded.

Spark's *The Girls of Slender Means* focuses on 1945 but from the perspective of the early 1960s, after the death of Nicholas Farringdon as a missionary in Haiti. Columnist Jane Wright rings acquaintances from the May of Teck club who knew him, while the main narrative relives those days in the club as a tissue of disjointed quotations: Joanna Childe's elocution lessons quoting Hopkins and Shelley; Winston Churchill speeches on the radio in the election campaign; bickering old maids; ambiguous screams for help or of hilarity; the two-sentence mantra of the five-guinea Poise Course and Dorothy Markham's 'waterfall of débutante chatter':

> 'Oh hell, I'm black with soot, I'm absolutely filthington.' She opened Jane's door without knocking and put in her head. 'Got any soapyjo?' It was some months before she was to put her head around Jane's door and announce, 'Filthy luck. I'm preggers. Come to the wedding.'[24]

The overlapping discourses of the hostel hypnotise Farringdon enough for him to bring a tape recorder from his army intelligence work to record it.[25]

What is most radical in the sixties avant-gardists' work is the different ways they pay attention to and consciously manipulate the discourses that surround and shape their characters. This focus on polyphony is clearly visible in Alan Burns's found and adapted texts; in J. G. Ballard's visual collages and in *The Atrocity Exhibition* (1970); in the decontextualised quotations used in Ann Quin's *Passages*; in the language of astronomy in Brooke-Rose's *Such*, the multilingual narration of *Between* and the co-option of literary theory in *Thru*; in Johnson's use of pupil essays in his *Albert Angelo*, and quotations from Erich Neumann's *The Great Mother* and colonial histories in *See the Old Lady Decently* (1975). Pervasive discourses around gender are confronted and inverted in Duffy's *The Microcosm* (1966) and more widely through her refusal of gender specificity, while the inability to communicate is the focus in Figes's *Konek Landing* (1969) and Heppenstall's *The Shearers* (1969). Ambiguity is introduced and the impulse is often to resist clarity in language.

To pluck out an example, I will glance at Quin, whose striking debut, *Berg* (1964), does not distinguish between speech or thought in its narration in relating an ineptly pursued Oedipal revenge. In *Passages* (1969) she goes further, using a parataxis (the juxtaposition of discourses) as a technique for half of its length, as a man's diary appears with quoted excerpts of an unacknowledged source alongside treating pagan mythology and its bloody symbolism. The juxtapositions of erotic dreams and ancient practices are disturbing enough but the diary as diary is utterly elliptic and inconclusive. What are we to make of the following?

> He had forgotten the revolver was loaded. He played with the safety catch as usual. At last, he said, as he heard the gun go off inside his head.
>
> A note on the door: Go Away I Have Shot Myself. They go away.[26]

In a text saturated with suicide is this a significant moment or not? The diary continues. Who does it happen to, if anyone? Who is he, who are they? To what extent can it be read literally, since 'inside his head' might indicate it is imagined? There are more questions than answers line by line as we swirl in dark waters, but also a distinct current of black comedy. Readers are implicated in these texts without clear cues as to how they should react.

As the decade ends, others among these avant-garde writers are also pushing the boundaries of acceptable material further in less oblique forms but equally dark tones. Johnson's urban terrorist Christie Malry takes extreme steps to get back at society, but Spark's *The Driver's Seat* (1970), a story of a woman on holiday, is even more perversely insinuating and disturbing in its moral ambivalence.

A Novel Experience for Criticism (Some Wailing and Gnashing of Teeth)

The iconic moments of the sixties that must have surrounded the writing of these novels are almost entirely absent. Their key moments are not the assassination of John F. Kennedy, the success of the Beatles or the Moon Landing, but the moments of composition, the incandescent coal of inspiration fading before the author can get it down. I do not want to claim, though others may have claimed it during this book, that the value of this volume, and of rereading these authors' work, lies in the way it expands or reorients our knowledge of the sixties, important though that understanding may be. I will also suggest, quite oddly for a collection structured around authors, that ultimately I consider the author's intentions to be neither here nor there, certainly not authoritative. It is what the texts mean for us now that counts.

The avant-garde authors discussed in this book grappled with the concerns of their times but that does not mean they are merely loose ends remaining to be properly historicised. This avant-garde is about diversity, in gender, class and backgrounds, and it told the criticism of its day – explicitly and not so explicitly – that its categories were wrong, its preferred themes were wrong and that literature was something capable of affecting the future. Tamed or untamed, through their work these writers are the unacknowledged legislators of a decade where things did change.

But they did not change in a way that benefited either avant-garde writers or their texts. By the end of the 1960s, the idea that writers, especially avant-garde writers, could make significant interventions in contemporary debates and set the agenda is revealed as clearly illusory. In *Christie Malry's Own Double-Entry* (1973), Johnson has his protagonist berate his author: '"you shouldn't be bloody writing novels about it, you should be out there bloody doing something about it".'[27] Johnson participated in an (unsuccessful) trades union campaign against changes to employment law as a film-maker. It cannot have escaped Johnson's notice that Ken Loach's *Cathy Come Home* (1966) had affected late sixties housing policy. Loach's indictment of austerity Britain, *I, Daniel Blake* (2016), shows that campaigning role is still there but there is nothing avant-garde in it. Johnson's most successful excursion into television, *Fat Man on a Beach* (1973), which is playfully avant-garde, was not broadcast until after his death.[28] In the continued hostile environment for literary innovation, writers had to battle on (think of Angela Carter's 1970s) or find ways out. Brooke-Rose published only one novel but established herself in French academia. Meanwhile, the dominant paradigms in English-speaking literary criticism continued to be oriented towards tradition while their critical antagonists turned towards theory. Neither offered any room for the sixties avant-garde. The importance of this material is that, in many ways, these texts and their reception prefigure the problems ahead.

Joseph North argues in his compelling recent polemic *Literary Criticism* (2017) that the eventual overthrow of the Leavisite Great

Tradition and their critical practice was a deceptive victory after which literary academics became marginal in neo-liberal culture:

> [T]he currently dominant mode of historicist / contextualist scholarship, for all that it was argued for by the left, has in its most salient aspects constituted a depoliticizing retreat to cultural analysis as a result of the spread of neoliberal forces in the wider economic and political sphere.[29]

While I think North's account underplays the ferocity of the battle to overthrow the forces of tradition, his identification of a discipline now mired in complacency rings true. Literary academics imagining scholarship affects anything beyond its ivory towers are assuming a progressiveness on the back of perceived associations with the radical changes of the 1960s and thus ignoring the rise to dominance of neo-liberalism in the late 1970s ('The magnetic appeal of the 1960s still throws compasses out').[30]

We come back to the sixties avant-garde because these are the texts that got left behind during the battle for ascendancy. The novels of the sixties avant-garde do not offer us a way out of the mire but they do offer us a diverse set of rule-breakers set on subverting the dominant paradigm of their era, something that the avant-garde writers of today's literature seem already to have discovered.

'Let the dead live with the dead' is Johnson's crude mantra about literary criticism.[31] He prefaces it with a slightly shrewder objection: 'the only use of criticism was if it helped people to write better books'.[32] From the point of view of criticism this author-centric view will not do either, though it will serve very well for anyone teaching creative writers. The purpose of criticism might be better encapsulated not as focusing on production but as helping *readers* read outside their comfort zone rather than consuming a literary diet that confirms the pre-existing worldview and reading habits.[33] The writing of the British sixties avant-garde is a toolkit to do so; the instructions to get started are in your hands.

Notes

1. B. S. Johnson, 'Introduction', in *Aren't You Rather Young to be Writing Your Memoirs?* (London: Hutchinson, 1973), p. 29. The list is quoted in full in footnote 9 in Nonia Williams's essay on Ann Quin in this volume.

2. For self-interest see Rubin Rabinovitz, *The Reaction against Experiment* (New York: Columbia University Press, 1967); for class prejudice see Philip Tew, *The Contemporary British Novel*, 2nd edn (London: Continuum, 2007) and John Driscoll, *Evading Class in Contemporary British Literature* (Basingstoke: Palgrave, 2009).
3. See, for example, Malcolm Bradbury's selection and overview in *The Novel Today: Contemporary Writers on Modern Fiction* (London: Fontana, 1990), and Andrzej Gąsiorek *Post-War British Fiction: Realism and After* (London: Edward Arnold, 1995). D. J. Taylor's *A Vain Conceit: British Fiction in the 1990s* (London: Bloomsbury, 1989) has no time for the sixties avant-garde, except to introduce the parlous plight of the authors he identifies as the followers of their 'dismal fate', pp. 69–73, p. 73. No novelist who might be called avant-garde features at all in Taylor's *After the War: The Novel and England since 1945* (London: Flamingo, 1993).
4. Those recognising the value of sixties avant-garde writers include Ali Smith, Joanna Walsh and Deborah Levy, and American writers such as Mark Z. Danielewski, David Foster Wallace and Jonathan Safran Foer. The reputation of so-called experimental writing of the period has begun to be revised since the millennium.
5. Glyn White, '"YOU ARE HERE": Reading and Representation in Christine Brooke-Rose's *Thru*', *Poetics Today*, 23:4 (2002), pp. 611–31; John Lanchester, 'Foreword', in B. S. Johnson, *Christie Malry's Own Double-Entry* (London: Picador, 2001).
6. Rabinovitz, *The Reaction against Experiment*, p. 169.
7. Johnson, 'Introduction', p. 15.
8. Martin Ryle, '"Educated and Intelligent, if Down at Heel": John Wain's *Hurry on Down* and B. S. Johnson's *Albert Angelo*', in *B. S. Johnson and Post-War Literature: Possibilities of the Avant Garde*, ed. Julia Jordan and Martin Ryle (Basingstoke: Palgrave Macmillan, 2014), pp. 103–17.
9. See, for example, Blake Morrison, *The Movement: English Poetry and Fiction of the 1950s* [1980] (London: Methuen, 1986), and Rabinovitz, *The Reaction against Experiment*.
10. For Johnson see his 'Introduction' to *Aren't You Rather Young to be Writing Your Memoirs?*, pp. 11–12 and 30. For Brooke-Rose see her own account of her career in *Invisible Author: Last Essays* (Columbus: Ohio State University Press, 2002).
11. Lynn Wells, 'What's New, Again? B. S. Johnson's Experimentalism', *Critical Engagements: A Journal of Criticism and Theory*, 4:1/4:2 (2011), pp. 27–36, p. 33.
12. Johnson's papers are held in the British Library.
13. At least in the cases of *Trawl* (1966) and, to a lesser extent, *The Unfortunates* (1969). See 'Introduction', in *Aren't You Rather Young to be Writing Your Memoirs?*, p. 14.

14. Linda Hutcheon, *A Poetics of Postmodernism: History, Theory, Fiction* (London: Routledge, 1988).
15. See Glyn White, *Reading the Graphic Surface: The Presence of the Book in Prose Fiction* (Manchester: Manchester University Press, 2005), and Glyn White, 'Outside Postmodernism: B. S. Johnson Before, During and After', in *The Cambridge Companion to British Postmodernism*, ed. Bran Nicol (Cambridge: Cambridge University Press, 2018 (forthcoming)).
16. Kurt Vonnegut, *Breakfast of Champions* [1973] (Frogmore: Panther, 1974), p. 180.
17. Samuel Beckett, *The Beckett Trilogy: Malloy, Malone Dies, The Unnamable* (London: Picador, 1979), p. 382.
18. Anthony Cummins, 'Man Booker Prize 2017: *Lincoln in the Bardo* by George Saunders: A Strange Beast', *The Telegraph*, 17 October 2017, available at <https://www.telegraph.co.uk/Culture/Books/What to Read> (last accessed 2 June 2018).
19. B. S. Johnson, *Albert Angelo* (London: Constable, 1964), p. 169; Johnson, 'Introduction', in *Aren't You Rather Young to be Writing Your Memoirs?*, pp. 14–15.
20. See David James, 'The (W)hole Affect: Creative Reading and Typographic Immersion in *Albert Angelo*', in *Re-reading B. S. Johnson*, ed. Philip Tew and Glyn White (Basingstoke: Palgrave, 2007), pp. 27–37.
21. Johnson, *Albert Angelo*, pp. 163, 169.
22. See Glyn White, 'The Sadism of the Author or the Masochism of the Reader?', in Jordan and Ryle (eds), *Johnson and Post-war Literature*, pp. 153–66.
23. Muriel Spark, *Loitering with Intent* [1981] (London: Penguin, 2012), p. 55.
24. Muriel Spark, *The Girls of Slender Means* (London: Penguin, 1966), p. 44.
25. Lyndsey Stonebridge has written on voices in Spark (and others) in 'Hearing Them Speak: Voices in Wilfred Bion, Muriel Spark, and Penelope Fitzgerald', *Textual Practice*, 19 (2005), pp. 445–65.
26. Ann Quin, *Passages* [1969] (London: Marion Boyars 2009), p. 95.
27. Johnson, *Christie Malry's Own Double-Entry*, p. 180.
28. See Jonathan Coe, *Like a Fiery Elephant: The Story of B. S. Johnson* (London: Picador, 2004), p. 2.
29. Joseph North, *Literary Criticism: A Concise Political History* (Cambridge, MA: Harvard University Press, 2017), p. 18.
30. Ibid. p. 58.
31. B. S. Johnson, *The Unfortunates* (London; Picador, 1999). Given that the novel consists of a number of sections each with their own pagination starting at 1, it is customary to give the first three words of the start of the section quoted from before the page number, in this case 'The opera singer. . .', p. 2. Johnson also uses this phrase in his 'Introduction' to *Aren't You Rather Young to be Writing Your Memoirs?*, p. 15.
32. Johnson, *The Unfortunates*, 'The opera singer . . .', p. 1.

33. Here I am taking up North's interest in what literary criticism should be doing, which goes back to I. A. Richards (accepting no substitutes) and the ideas of practical criticism and what literature can do: 'a central part of Richards' project is motivated by a will to use literary texts, together with contemporary readers' responses to them, as diagnostic instruments to determine the state of culture' (North, *Literary Criticism*, p. 34).

Notes on Contributors

Chris Clarke is an independent researcher based in Southampton. In 2017, he worked as a part-time tutor in the English Department at the University of Southampton, having also completed his doctoral thesis there. His recent publications include '"Unconsciously Influenced": Alan Burns, Ian McEwan, and the Lasting Legacies of Postwar British Experimental Fiction', *MFS Modern Fiction Studies*, 64:1 (Spring 2018). His current research explores the imprint of postwar experimental fiction on contemporary literature and culture.

Joseph Darlington is Programme Leader for BA(Hons) Digital Animation with Illustration at Futureworks Media School. He completed a PhD on 1960s experimental writers in 2014, won a Harry Ransom Fellowship for his work on Christine Brooke-Rose and is editor of *BSJ: The B. S. Johnson Journal*.

Kieran Devaney is an independent scholar and novelist based in Birmingham, UK. His first novel, *Deaf at Spiral Park*, was published by Salt in 2013. His most recent publication is the short story Sitcom, published on thefanzine.com.

Natalie Ferris is a Leverhulme Trust Early Career Fellow in the School of Literatures, Languages and Cultures at the University of Edinburgh. She was a Junior Teaching Fellow 2018 at the Ashmolean Museum, Oxford, and completed her Arts and Humanities Research Council-funded DPhil project, 'Ludic Passage: Abstraction in Post-War British Literature 1945–1980', at the University of Oxford, which she is currently revising as a monograph. She is Deputy Editor of the *Cambridge Humanities Review*, the English Editor of the architecture journal *SPACE*, and co-founder of the Christine Brooke-Rose Society. She is also a published arts and literary critic, contributing to publications such as *Frieze*, *The Guardian*, *Tate Etc.*, *The Times Literary Supplement* and *The White Review*, and catalogue essays for artists such as Veronica Hauer and Allen Jones.

Len Gutkin is a member of the Harvard Society of Fellows (2014–18) and an Associate Editor at the *Chronicle Review*. His articles have appeared in *ELH*, *Contemporary Literature*, *Genre* and elsewhere.

David Hucklesby is a part-time Lecturer in English Literature at De Montfort University, Leicester. David's PhD thesis examined the 'New Fiction' of mid-twentieth-century Britain, considering the post-millennial growth in critical readership of B. S. Johnson, and contemporaries such as Giles Gordon and Ann Quin, in relation to the emergent technological concerns of American novelists in the early 2000s, including Mark Z. Danielewski and Jonathan Safran Foer. His current research interests include resistances to the critical terminology of experimentalism, participatory storytelling in video games and live entertainment media, and innovative British women writers of the twentieth century.

Stephanie Jones is an independent scholar specialising in the work of Christine Brooke-Rose, postwar British literature, modernism and postmodernism. She graduated in 2016 with her PhD from Aberystwyth University, where she was a part-time tutor in the English and Creative Writing department. She is currently working at the University of Worcester as a sessional lecturer in the Institute of Humanities and Creative Arts and in The Hive as a Library Team Leader.

Eveline Kilian is Professor of English at Humboldt-Universität zu Berlin. Her major research areas are metropolitan cultures, modernism and postmodernism, life writing, trans/gender and queer theory. Her book publications include *Life Writing and Space* (ed. with Hope Wolf; Routledge, 2016), *Queer Futures: Reconsidering Ethics, Activism and the Political* (ed. with Elahe Haschemi Yekani and Beatrice Michaelis; Ashgate, 2013), *London: Eine literarische Entdeckungsreise* (Wissenschaftliche Buchgesellschaft, 2008), *GeschlechtSverkehrt: Theoretische und literarische Perspektiven des gender-bending* (Helmer, 2004), *Momente innerweltlicher Transzendenz: Die Augenblickserfahrung in Dorothy Richardsons Romanzyklus Pilgrimage und ihr ideengeschichtlicher Kontext* (Niemeyer, 1997).

Marina MacKay is Associate Professor of English and Fellow of St Peter's College, University of Oxford. She has published widely on mid-century British literature and culture, and her most recent book is *Ian Watt: The Novel and the Wartime Critic* (Oxford University Press, 2018).

Kaye Mitchell is Senior Lecturer in Contemporary Literature and Co-Director of the Centre for New Writing at the University of Manchester. She is the author of two books – *A. L. Kennedy: New British Fiction* (Palgrave, 2007) and *Intention and Text: Towards an Intentionality of Literary Form* (Continuum, 2008) – and editor of a collection of essays on the British author Sarah Waters (Bloomsbury, 2013) and of a special issue of *Contemporary Women's Writing* (Oxford University Press, 2015) on experimental women's writing. Her current work in progress includes a monograph on the politics and poetics of shame in contemporary literature, for which she received a Humboldt Foundation Research Fellowship for Experienced Researchers in 2014–15.

Philip Tew is Professor in English (Post-1900 Literature) at Brunel University London and a fellow of the Royal Society of Arts. His main publications include *B. S. Johnson: A Critical Reading* (Manchester University Press, 2001), *The Contemporary British Novel* (Continuum, 2004), *Jim Crace* (Manchester University Press, 2006) and *Re-reading B. S. Johnson* (Palgrave, 2007), the latter co-edited with Glyn White. Tew is Director of the Brunel Centre for Contemporary Writing and Hillingdon Literary Festival, and additionally founding Director of the B. S. Johnson Society. Among more recent books are *Zadie Smith* (Palgrave, 2010); a multi-authored policy report on ageing, *Coming of Age* (Demos, 2011); with Nick Hubble, *Ageing, Narrative and Identity: New Qualitative Social Research* (Palgrave, 2013); *Reading Zadie Smith: The First Decade and Beyond* (Bloomsbury, 2013); and with Jonathan Coe and Julia Jordan, *Well Done God! Selected Prose and Drama of B. S. Johnson* (Picador, 2013).

Hannah Van Hove completed her PhD on the fiction of Anna Kavan, Alexander Trocchi and Ann Quin at the University of Glasgow and is currently working on a research project which focuses on British postwar experimental women's writing. She is Secretary of the Anna Kavan Society. Her publications include reviews and articles on mid-twentieth-century avant-garde fiction, as well as translations of some of Flemish modernist Paul van Ostaijen's poetry.

Christopher Webb is an Arts and Humanities Research Council-funded PhD student at UCL (University College London), whose thesis, 'The Concept of Work in Post-War British Experimental Writing', examines why contemporary issues surrounding work came to shape and preoccupy the writings of several key postwar British experimental writers. It focuses on the work of Eva Figes, B. S. Johnson and Alexander Trocchi, and proposes that only with an understanding of these writers' engagement with the idea of work and other related concepts (such as leisure, public debt and forms of neglected labour) can we fully appreciate both their contribution to the development of the modern British novel and, more broadly, late modernism's relation to realism.

Glyn White is a Senior Lecturer in Twentieth Century Literature and Culture at the University of Salford, Manchester. He has written on Laurence Sterne, Samuel Beckett, B. S. Johnson, Christine Brooke-Rose and Alasdair Gray in *Reading the Graphic Surface: The Presence of the Book in Prose Fiction* (Manchester University Press, 2005), and has published further chapters and articles on Johnson, Brooke-Rose, Gray and Mark Z. Danielewski. He is also the co-writer (with the late John Mundy) of *Laughing Matters: Understanding Film, Television and Radio Comedy* (Manchester University Press, 2012). He has taught B. S. Johnson and Christine Brooke-Rose to undergraduates for more than a decade.

Nonia Williams is a Lecturer in Literature in the School of Literature, Drama and Creative Writing at the University of East Anglia (UEA). Nonia researches intersections between twentieth-century experimental aesthetics and forms, representations of gender and sexuality, and questions of wider twentieth-century cultural and political contexts. She completed her doctoral thesis on the life, writing and cultural milieu of Ann Quin at UEA in 2013. She has recently written on madness, formal experiment and cliché in Ann Quin for *Textual Practice* (2018) and is a reviewer for *Women: A Cultural Review* and *Modern Fiction Studies*. Nonia is currently researching Doris Lessing and Muriel Spark materials in the British Archive of Contemporary Writing at UEA.

Index

Ackroyd, Peter, 54
Adorno, Theodor, 171–2
  Aesthetic Theory, 171–2
advertising, as competitor or influence, 8, 125, 127, 131–2, 134, 171
Aldiss, Brian, 110, 112
Alloway, Lawrence, 125
Ambit Magazine, 130, 133, 134, 137
Amis, Kingsley, 60, 70n4
Angry Young Men, the, 8, 161, 211, 251
anti-novel, the, 5, 10, 12–13, 31, 83, 84, 214; see also *nouveau roman*; Robbe-Grillet, Alain
anti-psychiatry, 110, 115, 116–18, 203; see also Laing, R. D.
Antonioni, Michelangelo, 144
apocalypticism, 3, 4, 16
Apollinaire, 4
Arendt, Hannah, 23, 31
ARK (RCA magazine), 130
Arp, Jean, 12
Arts Council, the, 104n7, 176, 253
Attridge, Derek, 179–80
Avant-garde, the
  Beyond the Words anthology, 54, 55–61, 62, 63, 64, 65, 66, 68
  British avant-garde coterie, 2, 15–16, 54–5, 68–9, 113–14, 144, 176–7, 210, 211–13, 242, 248–9
  Bürger's *Theory of the Avant Garde*, 160–1, 165–6, 167, 168, 173, 174
  and chance/aleation, 10–11, 51, 129, 133, 152, 165
  as 'cute', 171–2
  difficulty, as characteristic of, 9, 21, 83, 86, 114, 145, 150, 153, 155, 156, 157, 163, 167, 193, 194, 196, 205, 207, 249, 250
  exhaustion of, 7, 8–9
  vs. 'experimental', 2, 3, 4–5, 8, 56, 57, 68–9, 144, 248–9
  and irrationalism, 10, 119–20
  as label, 3, 4–5, 249
  legacies of the, 249–51
  vs. the 'mainstream', 8–9, 59, 69, 237, 248–50, 251
  modernism, relationship to, 6, 16, 60, 81, 109, 226, 251–2
  and obscenity, 9, 10, 96
  overseas influences on, 11–12, 144
  and politics, 160ff, 257
  popularisation of, 8–9
  suspicion of, 6–7
  TLS issues on, 3, 4, 6, 8–9, 11–12, 13
  see also Bürger, Peter; experimental; modernism; postmodernism
Austen, Jane, 21, 75

Bailey, James, 21
Ballard, J. G., 5, 6, 113, 117, 125–42, 250, 252, 255
  Atrocity Exhibition, The, 17n18, 134–6, 137
  Burning World, The, 130–1
  collage, use of, 127–30, 132
  Crash, 17n18
  Crystal World, The, 130–1
  Drowned World, The, 130–1
  'Invisible Years, The', 137
  'Overloaded Man, The', 136
  Paolozzi, Eduardo, collaboration with, 132–3, 136–7
  Project for a New Novel, 127–8, 129, 134, 138
  and science fiction, 130, 132

'This is Tomorrow' exhibition, influence of, 125–6, 129, 136
'Which Way to Inner Space?', 130
Wind from Nowhere, The, 130–1
Banham, Reyner, 126
Barber, Dulan, 147
Barnes, Djuna, 237
   Nightwood, 237
Barth, John, 6, 87n4
   Giles Goat-Boy, 6
Barthes, Roland, 22, 52n17
Bataille, Georges, 222
Baudelaire, Charles, 74
Bax, Martin, 127, 130, 134, 136
Baynes, Ken, 9
Beardsley, Aubrey, 72, 74, 84
Beats, the, 11, 12, 13, 105n39
Beckett, Samuel, 12, 16, 22, 32, 93, 101, 104n12, 114, 144, 145, 158n9, 177, 178–9, 181, 189n23, 194, 195, 196, 197, 198, 253
   Molloy, 195, 198
   Not I, 22
Behn, Aphra, 231
Benjamin, Walter, 165–6
Bentley, Nick, 32
Berger, John, 158n9, 184
Bergonzi, Bernard, 3, 4, 7, 8, 9–10
Berry, R. M., 5
Binswanger, Ludwig, 119
Birch, Sarah, 199, 202, 206
Black Mountain Poets, the, 12, 13
Booth, Francis, 5, 8, 214
Borges, Jorge Luis, 253
Boxall, Peter, 178, 181
Bray, Joe, 13
Brée, Germaine, 15
Breton, André, 165
   Nadja, 165
Brittain, David, 133
Brooke-Rose, Christine, 2, 5, 6, 12, 13, 14, 15, 16n14, 19n72, 21, 36, 158n9, 193–209, 242, 249, 250, 251, 252, 255, 257
   Between, 193, 204–7, 255
   Gold, 193
   Invisible Author, 195–6
   nouveau roman, influence on, 196, 197–8
   Out, 12–13, 193, 195–200, 204, 207
   Stories, Theories & Things, 204
   Such, 193, 200–4, 207, 255
   Thru, 6, 13, 194, 207, 250, 255

Brophy, Bridget, 4, 8, 13, 14, 15, 19n72, 72–89, 158n9, 194, 207, 242, 249, 250
   aestheticism and decadence in the work of, 72–3, 77–9, 81–2, 83, 84
   Black Ship to Hell, 72
   camp in the work of, 73–6, 83, 85–6, 87n4
   Finishing Touch, The, 73, 79–80, 82
   Flesh, 77–9
   Hackenfeller's Ape, 8, 76
   In Transit, 4, 13, 73, 76, 82–6, 207, 242
   King of a Rainy Country, The, 76
   Palace Without Chairs, 72
   Prancing Novelist, 72, 74–6
   Snow Ball, The, 76, 79, 80–2
Brownjohn, Alan, 133
Buckell, G. J., 210, 211, 214, 216, 226
Bürger, Peter, 160–1, 165–6, 167, 168, 173, 174
   Theory of the Avant Garde, 160–1, 165–6, 167, 168
Burgess, Anthony, 54, 158n9, 250
Burns, Alan, 2, 5, 11, 13, 14, 40, 45, 65, 69, 129, 135, 144–5, 152, 157n7, 160–75, 176, 184, 212, 221, 226, 248, 255
   Angry Brigade, The, 164, 172–3
   Babel, 161, 163–4, 166–8, 170, 173
   Buster, 161, 164
   Celebrations, 161, 162–3, 221
   collage and montage, in the work of, 164–70
   Dreamerika!, 161, 164, 170–2, 173
   Europe After the Rain, 11, 161–2, 164–5, 166, 168, 170, 221
   Jeanette Cochrane [script], 168–9, 170
   Palach, 168, 169–70
Burroughs, William, 10, 18n51, 87n4, 105n39, 129, 136, 144, 166
   Naked Lunch, 10
Burstein, Jessica, 82
Butler, Judith, 232, 234, 243
Butor, Michel, 211

Cage, John, 144, 158n13
Calder, John, 11, 12, 91, 96, 97–8, 100, 161, 211, 253
Calvino, Italo, 5
Campos, Augusto de, 12, 13
Carter, Angela, 6, 8, 117, 158n9, 250, 253, 257
   Nights at the Circus, 253
   Several Perceptions, 117
celebrity culture, critique of, 167–8, 172
cinema
   as competitor for the novel, 7, 45, 56
   influence on experimental writing, 42, 130, 144

Cixous, Hélène, 210
Cobbing, Bob, 134
Coe, Jonathan, 36, 44, 55
Coleridge, Samuel Taylor, 239
Colette, 80
  Claudine, 80
collage, 5, 13, 126, 127, 128, 129–30, 133, 134–5, 137, 148–9, 155, 161–2, 164–70, 214, 231, 232, 255
colonialism and the British Empire, 2, 163, 250, 255
Compton-Burnett, Ivy, 8
concrete poetry, 12, 13, 64, 134
Connolly, Cyril, 107
Conquest, Robert, 60, 70n4
Cooper, William, 210–11
Coover, Robert, 5, 87n4
Creeley, Robert, 13, 144, 158n13

da Vinci, Leonardo, 152, 153
Dada, 4, 12
Dante, 233, 237–8
  Inferno, 233, 237–8
Davie, Donald, 60, 70n4
Davie, Elspeth, 5, 65–6
Debord, Guy, 93, 105n37
Deleuze and Guattari, 145
Drabble, Margaret, 117, 212
  Waterfall, The, 117
Duffy, Maureen, 2, 4, 15, 231–47, 249, 255
  Capital, 237
  gender and sexuality in the work of, 231–2, 232–7, 238–42, 243
  Londoners, 232, 237–9, 243
  Love Child, 232, 239–42, 243
  Microcosm, 231, 232–7, 238, 239, 243, 255
  Rites, 235, 240
  Single Eye, The, 231, 243
  That's How It Was, 231
  Wounds, 237
Duras, Marguerite, 144, 214
Dutheit, Georges, 178

Eliot, T. S., 77, 238
Ellmann, Richard, 60
Englishness, 11–12
Enright, D. J., 60, 70n4
Ernst, Max, 131, 161
experimental
  connotations of term, 2, 3–5, 9, 20–1, 55, 56–7, 58–9, 63, 68–9, 108, 113, 144–5, 158n12, 248
  linked to failure, 5, 56, 69, 144

  reaction against experiment, 7, 14
  vs realism, 7–8, 14
  see also Avant-Garde, the

Faulkner, William, 181
  The Sound and the Fury, 181
Feidelson Jr, Charles, 60
Feinberg, Leslie, 243
  Stone Butch Blues, 243
feminism, 14–15, 109, 173, 176, 177, 187–8, 235, 236
Fiedler, Leslie, 10
Figes, Eva, 15, 65, 101, 157n7, 158n9, 176–92, 212, 226, 242, 248, 249, 255
  B, 176
  Beckett, influence of, 177, 178–9
  Days, 176
  Equinox, 176
  failure, treatment of, 178–81, 188
  Holocaust, family experience of, 176, 184
  Journey to Nowhere, 184
  Konek Landing, 176, 177, 184–7, 188, 255
  Little Eden, 184
  Nelly's Version, 188
  Patriarchal Attitudes, 176, 187–8
  Tales of Innocence and Experience, 184
  Winter Journey, 176, 177, 181–3, 184, 187, 188
Finlay, Ian Hamilton, 13
Firbank, Ronald, 72, 73–6, 79, 80
  Vainglory, 75–6
First World War, 67
Forbidden Planet, The, 125
Forster, E. M., 238
Foster Wallace, David, 156
Foucault, Michel, 117
  Madness and Civilization, 117
Fowles, John, 6, 8
  Collector, The, 8
  French Lieutenant's Woman, The, 6
Freud, Sigmund, 72, 131, 202
Friedman, Ellen G., 14–15
Fuchs, Miriam, 14–15

Garrity, Jane, 109
Gąsiorek, Andrzej, 133, 211
Gautier, Théophile, 80, 83–4
  Mademoiselle de Maupin, 80
gender, 4, 14–15, 73, 75, 76, 79, 80, 82–5, 109, 171, 175n27, 187–8, 201, 204–5, 207, 231–2, 232–7, 238–43, 248, 249, 252, 255, 257; *see also* feminism

Genet, Jean, 93
Ghose, Zulfikar, 47, 250
Girodias, Maurice, 91, 93
Goethe, Johann Wolfgang von, 217
Gomringer, Eugen, 12, 13
Goodman, Jonathan, 211
Gordon, Giles, 54–71, 144, 158n9, 164, 248
  About a Marriage, 66
  Aren't We Due a Royalty Statement?, 54, 59
  Beyond the Words: Eleven Writers in Search of a New Fiction, 54, 55, 57–9, 60, 64, 65, 164
  Girl with Red Hair, 55, 66–8
  Pictures from an Exhibition, 55, 61–6, 67
  Umbrella Man, The, 66
Graham, Billy, 166–8
Grass, Günter, 12, 179, 190n30
Green, Jeremy, 212
Greenberg, Clement, 125
Gregson, Ian, 30
Groes, Sebastian, 5
Gysin, Brion, 129

Halberstam, J., 232, 235, 243
Hall, Radclyffe, 236
  Well of Loneliness, The, 236
Hamilton, Patrick, 237
  Hangover Square, 237
Hamilton, Richard, 132
Harris, Wilson, 114, 158n9, 250
  Palace of the Peacock, 250
Harrison, Jane Ellen, 154–6
  Prolegomena to the Study of Greek Religion, 154–6
Hassan, Ihab, 10
H.D., 156
  Helen in Egypt, 156
Heppenstall, Rayner, 2, 6, 129, 158n9, 210–30, 250, 255
  Blaze of Noon, The, 214
  Connecting Door, The, 210, 214–18, 219
  Fourfold Tradition, 211
  Intellectual Part, The, 215
  London Consequences, 212
  Master Eccentric, The, 211, 212
  relationship to other British experimental writers, 211–13
  Shearers, The, 210, 214, 219, 223–6, 255
  Two Moons, 225
  Woodshed, The, 210, 214, 218–23
Higdon, David Leon, 216, 219, 221
Hobson, Harold, 169
Hockney, David, 133
Hodgson, Jennifer, 5, 14

Hoggart, Richard, 43
Holocaust, the, 177, 184; *see also* Second World War
Holub, Miroslav, 12
homosexuality, 74–5, 80, 92, 232–7, 238, 243
Horace, 238
Horvath, Brooke, 85
Hucklesby, David, 39
Hutcheon, Linda, 242–3
hypertext, 16

Independent Group, The, 126
Institute of Contemporary Arts (ICA), 126
Ionesco, Eugène, 93
Irigaray, Luce, 223

Jacques, Juliet, 215, 217, 218, 223
James, David, 56
James, Henry, 114
  Golden Bowl, The, 76, 78
Jameson, Fredric, 137
jazz, 12, 13
Jenner, Sebastian, 51
Jennings, Rebecca, 235
Johnson, B. S., 1–2, 3, 4, 5, 6, 13, 14, 20, 21, 36–53, 54–9, 60, 61, 62, 63, 64, 65, 68–9, 101, 130, 133, 144, 157n7, 176, 196–7, 204, 212, 213, 221, 226, 242, 248–9, 250, 251, 252, 254, 255, 256, 257, 258
  Albert Angelo, 5, 13, 37–9, 45, 251, 254, 255
  'Aren't You Rather Young to be Writing Your Memoirs?', 43, 44, 45, 55–6, 249
  book as dynamic object in the work of, 37–42
  Christie Malry's Own Double-Entry, 38, 41–2, 45–6, 250, 256, 257
  House Mother Normal, 45
  politics in the work of, 36–7
  See the Old Lady Decently, 221, 255
  Travelling People, 39, 47, 51n4
  Trawl, 196, 204, 221, 252
  truth in the work of, 36–7, 40, 42–4, 47, 50
  Unfortunates, The, 36, 37, 45, 47–50, 53n38, 197, 221
  working-class origins of, 36, 42–4
Jones, Dr Maxwell, 119
Jordan, Julia, 2, 15, 44, 113, 177, 187, 196, 197
Joyce, James, 2, 18n51, 45, 56, 82, 114, 232, 236, 237, 251
  Ulysses, 82, 114, 237

Kafka, Franz, 11, 114
Kavan, Anna, 4, 6, 8, 15, 19n72, 107–24, 204, 249, 250, 252
  Asylum Piece, 108, 110, 119–20
  Bright Green Field, A, 114
  I am Lazarus, 110
  Ice, 110–18, 120–1, 249
  Sleep Has His House, 110, 113
  Who Are You?, 114
  writing as Helen Ferguson, 108–9, 112–13
  see also anti-psychiatry; Laing, R. D.
Kenedy, R. C., 5
Kennedy, John F., 131, 164, 170–2, 256
Kermode, Frank, 3–4, 10, 83, 194
Kierkegaard, Søren, 215, 216, 219, 226
Killing of Sister George, The, 236
Kolocotroni, Vassiliki, 30

Laing, R. D., 105n40, 110, 116–18, 119, 203–4
  Divided Self, The, 116–18, 119, 203
  Politics of Experience, The, 117
  see also anti-psychiatry
Lanchester, John, 21
Larkin, Philip, 60, 70n4
Last Year in Marienbad, 114, 149, 150, 211
Lawrence, Karen, 200, 201, 202, 203
Le Corbusier, 39–40
Lessing, Doris, 112, 117
  Golden Notebook, The, 117
Lettrism, 12
Levinas, Emmanuel, 177, 180–1, 185
Lewis, Wyndham, 81
Lodge, David, 7, 10

McCaffery, Larry, 5
McCarthy, Tom, 216
McHale, Brian, 6, 13, 38, 67
McLuhan, Marshall, 10, 126
  Mechanical Bride, The, 126
Marowitz, Charles, 169
Marriott, Raymond, 107, 108
Marx-Scouras, Danielle, 12
Mauriac, Claude, 144
May 1968, 169, 173
metafiction, 1, 5–6, 8, 16, 21, 41, 76, 82–3, 85, 194
Miller, Henry, 144
Miller, Jonathan, 3, 9
Miller, Karl, 55, 59–61, 63, 65, 69
  Writing in England Today, 55, 59–61, 63

modernism, 2, 3–4, 5–6, 10, 14, 16, 22–3, 39, 44, 55, 58–9, 60–1, 63, 65, 69, 109, 137, 187, 190n24, 211, 226, 249, 251
Moorcock, Michael, 133
Morgan, Edwin, 10, 13, 101, 134
Morrisette, Bruce, 156
Movement, The, 60, 211, 251
multimodalism, 16
Murdoch, Iris, 8
  Under the Net, 8

Nabokov, Vladimir, 5
New Worlds [magazine], 133
New York School, the, 13
Ngai, Sianne, 83, 143, 171–2
Nico, 168
Norman, Donald, 40
nouveau roman, the, 11, 12, 21, 32, 33n5, 77, 81, 83, 144, 156, 195–6, 197, 210, 223, 251; *see also* anti-novel, the; Robbe-Grillet, Alain
nouvelle vague, the, 144, 149; *see also Last Year in Marienbad*; Resnais, Alain
Nuremberg Trials, the, 164–5, 170
Nuttall, Jeff, 130
  My Own Mag, 130
Nye, Robert, 65, 154, 158n9, 164, 177, 181, 250

Orlovitz, Gil, 114
Orton, Joe, 238
  and Kenneth Halliwell, 238
Orwell, George, 23, 25, 213
Ovid, 241
  Metamorphoses, 241

Paolozzi, Eduardo, 132–3, 134, 136–7
  Metafisikal Translations, 133
Pater, Walter, 82, 84
  Renaissance, The, 84
Pellicer-Ortin, Silvia, 177, 182
Pero, Allan, 76
Pinget, Robert, 144
Pink Floyd, 168
Plante, David, 68
Pop Art, 129, 132
postmodernism, 6, 14, 21, 22, 38, 66, 67, 228n15, 242–3, 253
Pound, Ezra, 194, 251
Powell, Anthony, 27
Prague Spring, the, 169
Proust, Marcel, 80, 180, 214
  Albertine disparue, 80
  In Search of Lost Time, 180

psychoanalysis, 119, 200; *see also* Freud, Sigmund
Purcell, Henry, 231
Pynchon, Thomas, 5

Quin, Ann, 2, 4, 5, 6, 11, 13, 14, 15, 19n72, 54, 56–7, 59, 61, 63, 65, 67–8, 69, 117, 129–30, 143–59, 178, 204, 212, 213, 221, 226, 248–9, 255, 256
  Berg, 11, 12, 19n72, 56–7, 63, 67–8, 143, 145–7, 148, 150–6, 204, 212, 256
  'Every Cripple Has His Own Way of Walking', 146
  'Leaving School', 146
  'Never Trust a Man who Bathes with His Finger Nails', 145
  Oedipus, in the work of, 146–7
  Passages, 117, 143, 145, 147, 150–6, 221, 255
  source texts, inclusion of, 154–6
  Three, 13, 143, 145, 147–50, 155, 221
  Tripticks, 156–7
  Unmapped Country, The, 143
  Writers Reading Collective, The, 144

Rabinovitz, Rubin, 7, 251
Rauschenberg, Robert, 136
Read, Herbert, 125
realism, 7–8, 14, 21, 31, 36, 45, 55, 56, 57, 58, 59, 60, 63, 64, 65, 66, 68, 69, 76, 77, 83, 107, 178, 210, 216, 222, 231, 232, 242, 251
Resnais, Alain, 149
Rhys, Jean, 8
Richardson, Dorothy, 15
Ricœur, Paul, 223
Robbe-Grillet, Alain, 11, 12, 21, 30–1, 32, 33n5, 81, 83, 144, 149, 194, 195, 197, 198, 200, 211, 214, 216, 251
  In the Labyrinth, 81
  Jealousy, 12, 198, 216
  Last Year in Marienbad, 114, 149, 150, 211
  Towards a New Novel, 12
  Voyeur, The, 198, 211
  see also anti-novel, the; *nouveau roman*, the
Robson, Leo, 21
Ross, Maggie, 65
Rumney, Ralph, 130
  Other Voices, 130
Rushdie, Salman, 6, 253
  Midnight's Children, 253
Ryle, Martin, 251

Saporta, Marc, 39
Sarraute, Nathalie, 12, 15, 144, 195, 211, 214, 220–1, 251
  Age of Suspicion, The, 220–1
  Planétarium, Le, 195
  Tropisms, 12
Sartre, Jean-Paul, 32, 93, 145
Saunders, George, 254
  Lincoln in the Bardo, 254
Schiele, Jinny, 169
Schmidt, Michael, 13
Scholes, Robert, 7
Second World War, 22, 107, 119, 161, 171, 187, 205–6, 210, 214–15; *see also* Holocaust, the; Nuremberg Trials, the
Seddon, Melanie, 50
Sedgwick, Eve Kosofsky, 74
Shakespeare, William, 38, 240
  Othello, 240
Shaw, George Bernard, 73–4
Siegfried, Detlef, 97
Sigal, Clancy, 9
Simon, Claude, 214
Situationism, 12, 93
Smith, Patricia Juliana, 76
Smith, Roch C., 198
Smith, Stevie, 133
Smithson, Alison and Peter, 40
Sontag, Susan, 85, 87n4
Sophocles, 146
  Oedipus Rex, 146
Spark, Muriel, 8, 12, 15, 19n72, 20–35, 73, 178, 194, 226, 250, 255, 256
  as mid-century writer, 22
  Bachelors, The, 26
  Ballad of Peckham Rye, The, 25
  cliché, treatment of, 21, 22, 24–5, 26–7, 30, 32
  Comforters, The, 8
  Driver's Seat, The, 12, 32, 256
  Far Cry from Kensington, A, 24–5
  Girls of Slender Means, The, 23, 29–30, 255
  Loitering with Intent, 20, 22–4, 25–6, 32
  Mandelbaum Gate, The, 31–2
  Memento Mori, 21, 26
  Prime of Miss Jean Brodie, The, 21, 27–9, 31
  speech and violence in the work of, 29–32
  voice in the work of, 22–5, 30
  Voices at Play, 22
Stein, Gertrude, 62, 63
  Tender Buttons, 62
Sterne, Laurence, 39

Stevick, Philip, 15
Stewart, Victoria, 21
Stonebridge, Lyndsey, 23, 30
Stuby, Anna Maria, 176
Sturm, Jennifer, 109
Sugnet, Charles, 160, 161, 164, 166, 172, 174
Surrealism, 8, 10, 12, 129, 131, 132, 133, 165
Sutherland, John, 96
Sward, Robert, 145
Swift, Graham, 253
  Waterland, 253
Swift, Jonathan, 238

Tease, Amy Woodbury, 23
Themerson, Stefan, 157n7, 158n9, 212, 250
Thomas, D. M., 253
  White Hotel, The, 253
Times Literary Supplement, 3, 4, 6, 8–9, 11–12, 13, 152–3, 193, 224
Townsend, Sue, 54
Trilling, Diana, 113–14
Trocchi, Alexander, 1, 4, 6, 11, 90–106, 249, 250, 252
  Cain's Book, 90, 91, 93, 94–6, 97, 98, 99, 100, 101, 102, 103, 249
  Helen and Desire, 92–3
  Long Book, The, 91, 98–103
  project sigma, 93, 95, 97–9, 101
  Young Adam, 91, 93–4, 103
Tucker, Eva, 176

Varon, Jeremy, 173
Verdon, Cheryl, 177

Vietnam War, the, 133, 137, 163, 168
Villon, François, 238, 239
Vonnegut, Kurt, 253
  Breakfast of Champions, 253

Wain, John, 60, 70n4, 251
Walker, Victoria, 109
Wardle, Irving, 113
Waugh, Patricia, 5, 113, 117, 118, 194
Webb, W. L., 183
Weiss, Peter, 114
Weldon, Fay, 54
White, Glyn, 6, 36
Whittier-Ferguson, John, 22
Wilde, Oscar, 74–5, 77, 238
  Picture of Dorian Gray, The, 77, 79, 82
Williams, Raymond, 7
Wilson, Harold, 44
Winterson, Jeanette, 243
  Written on the Body, 243
Wittig, Monique, 15, 235
women experimental writers, 14–15
Wood, James, 156
Woolf, Virginia, 15, 22, 67, 232, 237, 238, 239
  Jacob's Room, 67
  Orlando, 237
  To the Lighthouse, 237
  Waves, The, 237
Wordsworth, William, 239

Young, Marguerite, 15

Zambreno, Kate, 108–9
Ziarek, Ewa, 179

EU representative:
Easy Access System Europe
Mustamäe tee 50, 10621 Tallinn, Estonia
Gpsr.requests@easproject.com

www.ingramcontent.com/pod-product-compliance
Lightning Source LLC
Chambersburg PA
CBHW061345300426
44116CB00011B/2003